AMERICAN TRIUMVIRATE

AMERICAN TRIUMVIRATE

SAM SNEAD, BYRON NELSON, BEN HOGAN,

AND THE MODERN AGE OF GOLF

JAMES DODSON

ALFRED A. KNOPF  NEW YORK 2012

THIS IS A BORZOI BOOK

PUBLISHED BY ALFRED A. KNOPF

Copyright © 2012 by James Dodson

All rights reserved. Published in the United States by Alfred A. Knopf, a
division of Random House, Inc., New York, and in Canada by Random
House of Canada Limited, Toronto.

www.aaknopf.com

Knopf, Borzoi Books, and the colophon are registered trademarks of
Random House, Inc.

Library of Congress Cataloging-in-Publication Data

Dodson, James.

American triumvirate / James Dodson.

p.   cm.

"This is a Borzoi book."

ISBN 978-0-307-27249-2

1. Golfers—United States—Biography.   2. Golf—United States—
History—20th century.   3. Nelson, Byron, 1912–2006.

4. Snead, Sam, 1912–   5. Hogan, Ben, 1912–1997.   I. Title.

GV964.A1D64 2012

796.3520922—dc23

[B]   2011043446

Frontispiece: Ben Hogan, Byron Nelson, Arnold Palmer, and Sam Snead
Front -of-jacket images (left to right): *Sam Snead.* Augusta National/
Masters Historic Imagery/Getty Images; *Byron Nelson.* Bettmann/Corbis;
Ben Hogan. Augusta National/Masters Historic Imagery/Getty Images

Jacket design by Jason Booher

Manufactured in the United States of America

First Edition

For Bill Campbell, John Derr, and Rayburn Tucker,

a true American Triumvirate,

with my deepest gratitude

No one has tasted the full flower of life until he has known
poverty, love, and war.

—O. Henry

When I look back at those days, I was lucky to have had ol'
Ben and Byron to play against. Damn straight they made me
a better player, and I hope they feel the same way about me.

—Sam Snead

Contents

AMERICAN TRIUMVIRATE

Billy Joe Patton, Ben Hogan, Bobby Jones, and Sam Snead

ODE TO BILLY JOE

L ET'S BEGIN WITH PERHAPS the most memorable Masters ever played, the last time Sam Snead, Byron Nelson, or Ben Hogan won a major golf championship.

The year was 1954, and the unlikely star who outshone the three greatest players since Bobby Jones was a genial, wisecracking, thirty-two-year-old lumber broker from the foothills of North Carolina's Blue Ridge Mountains, an unknown amateur named William Joseph Patton—"Billy Joe" to his friends back home in tiny Morganton.

Prior to his unlikely summons to Augusta, the most outstanding items on Billy Joe's résumé were lone victories in the Carolina Amateur and the Carolina Open and a somewhat surprising appointment as an alternate to the 1953 Walker Cup team, which netted him the Masters invitation. He was known for his sharp wit and infectious storytelling, his blazing backswing and go-for-broke style of play that often sent his drives anywhere but the fairway. His buddies back at the Mimosa Hills Country Club were almost as amused as they were impressed by his unexpected new honor. Several made a point, in fact, of asking Billy Joe to at least bring home an autograph by Ben Hogan or Sam Snead.

Five decades later, not long before he passed away, Billy Joe Patton sat on a pretty terrace at the retirement home where he lived in Morganton, and recalled the most remarkable week of his life.

"I drove down to Augusta on Monday of Masters week very excited that I would finally get to meet Snead, Hogan, and Nelson. I'd only seen Byron and Ben play in Greensboro and Asheville. I also decided that, with nothing to lose, I would just try to have some fun. The instant I turned up Magnolia Lane, though, my heart was racing like you can't believe.

"In those days, players parked right in front of the clubhouse. So I parked and got my clubs out of the trunk and noticed a Cadillac convertible sitting nearby with a fella wearing a banded straw hat sitting there talking to a lady. 'Oh, my God,' I said to myself. 'That's Sam Snead.' I tried not to disturb them, but as I passed Sam Snead looked over at me, winked, and tipped his hat.

"I knew it was going to be a fun week," Billy Joe recalled fifty-five years after the fact, with a roguish little twinkle in his eyes. "That was the first time I ever saw Sam Snead."

But it wouldn't be the last. With a homemade golf swing that was quicker than a frightened hummingbird, Billy Joe entered the tournament's annual long-drive contest on Wednesday afternoon and won it with a poke of 338 yards, the first time an amateur had ever done so. Members of the press swarmed around the well-dressed Carolinian with gray-flecked hair and neat rimless eyeglasses, discovering a fellow who was not only having the time of his life but also charming fans with every utterance and unorthodox swing. "Are you planning to hit the ball that hard in the tournament?" one of them demanded. Billy Joe smiled. "Well," he drawled pleasantly, "I didn't come this far to lay up, that's for sure. You didn't pay to see me play it safe."

He followed up this disarming swagger by shooting 70 on a cold and blustery opening day to tie veteran E. J. "Dutch" Harrison for the first-round lead. Only two other players in the field, Lloyd Mangrum and Jack Burke Jr., managed to shoot under par that day. Defending champion Ben Hogan got around the course in 72, former champion Sam Snead in 74. And Byron Nelson, who retired from competitive golf at the end of the 1946 season but never missed an opportunity to compete in the Masters, split the difference between his great rivals with an opening 73.

Going in, these three were the unchallenged favorites at golf's most prized invitational event, more or less in that order. Each, after all, had won the Masters twice. Between them they owned twenty-one major championships, nine Vardon trophies for the year's lowest scoring average, eleven Player of the Year honors, fourteen Ryder Cup appearances and no fewer than thirteen PGA Tour records. But on the heels of his extraordinary year in 1953, when he won five of the eight events he entered and captured the Masters, U.S. Open, and British Open, Ben

Hogan had announced his plans to dial back his appearances and join his longtime friend and rival Byron Nelson in retirement.

Many felt Slammin' Sammy Snead wouldn't be far behind. Though he still displayed the silkiest natural swing ever seen in championship golf, within a month he would turn forty-two, an old man by tour standards. For the record, Byron had already reached that mark, and Hogan would hit it later that year in August.

"There was an unmistakable feeling that an era was ending that year at Augusta," says Bill Campbell, the other outstanding amateur in the field that week, a thoughtful West Virginian playing in his fourth Masters. Something of a protégé of Snead's, he would go on to anchor eight Walker Cup teams and eventually serve as president of the United States Golf Association. "Everyone knew why Sam and Ben and even Byron were there. Each one wanted one more major title, ideally the Masters, because they each owned two titles and together they had more or less put the Masters on the map. Everyone was watching to see who would take the rubber match, so to speak. But that's what makes what Billy Joe accomplished all the more wonderful. He stole the show from the three greatest players who ever played at one time, on the greatest stage in golf."

On day two, when the weather turned colder and gustier, Harrison carded a 79 and Hogan slipped back a stroke to 73, leaving Billy Joe alone atop the leaderboard at the halfway mark with 144. Cary Middlecoff, who was five strokes off the lead, took a glance at the board with the easygoing amateur in first and sourly grumbled, "If that guy wins the Masters, it will set golf back fifty years." One veteran wire service reporter aptly dubbed the colorful amateur the "Falstaff from the Foothills."

The fans couldn't have disagreed more. As he strolled Augusta National's lushly groomed fairways, at times twirling a club and whistling out loud, Billy Joe waved to friends from back home in the gallery and exchanged warm greetings with any stranger who cheered him on, and shook every hand offered from behind the ropes. "Always wink at the crowds," he advised a young player making a similar debut decades later. "That way everybody thinks you're winking at them."

Ben Hogan wasn't the least bit pleased to be paired with the talk of the tournament for his third round. Since his miraculous return from a terrible car accident that nearly took his life in late 1949, he had won six major championships and achieved mythic stature in American sports. Long considered the coldest and most methodical player who ever played, and quite possibly the finest shotmaker of all time, he was a legend whose personal omerta was a code of silence that suffered no fools and certainly not a gabby amateur, and everything Billy Joe did that day irritated the poker-faced Hogan, starting with the fact that he, like millions of Americans, seemed to play golf purely for the fun of it. For Ben Hogan, golf wasn't merely a source of livelihood and fame; it was his sole means of survival. Fun never entered the equation.

The amateur's first big sin was outdriving his playing partner on the opening holes. Then, as they were walking together to the fourth tee, one of his High Country pals playfully called out, "Hey, Billy Joe, who's that little guy in the funny white cap?"

The comment probably wasn't meant to be malicious or insulting, most likely just an attempt to help keep his friend loose and free-swinging. But as Billy Joe predictably began spraying his drives right and left, the "Wee Ice Man"—as admiring Scots in 1953 at the British Open had nicknamed Hogan—refused to pay the amateur any attention, and his expression grew even more glacial after Billy Joe executed several near-impossible recovery shots from deep trouble to save par, prompting Hogan to mutter as he trudged off the ninth green, "I can't *stand* this."

True to form, however, Hogan buckled down and finished with a 69, while Billy Joe ambled into the house wearing the same catfish smile, lucky to have carded a 75, but still the new darling. "Billy Joe had put on a wonderful display," Bill Campbell remembers, "but the feeling around the tournament was that it was time for the amateurs to step aside and let the legends take over and settle the matter. That would most likely be Sam or Ben."

Snead's third-round 70 could easily have been three shots better, but he was still in the thick of it. Nelson, on the other hand, followed an untidy second-round 76 with a 74 that pretty well took him out of contention for a third title. He would, however, rally in the final round and finish tied for twelfth, not bad, Herbert Warren Wind later noted, for a man who'd retired nearly a decade before.

As Ben Hogan strode down the fairway of the fourth hole in the final round, bound tightly in adhesive leg bandages from groin to ankle and wrapped in his own secure world of absolute mental isolation, a thunderous roar came off the sixth hole ahead, causing him to do something he rarely did in the heat of competition. Spotting a wire service reporter, he walked over to ask what had just happened. The reporter held up one finger.

"Billy Joe just made an ace on six," he said. Hogan showed no emotion.

At the sixth tee, a second sustained roar echoed through the pines. Billy Joe, Hogan learned, had just birdied the eighth hole. And after his drive on seven found the heart of the fairway, he heard another roar come from the direction of the clubhouse. That turned out to be Billy Joe's birdie at nine.

The greatest player of the age and the amiable amateur were now tied for the lead in the eighteenth edition of the Masters.

As Hogan stood on the eleventh tee, Billy Joe hit his drive on the famous par-five thirteenth, a low slice that stopped in the pine trees bordering the fairway. From this spot, most experienced players intent on winning a major championship would chose wisdom over valor and lay up short of Rae's Creek, allowing themselves a short pitch to the green and a decent shot at birdie.

Billy Joe, however, hearing the summons of the gods in his ears, gambled on a different path to glory. All week long his fans had been issuing glandular rebel yells and patting him on the back, urging him to go for every risky shot on this notoriously unforgiving golf course. One bit of fanciful Augusta lore holds that as he was trying to decide between going for the green or laying up, a big-time gambler—who stood to lose a fortune if one of the favorites got upset by some good-time hacker—took Billy Joe's elbow and informed him that his mama had been rushed to the hospital back home, hoping this news might derail his freight train.

No one knows for sure if that really happened, but Billy Joe chose to go for the green and knocked his second shot into the creek. After retrieving his ball from the water, choosing to play the chip in his bare feet, he slipped and dumped his ball in the water for a second time in ten minutes. The huge gallery went deathly quiet, witnessing every amateur's nightmare being played out before them. Unsmiling for the first time that week, Billy Joe wound up with a double-bogey seven on the hole.

Back on hole eleven, meanwhile, unaware of Billy Joe's troubles ahead, Hogan made a rare tactical error by attacking a flag tucked in the lower front portion of the green; his approach shot trickled into the pond, producing a Greek chorus of groans from the vast galleries assembled on three pivotal holes in what Herb Wind would soon christen "Amen Corner."

Hogan took six there, but Billy Joe's adrenaline and poor choices resulted in a costly bogey on fifteen. As he was tapping in for his seven at fifteen, three holes ahead Sam Snead finished his round with a workmanlike 72 that put him in the house at 289—and, for the moment at least, in sole possession of the lead. His partisans were going crazy up on the hilltop by the clubhouse. Just under an hour later, however, Hogan limped home with an unhappy 75 that tied him. At this stage of his life and career, the last thing Ben wanted to endure was a playoff—especially against his greatest remaining rival. On the other hand, he was relieved that he wouldn't have to battle an amateur with a wild swing and a free spirit for his third Masters title.

By that point, Billy Joe Patton was standing under the famous oak tree by the clubhouse, enjoying a cold beverage and signing autographs and soaking up the congratulations of every Masters patron who passed by. A few minutes before, having just missed an eighteen-foot putt for birdie that would have put him in the playoff for the 1954 title, Billy Joe had dropped his head in disappointment—but quickly raised it again and beamed at the crowd, as if he still heard the angels singing.

"They all wanted to shake his hand," remembered CBS broadcaster and fellow North Carolinian John Derr. "Billy Joe was suddenly every ordinary golfer's hero—a guy who'd nearly beaten the two finest players of the age on what was becoming the single most admired setting in golf."

The next day's playoff shaped up like a golf junkie's dream come true, the two reigning titans of the game in a head-to-head rubber match for glory with all the intimacy of a country club match-play final.

As events unfolded, however, they both played careful and fairly uninspired golf through twelve holes, but Snead made his move by making a birdie at thirteen. Showing visible signs of fatigue, Hogan three-putted on sixteen for a bogey four. During their match, it would be remembered, he reached every green in regulation whereas Snead hit only fourteen. But he needed thirty-six putts against his opponent's thirty-three, and therein lay the winning margin. Ben shot 71, Sam a stroke better.

At the presentation ceremony, as they posed with Bob Jones for a photograph with the real star of the week—the tournament's low amateur—Snead grinned and said, "Hey, Billy Joe, you damn near got the whole turkey."

"Well, Sam, I gave it my best." Billy Joe was still in a daze, he admitted later, because he'd learned his performance meant he would be invited back next year.

Snead turned to Hogan. "It's nice of you to let me have another one," he drawled as Bob Jones helped him slip on his champion's green jacket, then added playfully, "Hey, brother, I thought someone said you were going to retire. Did you forget?"

Hogan smiled, always gracious in defeat. "Only how to putt, Sam," he replied.

The comment was telling. Neither man would win another major championship.

From this moment, an officially "retired" Ben Hogan's public appearances became much rarer events, highlighted by a pair of near-wins in the next two Masters and a trio of breathtakingly contested U.S. Opens in '55, '56, and '60. He would win only one more tournament—his fourth Colonial National Invitational in 1959. At this point his vaunted skills would sharply taper away and his tournament entries would dwindle until they ceased altogether in 1971.

The seemingly ageless Sam Snead, on the other hand, enjoyed something of a playing renaissance, winning fourteen more tour events and another six times on the senior tour. Similar to Hogan, he made bold runs at four more major championships only to come up just shy. Before he was finished, however, he would win five World Senior titles and continue to tour and give exhibitions until he became the pro emeritus at his beloved Greenbrier Resort in West Virginia, the first man to win a PGA event in six different decades.

Whatever else is true of the 1954 Masters, the real winners that remarkable week were the Masters tournament itself and the game's popularity in America at large. Patton's play and the hugely anticipated battle royale between Hogan, Snead, and Nelson generated more press coverage around the world than any time since Jones left the game—confirming a growing belief that the Masters had finally achieved major parity with the British and American opens and the PGA Championship, bringing out the best in pro and amateur alike on a course that would soon be familiar to every golf fan on the planet.

Billy Joe's smiling mug appeared on the cover of *Newsweek* magazine, and golf writer Charlie Price declared that golf had a new "Give 'em hell people's hero," the kind of guy any fan could relate to. In the tournament's afterglow, golf clubs across the land reported a significant uptick in membership inquiries, while driving ranges and public courses that summer reported record turnouts.

The end of an era that Bill Campbell had sensed was real. In the same summer, a younger Coke-swigging amateur from western Pennsylvania won the United States Amateur Championship in Detroit and decided to try to make a living in professional golf. He, too, had a go-for-broke style that every golf fan could relate to. In some ways, Billy Joe Patton had merely been the warm-up act for Arnold Daniel Palmer.

Within two years, the Masters would be televised for the first time; and two years after that Palmer would capture his first green jacket and the hearts of millions of American golfers.

"If a single golf tournament ever had a more magical week I simply can't name it," Herb Wind told me one cool April afternoon in 2001, during what had become an annual post-Masters lunch at his retirement village north of Boston. "I agree with those who say Billy Joe's Masters represented a turning point in the game of golf. Ben, Sam, and Byron, after all, had set the stage for golf's greatest period of expansion. But they were just leaving that stage, passing the torch, if you will, to Arnold and Jack Nicklaus and eventually all the rest. Now we have young Tiger Woods."

Woods had won his first Masters in 1997, and this was our third spring luncheon, but I wasn't there to talk about golf's most exciting newcomer. I was there to collect Wind's thoughts about Ben Hogan, Byron Nelson, Sam Snead, and the era of golf he perhaps understood better than anyone.

Not long after I helped Arnold Palmer write his memoirs in 1998, Ben Hogan's estate invited me to write an authorized biography of the most elusive superstar in the game's history. Before I officially said yes, I wanted to talk with Herb in depth about Hogan's career and to see if he shared my growing belief that Hogan, along with Snead and Nelson, had shaped modern golf in a number of ways.

This wasn't just my own theory. During my decade at *Golf Magazine*, and another ten years as golf correspondent for *Departures*, I'd spent a nice chunk of time interviewing early tour stars like Gene Sarazen, Henry Picard, and Paul Runyan, as well as a host of younger pros including Tommy Bolt, Cary Middlecoff, Jack Burke Jr., Mike Souchak, Bob Rosburg, Dow Finsterwald, Dave Marr, Don January, Ken Venturi, Jack Fleck, Eddie Merrins, amateur legends Bill Campbell and Harvie Ward, and, of course, the incomparable Arnold Palmer. To a man, in some form or another, they pointed to the galvanizing effect that Hogan, Snead, and Nelson had on the game.

In 1994, I spent two days chatting with Byron Nelson at his Fairway Ranch in Roanoke, Texas, ostensibly to gather insights for the fiftieth anniversary of his remarkable year in 1945, when he captured eleven tournaments in a row and won a total of eighteen in all. Much of our conversation dwelt on Byron's early career and his relationship with his leading two rivals. Remarkably, they were all born in 1912 and broke through in quick succession to revive public interest in golf in the midst of the darkest days of the Great Depression.

A few months later, I called on Sam Snead at the Greenbrier and enjoyed two days of golf and conversation with one of the most colorful, beloved, and controversial players of his time. Sam's seven major titles and eighty-two official victories made him the winningest player in PGA history, but I sensed that, not unlike his old rival Byron, he felt a little forgotten by writers and fans of the modern age. When I pointed out that I had just been hired to help Palmer write his long-awaited memoirs, Sam laughed and said in a low growl, "Well, you tell Arnold if it hadn't been for me and old Ben and Byron, hell, nobody would've ever heard of him!" He graciously invited me to come visit him up at his home in Hot Springs, Virginia, when I finished this project so we could "talk some more." I assured him I would love nothing better.

This was the background for my lunch visit with Herb Wind in 2001, when I wanted to hear what the dean of American golf writers, and coauthor of Ben's best-selling *Five Lessons: The Modern Fundamentals of Golf*, had to say about his mythic friend, but also about Sam and Byron.

Herb laughed when I told him what Sam had told me to tell Arnold Palmer, and smiled rather knowingly when I suggested it was a shame that up until then no one had produced major biographies on Sam and Byron like the one I was embarking upon with Ben. The deeper I got into my subject, the more I realized the critical roles Snead and Nelson played in shaping Hogan's life and golf game—not to mention reviving the game at a time when professional golf could easily have slipped back to little more than a second-rate sport.

"You're quite right. Both Byron and Sam, I think, perhaps feel a little forgotten in light of the so-called Hogan mystique." He paused to taste his chilled cucumber soup in the empty, sun-filled dining room. We were sitting by a large picture window, and through the glass the first brave tulips were poking up their heads to face yet another reluctant New England spring. "There's no question that Sam feels slighted by history and the golf establishment at large. Most of that stems from his painful record in the Opens. He never won our Open and, in fact, managed to lose several of them in the most agonizing ways possible. Generally speaking, no player is regarded as truly great unless he wins the tournament believed to be the hardest of all to win—our own Open. Sam could easily have won several of them, five or six by his own count, but he always seemed to author a different way to lose it. In doing so, he became convinced, as he once told me, that he was terribly jinxed. That's why winning that final Masters in 1954 meant so much to him."

I asked if Sam's colorful personality might have contributed to his image problems. Growing up in his adopted home of Greensboro, I'd heard enough darkly amusing stories about the Slammer to know that while his unfiltered backwoods showmanship appealed to millions of fans, some of his less savory comments and antics, rubbed others the wrong way. His off-color humor, for instance, was legendary. At one point, I asked Arnold Palmer about the annual Champions Dinner at Augusta, a tradition Ben Hogan started with money from his own pocket in 1953. Arnold smiled, shook his head, and said, "The dinner is never complete until Sam displays his physical prowess by kicking the top of the door and tells an even worse joke than the year before—at which point Byron politely excuses himself and goes home to bed."

At the other end of the spectrum, however, I knew from many conversations with Sam's closest friends that he was a man of uncommon generosity, quietly assisting groups and individuals who needed a financial boost—belying his popular image as that of a wealthy skinflint who kept his money safely stashed in a tin can buried in his backyard. If you scratched the surface of town life in Hot Springs, one found such stories were quite commonplace, almost always involving a local youngster, family, or organization in financial need. Moreover, I knew from my own experiences around him that, depending on his mood and the circumstances, Samuel Jackson Snead could be as charming and smooth as a Spanish diplomat—or as chilly as the January wind. "The darker side of Sam's large charisma," his longtime friend Bill Campbell told me one winter afternoon at his home in West Virginia, "is that Sam is possibly the most unfiltered and honest fellow you'll ever meet. Sam never left any doubt about how he felt about a person or circumstance. In this way he was pretty simple—and yet, to my way of thinking, he might have been the most interesting and complex of the three."

Herb nodded. "Sam was an original, no question about it. That's what endeared him to so many at a time when the game desperately needed a bona fide star and headline maker. The tour was really struggling when Sam broke through out west and won a flurry of tournaments on the winter tour in 1937. He was a complete unknown, a plainspoken hillbilly from the Blue Ridge Mountains, as they portrayed him—but he gave golf a legitimate star at a moment when the tour could easily have gone under. That same year, Byron won his first Masters and Sam nearly won the Open. People really started to pay attention to them, and interest in professional golf suddenly grew. Two years after that, Byron Nelson won the Open and the year after that, of course, Ben broke through at Pinehurst and won three tournaments in a matter of weeks. Suddenly you had three hot players making headlines."

Herb sipped his cucumber soup again and added, "There's something else I find fascinating, and no one has really written about this effect. If you look at the long history of golf, any time there were two or three great rivals in the game, the game flourished. In early Scotland you had the famous challenge money matches of the Morrises, young and old Tom, and Allan Robertson and later the Dunns from North Berwick. Then came Britain's Great Triumvirate of Vardon, Taylor, and Braid. They created golf's first popular golf boom and exported the passion for the game to our shores. We soon had our own homegrown stars and great rivals in the form of Bobby Jones, Walter Hagen, and Gene Sarazen. Golf grew in boundless leaps during these periods—and so, I might add, did the technology. That seemed to advance significantly any time there was a trio of stars."

"So how," I asked bluntly, "do Sam, Byron, and Ben rank in terms of trios of rivals?"

He looked up at me, glanced out the window at the emerging tulips, pursed his lips, and gently shook his graying head, his spoon hovering midair. Every year, I knew from his caregiver, Herb's brilliant mind was a little more fragile. But his eyes had a sympathetic, alert look in them, and his mind seemed to be happily roaming the fairways of his glorious reporting days. It would be the last lunch we ever had together.

"Perhaps I'm not the most neutral of observers on this subject, but I always felt there were never three better players who came along at the same moment—and did so much to propel the game forward. Any one of the three would have made that time remarkable. But the fact that Sam, Byron, and Ben all three appeared at the same moment and effectively changed how golf was perceived in this country—not to mention launched it into the modern era in terms of equipment and the many things they innovated—sets them apart, at least in my judgment, as the finest trio of any time."

Before I could agree with him, my host added, with visible emotion, "You know they were all three born the same year—1912. What a remarkable year. Fenway Park opened and the *Titanic* sunk. The fact that two of the three came out of the same caddie yard down in Texas is extraordinary. Equally important, I think, is the fact that their individual personalities, playing styles, and personal values couldn't have been more different. That's why each generated his own large group of die-hard followers. They shaped the game and influenced every generation of players that followed them. They introduced practices and ideas that are commonplace today."

"I keep thinking somebody should write about them," I heard myself say, something I'd been thinking about for months. "A book, I mean, about the effect their trio had on golf."

"Theirs is an extraordinary story that deserves to be told," he said, then looked at me and smiled again. "I think of them, in fact, as *our* great triumvirate—the American Triumvirate."

When I mentioned Herb's comments to Byron a few days later in Roanoke, he merely smiled. His second wife, Peggy, had made us a delicious lunch and lit a crackling fire in their den. After lunch, he showed me some beautiful woodworking projects he was working on out in his shop—one of them being a small chest for Tom Watson's daughter, Meg—and now we'd settled in his den to continue our conversation about the early days of the tour. The afternoon had turned gray and cold and Peggy had placed a beautiful plaid blanket on her husband's legs.

"That's very kind of Herb to say," said Byron. "Looking back, it was an amazing time in golf. But I sometimes feel like it happened to someone other than me. I really think Sam and Ben deserve the lion's share of the attention because they won more tournaments than I did."

"But only because you retired so early," I suggested.

The official PGA Tour record book spoke for itself. Sam Snead is credited with eighty-two tournament victories, a number that includes seven major championships. Ben Hogan's official number is nine majors and sixty wins, spanning a career that reached its celebrated apogee atop golf's Mount Olympus in 1953. Byron Nelson's total of fifty-two wins and five major championships takes on deeper significance when you take a closer look at his historic final year: he won eighteen out of thirty tournaments, collected seven second-place finishes and produced a scoring average of 68.33 that stood as a record for more than half a century. A common but false assumption is that Byron, who was deemed unfit for active military service due to a congenital blood disorder, pulled off the feat while much of his competition was away in the service. In fact, Sam played in twenty-seven events in 1945 and Ben played in eighteen. Both stars played in more than twenty-seven events in 1946 while Byron—preparing to officially retire and start his cattle ranch—scaled back to twenty-one. Between the resumption of the tour in 1944 and his final appearance in late 1946, Byron won an astonishing thirty-five of his last seventy-six tournaments.

Moreover, between 1945 and 1953, at least one member of this American Triumvirate won a tournament or finished in the top three more than 60 percent of the time. The record for the most wins in a season was, of course, owned by Byron, with eighteen, but the second and third names on the record list belonged to Ben (thirteen in 1946) and Sam (eleven in 1950). Not even Tiger Woods has ever come close to these marks.

Finally, recordkeeping was at best sketchy and at worst nonexistent back then, and in fact all three won dozens more tournaments than they were officially given credit for by the modern Tour. Sam's partisans, for instance, insist he won more than 135 tournaments: he himself claimed the PGA Tour should have at a minimum recognized 115 wins. Likewise, Byron captured at least two dozen two- or three-day events that aren't included in his total, and Ben told friends he won eighty-five tournaments of some sort or another. So a rough count suggests some 276 victories between the three of them.

Byron Nelson was in his prime, just thirty-four, when he walked away from the game, not unlike his friend and hero Bobby Jones. So one can only imagine what his "official" number would have been had he competed another dozen years. Something else to consider is which of the three men—at his peak—was actually the best player. Fans of Byron point out he had five major championships under his belt when he retired in 1946—two Masters titles, two PGAs, and one U.S. Open.

Entering that season, Sam had laid claim to only one major title, the 1942 PGA, but went on to win the British Open at St. Andrews. Ben won his first major championship that summer, too, the first of his two PGA Championships. "If Byron had wanted to keep playing," Bob Rosburg once told me, "I have no doubt the record everyone would be chasing today would have belonged to him."

True to his gentle, self-effacing nature and deep Christian convictions that regarded earthly achievements as secondary to matters of personal faith, Byron shrugged off these points as I politely raised them in his cozy den.

"You know," he said in his flat Texas drawl, "I know this may sound kind of strange to some folks, but I always considered the things I did after my playing days ended really more significant. I became a good rancher and very active in my church life. I had time to help a few young players who were coming along about that time. Eventually I became a broadcaster and became involved with the golf tournament over in Dallas. I know folks remember me for that eleven in a row, but to tell the truth, nothing meant more to me than helping people."

Unlike Sam or Ben, who enjoyed sweetheart deals with leading golf clubs and resorts that required little more than the use of their names, Byron remained an active head club professional almost up to the day he left the Tour, making his professional feats even more impressive. The young players he worked with included Frank Stranahan, Ken Venturi, Harvie Ward, Dave Marr, Johnny Miller, Corey Pavin, and Ben Crenshaw. His work and close friendship with Tom Watson preceded Watson's breakthrough and evolution into a major champion.

"There's no question that Byron unlocked the mystery of the modern golf swing," Venturi told me over the phone a few days before I ventured out to see Byron in Roanoke for the final time. "As far as I'm concerned, he really is the father of the modern golf swing. His golf instruction books—like Ben's—shaped thousands of young golf swings, including my own, and they're still doing it today. But more importantly, Byron is the finest gentleman and perhaps the greatest ambassador golf has ever had. He represents everything that is good about the game and the people who love it. In that respect, he touched untold millions."

Indeed, his knowledge of the swing—and mastery of it—prompted the USGA to nickname its own testing robot "Iron Byron." Perhaps the straightest driver of the ball ever, he is credited with developing the techniques that moved golf from the hickory shaft to the steel shaft era. "Byron's divots are so straight," Dave Marr once remarked, "they look like dollar bills."

The first player to become a full-time TV commentator, he led the way for Venturi, Miller, and several others. Then he focused his energies on the tournament in nearby Dallas that became the first PGA event to be permanently named in honor of a player, the Byron Nelson Classic, helping the Salesmanship Club of that city establish the model of charitable giving that's standard on tour today. His tenure as an honorary starter at the Masters lasted twenty years, almost a decade longer than anyone else.

During our last afternoon together in 2001, Byron seemed both eager to help with my Ben Hogan biography and pleased and a little surprised when I told him that Herb Wind had given me a broader idea, the story of an American Triumvirate.

"I will say this," he told me as we stood outside in a warm Texas wind before we shook hands and said goodbye. "It always struck me as unfortunate that Ben Hogan never really permitted the world to see who he really was—and by that I mean to say not just the cold and intimidating figure so many people think of. But the nice man I knew growing up, and the friend I grew close to when we traveled the early tour together with our wives. We had some wonderful times. And Ben has been both a friend and an inspiration to this game. Millions have tried to copy his golf swing. Every year seems to bring a new book about his secret. That should tell you something."

"And what about Sam?" I had to ask, recalling Arnold's remark about the Champions Dinner, inwardly bracing for the response.

But Lord Byron just smiled. "Sam is Sam. People either love or dislike Sam. There's no in between. Part of it is Sam doesn't care for strangers. But if he knows and trusts you, he can be the sole of charm. He's a lot more complex than most people think, and I've always believed he's a little misunderstood. He was very good for the game—the first serious athlete who kept himself in top shape. They all do that on tour these days. But Sam was the first. There's never been a more gifted natural player."

Then he winked at me and added, "That's why he and I still show up to hit the first shots at Augusta every spring, you know. Sam still tries to outdrive me, though I tell him, 'Why shouldn't you, Sam? I've been *retired* from golf for over fifty years!'"

A little over a year after *Ben Hogan: An American Life* was published, I stopped off in Latrobe during the 2006 U.S. Open to see the new house my boyhood hero Arnold Palmer had built for his new wife, Kit, a gracious lady from California.

Following the Saturday afternoon telecast from Winged Foot, Arnold and I went to dinner at the country club where he'd grown up and his father, Deacon, had been the professional. We sat at a small table by the window and talked about his grandson Sam's pending matriculation from Clemson to the Tour, my recent relocation from Maine to my native North Carolina, and how Tiger Woods now owned the PGA Tour and it seemed only a matter of time before he bettered Jack Nicklaus's record of eighteen major championships.

Arnold seemed pleased to learn I was happy to be back in my old boyhood stomping ground—where I'd first seen him play at the Greater Greensboro Open—and congratulated me on winning the USGA's Herbert Warren Wind Book Award for my biography on Ben Hogan. Ironically, Herb Wind had passed away just one week before the start of the Open at Pinehurst in 2005, the event that prompted my relocation home to North Carolina. It felt as if a circle had been completed for me—though, as I admitted to Arnold, thanks to Herb, I still had some unfinished business with Sam, Byron, and Ben.

I told him about the triumvirate idea and wondered if he felt, as I did, that these three remarkable sons of 1912—so utterly different in every respect—had collectively saved the ailing professional golf tour, elevating it to heights it hadn't enjoyed since the days of Jones and Hagen, and set the stage, as it were, for the coming of a king.

Arnold pondered for a moment. "You know," he finally began, "when I decided to turn professional, as Pap warned me, there wasn't a great deal of money in the professional game. Only a handful of players made a good living at it. It was still something of a vagabond's life. Most guys went broke out there. But the three guys we all looked to were Sam, Byron, and Hogan. They'd proved you could make a good living just playing golf and they did things that nobody else had ever done before."

"Such as?"

"Well, let's start with Sam. I met him first. We had a lot of fun playing together. Sam was a serious athlete who made the game look easy and fun to play. People were naturally drawn to that. He was always clowning around, making people smile, which made him all the more popular. I was an athlete, too, and in that respect he became a role model for me. I saw how he took care of himself and extended his career for decades. When talk about starting up a senior tour got serious, Sam was the first guy they called. He's one reason I supported the senior tour so enthusiastically—now called the Champions Tour, of course. Sam was great for golf."

"Byron?"

"Well, for me, Byron was the definition of a gentleman, the greatest ambassador of the game I ever saw. There's no question his golf swing took the game into the modern era, and his year in 1945 will never be equaled, period. The work he did on TV and with his charity tournament were the models for those who came after him. Byron's real gift is for people. He loves people and they love him. Don't believe he's ever turned anyone down for anything, including an autograph or a speaking engagement. He cares deeply about the traditions and he's inspired so many great young players in the game. I'd say he really influenced me the most of the three."

"How about Ben?"

Arnold smiled. A commonly held view is that Hogan resented this brash and upstart kid from Pennsylvania whose style left nothing in the bag and the massive galleries he quickly generated—an army on the hoof, so to speak. Tellingly, in my presence at least, Arnold always referred to Sam and Byron by their first names, Hogan by his last.

"You know, Hogan and I actually liked each other. We had our differences but certainly had great respect for each other. He was a true professional in every respect of the word. I think the essential difference between us is that Hogan didn't need anyone but Hogan and I was more like Sam and Byron. I needed the fans. Still, you can't argue with the things he accomplished—the way he meticulously practiced and prepared for a tournament, the ability he developed to summon whatever was necessary to win, not to mention the really fine equipment company he created after he left the game. These were all important improvements, things taken for granted in golf today. And the difficulties he overcame also can't be overstated. Unless you've won a Masters or a U.S. Open or a British Open, you have no idea how difficult that is to do. Hogan earned his glory—and in doing so he made a lot of people pay attention to the game of golf."

Before I could ask him another question, Arnold said, "There's no question in my mind, they paved the way for the rest of us."

"You mean the Big Three?" I asked—referring, of course, to the triumvirate of Palmer, Nicklaus, and Player that dominated golf through the 1960s and early '70s, yet further proof of Herb Wind's theory about the power of three.

"No," Arnold came back. "I mean all of us. You. Me. Anyone who loves golf. Even Tiger Woods. We all owe them a big debt of gratitude."

This, coming from the most charismatic and influential figure in modern golf history, really meant something. And it seemed like both a good ending point for a fine evening with my boyhood hero and a great starting point for *American Triumvirate.*

1

YEAR OF WONDERS

A T SEVEN O'CLOCK ON a cool Indian summer Saturday evening, eager to catch a glimpse of the future, thousands of patrons began filing into venerable Mechanic's Hall on Huntington Avenue, happy to be among the first to see the wonders of the 1912 Boston Electric Show. "Electric devices unheard of just one year ago are to be exhibited in full operation," wrote a reporter for *The Christian Science Monitor*, "inventions which make the fable of Aladdin and his magical lamp seem prosy by comparison."

Emblematic of the affair, Mechanic's Hall was ablaze with forty thousand light bulbs, the largest display of incandescent lighting ever mounted; the creation of the Edison Illuminating Company of New Yorks outshone the "Great White Way itself," the company promised. Owing to the marvels of alternate electrical current, wide-eyed patrons wandered through the vast hall being serenaded by live opera and choir selections amplified by an invention called the *microphone* ("such a delicate instrument that by its agency the tread of a fly is magnified until it sounds like the clomping of a horse over the loose planks of a country bridge") and saw inventions designed to transform everything "from the farmyard to Main Street, from the shop floor to the housewife's kitchen." They viewed a dairy farm where cows were milked by automated machines, for instance, promising to make the drudgery of hand milking obsolete, and an electric forking machine that could unload two hundred bales of hay from a wagon and stack them in a loft in a matter of minutes rather than hours, reducing the need for hired labor.

There were special motion pictures displaying how the dedicated electrical current would soon transform businesses from accountancy to coal mining; how it would count money in banks and permit a clerk in one location to inquire about a customer's account balance in a separate building altogether, achieving a response within seconds; how bakers would never need to touch the bread they sold because machines would mechanically mold dough into perfect loaves and bake them by the clock to golden perfection; how lumber mills would use power saws to mill stockpiles of flawless high-grade lumber for the booming furniture and house-building trades in minutes, not hours; how darkened streets would soon be made bright as noon by municipal lighting soon coming to market, "pressing back the cloak of night and greatly reducing the scourge of crime and hoodlum behavior."

Perhaps the most popular aspect of the revolution on the doorstep, the show's organizers promised, would be the liberation of the ordinary housewife thanks to special electric appliances that would wash and sanitize dishes, eliminating the need for madam or a domestic to ever touch a single china plate that wasn't sparkling clean. Ovens would bake cakes and roasts according to an electric clock that would make expert cooking a snap at home. An exciting new commercial "electric refrigerator"—the world's first, being introduced that year by the General Electric Corporation—promised to make spoiled fruits, vegetables, and meats a thing of the past.

"This magical showcase at Mechanic's Hall fittingly serves as a capstone to a year that has seen one astonishment after another, all aimed at providing more leisure time for Americans to enjoy the bounty of their lives," declared *The Boston Evening Traveler*. "Many will look back and perhaps agree there has never been a year quite like it."

To be sure, it had been a year of human wonders.

Despite jitters about rising Anglo-German tensions over some obscure place called the Balkans in a faraway corner of Europe, most Americans were enjoying an unprecedented sense of prosperity and well-being, the afterglow of a Gilded Age that produced untold wealth for a few but also labor reforms that dramatically expanded the reach and power of a newly emerging middle class. Earlier that year in Detroit, Henry Ford revealed plans for the first moving assembly line, a concept that would revolutionize the manufacture of reasonably priced consumer goods and herald the arrival of a reliable automobile that almost any American with a good job could afford to own. Banks responded by offering new credit terms to qualified customers based on easy time-payment plans.

In January, New Mexico became the forty-seventh state; less than a month later, Arizona joined the union, too. The world's first "flying boat" took flight, Frederick Law made the first successful parachute jump from the Statue of Liberty, and a few weeks later another daredevil upped the ante by leaping from an airplane. For the first time ever that year, the 100 mph air speed barrier was broken and a transcontinental passenger flight was completed.

Daily newspapers, experiencing a surge in circulation, couldn't cover the emerging wonders of human achievement fast enough, including Amundsen's successful race to the South Pole and Scott's unfortunate demise, the establishment of China as a republic, and the exciting launch of the *Titanic*, said to be the most lavish and technically advanced ocean liner in history, all but unsinkable according to widely distributed reports.

With more time and disposable income on their hands, Americans read with interest about Mrs. Taft planting the first cherry trees along the Potomac in Washington, the formation of the Girl Scouts in Savannah, Georgia, and Columbia University's creation of something called the Pulitzer Prize. A record number of public libraries and more than one hundred movie theaters opened in 1912 alone, bringing the magic of the first Keystone Kops movie to small towns across the nation. That summer children were either playing a new craze called "marbles" or enjoying a fruit-flavored summer candy called "Life Savers" that was guaranteed not to melt in summer heat.

Professional sports were another lifesaver, particularly baseball. At least a half dozen records fell that year—for triples and stolen bases, attendance and consecutive wins. After multiple suspensions for fighting with fans and opponents, Ty Cobb publicly hinted at an early retirement from the game. After 511 wins, Cy Young actually did retire. Several state-of-the-art ballparks opened that year, including Tiger Stadium in Detroit and Boston's Fenway Park, where a sold-out crowd of 27,000 fans got to see the hometown Red Sox beat the New York Highlanders (soon to be the Yankees) 7–6 in a marathon season opener that lasted eleven innings.

Ironically, Fenway Park was knocked off the front pages of Boston's newspapers by news that the *Titanic*, on its maiden voyage, had struck an iceberg and sunk off the coast of Newfoundland, killing 1,500 passengers and crew.

In 1912, golf in this country was barely two decades old, played by roughly two million Americans on about fifteen hundred courses of widely varying quality in all forty-eight states. For the vast majority, it was simply a recreational pursuit with unmistakably patrician overtones, conveyed to these shores by a wave of immigrant Scottish professionals who accurately perceived that a comfortable living could be made promoting the game of their ancestors. Until fairly recently, Americans had been more comfortable as spectators than as participants at sporting events. But the surprising popularity of golf, particularly among the middle and merchant classes, suggested that a cultural sea change might be under way. In addition to the private clubs where it first took root, virtually every municipality of any size now offered a rudimentary golf course, most of which were crowded on any given weekend in fair weather months with men and women eager to learn about the game.

More telling, perhaps, at least eight different companies were now manufacturing hickory-shafted golf clubs, and a half a dozen more producing a newly introduced rubber-cored golf ball. Meanwhile, such seasonal resorts at places like Poland Spring in the highlands of Maine, Saratoga in New York, and Pinehurst down in the Carolina Sandhills—which was in the process of adding its third golf course under the guidance of Scotsman Donald Ross—helped establish the game as both a wholesome activity for the new leisure class and a serious competitive sport for any swell who had the gumption to try to excel at it.

All of this was the result of one man's international celebrity.

A dozen years earlier, in February of 1900, when Harry Vardon came strolling down a ship's gangway to begin his heavily publicized exhibition tour of America, he was greeted like a visiting head of state by a crush of reporters and photographers eager to learn everything they could about England's most acclaimed sportsman, an elegant, gracious man who'd been nicknamed "The Greyhound" because he typically bounded ahead of competitors in tournaments and rarely yielded ground. His only rival, every British schoolboy knew, was John Henry

Taylor, a quiet, dignified man from the windswept links at North Devon Golf Club, more popularly known as Westward Ho! J.H., as he was called by his friend Harry and other intimates, had won the British Open Championship twice, in 1894 and again the following year.

Vardon, the son of a manual laborer from the Isle of Jersey, began his working life as a gardener but quickly evolved into a club professional, employed at Ganton Golf Club in Lincolnshire. He was twenty-nine years old when he arrived in America, having already claimed three Open Championships with a slightly upright golf swing that was so deceptively smooth and refined that his irons and fairway woods rarely left more than a modest scuff on the turf. Opponents claimed Harry's tee shots were so maddeningly precise in tournament play they often wound up in the same spot where he had hardly left a mark from the day before.

His ostensible reason for visiting America was to play in the fledgling United States Open and conduct an extensive tour of public exhibitions to promote the Vardon Flier, a so-called gutty golf ball manufactured by the A. G. Spalding Company of Chickopee, Massachusetts. Mr. Spalding had a private course on his estate, and had agreed to pay Vardon a princely fee of $2,000 for ten months of exhibitions, on top of any appearance fees he could generate during the tour. Back home, J. H. Taylor had also confided to friends his intention to give chase to his friend the Greyhound and all comers at the National Championship of America, conducted that year at Chicago Golf Club in Wheaton, Illinois.

Whoever actually won the affair—accomplished thus far only by five Scottish immigrants, each gainfully employed as a club professional in America—would undoubtedly result in an avalanche of favorable press for the ball he used, for golf was not only increasingly shaped by both the men who played and those who knew that money could be made catering to the growing number of adherents.

For nearly half a century, the venerable gutta-percha ball had reigned supreme, dating from a famous dispute between golf's two most celebrated founding fathers. In the 1840s, Allan Robertson, a short, friendly Scot, was the first true professional and widely regarded as the finest player of his time; the son of a senior caddie at the Royal and Ancient Golf Club, he operated a thriving business making clubs and traditional feathery balls just off Links Road in St. Andrews. Although a new feathery ball could be driven great distances, the ball—made from a top-hat-ful of goose feathers compressed into a stitched leather orb—was fragile and subject to either losing its shape or breaking apart after only slight use. The balls were also expensive to produce, costing about half a crown apiece, thus attractive to the better-heeled classes.

Still, records show that Robertson and his shop assistants turned out 2,456 featheries in 1844 alone. Twenty-three-year-old Tom Morris—son of a local weaver, he'd taken to the game by batting a wine cork around the Auld Grey Toon, as locals called St. Andrews—had worked for Robertson since the age of fourteen, apprenticing in his shop for five years before becoming a journeyman salesman. By 1845 Morris was not only his junior partner but also nearly his equal on the links. The two steadfastly avoided playing a head-to-head match but frequently teamed up in big-money challenge matches against other leading professionals including Willie Park Sr. and the Dunns of Musselburgh. A famous match against Willie and Jamie Dunn with 400 pounds sterling at stake helped seal their reputations. Four holes down with eight to play, Morris and Robertson closed the gap and won on the final hole, earning the sobriquet "The Invincibles" among the golfing laity. News of the victory didn't hurt their business one bit.

In April of 1848, however, a man named Tom Peters stepped into Robertson's shop to show him a new kind of golf ball he'd acquired from a local divinity student named Robert Patterson. It was hard and perfectly round, made from the hardened milk sap of the *Palaquium gutta* tree of Malaysia. Three years before, Robert's father, Rev. Robert Adams Patterson, had discovered strips of this malleable substance used to pack a statue of the Hindu god Vishnu sent by a friend from the Far East. Being naturally thrifty, he boiled the material down and used sheets of it to resole his family's shoes, but his enterprising son saw a potentially better use for the waterproof material. Young Robert used the softened gutta to make perfectly round golf balls he promptly went out and played with on the links. Then, after years of tinkering with the formula, his brother came up with a ball that flew farther and straighter and kept its shape much longer than the traditional featheries. Moreover, the newly patented "gutty" ball could be made and sold at a fraction of the cost.

Peters declared that the day of the feathery ball was over, and Robertson—who'd introduced the use of iron clubs in competition, heads of earlier sets having been made of apple wood—agreed to give the new ball a try. He woefully hooked his first shot, perhaps intentionally, and reportedly dismissed the gutty ball with undisguised contempt.

The problem arose when mild and mannerly Tom Morris teamed with a member of the R&A in a match in the summer of 1851, and used these controversial new balls. When he heard of this betrayal, an outraged Robertson confronted his longtime partner and fired him on the spot. A short time later, Morris was hired by the Prestwick Golf Club to lay out and maintain its new course and serve as club professional.

Old Tom, as he was soon to be called, started his own equipment business, making clubs and balls and selling both featheries and gutties. He would also be instrumental in mounting the first Open Championship at Prestwick in 1860, a year after his fiery mentor, Robertson, had passed away, and himself captured the title four times from 1861 to 1867. By that time, the gutty was the preferred ball of better players, including his son, Young Tom Morris, who won his first of four consecutive Opens in 1868, a mere stripling of twenty who shattered scoring records and brought the game to new levels of brilliance and popular notice before his premature death following the sudden loss of his young wife and infant son while he was away playing a match.

The reign of Allan Robertson and Tom Morris *père et fils* was over, but the durable gutty prevailed for another many years in competition.

When J. H. Taylor, the current British Open champion, opened his locker at the Chicago Golf Club in early October of 1900, he supposedly found a complimentary tin of a new rubber-cored ball that was causing a major row on both sides of the Atlantic, the gift of a bicycle manufacturer named Coburn Haskell.

Haskell, a mediocre but passionate golfer, had a brainstorm one warm afternoon while sitting on the porch of the Cleveland Country Club, chatting with the head professional. As he squeezed a handful of rubber bands, the story goes, a revolutionary idea took shape. For all its popularity, the gutta-percha ball had its flaws—principally a certain deadness if it wasn't struck perfectly. Haskell contacted a friend named Bertram Work at the B. F. Goodrich plant in Akron, twenty miles south of Cleveland, and explained his idea of wrapping bands of rubber tightly around a solid rubber core, then covering it all with gutta-percha, thereby producing a much livelier golf ball. Work signed on and the two struck a deal to evenly split any proceeds from their innovation, which they patented in 1898. When the first "Haskell" was put into play a short time later, its superiority became immediately apparent.

The new ball flew twenty yards beyond the old gutty. Traditionalists both here and abroad quickly inveighed sharply against the new American golf ball—including Harry Vardon himself, initially dismissing them as "Bounding Billies" because they allegedly were difficult to control around the greens. But the swift acceptance by players forever in search of greater distance and any competitive edge guaranteed another major turning point in the game.

This happened just as three players were becoming dominant.

By the time Vardon and Taylor met at the Chicago Golf Club, they were the most famous golfers in the world. The reserved and dignified Taylor, a naturally quiet man prone to gnawing self-doubt, was nevertheless said to rarely yield a lead once he held it. He'd collected his third British Open trophy, the Claret Jug, just weeks before making this trip—in large part, like Vardon, to promote his own burgeoning business interests. Convinced beyond any doubt that golf had a bright future in America, he entered into a business agreement with a childhood friend named George Cann to start a club-making firm based in Pittsburgh. He'd also contracted *Golf*, America's first magazine devoted to the game, to write a series of instruction articles. For this he was paid $2,000, a large sum for an athlete's literary services.

Vardon's Open Championship run began at Muirfield in 1896, when he beat Taylor in a dramatic playoff; he then added back-to-back titles in the last two years of the century. His imperturbable grace and seemingly effortless swing made him the darling of America's raw and largely uninformed sporting press. This was the age of yellow journalism, when sensational headlines, political scandals, and sex crimes dominated the biggest newspapers, the reporters often inventing colorful details and nefarious intrigue when the simple facts seemed bland and banal. So it comes as no surprise that the widely reported blood feud between Vardon and Taylor didn't exist, neither of them paying spies to keep tabs on the other's whereabouts and practice habits. They were actually close friends, and frequent traveling partners back home in Britain, fellow professionals who aimed to elevate the game's stature within their own borders—and perhaps, however they could, in America.

Their playing styles, on the other hand, couldn't have presented a more striking contrast. Vardon's high, soaring, and gentle fades always seemed to settle with uncanny accuracy somewhere within the vicinity of the flag, whereas Taylor's low, right-to-left shots often ran along the fairway and invariably rolled onto the green, which proved particularly effective on a true links. There were personal differences, too. Taylor would visibly stew over a poorly executed shot whereas Vardon typically offered a faint nonchalant shrug and moved on. And while Taylor seemed tongue-tied when peppered with questions by members of the rowdy Yankee press, Vardon appeared to relish being in the spotlight. Indeed, aside from their friendship and mounting fame, perhaps the only thing they had in common was their stubborn devotion to the gutta-percha golf ball.

In an attempt to eliminate the bumpy putting surfaces that were common to American courses of that era, the Chicago Golf Club used a special machine that brushed the grass to a velvety consistency. Taylor, who putted miserably in the opening morning round of the championship, gently grumbled afterward that it was like putting on the head of a lad whose hair had been combed in the wrong direction. Even so, with a 76, he jumped out to a three-stroke lead over his friend and rival, Vardon shooting a 79. After J.H. struggled that afternoon to an 82 to Harry's 78, the two greats had reversed positions but still led the tournament. The rest of a fairly decent American-born field was never taken seriously and was ignored by the press.

Putting continued to bedevil Taylor over the concluding two rounds. Vardon extended his lead to four strokes in the third round and a seemingly insurmountable six by the start of the final nine. J.H. gamely nibbled away, however, and trimmed Harry's lead to two strokes through seventeen, but the Greyhound struck one of his patented brassie shots on the home hole and finished with 313 to Taylor's 315. Both, as predicted, were well clear of the field at the end. Dave Bell, a fine player from Chicago's Midlothian Club, finished seven strokes back, though in most accounts his name was never mentioned.

By any measure, Vardon's grand exhibition tour of America, capped by his victory, was an unqualified success. Wherever he went, vast and adoring crowds turned out to study his stylish technique, whether at the Jordan Marsh department store in downtown Boston (where an impressionable seven-year-old caddie named Francis Ouimet from Brookline saw him hitting balls into a net) or down in remote Pinehurst where more than three thousand spectators materialized in the heat of a longleaf wilderness to watch him play on a Donald Ross course that was more sand than grass. During his visit to New York, Wall Street suspended business so traders could attend an exhibition match at one of the country's first public courses. The Greyhound was feted by mayors, photographed with beauty queens, presented with the keys to a dozen different cities. In eighty-eight matches, competing against local club champions and head professionals who knew their courses like the back of their hands, he lost only once and set scoring records on half the courses he played.

The warmth of America and open personality of Americans charmed and relaxed Harry Vardon, prompting him, in light of a dry and unhappy marriage back home, to seriously consider immigrating with his brother Tom (also a fine player and club professional at Sandwich) to the States. In clubhouses where no professional had ever set foot, Harry was not only an honored guest of the membership but was treated as a first among equals and a conquering hero.

He suffered but one disappointment—the Vardon Flier he so tirelessly promoted was a commercial flop. The gutty was soon as extinct as the feathery, given the Haskell ball's mounting success in major championships and popularity in everyday play. Its gutta-percha cover was replaced by balata, and the patterns and dimples on its surface were now stamped by machines, not by hand. Coburn Haskell's basic design proved to be a revolutionary advance in golf, persisting until the 1970s and becoming known as the "modern ball."

Against the surging popularity of the Haskell ball, the Vardon Flier sunk like a stone, but that was Vardon's only failure.

In every other respect, Harry Vardon's barnstorming in 1900—enhanced by J. H. Taylor and his own promotional efforts—helped to alter the perceptions of a game and the sports consciousness of a nation. Within a year, more than two hundred new golf clubs had been organized and close to one million Americans had taken up the game (many using an overlapping grip the press mistakenly attributed to Vardon, who actually picked it up from a top amateur named Findley). Golf in this country had never experienced such a surge of growth and popularity.

Eleven years later, at the Chicago Golf Club, Johnny McDermott of Atlantic City finally picked the British lock on the United States Open, becoming the first homebred professional to win the national championship, a feat he would successfully duplicate at the Country Club of Buffalo in 1912. Watching closely from the gallery that week was a cocky unknown assistant club pro from Rochester named Walter Hagen, who had recently turned down a baseball contract to play with the Philadelphia Phillies.

With two Opens under his belt, the brash and chesty McDermott openly boasted that he would happily take on all comers—including the great Harry Vardon, J. H. Taylor, and a surging James Braid, a Scotsman who since 1901 had collected five Claret Jugs and narrowly missed claiming two more. During these years, in a brilliant series of foursome matches staged across England and Scotland, Vardon and Taylor played Braid and Sandy Herd of St. Andrews, and when a Lincolnshire newspaperman described the three Open winners as the "Great Triumvirate," the Fleet Street press snatched up the phrase and ran with it.

In part because of McDermott's challenge, but also because he harbored deep affection for Americans, Vardon was finally persuaded to make another tour—this one with his friend and fellow professional Edward "Ted" Ray—for the U.S. Open at Brookline, America's oldest country club.

By now, however, things had changed. Shortly after winning the British Open in 1903, scarcely a month after the R&A chose not to ban the controversial Haskell ball in its Open Championship, Vardon had returned to his new post at the South Herts Golf Club in the London suburbs to rest and recover from a tournament that had visibly aged him. Within a fortnight, while playing a casual round with members, he suffered a massive lung hemorrhage that sent him to a Norfolk sanatorium for months. Tuberculosis was the diagnosis. Fleet Street insisted he'd picked it up on his American tour.

Though his beautiful swing and tempo were intact, Vardon was slow to recover his championship form. His hand visibly shook over putts, for instance, and his stamina waned in the closing stages of rounds. Perhaps for this reason alone, the first decade of the new century belonged almost entirely to James Braid, who in 1910 passed both Vardon and Taylor in Open totals with five. But the Greyhound finally came charging back in 1911. Amid swarming crowds at his brother Tom's club at Sandwich, Harry found his old magic and beat the formidable Frenchman Arnaud Massy in a thirty-six-hole playoff, hoisting a fifth Claret Jug himself. American newspapers heralded this victory as if one of their own had come back from the dead.

Following an exhibition tour comparable to that of 1900, Vardon and

Ray arrived in Brookline for the U.S. Open, whose field boasted Taylor but also Johnny McDermott and young Walter Hagen.

After fifty-four holes, the favorites Vardon and Ray were tied at 225. The only real surprise was that a young local kid was also at 225. Francis Ouimet, twenty years old and the Massachusetts Amateur champion, was unknown outside the Boston area. He'd grown up right across the street from the country club where he'd caddied for years and now found himself tied with two of the finest players in history. Nobody gave him any chance whatsoever against such legends.

What happened next changed the history of golf in America. Defying the odds and common sense, Francis Ouimet tied Vardon and Ray in the final round, then beat them by five and six strokes respectively in the eighteen-hole playoff. An ecstatic gallery lofted the heroic young amateur on its shoulders and celebrated for days.

Gracious in defeat, after hailing young Ouimet's historic achievement, the Englishmen set sail for home. Less than a year later, the Great Triumvirate—tied at five Opens apiece—would reconvene in high British summer at Prestwick, the Open's birthplace, for another shot at immortality. Both Taylor and Braid widely acknowledged that Vardon ranked first among them, and in fact he beat his old friend by three strokes, and the younger Scot by ten, becoming the first man to hoist the Claret Jug six times, a record that still stands ninety-five years later. But with the outbreak of World War I only weeks away, the R&A suspended the British Open Championship until further notice.

The Great Triumvirate's glorious run was over.

Meanwhile, back in the States, one giddy Boston editorialist confidently predicted that thanks to Francis Ouimet's astonishing triumph, the day would not be too distant when America produced its own great triumvirate. This story continued to reverberate throughout the country, to the rolling farmlands of central Texas and even the deepest hollows of Virginia's rugged Blue Ridge Mountains—penetrating the heartland of an awakening nation where, in due course, three remarkable young men—born just months apart in the wondrous year of 1912—would indeed fulfill that bold newsprint prophecy.

2

THE POWER OF THREE

IS THERE ANY SIGNIFICANCE to the fact that the three greatest play-ers of their era, and perhaps the entire twentieth century itself, were born on three consecutive days of the week, three months apart from each other?

Sam Snead thought so. "One time Ben Hogan come up to my tour-nament at the Greenbrier and I was showin' him around town and we got to talkin' about how we each come up in golf," Sam once explained. "Ben didn't let out much about himself, you know—people got the impression he was just unfriendly that way. But this time we got to talkin' and I learned we'd been born about the same time in the same year, except I was born in spring and he come along in late summer. Later I learned Byron Nelson was the same age. He was born sometime that winter, see, which mean we come along one, two, three. That's kind of how we got known out on tour, too, Byron first, then me, then Ben. He didn't put too much stock in that but my mama thought num-bers were important, if you know what I mean. And so do most golfers."

Across the ages, in every known human society, the number three holds an uncommon power in human affairs, a symbol of balance and divine fullness. It's frequently a sign of transformation and perfection itself.

In all of nature there are three stages of existence: birth, life, and death. Time itself represents a triad: past, present, future. In the Bible, three magi come from the East seeking the newborn Jesus, who three days after his crucifixion is resurrected. Not surprisingly, Christianity organized itself around the concept of a Holy Trinity, the Father, the

Son, and the Holy Ghost. But the number also dominates other ancient cultures and religions as well. In Egypt, for instance, it was regarded as the purest articulation of the cosmos, best symbolized by the three great pyramids of Giza. The Greeks believed man's life was shaped by three Fates, three Graces, and three Furies. In Chinese, three represents absolute harmony, a symbol found prominently displayed on the walls of the Temple of Heaven in Beijing. Across medieval Europe, symbols of three graced the shields of Templar knights and cropped up repeatedly in everything from Shakespeare's plays to nursery rhymes and fairy tales, meant to entertain but instruct in the ways of the world—three little pigs, three bears, three witches, three wishes.

Not to put too fine a point on the subject, modern science tells us there are three primary colors from which all others—including white—are derived. In music, three basic notes dominate the musical scale. Pythagoras, the father of math, declared three the perfect number because it contains its own beginning, middle, and end.

In the context of our story, perhaps all of this means absolutely nothing and is simply a happy coincidence—except that scientific methodology regards the number two as a statistical coincidence, three as evidence of a significant evolutionary pattern.

Whatever one might choose to make of this numerical phenomenon, simple coincidence or cosmic design, the first of the three, John Byron Nelson Jr., was born at home just outside Waxahachie, Texas, on a cold, overcast Sunday evening in February of 1912, the first of three children belonging to Madge Allen Nelson and her quiet but hardworking farmer husband, John.

Samuel Jackson Snead was Monday's child, the last of six born to Harry and Laura Snead at home in the tiny Blue Ridge hamlet of Ashwood, Virginia, three miles from the leafy resort village of Hot Springs, on May 27, a beautiful Appalachian spring day.

Finally, on August 13, 1912, Clara Hogan gave birth to her third child on a Tuesday at the new Women's Clinic in the county seat of Stephenville, Texas. For reasons unclear—possibly having to do with a lingering Western superstition that all newborns should be properly named at home, where more than half of Americans were still born in 1912—she chose not to name her new baby son until she brought him home to the modest wood frame house she and husband Chester rented on Camden Street in Dublin, a small town that boasted a tidy opera house and a couple of popular saloons, six miles from what not so long before was considered Comanche territory.

The strong-willed, unsentimental daughter of a successful cotton broker and prominent member of the Dublin Baptist Church, Clara's considerable social aspirations were possibly compromised by marriage to the handsome heir to the village blacksmith shop, a pleasant and if somewhat dreamy fellow called Chester Hogan. She gave her first two children the rather fanciful names of Royal and Princess but chose to name her third William Ben Hogan after his two grandfathers, Chester's blacksmith father, William Hogan, and her own father, Ben Williams, a fastidious dresser who was known to have an excellent head for numbers. She called the new baby "Bennie" for short. Clara was just eighteen years old.

Of the three who would, in time, constitute the greatest triumvirate ever in competitive golf, Nelson's was the only one whose birth was difficult. "My mother once told me the labor took all day and into the night," Byron recounted in his memoir *How I Played the Game*. "It took so long the doctor who came out from town was all but certain that I would not survive being born. But my mother was a determined woman who wouldn't give up. He finally had to use forceps to get me out. It broke my nose and I still have these little dents in my skull, you see, from that ordeal. I must have been pretty still because the doctor assumed I hadn't made it and just set me aside, on a table. While he worked to save my mother my Grandmother Allen, my mother's mother, took care of me. The story I always heard was that she got me cleaned up and I took a breath and she yelled out, 'Doctor, this baby is *alive!*' The toll on my mother was heavy, though. She needed a long time to get back on her feet. There were no antibiotics and medicines available back then. She just rested and slowly regained her strength. I weighed twelve pounds, eight ounces. I believe that doctor told my mother he'd never delivered a baby that large. Anyway, that's the way I came into this world."

Madge Nelson was nineteen, a spirited, highly intelligent and religious girl, still an infant when her family moved from East Tennessee to the Lone Star State two decades after the Civil War, much as the Hogans fled to Texas from the poverty of Mississippi immediately after the war. She was a crack Bible scholar and schoolteacher when she married John Nelson, four years her senior, in February of 1911. Their married life started on the 160-acre cotton farm he'd inherited when he was just six, after his father died of tuberculosis, five and a half years after the same disease—then called consumption—had claimed his mother. A pair of maiden aunts raised him on the family's farm in Long Branch, a small farming junction just outside Waxahachie, in a stark and simple farmhouse heated by a large woodstove in winter and shaded by a pair of large cottonwoods in the blazing summers. Madge had an uncommon fondness for the Book of Proverbs and the poetry of Lord George Gordon Byron, which is why she called her son "Byron."

Byron was seven when his sister, Ellen, was born. By then his father had sold their farm and leased a 240-acre cotton farm on the bluffs above the San Saba River in south-central Texas. With its handsome columned courthouse and lush groves of pecan trees that locals claimed predated Columbus's arrival in the New World, San Saba was a beautiful town with half a dozen churches and a violent cowboy past—famous for the "Mob Rule" violence that required the Texas Rangers to keep the peace, resulting in the deaths of forty-three gunslingers. The year the Nelson family moved there hoping to expand their fortunes, 3.5 million pounds of pecans were shipped out of San Saba, more than twice as many as anyplace else in America. The town called itself the "Pecan Capital of the World."

The Nelsons lived a dozen miles out in the country in a thin-walled sharecropper's house that overlooked the fields and river. One summer Byron's family killed sixty-five rattlesnakes around their house, and Byron recalled first putting on shoes about age eight and joining his father's hired hands in the cotton fields, weeding rows of the state's leading cash crop through summer and picking the prickly balls with sticky resin in the fall. "I can't say I ever liked picking cotton much because it made your hands bleed and it was powerful hot, hard work," Byron recalled nearly eight decades later. "But my parents encouraged me to work hard because they knew our field hands would work harder when they saw a child my size working like I did."

Until then, out of necessity, Byron was educated at home, but when a new primary school opened three miles away, he was permitted to ride a coal-black horse to class over the objections of his maternal grandmother, who came to stay with the financially struggling Nelsons from time to time. Because Byron already knew how to read and write and do his multiplication tables up to twelve, the principal promoted him to the third grade. He earned constant As in spelling and penmanship. "I missed being outside all day. And I missed being at home with my folks, particularly my mother. My father was one of the finest hardworking men you ever met, but I'd have to say it was my mother who really helped shape my outlook the most. She was such a strong but gentle person who knew her Bible and taught me early that its messages were the only way to live your life, to do right, to be strong."

Lack of money was always an issue for the family, in part because the boll weevil devastated Texas cotton crops during the first two decades of the century until a formal eradication program was established by the state, but also because the prosperity that was beginning to light up the country's larger cities and prompt record numbers of Europeans to immigrate had yet to filter down to the remote, hard-scrabble Southwest.

Complicating matters, when America entered the First World War in 1917, John Nelson was drafted but then turned down for active service due to a mild case of tuberculosis. After less than a year in San Saba, he moved his family a hundred miles farther west to the prosperous railroad town of San Angelo, the county seat of Tom Green County, which had the largest sheep and lamb livestock yards in Texas and also one of the largest sanatoriums in the Southwest. They lived in a house rented by Madge's parents, the Allens, who'd temporarily relocated from Fort Worth to the "Oasis of West Texas" in order to be near their son Benton, Byron's uncle, who was under treatment at the sanatorium. John found part-time work loading bundles of mohair wool onto freight cars on the Santa Fe Railroad and hauling gravel for the state crews that were constructing a new paved highway north to Fort Worth. When he found himself too far away to get home for the night, and unable to afford staying in a boardinghouse, he often took to sleeping in an empty piano crate he carried along with him. "Our family," Byron recorded in his memoirs many years later, "knew what poor meant."

After Benton died of TB, Byron's baby sister, Ellen, was also diagnosed with traces of the highly communicable disease. The family moved north for a time to the Allens' permanent home in Alvarado, twenty-six miles south of Fort Worth, then into a small frame house in a mixed-race, working-class neighborhood called Six Stop, so named because it was the sixth stop on the bus line that linked the most famous cowtown in the West to Dallas. John found a job driving a delivery truck for White Swan Foods but got laid off during an economic slump that followed the great influenza pandemic that killed between 50 and 100 million people—3 percent of the world's population—between March of 1918 and summer of 1920. Fortunately, he soon found a better job making delivery runs for the Dyer Feed Company on 15th Street in Fort Worth, a job he kept for many years. Known to be a fair boss, Mr. Dyer was an unsentimental character who swore like a ranch hand and drank hard liquor. Under the influence of his hardworking Christian delivery man, or so the family lore held, Mr. Dyer eventually reformed his ways and softened up.

"I think it was those early years when we moved to the city that I began to think about someday just having a ranch of my own out in the country," Byron Nelson mused many decades later one afternoon at his ranch in Roanoke. "My earliest and happiest memories, after all, were all associated with being out in the country, shoeless and as happy as could be, a little fella riding that coal-black horse to school and back. That sort of thing stays with you, don't you know. Life in Fort Worth was very different, very tough at times."

During this flight from disease and poverty, a third child, Charles, appeared—yet another mouth to feed—and Madge Nelson turned to her faith for strength, joining the local Church of Christ community and rarely missing dual Sunday services, which not only shaped her oldest son's spiritual values but probably saved his life. While playing with a puppy that belonged to some neighbor children, Byron was exposed to rabies and sent for twenty-one days to stay at a state mental hospital in Austin, where the cost of treatment—a series of painful daily shots administered with a large needle into the abdomen—would be covered by the state. About halfway through, after developing severe headaches and high fever, he was sent home to Fort Worth. The instant his mother touched his burning head, she looked at her husband and declared, "This child's got typhoid fever."

While he battled the dreaded salmonella bacteria—generally associated with the ingestion of contaminated water, a disease that supposedly once wiped out a third of Periclean Athens—Byron's body weight dropped from 124 to 65 pounds in a matter of weeks. A lanky five-foot-eight, he'd lain in bed gazing at his own gaunt pelvic bone, and wondering if he would ever regain his strength, sneaking malted milk balls whenever his mother was out of the room. He grew even sicker, and when his temperature topped 106, the doctor had him packed in ice and advised his parents they should prepare for the worst.

At which point a friend from their church saved his life by means of cleansing enemas, treating him twice daily for ten days, until he slowly began to recover. During this winter of 1924 he turned twelve years old, but owing to the effect of the damaging high fevers he could never recall his twelfth birthday or really much else, save for fond memories of his prior life, barefoot and riding a horse across the wide-open plains of West Texas.

"The fact that I survived rabies and typhoid fever left me with a strong sense of gratitude," Nelson reflected years later. "I was happy to have my life back. I got baptized and joined the church myself about that time. I knew God had saved me for some reason and determined I would never be unhappy again. I also heard from some boys at school about the money they were making over at the Glen Garden Country Club. They were working as caddies. I had no idea what that meant, but I thought it was worth investigating just to see what it was all about."

Like Byron Nelson, Samuel Jackson Snead was unusually close to his mother. Laura Dudley Snead was forty-seven years old when she delivered the last of the six children she had with her quiet, deeply religious and somewhat emotionally remote husband. They named the baby for both his maternal grandfather and the famed Confederate general Stonewall Jackson, a distant relative. Before him had come Lyle, Homer, Janet, Jessie, and Welford, whom everyone simply called Pete. Sneads had inhabited the tiny hamlet of Ashwood since before the Revolutionary War, dating from an ancestor named Richard Snead's land grant from the king of England. Harry Snead, after failing to make a go of farming on the rich valley land he and a brother had inherited, moved his family to a six-room farmhouse a block behind the village's primary school and went to work three miles away at the Homestead, one of the oldest resort hotels in America, maintaining its boilers and performing other maintenance jobs for $125 a month. Sam would recall his father rising early six days a week and putting on one of the two fancy three-piece suits he owned and walking to the hotel, where he would change into work coveralls and shovel coal and repair things in the hotel's maintenance workshop with the skill of a mechanical polymath. On Sunday, he put on his finest three-piece suit and walked the same three-mile stretch to services at the Ashwood Methodist Church in the shadow of the Homestead.

Healing water was the source of the area's first prosperity, for the hot mineral springs that burbled abundantly out of the steep and craggy slopes of Bath County were believed to cure any malady of body or spirit. In 1755, at the age of twenty-three, George Washington encountered them as a captain in the Virginia Militia, and the following decade a rudimentary hotel was erected by a large hot springs pool. By the 1880s, when J. P. Morgan financed a complete renovation of the hotel, the Homestead was considered the country's finest mountain retreat and catered to an elite patronage that included presidents and titans of industry. Thomas Edison, a frequent visitor, designed the famed mountain retreat's state-of-the-art electrical plant, and presidents Harrison, McKinley, and Taft all came there to play on the resort's six-hole golf course. Nine months after Sammy Snead was born, Scotsman Donald Ross completed an expansion of the original layout to eighteen holes, popularly called the Old Course. Two years later, Woodrow Wilson honeymooned at the Homestead with his second wife, Edith Bolling.

Throughout his life, especially whenever a big-city reporter was within earshot, Sam was fond of emphasizing his impoverished hillbilly heritage. His large and lively clan, as biographers and family friends have amply noted, was by no means well off; Harry augmented his income at the hotel by raising chickens and a few cows on the original Snead property just outside Ashwood, and every son was expected to find a job of some kind to contribute to the family pot. But the Sneads were far from the indigent mountain folk who inhabited the deeper recesses of one of the surrounding hills and hollows. Sam's proud, hardworking, churchgoing father wore a fashionable handlebar mustache and expressed his vanity with the fine store-bought suits and starched white collars he favored well into his dotage, and enjoyed additional stature in the community serving as the captain of the Hot Springs hose-and-reel brigade.

Like his father before him, Sam eventually relied financially on wealthy sporting and society types who stayed at the Homestead. Yet unlike Harry Snead, who knew his place, as it were, his son came to feel resentment of the privileged classes. He wouldn't be the first working boy ever driven by class envy, though whatever slights he suffered early in life would later manifest themselves in an undisguised contempt for snobbery in any form and a willingness to skewer and at times openly exploit the idle rich that his father held in such high regard.

Once famous as America's golfing hillbilly, whenever asked about his parents Sam would invariably talk about his mother with almost biblical reverence, explaining how this true daughter of Appalachia had overseen this strapping, athletic family, cooking all their meals, maintaining a clean and Christian house, and making sure her sons all behaved. From his father, on the other hand, he received only one modest piece of advice. "A man who keeps his shoes polished and his fingernails clean," Harry Snead liked to say, "can get by with the rest." Ironically, Sam was destined to also become a smart dresser himself, given to banded straw hats and perfectly tailored silk sports jackets that echoed the lessons he'd learned as a raw-boned, barefoot "pecker-wood kid." Thanks to both of his abstemious parents, from childhood he forswore the evils of drinking and smoking.

It was Laura Dudley Snead who had the final say and wielded the greatest influence on her youngest boy. Sam liked to say she was already an "old woman when I first knew her," and he grew up exercising the prerogative of the last-born, doted-upon baby, by his own admission "running a little wild in the hills," which meant fishing and hunting and trying to avoid being shot by the numerous moonshiners whose stills were in his favorite coon-hunting hollers. He found and kept a young buck deer as a pet for a time, and learned how to slaughter hogs in the fall. "When the chores was finished," he wrote in *The Education of a Golfer,* his splendid 1962 memoir, "all us Snead kids scattered for the hills. We were rounded up on a Sunday the way they call hogs. My mother, who had a good strong voice, would let out a war whoop that could be heard over the next mountain, and when we straggled in they scraped off the mud and wood ticks and put us into clean clothes for churchgoing."

Sam's affection for his mother bordered on adoration. "Long after she died, he spoke of her often and with no little reverence," Al Barkow notes in his thoughtful biography of Sam, offering a deeper insight on her in his terrific *Gettin' to the Dance Floor: An Oral History of American Golf:* "I'd like to have had all my characteristics and character from my mother. She was one of the few people I ever knew who had front sight as well as hind sight. We never went to my dad for anything." Barkow speculates that he played so well just down Highway 220 at the Greater Greensboro Open, which he captured a record eight times, because it was the last stop on the winter tour and only a few hours from his mama's front porch and home cooking.

Sam's prodigious physical gifts were clearly a family trait—huge hands, powerful muscular control, topped by astonishing range of motion that would grant him the ability well into his seventies to stand flat-footed on the floor and touch the top door jamb with a kick that would make a Radio City Music Hall Rockette split her tights with envy. His brothers were similarly gifted, particularly Homer, twelve years Sam's senior and his personal hero. A high school star in football, swimming, and boxing, he could slug a golf ball farther than his famous kid brother for many years. But to bring in additional income, Homer left school early to work as an electrician and amateur inventor. For decades, residents of Hot Springs claimed Homer Snead built the first radio ever heard in the county and even developed a technology that eliminated the all too common static only to have an enterprising Homestead guest steal his brilliant idea and make a fortune selling it to an outfit called RCA, or so the story goes. Homer's real love, though, was golf, and when Sam was seven Homer began letting his kid brother shag balls for him on summer mornings in a meadow above their house before he hiked off to work in town. Because Homer always carried his one hickory-shafted club wherever he went, Sam had no option but to improvise by cutting a swamp-maple limb and using the knotty end to bash around anything that resembled a golf ball, including rocks, dirt clods, and hickory nuts. One day, he recalled in *The Education of a Golfer,* "The organ was finishing off the sermon when I came down the road, swinging at rocks and dried-up manure. One of the rocks took off like a bullet, even went through the church window, and sprayed the congregation with glass. The preacher, whose name was Tompkins, was the first one out the door, but all he found was an empty road. I stayed in the woods until dark, then wouldn't admit a thing when they gave me the third degree. They never did prove it on me."

Despite the colorful shadings of Appalachian poverty he applied to what he fondly called his "backwoods boyhood days," Sam Snead's childhood was in fact something of a rural idyll. Barefoot and armed with his swamp stick, before long he could hit a golf ball for "twenty fence posts," or approximately 125 yards, or so he later claimed. He experimented with grips and stance until the club just felt natural in his hand and the ball more or less stayed true to his aim.

When he was seven years old, a black kid he often played with, Franklin Jefferson Jones, proposed they steal some candy from a local shop, and they did so, but Sam was overcome with remorse and tearfully insisted they take it back. "Frankie thought I was out of my mind but suggested that we could earn candy money by packing clubs over at the Homestead Hotel links in Hot Springs. A set of clubs weighed nearly as much as my sixty-five pounds. Since my shoulders weren't wide enough to support a bag, I hung it around my neck and staggered along after the golfers."

He earned fifty cents a loop, but eighteen holes exhausted him. Around his eighth birthday, with snow still on the ground, a hotel guest hired barefoot Sammy to carry his bag, which he did before he lost all feeling below the shins, promptly dropped the bag and staggered back to the caddie house, where he warmed his feet by the caddie master's woodstove. The verdict was frostbite on all ten toes, and he was fortunate to keep them. A year or so later, he disappeared to caddie for most of a Sunday, missed supper, and came home at dusk to find his furious mother waiting for him. "I wound up gettin' one of the worst lickin's I ever got. I hadn't told a soul where I was all day and she had my brothers out lookin' over half the county. After that, I made sure she knew where I was when I was caddying."

"That hurt," he amplified in *The Education of a Golfer*, "because I was a hurrying kid with ambition. Horsehair Brinkley and Piggie McGuffin, two pals of mine, had to run to keep up with me. I tried every which way to learn to play golf on a real course, but when I was ten or twelve years old there wasn't a chance. The Homestead and Cascades Hotel courses were for wealthy tourists only. Anytime we peckerwoods sneaked onto the local 'Goat Course,' which was a nine-holer for hotel employees, a cop would holler, 'Hey, you little bastards!'—and we'd have to scatter for the woods without even time to putt out."

So he practiced his golf swing in a family pasture in Ashwood, improvising an improbable homemade club from a buggy whip a local blacksmith gave him, to which he attached a clubhead he'd picked up from his uncle Ed Dudley, using small wood screws—or so Sam always spun the tale. Given the supple flex of this makeshift "shaft," he developed a slow, unhurried tempo, learning to "wait" on the swing, and was soon able, he claimed, to hit a ball two hundred yards. He also sank empty tomato cans in his backyard, creating a five-hole course where he could chip and putt.

Throughout his teens, whenever he wasn't helping slaughter hogs, running his own trap lines, hunting wild pigs or trout fishing in the surrounding hollers and creeks, he was making money caddying and occasionally tagging along with his brothers Homer and Pete when they played matches. Pete, the closest to Sam in age, was his only brother who also made a living out of golf, eventually becoming head professional at the Homestead.

The household Sam grew up in was, for the most part, harmonious and even musical. His mother played the guitar, his father the trumpet, brother Pete played the saxophone; all were self-taught. Along with Laura's half-brother Ed Dudley, who owned a restaurant on Main Street, the family sometimes picked up extra money by playing for dances at the Homestead. At age ten, Sammy began fooling with Harry's trumpet and taught himself to play, and down the road a bit he soloed with some of the featured bands at the resort. Even after his fame and fortune arrived, one of his favorite things to do was slip off to a popular "jazz shanty" outside White Sulpher Springs and blow the trumpet till the wee hours. Or, as his son Jack would recall, he'd just pick up his old trumpet and a mute, then disappear to a back room where he would play along with big band records for hours. "I think that was something Dad loved doing since he was a kid," said Jack. "He always told me he learned most of what he knew in life when he was a boy—including that trumpet."

"You know, I read somewhere once that your first dozen years shape the rest of your life. Well, when I look back on my childhood I realize how pretty fortunate I was overall," Sam remarked to a writer who called on him at the Greenbrier in the early 1990s. "An awful lot of what I later applied to my golf career came from either home or those woods around Hot Springs. Hunting and fishing taught me a helluva lot of patience and even basic psychology. I learned to watch what was happening around me and rely on my own hunches about everything. We weren't the poorest folks in town and we sure weren't the richest. No way. But I'd say we did all right. We were close, and I never felt like I was missing a whole lot. Just about anything I put my head to, why, I could do it."

Contrary to accounts of Ben Hogan's obscure early life that began to emerge about the time his fabled playing career was drawing to a close—suggesting a childhood marked by poverty and hardship—much of Ben's boyhood was, in fact, normal, happy, and reasonably prosperous by the standards of the rural Southwest. Family and friends recalled Ben and his siblings playing games on the oak-shaded streets of lively little Dublin, Texas, playing in nearby

Clear Creek and attending picnics at the Dublin Baptist Church, where their mother had strong ties.

For a time prior to and just after Bennie's birth, Chester Hogan abandoned his father's blacksmith shop and hired on with Sam Houston Prim, a former bookshop owner who'd opened a firm that bottled a sweet cherry-flavored concoction called "Dr Pepper" and shipped it all over West Texas. It was Chester's job to wash used bottles then refill and cork them before loading the fresh crates onto delivery trucks and the Fort Worth–Rio Grande Railroad. The work paid decently, but Chester missed working with horses and the people who owned and loved them. Once his father died, he returned to run the town's principal livery stable, the place he was always happiest.

An advertisement for the family business, from the *Dublin Progress* in about 1915, shows a pony wagon carrying the three young Hogan children and draped with a Fourth of July parade banner that cheerfully proclaims: PAPA'S A BLACKSMITH. LET HOGAN SHOE YOUR HORSE! The oldest son, Royal, would be remembered as a natural athlete who pitched a mean sandlot baseball game and helped organize the town's first team. Princess, who had her mother's stern good looks and no shortage of the Williams gumption, sang at church and even won a few choice parts in productions at the Dublin Opera House. She and her brothers were regulars at the open-air movie theater on Friday nights, where they watched the Keystone Kops and Charlie Chaplin, a world far removed from a dusty square in the frontier West.

Neighbors recalled that Bennie—like his father, quiet and undersized—was his papa's little boy clean to the core, a bit of a happy loner who preferred to spend his free time hanging around the blacksmith shop, where he calmed the horses as they were waiting to be shoed and fed scraps to the village dogs that always congregated there. Decades later, Ben Hogan's most cherished possession was a small black-and-white photograph that shows him sitting astride a chestnut mare with his father, cradled between Chester's belt and the saddle horn. He was no more than a year old. Both father and son are looking away from the camera—a rare pose in those days, as if they'd been suddenly distracted, glancing at something in the distance. Their expressions, in this haunting photograph, in any case, are calm and nearly identical, and the spiritual connection is unmistakable. "Ben's father was his hero," his wife, Valerie, once told Dave Anderson of *The New York Times*.

The year Byron Nelson's family moved to a rented house in San

Angelo, a fresh new start that soon had the elder Nelson sleeping in an empty piano crate, Bennie Hogan's own life took a sharp and fateful turn.

By 1921 there were more than nine million automobiles on America's ever-expanding network of paved roads and highways, as Secretary of Labor Herbert Hoover liked to boast. The state of Texas alone paved more than a thousand miles of new highways that year. Not surprisingly, a record number of businesses catering to the traditional horse trade shut their doors for good that year; within five years, it's been estimated, more than half the remaining livery stables in America failed. The summer Bennie Hogan turned nine, his mother suddenly packed their belongings, put their Camden Street house up for sale, and moved her family into a small wooden rental house on the southeast side of downtown Fort Worth, Texas's rowdiest city.

Clara Hogan wasn't oblivious to the village talk that her quiet husband's smithing business had simply become a victim of changing times. But the problem went deeper than that. Even if she'd felt obliged to explain their turn in fortune—not likely, given that she was so silent on private matters that her own children and grandchildren knew virtually nothing about the family's history for decades—her prime objective was to try to stave off her husband's grievous mental depression that deepened every month as debts mounted and his business dried up like jimsonweed.

During the early months of 1921, Chester Hogan had ceased attending church and sometimes never even left the house to open up his stable. Clara Hogan's hope was to have Chester "treated" at the only facility in all of West Texas equipped to handle issues of mental health, a large mansard-roofed institution on the eastern flank of Fort Worth. The determined and pragmatic Clara—a gifted seamstress—took matters into her own hands by doing contract alterations for Cheney's downtown department store, which catered to the tastes of the city's well-to-do matrons.

It seemed, for a short while, that they would be fine. Fort Worth was the celebrated "Cowtown" of Texas, the place where the Santa Fe Trail began, the self-described "Queen of the American Prairies" and "The Place Where the West Begins." The city had a burgeoning population of more than 150,000, at least thirty saloons the Baptists had failed to get shut down, a booming cattle market and an ornate Texas & Pacific train depot that saw more than seventy trains a day pass through.

Submitting to his wife's iron will, Chester agreed to treatment regimes at the sanatorium in Arlington Heights—alkaloid tablets, calming mineral baths, and mild electrotherapy, therapies that had been around since the late nineteenth century—and found a job training to become an auto mechanic. Clara installed their children in the local public schools and took a bus to Cheney's six days a week. Royal found an afternoon job delivering prescriptions for a druggist. The rent got paid and Chester showed marked improvement, his black moods gradually easing.

Five months into this new life, in fact, he pronounced himself cured and declared he intended to return home and reopen his shuttered livery stable. Clara, however, wanted no portion of this plan. Dublin held only the specter of their failed hopes, whereas Fort Worth afforded the anonymity her extremely private nature craved, as well as the financial opportunities that were luring historic numbers of rural Americans from the farm to the city. So Chester returned to Comanche County alone, and within a month neighbors reported he was in a visibly upbeat mood, informing anyone who would listen that he'd "soon bring Clara and the children home for good."

On the dank, drizzily eve of St. Valentine's Day, 1922, he returned to Fort Worth by train to convince his unyielding wife it was time to do just that. A bitter argument erupted in the front parlor of the tiny frame house at 305 Hemphill Street. According to family accounts, the children stood mutely in a bedroom listening to their parents argue. At some point, Chester picked up his carpetbag and stalked from the room, addled by the demons of self-loathing unleashed by Clara's belief that Dublin held nothing but failure for them all. As his youngest son rushed into the room to try to comfort his father, Chester pulled a .38 pistol from his bag, placed the barrel to his upper chest, and pulled the trigger.

A dozen hours later, a headline in the Valentine's Day edition of the *Fort Worth Record* read: "Child of Six Sees His Father Shot." Shootings were a daily occurrence in the Queen City of the Prairies, and the brief article reported that "while his condition is critical he has a good chance for recovery."

The son was Bennie, of course, and he was nine. By the time the paper hit the streets, his father and hero, who'd turned thirty-seven just days before, was already dead. A slightly clearer (if also inaccurate) account of the shooting appeared a few days later in the *Dublin*

Progress, based on details Clara Hogan probably provided, explaining that it was the family's "twelve-year-old son" who witnessed the suicide. Royal Hogan, in fact, was thirteen. Among those who knew the Hogans best, the abiding impression was left that, in an attempt to shield the younger and more impressionable Bennie from the cascade of sorrow and natural curiosity that was bound to follow, Mama Hogan had placed her older and much more resilient son in the room where their father committed his desperate act.

In any case, Bennie refused to attend the funeral. Decades later, near the end of her own life, Valerie explained to the *Times*'s Dave Anderson that they'd been married for "many years" before she learned of Chester's suicide, the singular event that shaded her husband's life and worldview. "And his father's death just hurt Ben so much," she'd added, "they were not able to get [him] to go to the church. He couldn't bear to see the casket."

A short time later, Clara Hogan picked up extra piecework at two other downtown department stores and moved her family to a house on East Allen Street, in a slightly better neighborhood called Morningside, just a few miles south of the Texas & Pacific train depot. To provide a bit more social stability, she placed her two youngest children in the Sunday school of a local Baptist church. Royal quit the drugstore and dropped out of school to take a full-time job delivering office supplies on his bicycle; he also sold copies of Amon Carter's Fort Worth *Star-Telegram* at the Westbrook Hotel and pumped gas on Lancaster Avenue. "He became my rock of Gibraltar," Mama Hogan boasted to a reporter three decades later, attempting to clarify rumors about her youngest son's troubled early life. "Without him I hate to think what might have happened to us."

When Bennie, then a fourth grader, volunteered to help out by hawking late editions of the newspaper on the boarding platform at the sprawling Texas & Pacific depot, Clara let him. Princess made her contribution by baby-sitting and working part-time at the same drugstore where Royal had worked.

Immediately after school, barely four feet tall and weighing seventy pounds, young Bennie Hogan hustled to the depot and sometimes worked all night to peddle his bundle of papers; he could occasionally be found curled up asleep on a waiting room bench by dawn's first light, his large aviator's cap pulled over his face. Many decades later, any time the aging golf legend happened to see a Fort Worth newsboy working late on the streets of Cowtown, according to his longtime secretary and closest friends, he would pull over and purchase the kid's unsold papers and send him home.

"That station was where I learned to take pretty good care of myself," Hogan reflected gently, almost fondly, to a reporter in the early 1950s. "It toughened me up real fast. You either fought for your turf and won or you went someplace else. I wasn't about to give it up."

By age ten, Bennie Hogan's childhood was over. Two years later, he heard Royal, whom he called "Bubber," say that local boys were getting sixty-five cents just to carry a golf bag around eighteen holes at the Glen Garden Country Club. And had Ben's brother—then sixteen, with his maternal grandfather's head for numbers—not been working full-time at the office supply, he might've headed straight for the country club himself. Though he'd never seen the game played, Bennie had read about golf in the sports pages of Amon Carter's famous newspaper, particularly the splendid exploits of colorful touring professional Walter Hagen, and the admirable amateur Bobby Jones, who won his first U.S. Open Championship on Long Island in the summer of 1923.

Located on the southeastern fringes of the city, not far from the interurban bus line where Byron Nelson's family lived in Six Stop, Glen Garden wasn't Fort Worth's best private golf club, but it was very popular with Cowtown's growing ranks of middle-class golfers and also within walking distance of East Allen Street.

Shortly before his twelfth birthday, Bennie Hogan went over to see what all the excitement was about—just two weeks after a sunny, cheerful kid named Byron Nelson had shown up, wide-eyed and eager to know more about golf.

3

The Golden Age

THE LUCKIEST THING THAT happened to American golf, someone once said, was the unexpected coming of Francis Ouimet, the personable former caddie who crossed from the wrong side of the street to win the U.S. Open in 1913. Almost overnight, golf ceased being principally viewed as a rich man's game and became something within reach of anyone who dared to try and become good at it.

Within a decade, sprinkled by the gold dust of Ouimet's incomparable triumph, there were an estimated seven million new adherents and more than a thousand new golf clubs and public courses scattered across the nation, reflecting a sudden mass democratization that shifted the balance of power from Britain to America.

In 1916, as Europe disappeared into the fog of the so-called Great War, the Professional Golfers' Association of America organized itself with the stated mission of promoting the sport's recreational benefits to people of all means and social standing, staging its first championship. Once the country entered the war in 1917, the fledgling PGA urged its members to conduct public exhibitions free of charge to enhance the game's popularity and raise money for the Red Cross and other war-related charities. Amateur star Chick Evans logged more than 26,000 miles and visited forty-one cities, raising more than $300,000 for the cause, and a talented if tempestuous teenager named Robert Tyre "Bobby" Jones Jr. played a full exhibition circuit with U.S. Women's amateur champion Alexa Stirling and Perry Adair, Bobby's boyhood rival. While he waited for induction into the army, Francis Ouimet participated in dozens of Red Cross exhibitions across New England.

Largely as a result of the record amounts of money they helped generate for worthy home causes, professional golfers achieved a surprising new status in the eyes of ordinary Americans, who closely followed the tournament exploits of Jock Hutchison, long-hitting Jim Barnes, and a suave and flamboyant Walter Hagen. The rangy Barnes hailed from Cornish, England; the fidgety and philosophical "Hutch" came from St. Andrews, Scotland. But because they developed their games on American shores, they were embraced by American fans hungry for a pure homebred star. After Barnes captured the first PGA Championship in 1916 and followed with a U.S. Open title in 1921, President Warren Harding personally presented him with the trophy and declared that professional golf was the fastest-growing sport in America.

It was "The Haig" who achieved stardom as a native-born pro, however, grabbing the public's attention like no other before him. Only a year out of the pro shop, he'd finished a respectable fourth behind Ouimet, Vardon, and Ray at Brookline, then turned up at the venerable Midlothian Club in suburban Chicago—sporting a rakish summer straw boater—and set a new competitive course record with a 68 in the first round of the U.S. Open. Hometown favorite Chick Evans kept it close until the end, urged on by partisan fans who actually applauded when Hagen stubbed his chip on the seventieth hole of the championship. On the next hole, however, he smoothly drained a monstrously long birdie putt, then rolled in another birdie to win by a stroke. Golf was still provincial enough for galleries to root for their hometown favorite, but when Hagen peeled off his straw hat and bowed theatrically when presented with the trophy, brilliantined hair gleaming in the fading sunlight, the crowds gave him a rousing cheer. A national hero was born, and a natural showman as well.

The cognoscenti uniformly dismissed his broad stance and unorthodox swing, which had a noticeable sway and finished with a wholly unrefined leaning stance. He looked, in this regard, more like a baseball hitter than a peerless ball striker like Harry Vardon or Chick Evans. The press found the Haig's flamboyant style entertaining, but confidently predicted he would be a flash in the pan. He was, after all, always in and out of the brambles and scrambling to make par or having to make outrageous putts just to keep within reach of Barnes and Hutchison or even Chick Evans.

What the experts failed to grasp, however, was that in a nation struggling to come to grips with the most maddening sport, Walter Hagen seemed like one of their own who'd somehow found the key to success, a genial fellow who excelled at the game but at times made it look as hard as they understood it to be. Adding to his Everyman appeal was the fact that he broke through when the last generation of the Scottish pros who'd immigrated to this country were beginning to fade away like Brigadoon at dawn. Hagen represented something never seen before on American ground: a native professional whose star power could match that of any invading Brit, including the great Harry Vardon himself.

With an olive complexion that tanned easily to a rich mahogany hue and slightly inscrutable Asian features, Hagen was a beguiling combination of confidence and grace under fire, supremely assured without giving lasting offense, a dapper charmer who never seemed rushed or flustered by a wayward shot or unlucky break, always on the verge of disaster yet somehow able to summon recovery shots that left fans breathless—especially the beautiful young women who seemed to regularly turn up whenever the Haig was in the hunt.

When the U.S. Open resumed after its two-year wartime hiatus outside Boston at Brae Burn in 1919, twenty-seven-year-old Hagen needed to cover the last nine holes in even par in order to match popular hometown favorite Mike Brady, who had already posted a score of 301. With seven holes left to play, he hooked a tee shot out of bounds and cost himself a valuable stroke. During his slow walk to the next tee, a young sportswriter saw him wink at a friend and casually remark, "Don't worry, I'll get another birdie to make up for that little error." Two holes later, he did—and then he did the sort of thing that would seal his image as the game's greatest showman and make him the biggest draw in the game.

On the last hole, after hitting a high-risk long iron to the dangerous, two-tiered green, and leaving his ball just eight feet from the cup, he paused and asked for Brady to be summoned from the clubhouse to observe the finish—or witness his own funeral, as many interpreted it afterward. A bit anticlimactically, the short putt lipped out and he was forced to beat Brady the following day in a playoff that went right to the final hole, the Haig winning by a single stroke. Asked by a reporter what he and pal Al Jolson had done the night before, the newly divorced national champion smiled and replied, "Why, enjoyed ourselves till the sun came up. Didn't want to be late to the tee."

Nineteen twenty was a watershed year in America, the dawning of an extraordinary decade that would not only produce a radical revolution in manners and morals but shape the values of generations to come through the birth of mass-market consumer culture. Many of the defining features of modern life first appeared in the Roaring Twenties: talking films, radio broadcasting, book clubs, comic strips, fad diets, celebrity gossip magazines, air travel, home mortgages, department stores, beauty pageants, national advertising, and—perhaps above all—spectator sports.

After four long years of war, a Red Scare, and the failure of Woodrow Wilson's lofty dream of a League of Nations, Americans everywhere wanted simply to make and enjoy a better life. When the Eighteenth Amendment went into effect that January—a misguided attempt by Christian temperance forces to curb the nation's insatiable thirst for alcohol—an estimated forty thousand saloons shut their public doors and opened private ones, devastating the legitimate distillery and brewing industries, giving birth to a thriving industry of speakeasies, crime bosses, and bootleggers.

The presidential election that fall—the first in which women were entitled to vote—resulted in the largest lopsided victory but the poorest voter turnout in more than a century. Only 49.3 percent of registered voters bothered to turn out, sending Warren Harding to the White House, a small-town Ohio newspaperman who promised "normalcy" instead of "normality," a symbolic slip of the tongue that appealed to the country's new isolationist mood and domestic ambitions. On November 2, 1920, both election day and his fifty-fifth birthday, Harding stressed the point that Americans desired "serenity over surgery," then went out with his business cronies for a round of golf, inviting the press along, promising more of the same fun to come.

That same evening, the first commercially licensed radio station— KDKA in Pittsburgh—broadcast the election results. Just weeks before, Westinghouse had put the first mass-produced radios on sale in urban department stores for ten dollars. Within five years, a third of American households would have one, fueling an explosion of information, news, and the new phenomenon of leisure time entertainment. Mamie Smith, formerly a black gospel singer, sold a million copies of "Crazy Blues" within six months, prompting sales of phonographs to soar, which in turn caused sales of pianos to severely slump for the first time ever.

Walter Hagen's pal Al Jolson was at once America's first Jewish entertainer and a tireless promoter of equal access for black jazz and blues artists. Credited with making that music respectable to white people, he was the toast of Broadway in 1922, selling out his fifth Winter Garden concert the same summer. F. Scott Fitzgerald coined the term "Jazz Age" to characterize the anything-goes era of flappers, bootleg whiskey, and the general decline of public morality. Hollywood began cranking out about seven hundred movies a year, weekly attendance growing from about fifty million in 1920 to ninety million, or three fourths of the nation's population, in 1929—reportedly more than went to church.

By 1925, Americans were having fifty million telephone conversations a day, and Henry Ford—named the greatest historical figure of all time after Napoleon and Jesus Christ, according to a poll of college students—was turning out a car every ten seconds, which workers—making roughly twice as much as previous generations could—were able to purchase on installment plans offered by banks for the first time. Aiming to further capitalize on the home-building boom that was creating something called "the suburbs," commercial lending institutions also introduced home mortgages. Fueled by easy credit and an unflagging faith in capitalism, grand hotels and resorts were conceived and completed in record time. In New York City alone, the Empire State Building, the Chrysler Building, and Rockefeller Center all jumped from the architect table to reality in a matter of a few years. Meanwhile, the state of Florida—largely written off as a swampy, uninhabitable wilderness just a decade before—was enjoying a land boom that attracted real estate speculators and empire builders from all over the world.

Warren Harding died after 882 days in office, and the taciturn Vermonter Cal Coolidge was awakened in the middle of the night by his father on the family farm in Plymouth Notch to take the oath of office. Despite the scandals that plagued the current administration, Coolidge continued the laissez-faire policies that permitted Wall Street to soar and allowed crossword puzzles, Ouija boards, and a Chinese craze called mah-jongg to surge into every household across the country. Ivory Soap sponsored the first national radio broadcast, and the *Chicago Tribune* routinely covered the faux-heroic antics of gangster Al Capone, who supposedly tipped hatcheck girls $100 and underwrote a soup kitchen in his old neighborhood with a check for twelve grand.

This new embrace of consumerism and liberation from the Victorian past also brought unprecedented social turmoil—violent strikes, gangland murders, race lynchings, a strong resurgence of the Ku Klux Klan—and was underscored by a pervasive spiritual emptiness depicted in best-selling books by Sinclair Lewis, Ernest Hemingway, and F. Scott Fitzgerald. But one leading economist saw no end to the gold rush, or the good times. "The business of America is business," President Coolidge evangelized. "The man who builds a factory builds a temple," he emphasized. "And the man who works there worships there."

Perhaps more than anything else, the birth of sports as mass entertainment symbolized the mythic hopes and personal aspirations of this evolving nation. In an ever-mobile society that felt increasingly bureaucratic, uprooted, and isolated by its own liberated values and free spirit, especially against the backdrop of movie villains and real-life crime bosses, the success of hometown sports heroes touched a sentimental chord in millions of ordinary Americans, and thus took on disproportionate meaning in everyday life. Not surprisingly, this became the age of overnight sports heroes.

"Ballyhoo artists—promoters, press agents, and public relations experts—ranked second only to sportswriters in influencing the public," wrote Michael Bohn in *Heroes and Ballyhoo,* his fine account of the decade's sports obsessions. "Without a thought of accuracy or balanced reporting, they flogged their athlete or event with undiluted fervor."

Football, for example, went nowhere until Notre Dame coach Knute Rockne's phenomenal success produced five undefeated seasons and six national championships in the span of just thirteen years. Rockne and his seemingly invincible "Four Horsemen" prompted the construction of football stadiums at colleges like Stanford, Ohio State, Michigan, and Illinois—where, it just so happened, a freshman named Harold Edward "Red" Grange reluctantly put on a jersey and became the most gifted, publicized breakaway runner of his time. Before he left Illinois, pro football was only of minor interest to American sports fans. After graduating and signing with the Chicago Bears, he made a small fortune appearing in motion pictures, making commercial endorsements, and collecting personal appearance fees. He also put professional football on the map to stay.

Much the same thing—the charisma of a single player igniting a frenzy of idolatry—occurred in baseball. In 1921, after signing the largest contract in the sport's history, and moving from the Red Sox to the Yankees, Babe Ruth swatted fifty-nine home runs, more than any other *team* in the league. So the next year, the Yankees broke ground on a $6 million stadium that would seat 62,000 fans, based purely on the Bambino's drawing power. Ruth's popularity and winning personality made him a regular feature in Grantland Rice's nationally syndicated "Spotlight" newspaper column, read by millions every day over their Corn Flakes, a new Kellogg's breakfast cereal.

In prizefighting, Jack Dempsey, who'd won forty-seven of his sixty-nine fights by knockouts, lost his title to Gene Tunney in 1926, only to come back a year later in a "grudge match" that drew more than 150,000 spectators to Soldier Field in Chicago. Won by Tunney in a controversial decision, the bout netted organizers the largest sports payday ever—$3 million.

In this frenzied Golden Age of sports—or the "Decade of Deception," as H. L. Mencken labeled it—each and every sport seemed to have a colorful presiding champion. In tennis, tall, lean Bill Tilden won seven Davis Cup titles and dominated play throughout the 1920s, recasting the sport as a power game rather than a country club pastime. Swimmer Johnny Weissmuller won five gold medals and set sixty-seven world records between 1921 and 1929, establishing himself as the logical choice for the starring role in sixteen Tarzan movies that would soon begin filming in Hollywood. Even horses got in on the hero worship. The fiery stallion Man O'War won twenty of twenty-one starts and retired early to stud having earned a record quarter of a million dollars at the track, setting attendance records wherever the "Greatest Horse of All Time" turned up.

Perhaps no single sport, however, reflected the country's social aspirations more than golf. If Ouimet's Brookline triumph more or less democratized the game, the coming of Jazz Age prosperity—heralded by the completion in 1918 of the Pine Valley Golf Club in the Pine Barrens of southern New Jersey as a new decade dawned—accelerated the construction of nearly a thousand public and private golf courses, including many of the nation's premier layouts. Almost overnight, the concept of the "country club"—a strictly American innovation—came into the lexicon. "Membership in an exclusive club," Herbert Warren Wind noted, "was the salient badge of distinction in the Twenties."

In Chicago, a thousand Shriners pooled their money to build the majestic Medinah Country Club at the unprecedented cost of $1.5 million only to see it get trumped by the even grander Olympia Fields on the city's working-class South Side—the first club to offer seventy-two holes to its members, plus a Tudor-style ballroom that would comfortably seat eight hundred.

Down in Pinehurst, meanwhile, Scotsman Donald Ross completed fifty-four holes for his employer, Leonard Tufts, then went on to build another three hundred or so layouts. After helping shape Pine Valley, Ross's friendly rival A. W. Tillinghast created several hundred distinctive courses of his own, including the spectacular layouts at Winged Foot, Baltusrol, and the San Francisco Golf Club. Another transplanted Philadelphian, George C. Thomas, brought forth such classics as the Los Angeles Country Club, Bel-Air, and Riviera. William Flynn produced timeless venues at Cherry Hills outside Denver, the Philadelphia Country Club, and the new Cascades golf course at the Homestead in Virginia, where a former caddie named Sam Snead would soon find his first clubhouse employment.

In California, Bobby Jones was introduced to the sublime courses that Marion Hollins, the 1921 Women's Amateur champion, had convinced Dr. Alister Mackenzie to create at Cypress Point and Pasatiempo. Jones lost his quest for a fifth U.S. Amateur title to Johnny Goodman at Pebble Beach but found the designer he wanted to collaborate with on the dream course he was hoping to build on the grounds of a defunct plant nursery in Augusta, Georgia.

More important, this so-called Golden Age of golf course construction also saw a major changing of the guard at the highest competitive level. The revolution began, at least symbolically, in June of 1920, at the revival of the Open Championship at Deal, England. The pre-tournament favorite Walter Hagen, one of the few Americans who bothered to cross the water, had never played on a linksland course before, and finished a dismal fifty-third in a field of seventy-seven. But he endeared himself forever to both his fellow competitors and fans everywhere by knocking down one of the game's most stubborn social barriers.

A long-standing tradition permitted only members and invited guests inside clubhouses, and professional golfers were treated like a yeoman class of servant. Hagen rented a Daimler limousine, hired a footman, and used the car as his personal locker room, parking within sight of the club's main dining room, and changing his shoes just yards from the front door. He also arranged for lunch to be served to himself, Jim Barnes, and other competitors, provoking a gale of criticism from offended members but making himself something of a sporting Robin Hood in the eyes of the Fleet Street press, who ate up every delicious morsel provided by "Sir Walter."

Hagen's intention was to send a message that he wasn't merely a club pro trying to pad his income by winning a major championship, that he was a professional sportsman dedicated to making a living by playing exhibition matches and tournament golf. The Haig was, in his mind and soon everyone else's, the world's first entirely professional golfer.

The test at Deal proved too much for him, but true to form, he made no excuses for his unusually poor showing. "I tried too hard," he remarked afterward, "just like any duffer." Commenting on Hagen's courage in the London *Times*, Harry Vardon predicted he would soon return and "win several of our Opens." Indeed, just two years later at Royal St. George's in Sandwich, the Haig proved Vardon a prophet by claiming the first of his four Claret Jugs—becoming the first American to win the championship. Despite the grumbling of members who believed that opening their exclusive doors to the likes of Hagen was tantamount to the end of civilization as they knew it, clubs across Britain soon began revising their rules and welcoming club pros inside.

Barely a month later, along the windy shores of Lake Erie, members of the venerable Inverness Club of Toledo, host of the U.S. Open of 1920, felt the winds of social change blowing into their own heretofore cloistered world, and broke with tradition by inviting the contestants into their clubhouse and granting them unrestricted use of all facilities, even the dining room. The impressive field included Jock Hutchison and "Long Jim" Barnes, fresh off a win at the Shawnee Invitational, and was highlighted by the sentimental return of Vardon and Ted Ray, this concluding another exhibition tour. Both the public and the press showered these aging legends with grateful affection.

In his two qualifying rounds at Inverness, the fifty-year-old Vardon was paired with a polite young man from Atlanta who was studying mechanical engineering at the Georgia School of Technology. Bobby Jones was eighteen. They were the oldest and youngest men in the field. Not until a graying Ben Hogan played alongside a raw Ohio youngster named Jack Nicklaus at Cherry Hills in 1960 would the golf world see another twosome as historic as Harry and Bobby.

Hagen's defense of his Open title on a difficult Donald Ross course started promisingly. By the halfway point, however, the issue lay between Hutchison and Barnes, the leaders at 145 and 146 respectively, with a dogged twenty-one-year-old pro named Leo Diegel tied with Barnes. Hagen lurked just two strokes back, drawing immense crowds as he sallied forth, chatting with friends in the gallery and winking at pretty girls—Sir Walter at his charming best. But his hopes were dashed when he went out in the morning and cobbled together a woeful 41 on the outward leg, losing whatever momentum he'd built. The Haig was never really a factor after that.

As if to punctuate the end of an era, six-time Open champion Harry Vardon put on a gallant effort to capture the coveted American title he'd won two decades before, producing one flawless shot after another and leading by four with seven holes to play.

The gallery was with the great man every step of the way, which made what happened next all the more poignant. The Greyhound found himself agonizing down the stretch over several putts, his right forearm twitching so violently that he lurched at the ball, and sent it shooting past the hole. Over the three days he had played peerless golf, 36 in qualifying and 65 in the championship itself, displaying the stamina of a man half his age. But when his putting stroke yielded to nerves, so did his confidence. With the championship his to claim, Vardon lost seven strokes over the closing seven holes and finished with a respectable, if heartbreaking, 296. If there was to be any consolation to be had that afternoon, it was that Harry's dear friend and long-time traveling companion Ted Ray slipped past Hutchison and Diegel to become the oldest man to win a U.S. Open.

Nine thousand spectators—a record turnout—saw these two thick-waisted Englishmen perform their hickory-shafted artistry one final time. Then the Greyhound tipped his hat to the adoring gallery and sailed home to England, never to return. Hagen took up a collection from his fellow pros and paid for a beautiful handmade chiming clock to be shipped to the members of Inverness, in gratitude for welcoming them so graciously. And Toledo police noted a curious new phenomenon in relation to a golf tournament: a traffic jam.

Over the next decade, championship golf would essentially belong to three names, a dynamic if somewhat uneven new triumvirate: Hagen the dashing stylist, the brilliant amateur Bobby Jones, and a strutting cock robin named Gene Sarazen. There were, to be sure, great supporting players like Leo Diegel, Tommy Armour, Johnny Farrell, Joe Turnesa, "Wee" Bobby Cruickshank, "Lighthorse" Harry Cooper, "Wild" Bill Mehlhorn, and mild-mannered Boston pro Denny Shute. At any given moment, any one of them could get a red-hot putter and steal the prize. But as the Twenties roared on, the readers of America's sports pages couldn't get enough of Sir Walter, the upstart Sarazen, and the well-mannered amateur who would rewrite all the record books and become immortal in the process.

The flamboyant Haig—always stepping from a chauffeured limousine, always a little bit late by design—claimed his second Claret Jug at St. George's, Sandwich, in 1922, then three more—at Hoylake in '24, back at St. George's in '28, at Muirfield in '29—before the decade drew to a close. In the PGA Championship's match-play format he was even more formidable, using his bag of mental tricks to seize five PGA titles, including four in a row. In the winter of 1926, when Bobby Jones was playing his finest golf, Hagen agreed to a seventy-two-hole one-on-one exhibition ballyhooed by the press as "the Match of the Century" over two courses in Florida, and easily obliterated the young Atlantan, twelve and eleven, pocketing $6,800 for his trouble. The following year, he was the obvious choice to serve as captain of America's inaugural Ryder Cup team; he went on, in fact, to captain the squad for a decade, winning four of the first six events and amassing an individual record of 7-2-3 in singles, four-ball, and alternate-shot foursome matches.

For Bobby Jones, whose rapid maturity made him the world's greatest amateur sportsman, drubbings like the one he took against the Haig in Florida helped him refine his game, dampen his fiery playing temperament and harden his nerves for combat against the two toughest professional competitors America had ever produced. A great many fans held that golf's sanctity as a sport was tarnished by pros who played for an unholy marriage of trophies and cash, and he was their standard-bearer.

Knute Rockne, for one, used the rise of Bobby Jones to rail against the rampant commercialism creeping into all sports. "A true gentleman," he told his friend Grantland Rice, "never plays for money, directly or indirectly." And Harvard professor Ralph Barton Perry fumed in the pages of The Atlantic magazine: "Just what is it a man must not sell? It would be agreed that a man must not exhibit his game for gate receipts or impart his skill for hire, or play to win for stakes. The true golfer believes in noblesse oblige, not the sordid code of barter."

But it was more than just money. Jones—who began the decade by edging ever closer to a major championship only to fall maddeningly short—also represented the golden ideal of American youth, and was admired as much for his sterling character as his playing skills. "Bobby Jones had the face of an angel and the temper of a timber wolf," says his modern biographer, Sidney Matthew. "The fact that he sometimes lost his temper, early on at least, and threw clubs into trees, was mitigated by his unfailing courtesy to fellow competitors, fans, and tournament sponsors. His natural modesty and social grace covered a lot of sins."

Bobby's first notice of the former Eugenio Saraceni came in 1922, at the U.S. Open in suburban Chicago. Born only a month before Jones in 1902, he was a young man who'd grown up caddying at the Apawamis Club in Rye, New York, and gravely disappointed his immigrant father by choosing the uncertain life of an assistant club pro over the family trade of carpentry, and then compounded the sin by Americanizing his name. After three rounds on the comparatively easy Skokie Country Club course, twenty-year-old Jones and veteran Wild Bill Mehlhorn were the co-leaders at 216. All but unnoticed four strokes back was the five-foot-five Gene Sarazen, who'd recently accepted the head professional job at the Highland Country Club in Pittsburgh and confidently assured betting friends that he was the man to bet on in Skokie. Here, in order to finance the championship's growing purse, with $500 and a gold medal going to the winner, the USGA charged spectators gate admission for the first time—a dollar a head.

Even as Mehlhorn tapped in to finish with 290, an explosive cheer was heard far out on the course where the unheralded Sarazen had gone out in 33, picking up four strokes on the leaders. His brilliant back nine brought him home in 68, the lowest final-round score recorded up till then in the championship, giving him a 288 total and a two-shot lead over Mehlhorn. He finished a full hour ahead of the popular amateur, and retreated to the locker room to sweat it out, worried that his 288 simply wouldn't hold up. "How could I win?" Gene fretted to veteran Leo Diegel, displaying a rare moment of uncertainty. "I'm just a kid, just been a pro three years, and everything I learned about golf I learned caddying. Out there are the best in the world."

Marching ahead of a swarming army of fans—three thousand more than turned out at Inverness the year before—Jones needed a 71 to win; he shot 73 and finished an agonizing stroke short. America's newest national champion was also its youngest ever. In the *Chicago Tribune,* Gene Sarazen was described as "A fresh kid . . . laughing at anything that happens, one of the most lovable youngsters in the world."

A month later, the champion himself struck a more humble note in *Golf Illustrated:* "In the press there have been comments to the effect that my success should prove to be an inspiration to other caddie boys. All I can say is that if my winning of the National Open championship acts as an incentive to any other boy to develop his game of golf, then I will feel that I have accomplished something really worthwhile. As J. H. Taylor, the great English professional, told me the other night, I have a great responsibility and I hope that my youth and inexperience will not be drawbacks in my upholding the highest traditions of the game of golf and the prestige of being an American Open champion."

But when the PGA Championship got under way at Pittsburgh's Oakmont Country Club on Monday morning, August 14, 1922, the new national champ was nowhere to be seen.

Following his victory at Skokie, Sarazen had embarked on a lucrative but hastily arranged exhibition tour that carried him around the Northeast and Midwest. He happened to be having dinner in Dayton, Ohio, that Sunday evening when a fan casually inquired how he expected to do on difficult Oakmont, noting that the PGA was scheduled to begin the following morning in Pittsburgh. "I'd completely forgotten about it," Sarazen later admitted, explaining how he'd caught the last train to Pittsburgh only because it got fortuitously delayed—and had arrived at the championship in a taxi cab, thirty minutes late for his first scheduled match. Owing to his brand-new stature, and the event's need for good publicity, officials relaxed the rules and let him play anyway.

Among the subsequent surprises were the early departures of two-time PGA champ Jim Barnes and former U.S. Open winner Johnny Farrell, a childhood friend of Sarazen's. Another was that a first-time contestant—Charlie Rowe, Oakmont's head professional—showed up sporting a driver with a steel shaft. Several players lodged protests with PGA president George Sargent, claiming it provided an undue advantage; somewhat reluctantly, he concluded that no "official" rule barred use of a steel-shafted club. But perhaps the biggest surprise was Sarazen's performance. After nosing out Jock Hutchison three-and-one in the quarterfinals, he fired a 32 in his opening semifinal nine—breaking the course record—to get past Bobby Cruickshank. In the thirty-six-hole title match he faced Emmet French—ironically his clubhouse roommate for the week—and beat him with relative ease, four-and-three.

Newspapers hailed the arrival of a major new star, a charismatic player who loved the limelight as much as did his boyhood hero, Walter Hagen—who'd controversially skipped defending his title at Oakmont in favor of a private exhibition that paid $2,000 more than the PGA's thousand-dollar top prize. Within hours of Sarazen's victory, advance agents for both men were busy cooking up a seventy-two-hole challenge match they ambitiously labeled "The Championship of the World," trumping "The Match of the Century" between Hagen and Jones. Sarazen won that as well, mounting a furious comeback to pocket the $3,000 prize money.

During the heady days of the 1920s, a U.S. Open title was believed to be worth about $25,000 in resulting endorsement deals and exhibition fees, a PGA title slightly less. Weeks after winning at Oakmont, however, Sarazen, the first player ever to hold both titles simultaneously, cashed in by signing deals to open a correspondence golf school in New York and to represent and design golf clubs for the Wilson Sporting Goods Company. He was also paid to endorse everything from shotgun shells for trapshooting to automobile tires and razor blades, the first golfer to exploit these opportunities so thoroughly. He then accepted the highest salary ever offered a professional—estimated at $5,000 a year—from a swanky resort located north of New York City in Westchester County. Sarazen was having the time of his life, "riding sky-high," as he once put it, "in the classiest sport in the land."

Momentarily overshadowed by Sarazen's and Hagen's celebrity was the steady rise of Bobby Jones. Despite a poor break that cost him the Open in Skokie, followed a month later by a bitter loss to Yale undergraduate Jess Sweetser at the U.S. Amateur at Brookline, Jones was generally considered the most promising player in the game. His swing, after all, was a picture of efficient simplicity. He'd acquired it, starting about age of six, by mimicking Carnoustie-born Stewart Maiden's, head pro at his club, East Lake in Atlanta. A frail and shy boy, he'd suffered from digestive problems early on but quickly came to share his father's passion for all sports, particularly golf and baseball. The senior Bob Jones had starred at Mercer College and been offered a contract with the Brooklyn Superbas (later the Dodgers), which his father refused to let him accept. Young Bobby soon graduated from the creeks of East Lake, where he chased frogs and killed snakes, to the fairways where, by 1916, just fourteen years old, he developed into the hottest player on the Southern club circuit—with a temper to match. Besides throwing clubs, he could cuss up a storm whenever a shot failed to go his way. Years later, he explained, he'd learned how from his family's longtime yardman.

Back when Jones appeared at the Merion Cricket Club just outside Philadelphia for the U.S. Amateur in 1916, he didn't seem the slightest bit intimidated by the well-known names in the field. Matched against Eben Byers, another young club thrower, in the first round, he managed to prevail three-and-one, wryly theorizing later that he won only because Byers "ran out of clubs first." He also won his next match, but then lost to the defending champion, Bob Gardner, on the thirty-first green of a thirty-six-hole match. He was, however, the talk of the championship, and even made a strong impression on Walter Travis, amateur golf's grand old man. Upon being asked what improvements young Jones might make, Travis gave his interviewer a surprised look and a curt reply. "Improvement? He can never improve his shots, if that's what you mean. But he will learn a good deal more about playing them."

For all his lavish natural gifts, Jones wasn't a typical spoiled scion of the upper class. Off the course he was the soul of courtesy to everyone he met, an exemplary and well-read young sportsman whom the press found it a sheer pleasure to converse with, a Southern Baptist gentleman who was already developing a taste for classical opera and the reflections of Cicero. His outbursts of incandescent anger were directed at himself for making foolish mistakes or losing his focus. A gallery official addressing the gallery using a megaphone unbuttoned him at the U.S. Amateur at Oakmont in 1919. A pesky bee landing on the ball during his swing shattered his concentration and ruined his chances against Francis Ouimet in the semis of 1920.

By then—under the steadying influence of both his father and O. B. Keeler, the *Atlanta Journal* sportswriter and bon vivant who immediately recognized Jones's potential and took him under his wing—he was beginning to emerge as a spectacular talent. A famous incident at St. Andrews, however, marked his true coming of age. During the third round of the 1921 Open Championship, after going out in a woeful 46, he played five strokes on the short par-three eleventh, exploded with rage and picked up. The next day he was so ashamed of "quitting on the game and myself" that he vowed never to compete again unless he could maintain the highest standard of sporting comportment. This would prove to be a decision of historic importance.

As Walter Travis had predicted, Jones learned how to play the shots, and he mastered other factors as well. After he narrowly lost to Sarazen at Skokie in 1922, O. B. Keeler suggested he consider altering his diet. Between rounds, Jones had a predilection for heavy lunches topped off with sherbet or pie à la mode. Keeler—himself a well-fed man who hosted lavish suppers for his opera-loving friends back home in Atlanta—proposed that this caloric indulgence might well account for his tendency to lose his concentration and make poor decisions late in a match. After a childhood in which his digestive system prevented him from enjoying ordinary treats, good food and excellent whiskey were always important to Bobby Jones. Yet something was clearly denying him the breakthrough in golf he hungered for.

On a much deeper and far more private level, the courtly Atlantan wondered if he simply wasn't fated to ever win a major championship of any kind. "Very lately I have come to a sort of Presbyterian attitude toward tournament golf," he confided in *Down the Fairway*, the lovely coming-of-age memoir that Keeler helped him write, published when he was just twenty-five. "I can't get away from the idea of predestination."

After Skokie, he agreed to avoid the buffet table and stick to a diet of tea and buttered toast during the break between rounds. Yet even then he was actually mulling over the idea of retiring from competitive golf, which he found so grueling that he frequently lost weight regardless of what he ate. Years later, he would famously say there are two kinds of games of golf, the kind played for recreation and simple competitive enjoyment with friends—and the other kind played for tournament glory. He actually preferred the former. That autumn he entered Harvard College to study English literature, and his agile mind, if not full of sonnets, was certainly reeling with Shakespearean doubt about his own golfing future when he arrived at the Inwood Country Club on Long Island in June 1923 for the twenty-seventh U.S. Open.

The Inwood course was long and narrow, full of lurking disaster. Feeling the pressure as never before, Jones was feeling worse than ever about his competitive career despite a late-arriving telegram from his grandfather, who heretofore had been as supportive of his grandson's golf dreams as he'd been about his son's baseball aspirations. But he now urged his namesake to "Keep the ball in the fairway and make all the putts go down." Frisky Atlantic winds played havoc with his practice rounds, neither of them breaking 80. His qualifying rounds of 77 and 79 only darkened his mood and deepened his gloom. Keeler tried to bolster his spirits but privately conveyed to friends that he sensed a disaster in the making.

As play opened, however, Jones found himself in unusual command of his game. He finished the round with 71, one of just two sub-par rounds Inwood yielded during the championship. Following a 73 in the afternoon, he found himself comfortably lodged in second place, two back of Jock Hutchison and one ahead of Bobby Cruickshank, the infectiously cheerful Scot who'd survived a Great War POW camp and immigrated to America to make his fortune in golf. After the third round, as the others stumbled, Jones held a commanding three-stroke lead and appeared to have his first national championship safely in hand. In the afternoon, despite a lapse that cost him a double-bogey on the difficult par-three seventh, he arrived at the seventieth hole of the championship dead level par, needing only three pars to win. His confidence was surging.

What happened next reveals not only why the U.S. Open to this day remains the hardest major championship to win but also how heavy a toll it exacts on those who would claim it. Overwhelmed by nerves, Jones went bogey, bogey, double-bogey, the worst finish of his storied career. Having blown the door wide open for Cruickshank, he disappeared into the clubhouse to await the verdict. "Even the people closest to Jones," writes Ron Rapoport in *The Immortal Bobby*, "those who had been with him for years and seen his blackest moods, were shocked by his appearance as he came off the course." Grantland Rice, who came to feel like his adopted uncle, wrote that the young man looked as if he'd been mortally wounded. Keeler, struggling to put a good face on the collapse, told him he felt the score would likely hold up—though he didn't really believe it himself. "Well, I didn't finish like a champion," Jones snapped in response. "I finished like a yellow dog." Then he skulked to his room to wait in miserable solitude.

Back on the course, Bobby Cruickshank arrived at the thirteenth tee three strokes up with six to play, but then succumbing to the pressure gave four strokes back to par and, looking shell-shocked himself, came to the long and treacherous eighteenth hole needing a birdie to tie. From two hundred yards out, with the wind in his face, he fired one of the finest clutch shots in U.S. Open history and drained the six-footer to draw even with the inconsolable Jones. The following afternoon, before a crowd of more than ten thousand, the two men battled nip and tuck, swapping the lead back and forth, to arrive all square at the tee of the eighteenth hole. Both men hit poor tee shots, and Cruickshank chose to lay up in front of the lagoon that protected the eighteenth green.

With everything on the line, Jones quickly pulled a two-iron and struck his best approach shot ever, clearing the water and stopping six feet from the cup. The gallery exploded. Stewart Maiden, Bobby's aging East Lake pro, the sedatest of men by nature, nearly threw his new straw hat in the air. As the gallery broke and ran to surround the green, Francis Ouimet, Jones's roommate all week, protectively took his arm to escort him to his ball. Years later, Jones would write that he had no memory of this moment. Cruickshank's third found the bunker, and his recovery from it was poor; Jones two-putted for the victory. When the two competitors shook hands, Jones's eyes wobbled with shock and emotion. "My, what a golfer that boy is," Cruickshank told a swarm of reporters moments later. "He's the greatest champion of them all. To be defeated by him is glory enough."

These were extraordinarily generous and prescient words. Beginning at Inwood in 1923, Bobby Jones made the U.S. Open his own private affair. Over six of the next eight years, he either won it outright—twice—or finished in a tie for first that necessitated a playoff, two of which he lost, two of which he won. His total of four titles matched the record set in the early years of the century by a largely unknown Willie Anderson. In all, he won twenty-three of the fifty-two tournaments he entered during his fourteen-year playing career, and thirteen of twenty-one major championships he competed in between 1923 to 1930. "The first seven years brought Bobby nothing but anger and frustration," says his modern biographer Sidney Matthew. "Once he mastered his temper and learned how to win, the remaining seven brought him immortality."

Though some have accurately pointed out that the financial success of his leading rivals Hagen and Sarazen lured many of the top amateurs of his day into the pro ranks, Jones's record in these events was still breathtaking. "In seven cracks at our Amateur beginning in 1924 and through 1930," Herb Wind pointed out, "Jones was eliminated once in the third round, defeated once in the final, and was victorious the five other times in the final." Sportswriter Paul Gallico summed it up best when he observed that golf in the 1920s seemed to have been "invented for Bobby Jones."

The endless bathtub-gin party that was the Jazz Age came to a stunning halt on Tuesday, October 29, 1929, when the stock market collapsed under its own unregulated weight and $30 billion of American wealth vanished overnight, sending the country spinning into the dark and uncertain days of the Great Depression. As if to punctuate the end of golf's Golden Age, Walter Hagen won his final major earlier that summer, the 1929 Open Championship at Muirfield. Bobby Jones capped things off majestically less than a year later by capturing the amateur and open championships of both America and Britain, returning home to a hero's welcome and a pair of ticker tape parades that celebrated what O. B. Keeler would eventually name the Grand Slam. Days later, the finest symbol of amateur sports announced his retirement from competitive golf and went home to Atlanta to resume his law practice, commence the task of creating the Augusta National Golf Club, and make a dozen instructional films for Warner Brothers. Ironically, he netted anywhere from $300,000 to half a million from film work and public appearance fees during his first year away from the game—more than either Babe Ruth or Walter Hagen during their first year of stardom.

Gene Sarazen, Jones's exact contemporary, distracted by movie roles and big exhibition paydays of his own, narrowly lost the 1928 U.S. Open to his rival, the Haig, but continued to win tournaments at an impressive clip, though he wouldn't capture his next major championship until the Open Championship of 1932, at the low point of the Depression. The notion of an American triumvirate in golf more or less retired with Bobby Jones.

Despite a brief bull market rally in late 1930—symbolized by that year's hit song "Happy Days Are Here Again," a movie anthem intended to herald the impending repeal of Prohibition—banks were suddenly closing and country clubs losing members at a shocking rate. Within fourteen months, over two dozen major East Coast clubs shut their doors and a third of the public courses in America were turning into grassy fields. As unemployed men began to turn up on street corners selling apples to feed their families, the Golden Age—not just in golf—began to wither and die.

After losing the infamous "long count" rematch to Gene Tunney that made him a sentimental favorite to millions, Jack Dempsey fought a hundred more bouts purely for the money and watched the sport he resurrected from back alleys sink back into ill repute due to underworld infiltration; Dempsey went to New York and opened a restaurant across from Madison Square Garden that became the preferred watering hole of press agents and sportswriters. Red Grange abandoned football entirely in 1930 and started an insurance agency in Florida, hoping for a more stable life. Bill Tilden—who'd inveighed against athletes turning professional—began playing tennis for cash and turned pro himself. The great Knute Rockne, who despite his protestations against playing for money allowed his players to wager on their own games and made money himself writing pulp sports novels and using his fame to peddle Studebakers, perished in a plane crash in 1930 while flying to Los Angeles to discuss a football-themed movie with Universal Pictures. President Hoover proclaimed his death a national disaster.

The message of this tarnished age of sport wasn't lost on three impressionable caddies from the heartland.

"I suppose I was about age twelve around the time I went out to Glen Garden," Byron Nelson recalled to a visiting reporter in 1994. "I began to read a great deal about the sports stars of the Twenties—particularly golfers, Hagen and Sarazen and, of course, Bobby Jones. The things they were doing were pretty inspiring to a kid like me. They seemed to say you could go somewhere if you had the game and the opportunity. I went and got myself a copy of Harry Vardon's book on how to play golf and read it cover to cover several times. I think I still have it."

"I used to see the top players of that time come through Hot Springs to play at the Homestead," Sam Snead remembered. "And I used to tell myself that I could probably beat those fellas in a few years. You may think I'm joking, but I'm not. I started to believe it bad about then. Hagen, Sarazen and Jones were the very best, and I told myself, by God, I could be as good as them someday soon."

Late in life, Ben Hogan confided to his lunch companions at the Shady Oaks Country Club in Fort Worth that when he walked out to the Glen Garden Golf Club in 1924, and confirmed that boys his age were getting paid sixty-five cents a day for simply lugging some rich man's golf bag, he saw his life opening up before him—every step carrying him toward something better and further away from his father's desperate act, and the event that would shape his life.

4

THE CHRISTMAS MATCH

THE GLEN GARDEN COUNTRY CLUB was neither Fort Worth's first nor finest golf club. That distinction belonged to the Rivercrest Country Club, formed in the city's western suburbs in 1910 when a hundred prominent local members organized to purchase 625 acres and create a golf club. By 1920, Rivercrest was one of the premier clubs in Texas. Glen Garden, three years its junior, was three miles past the city limits on Cowtown's southeastern flank, built on 111 acres of hard-turf prairie land formerly owned by the OK Cattle Company, about one mile from where the family of Byron Nelson settled in a small frame house on Timberline Road. Glen Garden's original clubhouse—a rustic Craftsman-style ranch structure with a large porch supported by beams and stonework—opened in 1914 with 350 members, including many of Fort Worth's newest and most enthusiastic golfers. It quickly became known as a player's club, and it particularly appealed to young businessmen, civil servants and lawyers.

By the time twelve-year-old Ben Hogan wandered up to see what caddying was all about, members had recently voted to expand their nine-hole, sand-green layout. Gangly Byron Nelson had already been on the grounds for two weeks, trying to hustle up a bag. "Competition was pretty stiff," he recalled. "There were all sorts of boys out there for the same thing. Before Mr. Akey, the caddie master, would permit you to carry a bag, you had to learn about caddying, how to carry the bag and keep the clubs clean and keep your eye on the ball, that sort of thing. He called it caddie school and stressed that a caddie's job was to help a player but know when to stay out of the way. He told us we should watch good players to learn how to play, and maybe even read a book on the rules of the game. Some of the boys didn't think that was necessary but I took that lesson to heart."

Byron presented himself half a dozen times before Mr. Akey permitted him to have a bag of his own, and his first client was a visiting Rotarian from Dallas one Saturday after school resumed in September. "I was pretty nervous that first time out," he remembered. "My golfer was named Mr. Shute. On the first tee he told me that if I helped him avoid losing a ball, why, he'd give me an additional quarter. That would have been seventy-five cents—a lot of money to me. But on the first hole, wouldn't you know, he sliced one into the deep grass and I couldn't find that ball to save my life. He still gave me the fifty cents, though. So that was good."

Byron's general ease around people and eagerness to abide by the club's strict prohibitions against caddies cursing and smoking made him quickly stand out from the others and brought him to favorable attention from both the club's somewhat avuncular caddie master and the club's tyrannical manager, James Kidd, a stern Scotsman who went by the nickname "Captain Kidd." Weeks after he arrived—an indication of how quickly he made a positive impression—Byron was allowed to borrow a member's clubs and play the course for the first time. He shot 118 and soon acquired the first club of his own set, a hickory-shafted mashie iron (equivalent to a five-iron today). Unlike undersized and silent Ben Hogan, who accurately deduced he would have to battle his way into the Glen Garden's pecking order by being tougher than the other boys, Byron was largely spared much of the caddie yard's traditional hazing rite known as the "Kangaroo Court."

"It was like a fraternity initiation," said Byron. "They would form two lines and you had to run between them while each one gave you a good hard lick with a belt. Sometimes they'd get a barrel and put a new kid in it and roll it down a hill from the clubhouse. That was even worse than running the gauntlet, but for some reason they never did that to me. They did try to run the new boys off, but I didn't run off very well. After I became a regular caddie, I never did pick on the younger boys because I didn't like it when they did it to me and didn't think it was right."

Ben, on the other hand, was a natural target. His size worked against him—he was almost too small to carry a bag—and his brooding intensity made him an even more appealing mark. The larger boys snatched off his aviator's cap and shoved him into an iron-stayed wooden barrel and sent him rattling down the hard clay hill of the practice range, laughing and taunting the new arrival, a game that never failed to reduce the victim to tears. In his case, however, no tears appeared. Ben Hogan didn't cry for anybody, life had already made damn sure of that. When they forced him to fight an older kid who stood at least a full head taller, Ben used his oversized fists to quickly reduce the boy to a blubbering heap in the dust. After that, they left him alone. He'd found a hard-won, if uneasy, place for himself in the Glen Garden caddie yard.

Five decades later, with his place among the greatest names in the game assured and the equipment company bearing his iconic signature producing the most desired clubs in golf, he sometimes spoke wistfully of "Hennie Bogan" to his longtime secretaries Doxey Williams and Sharon Rae or his regular lunch pals at Shady Oaks. "Hennie Bogan was Ben's alter ego," his longtime friend, the insurance man Gene Smyers, explained, "and I always thought Hennie was the boy Ben wished he could've been. This may sound odd but Ben was proud of the hard things he'd endured. He genuinely believed the tough things he went through—from losing his father to having to fight his way into the caddie yard—only prepared him for being the best he could be in life. That's why he never showed a ripple of fear or intimidation to the world at large—and certainly not another golfer. If he did, he knew he wouldn't make it, might not survive. Hennie Bogan, on the other hand, had an easier time of it—a happy childhood, probably more like Byron's than Ben's. He even had Hennie's name on a desk plate someone gave him. He was very proud of that."

"I think Hennie Bogan was the boy Mr. Hogan always wished he could have been, but life never worked out that way," Sharon Rae added. "Sometimes he would sit and tell me stories about his childhood and actually call himself Hennie Bogan without even realizing it. That always brought tears to my eyes, I have to say. Hennie Bogan was very much a part of Mr. Hogan, the man who loved to help stray dogs and doing things for people down on their luck, never wanting anyone to know about it. I think he was really that boy deep inside."

There's no account of how long it took Ben Hogan to snag his first paying loop, and Byron had no memory of ever caddying with him, though he saw him frequently on the practice range. But by the spring of 1925 Ben had somehow acquired an old hickory-shafted cleek and a mashie iron of his own and was regularly competing in weekend caddie games on the range. In one game, players hit from one end of the practice area to the other, and whoever struck the shortest shot had to pick up the balls; in another, every competitor had to bet a nickel, and the longest driver won the pot. Unlike Byron, who was earning regular money on weekends by caddying for Judge J. B. Wade, Ben Hogan had no regular client, and because every scrap of cash was needed at home, he didn't pitch pennies with the other boys whenever Captain Kidd or Harold Akey were out of sight. He spent his idle moments on the practice range, hitting balls. Whatever he learned, he picked up purely from mimicking more skilled players and beating his own rudimentary game out of the baked dirt on the range. "He would stay out there practicing till dark sometimes," a member named Rawlings remembered in the 1960s. "Even practicing was harder for Ben. Byron lived just a mile from the club and members sometimes gave him a ride home. Ben would stick around and hit balls and walk home in the dark. I reckon it was six or seven miles home for him."

In early 1940, in the glow of his first solo win at Pinehurst, Ben came out with the surprising revelation that he was naturally left-handed, but had switched to playing right-handed when his older brother, Royal, assured him no great champion had ever played from the other side. This transition apparently took place not long after Ben joined the caddie ranks at Glen Garden. "My brother would slap me every time he saw me use that right," he told a reporter, adding that left-handed clubs were so scarce he was forced to learn with conventional clubs. Byron never saw evidence of this switch, though he did recall that Ted Longworth, Glen Garden's affable head professional, repeatedly tried to fix Ben's "hog killer" grip on the club. Others maintained that it was actually Longworth's assistant Jack Grout—a young player with sizable tournament ambitions of his own and the future teacher of Jack Nicklaus—who finally sorted out young Bennie's grip. At any rate, he learned early that if he shifted his left hand over on the club, adopting a "strong" grip on the shaft, and made a long and relatively flat swing with a strong cocking of the wrists, he could produce shots that matched the length of the larger boys. "That's probably what kept me going," he reminisced to *Sports Illustrated* in the 1950s. "I began copying the good players and I began hitting a much longer ball. . . . You learn to take care of yourself and how to think when you're out on your own. I was too old for thirteen."

"Mr. Hogan told me that once he figured out how to do this, he hit low-running drives that beat the other boys," Sharon Rae remembered. "That's how he learned to hook the ball and why, I guess, it caused him so much trouble later on. He told me he earned quite a few nickels that way, though."

Byron didn't need to play driving games for nickels. Within two years of his arrival, growing into a polite beanpole of a kid approaching six feet in height, he was regularly on the bags of Judge Wade and a member's wife, May Whitney, who was close to Longworth. What impressed both Whitney and the head pro most about Byron was not only his diligence as a ball hawk, but also the devotion he exhibited to his family. Byron's mother had a third child about that time and Byron convinced his mother to name the boy after Judge Wade—Charles Wade Nelson. Moreover, though his father was not much for church-going, he regularly attended with his deeply religious mother and, when he wasn't either caddying or doing his chores, looked after Charlie. His daily chores included milking the family's cow and goat before school and feeding their Leghorn chickens; he worked in his father's ample vegetable garden in the evenings and hauled produce and fresh eggs around in a small wooden wagon, selling them to local stores and to Glen Garden's chef. For a time, he also sold *Liberty* magazine and a hand cleaner called Hand Slick. Impressed by his personal industry and responsibility, Longworth invited Byron to work in his shop and showed him how to operate a buffing wheel to clean the rust off clubs, and how to replace broken or bent hickory shafts. Byron earned an extra three dollars a week and grew so skilled at reshafting clubs that Longworth invited him to work on his own hickory set before he went to play the U.S. Open at Oakmont in 1927.

"He'd already qualified," Byron remembered. "So we got right to work on those clubs. He'd select the hickory shafts out of the barrel of shafts we had, making sure each one was good and straight and strong. Then I'd work down the end of the shaft so it would just fit good and tight in the hosel of the clubhead. I'd drive the shaft in with a maul, and put a pin or nail through the small hole on the side of the hosel to hold it in place. He took those clubs with him to Oakmont and played pretty well. I felt real proud of him, and happy I'd been able to help with his clubs."

A big thrill came later that summer when Longworth invited his cheerful shop assistant along to watch the semifinal match between

Walter Hagen and Al Espinosa for the PGA Championship over at the Cedar Crest Country Club in Dallas. With no ropes to keep spectators apart from players, the fifteen-year-old Byron was able to tag along in the shadow of the great Haig. At one point during the back nine, Hagen paused and squinted into the sun, having trouble determining where to aim his shot, and Byron spoke up.

"Would you like to borrow my cap?"

The winner of eight major championships glanced over and smiled.

"Yes," he said, taking the offered ball cap. "Thanks, son."

Slipping it on, Hagen hit his approach shot to within eight feet of the cup, then handed the cap back to the friendly kid, thanking him again with a wink. Moments later, Sir Walter rolled in the birdie putt and went on to eliminate Espinosa on the thirty-seventh hole. The next day, Hagen won his fifth PGA Championship title, one-up over Joe Turnesa.

Many years later, a reporter asked Byron if he'd kept the cap as a memento or a souvenir. He laughed and replied, "You'd think I would have kept that cap, but I haven't. I've never kept clubs or balls I won tournaments with or anything like that. Just not sentimental that way, I guess. But I wouldn't mind seeing that old cap again."

Every year at Christmas, Glen Garden staged its annual Caddie Championship, which many members regarded as the capstone of the season and the most entertaining event of the year. By tradition, caddies signed up to use members' clubs and members not only volunteered to carry the bags of their favorite loopers but also made handsome side bets on their players and threw a lavish turkey dinner for all the boys afterward, complete with small gifts.

Despite his evening job selling the *Star-Telegram* at the train depot, and Mama Hogan's firm insistence that golf was an idle rich man's game that could never take him anywhere of value, Bennie Hogan had managed to carve out something of a niche for himself at Glen Garden by regularly caddying for Ed Stewart, perhaps Fort Worth's most accomplished amateur player at that time, and for a boy about his own age named Dan Greenwood, a realtor's son who often let him hit shots with his matched Spalding clubs as they went along the course; this violated one of Captain Kidd's cardinal rules, but Bennie was willing to risk it since it gave him a chance to play with quality equipment. Even more important, one early summer morning in 1927 he began carrying the bag for a decidedly nonathletic new member who'd joined Glen Garden out of the blue on his doctor's advice to get some fresh air and exercise before he dropped dead of physical exhaustion.

Polite and dignified, Marvin Leonard was thirty-two years old and already something of a retail legend when he took up golf. Having failed twice earlier in his career to run a general merchandise business in North Texas, at a time when most Fort Worth retailers were aiming to exploit the city's new oil-driven wealth by catering to upscale buyers, Leonard and his brother Obie had decided to concentrate on selling a vast array of everyday commodities to ordinary folks from an unpretentious general store on Cowtown's busy North Houston Street, almost in the shadow of the ornate Tarrant County Courthouse.

Despite Prohibition, the Queen City of the Prairies was awash in speakeasies and flush with big-oil money, believed by many to be the most affluent city in Texas. At one point amid the frenzy of rising oil prices, petroleum speculators seized control of the lobby at the Westbrook Hotel (where Royal Hogan sold his newspapers before he headed off to his evening accounting classes) and chased out guests, pitching every piece of furniture and a large Greek statue into the street to make room for a makeshift trading floor. "Fort Worth," according to historian Oliver Knight, "was drunk at the shrine of the oil goddess."

The Leonard Brothers department store bucked the trend, specializing in basic goods and bargain prices, from slightly dented cans of condensed milk and surplus oranges, to roof nails or rubber work boots. Marvin and Obie Leonard acquired whatever commodities they could acquire by the cheapest means, typically from damaged freight or the inventory of a belly-up competitor, passing savings along to their growing ranks of devoted customers, stacking merchandise with a dash of imagination and wit that made their store something of an Old World shopping bazaar of cut-rate goods, a consumer cornucopia that tumbled exuberantly straight out the front door into the teeming streets of Cowtown—"laundry soap to range wire," as Marvin himself once explained to a reporter, "razors and cheese, cabbage and canned peas."

Within a few years of opening its doors, Leonard Brothers moved to a larger space farther up North Houston Street and kept expanding, fast becoming a retail destination for the working-class and farm families. Many consider Marvin Leonard the inspiration for Arkansan Sam Walton and others who saw the vast cut-price general store as the future of retailing. "Going to Leonard Brothers was like going to another world," Ben Hogan once remembered, "some place you liked to be, almost like home." Leonard Brothers was even famous for its fabulous window displays at Christmastime, and by the summer of 1927 Marvin and Obie were in the throes of further growth, taking over an entire city block. Marvin's doctor specifically prescribed golf, assuring him that "it will do you a world of good." Though he certainly could have afforded to join posh Rivercrest Country Club, he chose Glen Garden instead, bought a starter set of clubs from Ted Longworth, and took a few golf lessons, displaying an erratic and loopy swing he diligently attempted to refine. Like many late beginners, he had a tremendous desire to improve and began regularly showing up at dawn for a quick nine holes before work. In summer, Bennie Hogan arrived early, too, eager to get a loop in before Danny Greenwood or Ed Stewart showed up. One morning in late June, Marvin Leonard found him. "I'm not much of a player yet, son," Leonard apologized in advance, "but I'd be glad to have you go along."

"That's okay, sir," Ben told him. "Maybe I can show you something."

So off they went together, the runt caddie and the genteel storekeeper—an unlikely yet perfectly matched pair. Leonard had a soft spot for underdogs and kids; his own childhood had been a difficult one, and hard work had yielded first failure and now success beyond his wildest dreams. Something about the kid's inward solemnity reminded him of himself—though he had no inkling that he would soon become the father figure desperately needed to fill the cindered hole left by Chester Hogan's suicide. In Leonard, Hogan would find the decent, widely respected and transformative role model he needed to peer beyond the unremitting struggle of his past and present circumstances. Over the next thirty years—paralleling his own miraculous rise from a nobody to the most admired figure in golf—Ben Hogan (or maybe Hennie Bogan) would study men of means and substance like Marvin Leonard with the exactitude of a Swiss watchmaker, noting how they spoke, dressed, interacted with subordinates, and performed their jobs and ran their business affairs, with no detail too minor to take note of—especially the effect they had on others. His preference would be for extremely accomplished men who wore their success lightly, conveying an ease and social grace he secretly dreamed of attaining. In the fullness of time, both men would become legendary figures in their chosen and mingled worlds of commerce and golf, but the similarities went much deeper than that. Each valued honesty and personal friendship as among life's highest ideals, and each eventually married a pretty if emotionally needy woman who required constant attention and hid her social frailties from the world at large, a lifelong burden their devoted husbands carried with great dignity and composure. But that was still far down the fairway.

In the beginning, there was just ragged golf on a warmly flaring Texas morning and the two of them chasing the game and getting acquainted. Leonard never forgot those early days; they formed his fondest impressions of the game, and in time filled his imagination with greater possibilities. "Every morning I got up in time to be at the course about sunup and play nine holes," he explained many years later to a reporter who cornered him at the Colonial golf tournament he'd created at the beautiful club he'd founded on the banks of the Trinity River in Fort Worth. "Then I would go home and eat a big breakfast and sail off to work feeling like a new man. Golf not only saved my life, but it restored my health and gave me a new interest."

Ironically, about this time, *Star-Telegram* office manager Clyde Milliken began noticing a curious pattern in Ben Hogan's work habits. Whenever it rained, the kid was faithfully at his platform at the train depot selling papers to beat the band, but when it was sunny, he was nowhere to be found. Milliken soon discovered that on such days his teenaged news hawk was out at Glen Garden caddying and practicing, so he presented him with an ultimatum—golf or his job. Ben chose golf. Clara Hogan, when she heard the news from Royal, was neither pleased nor surprised. Golf, she predicted, would lead him nowhere fast. "Golf is nothing. And nothing divided by nothing," she liked to say, "is nothing."

Evidence that his mother might be wrong came that Christmas at the club's annual nine-hole Caddie Championship, when Bennie surprised everyone by shooting 39, two over par. He had the event sewn up until Byron Nelson sank a thirty-foot putt on the final hole to tie him—though years later Byron insisted their score was actually 40.

No matter. Captain Kidd declared a playoff and everyone marched back to the first tee with drinks and cigars in hand. The two young competitors shook hands, and Ben reportedly told Byron, "Well, good luck. I didn't think you could make that putt."

He probably meant no offense by his remark; was merely stating the unvarnished facts as he saw them—an evolving Hogan personality trait. And to be fair, he had to feel somewhat slighted by the fact that he'd achieved his first success of any kind only to have Glen Garden's golden boy rob him of the outright win at the last instant. To compound matters, both boys believed this was a sudden-death playoff. So when Bennie scored a four to Byron's six on the first hole, he assumed he'd won for a *second* time. Eager to keep the drama going, however, several Byron supporters firmly insisted on a full second nine, so they played on and Byron eventually drained another long putt on the final green to register 41 and a one-stroke victory. In a little ceremony, each player was presented the gift of a new golf club. Byron, Caddie Champion for 1927, received a small silver cup and a brand-new mashie, while Ben was given a driving iron. "Well, I already had a five and Ben had a two," Byron explained years later. "So we traded clubs."

After this, members recalled, everyone went into the clubhouse for dinner and Christmas celebrations—all except for Bennie, who melted away into the dusk. "I felt I had my party," he said later, "when I tied Nelson." Given Byron's social ease and sunny farm-boy charm, it's easy enough to see why members lavished their affections on the more popular young man, and why—like a Charles Dickens character peering through the frosted glass at the festivities within—his greatest rival would be unable, for the moment at least, to shake the feeling that he was naturally inferior, a boy who was always destined to stand outside in the cold.

Within months, Byron was working longer hours for Ted Longworth and playing a regular amateur circuit at the clubs around Fort Worth. Moreover, every spring Captain Kidd was asked to nominate a deserving caddie for a junior membership, which came with full playing privileges, and Byron was an easy choice in 1928. "He's the only caddie who doesn't drink, smoke, or curse," the pragmatic Scot summed up, conveniently overlooking Ben. "I think he should have it."

As a new junior member with a little spending money in his pocket, Byron soon won a junior match-play tournament at the Katy Lake Golf Course, beating another former Glen Garden caddie named Ned Baugh, and suddenly found himself invited to play at the better clubs of the Queen City on weekends. He was introduced to the area's better players—including a gangly soft-spoken young man from Dallas named Ralph Guldahl who slaughtered him the first time they met in a friendly caddie match, and a pair of seasoned brothers, Ray and Lloyd Mangrum, also from Dallas—and his game rapidly progressed. Some Glen Garden members believed Ben Hogan's game matched or exceeded Byron's by this point, but only Byron enjoyed the enthusiastic support of club members, many offering to drive him to weekend matches and pay his entry fees at a time when there were few restrictions on such things in amateur play.

As Byron's interest in golf grew, the attractions of school waned. "Math and geometry really confused me," he allowed. "I liked history and English well enough, but when I began playing hooky from school just so I could play golf my parents got very concerned about it and we had a serious discussion. Very few people I knew went on to college in those days. Formal education wasn't as important as it is today. I managed to convince them that the smart thing for me to do was to drop out of high school and get another job to supplement my daddy's income. I don't think my mother liked that idea much, but she eventually let me go ahead. She made me promise I would keep on reading books and learning as I went."

Sixteen-year-old Byron spent the summer hunting for work and mowing greens with a single-reel push mower every morning at dawn at Glen Garden. That autumn, through a member named Cecil Nottingham, he found a job as a file clerk for the Fort Worth–Denver City Railroad office, sorting and filing freight bills. Nottingham, both a sympathetic boss and a golfer, let him work on his game anytime the pace of office work slowed. But this arrangement lasted only about a year, since shortly after the stock market crash in October 1929 Nottingham was forced to let his favorite employee go.

During the spring of that year, however, having heard about Ben Hogan's work ethic from Marvin Leonard and others, Ted Longworth brought him into the shop and taught him the same skills Byron had learned there—solitary work Ben found deeply satisfying. Better yet, the club gave him playing privileges, too. "On weekends I polished clubs until three in the morning," Hogan recalled. "Boy, I would look at those clubs and they were the most beautiful things, Nickels and Stewarts, all made in Scotland. I found that working on those clubs, usually alone and sometimes late into the evening, gave me tremendous personal satisfaction and a much better understanding of the game."

To replace his lost *Star-Telegram* income, he took a second after-school job as the doorman at the Hippodrome Theater in downtown Fort Worth. Having reached his full height of five-foot-eight with a weight of 130 pounds, Ben finally began to resemble a man. His lean facial features were set off by a surprisingly broad smile, with unusually white, well-formed teeth, and a thick head with wavy dark hair. When he was a young boy in Dublin, he and Princess had been transfixed by the silent movies of Charlie Chaplin and Clara Bow that the town showed for free in the square on hot summer nights. Now, as a young man standing in the back of the darkened theater watching the light comedies of Pickford and Fairbanks or the popular gangster epics of the day, Bennie Hogan allowed himself to dream that even a no-name kid from rowdy Cowtown might someday go places.

The Christmas before, Clara Hogan had done something so out of character that her son would speak about it decades later with visible emotion. She used her extra sewing money to buy Ben his first set of matched golf clubs. "It meant more to me than anyone can know that she did that," Hogan told a Shady Oaks friend. "That she expressed some confidence in me meant the world."

Perhaps her support influenced Ben's decision to drop out of Central High after his sophomore year. Formal schooling held no appeal for him, either. He'd joined no social organizations, played no organized sports, even failed to show up for his class photograph in the yearbook. "He just stopped coming to school," a former classmate remembered. "We heard Ben planned to be a golfer." Ben understood, as Byron had pragmatically figured out before him, that college simply wasn't an option. But he possessed discipline and self-reliance shaped by Clara Hogan's iron will and natural gumption. "I feel sorry for the kids these days," he remarked in an interview with Ken Venturi in the 1970s. "They don't know what it's like to learn that you can survive almost anything."

The direct beneficiary of this decision was, of course, his golf game. He practiced on a regular basis and qualified for his first amateur tournament away from Glen Garden, the public links championship in Waco, securing a lift to the tournament from another promising amateur named Matty Reed. Ben played well, placed second, and won thirteen new golf balls—which he promptly sold to other competitors for two bits apiece before he and Reed rode home. The next summer, as his lone practice sessions grew lengthier, just prior to his seventeenth birthday, the Glen Garden shop assistant hitchhiked all the

The youngest caddie: Sam, age seven, at the
Homestead in Hot Springs, Virginia

Sam, with former U.S. Open winners Johnny Farrell and Billy Burke, at the Cascades Open in 1935, which he thought he should've won

With Audrey, whom he married in 1939

Perhaps the most iconic photograph of the most charismatic star of the prewar years on the PGA Tour

The good sport: Sam after losing the 1940
PGA Championship to Byron

His first U.S. Open disaster,
at Spring Hill in 1939

Sam brings home the claret jug, 1946

With the Hawk in the late 1940s, probably taken
at Augusta, both men in their prime

Following his record eighty-two PGA Tour wins, the professional emeritus at the Greenbrier, with his beloved dog, Meister, in 1992

Traveling buddies: Sam and his son, Jack, in 1995

GENE SARAZEN 92
BYRON NELSON 82
SAM SNEAD 81

Masters legends: Byron, Sam, Augusta chairman
Jack Stephens, and the ageless Gene Sarazen

The Slammer at Snead Links, where he and
Audrey are buried side by side

way to Shreveport, Louisiana, and made it to the finals of the South-western Amateur, losing out four-and-three to a sensational nineteen-year-old player from Dallas named Gus Moreland. After their match, the Shreveport paper noted that the long-hitting Hogan had been troubled off the tee by a hook that constantly forced him to scramble from the rough or the woods to stay in the match. Too broke to pay his caddie—an early glimpse of the moral code Hogan would adopt in all of life's transactions—he hocked the runner-up prize, a wristwatch, on the spot, then paid him and thumbed home to Fort Worth.

"After that," Hogan later explained, "I decided amateur golf was fine but, if I wanted to continue playing golf, I'd have to make some money."

At least in theory, his timing, like that of Byron and Sam, couldn't have been better—or worse. Through the balance of the summer and into the fateful autumn of 1929, Ben began showing up for "money" games in Fort Worth and Dallas against some of the area's better players. One reason Guldahl and the Mangrums appeared sooner than he or even Byron on Texas scoreboards, Hogan's Shady Oaks cronies later theorized, was the fact that they played so many more tough five-dollar matches that seasoned and prepared their games for tournament competition. Gus Moreland became a holy terror on the Texas amateur circuit, beating Byron, Ben, and every other significant amateur of the 1930s, even finishing second at the Texas Open. The upstart Hogan won a handful of these side games, too, prompting him to wonder how far the game might take him if he continued to diligently practice and play against the best competition.

During the last summer of the Jazz Age, a young man could have been forgiven for entertaining lofty golf dreams. Fueled by the material successes of Hagen, Sarazen and, most of all, Bobby Jones, the game was at its zenith of popularity, coming off its greatest growth period ever. Bernard Darwin, the grandson of the great naturalist whose theory of evolution sparked 1925's sensational Scopes trial, remarked in the London *Times* that America had eclipsed Britain in the sport. As summer moved on, a leading Wall Street light confidently declared there would be no end to the rampaging bull market, predicting it might actually extend its run "indefinitely owing to the insatiable American appetite for creating success upon success." Echoing this sunny forecast for the summer of 1929, *Vogue* magazine declared that next to acquiring a "fashionable sun tan, there is no better indication of one's social acumen than displaying a fine game of golf."

That autumn, Byron won several small amateur tournaments and some member-only events in the Dallas–Fort Worth area, arranged by Ted Longworth or Jack Grout, suggesting great things might follow in the near future.

Twelve hundred miles away in the Blue Ridge Mountains, the summer before his senior year at Valley High in Hot Springs, Virginia, Sam Snead was working as a short-order cook and cleanup man at his uncle Ed's restaurant, and occasionally caddying on weekends at the Homestead for spending money, and courting his high school sweetheart, Audrey.

Owing to his natural Snead athleticism and saturnine good looks, he was a popular student at the tiny high school (population: 150) though he rarely applied himself in the classroom. By 1929 he'd already lettered as a halfback on the football team and possessed a reasonably good sinker pitch in baseball. In basketball, his best sport, he was known for his deadly jump shot. He also ran track—able to clock the hundred-yard dash in ten seconds flat—and even boxed on the side to earn some extra money, once knocking out a journeyman Golden Gloves boxer who passed through town looking to score an easy payday against local contenders. Though golf didn't rival team sports in his estimation, Sam played that as well, entering two schoolboy tournaments on the sand-green nine-hole course at the prestigious private Woodberry Forest School during his junior and senior years, never finishing better than third place, but he was runner-up both times in the long-drive contest, belting the ball over three hundred yards using a driver he borrowed from Doc Ridgeley, the drugstore owner back in Hot Springs.

Team sports and prizefighting would fascinate Snead his entire life, as friendships with Ted Williams and Gene Tunney would attest. For a time, until he worried the mob connections could hurt his own reputation, he even owned a percentage of a prizefighter. Early on, though, his coach, Harold Bell, realized that golf held the best prospects for Snead. Virginia Polytech and even Mr. Jefferson's University of Virginia had already made inquiries about the versatile star athlete from Valley High, but Bell advised Sam that he might put these gifts to better use—and see quicker results—if he skipped college altogether and concentrated on golf. His reputation as a big hitter, Bell noted, was the talk of the county. Sam's frustration was how to make the jump from high school stardom and part-time caddying to something more substantial. "You've seen these small town star athletes who ran out of eligibility and don't marry a rich girl or land a job selling stocks and bonds and hang around the hometown pool hall and cigar store, wondering where the cheers went," he wrote years later. "That's the way I seemed to be headed."

To hear Sam tell it, his life changed forever the summer evening a stranger entered Uncle Ed's restaurant near closing time and ordered a hamburger. They chatted, Sam cooked the man's burger, and it turned out that the man was a good friend of Freddie Gleim's, the Homestead's head professional. Having heard of Sam's prodigious length, the man suggested Sam contact Gleim about a job—even offered to put in a good word for him.

Weeks later, toward the end of summer, Sam had an interview at the Homestead and was hired to clean clubs and keep the golf shop stocked and swept. Gleim was sufficiently impressed that he taught him how to repair and reshaft clubs—tasks that Sam, like Ben Hogan out in Texas, took a liking to. He learned to taper shafts with his pocketknife and strengthen them by rubbing them down with linseed oil and shellac, developing a good sense of a club's balance, feel, and flexibility. The job paid only twenty-five bucks a month but permitted him to use the practice range and sometimes even play the course when things were slow. That carried him into late October, when the course shut down for the winter. The day after they closed the shop, the stock market collapsed.

The following summer, however, after high school graduation, he got his job back and, two weeks later, while Gleim and his assistant pro were busy elsewhere, a bosomy matron steamed into the shop and demanded to have a golf lesson. Sam demurred, but she persisted. Finally, after the the starter promised to keep a look out for Freddie Gleim, the two of them went to the practice ground and he showed her the basics of grip, stance, and swing. "I got her so she could pelt it out there a little ways," he remembered. "Gave her a pretty good workout, though she wasn't in danger of being a good golfer anytime soon."

He was summoned into Gleim's office afterward, half expecting to be fired. Instead, he was informed that the deeply pleased guest had gone straight to the general manager to compliment the young man's courtesy and teaching abilities. Gleim "promoted" him to the Cascades Hotel course three and a half miles down the road. His new title would be "apprentice professional," which meant he drew no salary but was free to charge a dollar for any golf lessons he gave to guests.

The good news was that he now had almost free run of the resort's finest golf course and plenty of free time to work on his game. The bad news was that nearly one third of working Americans had either lost their jobs or soon would, so the affluent resort trade the Homestead and Cascades hotels relied upon pretty much dried up overnight. Sam spent the next three years working there, polishing his own game and giving the occasional lesson for minimal compensation, playing his trumpet at night and wondering if he'd been smart to choose golf over college football or baseball. "I was thin as a razorback hog," he recalled of his lean years in the Cascades shop, "and had sharpened into a long hitter with a fair amount of ability at chipping and putting—while not having a prospect in sight for getting up in the world."

When word spread that Sam was regularly shooting in the 60s on the tough Cascades course, Gleim brought him back to the Homestead shop at the start of the 1935 season, but kept him largely out of sight while he himself monopolized hotel guests' attention. This slight was magnified when Gleim refused to give his assistant a discount when he began putting together his own first set of matched golf clubs, buying them one club at a time, for five dollars each, the same price hotel guests paid. Moreover, on the few occasions Sam asked Gleim to take a look at his golf swing, Gleim snapped, "You're a professional now. You shouldn't have to ask anyone for help."

Sam got the message. "It was pretty clear to me he was holding me back, probably because there wasn't anybody around who could beat me on the golf course. I figured I just had to bide my time. The Depression was pretty thick on us all by then, let me tell you. Besides, there wasn't anywhere else to go. I thought a lot about trying to go out on the circuit, but I had no backing and no money of my own."

That winter, however, Gleim did invite Sam to his first "professional" tournament, the Miami Open. Using a two-wood on loan from his boss, he played well enough to earn $150. But afterward Gleim demanded the club back before the following tournament in Nassau, Bahamas. "So I don't have a club to play with, and have to go back home," Sam recounted to Al Barkow in *Gettin' to the Dance Floor.* "Gleim leaves for Nassau and I go look in the locker he was using. I just wanted to see if that club wasn't there. Well, it was there. Gleim didn't take it to Nassau; he just didn't want me to go."

The final indignity came when the Homestead hosted the Cascades Open the following summer, attracting an impressive field that included Bobby Cruickshank and a pair of U.S. Open champions, Johnny Farrell (1928) and Billy Burke (1931). Initially, the resort management refused to let its twenty-four-year-old apprentice pro compete, but Farrell and Cruickshank—eager to get a look at the long hitter they'd been hearing about—let it be known they might withdraw if the kid were snubbed. Sam was permitted to play.

He opened with a blistering 68 and after three rounds owned the lead. Before the final round, however, Gleim got summoned to the office of the Homestead's president, Fay Ingalls, and was informed in no uncertain terms that Snead should not be allowed to win the tournament. "Do whatever you have to do to prevent that from happening," Ingalls told him, sensing a public relations disaster in the making. At a time when hotels and resorts everywhere were struggling to keep their doors open, the last thing the Homestead needed was a no-name local assistant beating a pair of U.S. Open champions. The newspapers would either write it off as a fluke or ignore the tournament completely.

Before the final round, Gleim pulled Sam aside and advised him that his "flying left elbow" would ruin his chances under pressure. "How do you expect to ever be a pro with that left elbow coming out like that?" he said.

Sam realized Gleim was trying to unsettle him, that this was the same rank jealousy and gamesmanship he'd been dealing with on and off the course for almost five years. The idea that Gleim would sabotage his chances to win a tournament and get out of Hot Springs for good chewed deeply on his psyche. A photograph of Sam, Billy Burke, and Johnny Farrell taken as they strode down the first fairway shows the two Open champions smiling graciously, and Sam wearing an almost hangdog expression. "I was spitting mad inside at what that no-good bum was trying to do," he recalled years later. Even so, on the second hole, he tried to keep his elbow from flying and sliced his drive "halfway up the mountainside," requiring eight strokes to complete the hole, and 80 for the round; though he finished in third place, he still managed to put $358.66 in his pocket.

"That was a lesson I learned two ways. First was that I let my anger take ahold of my game and distract me—that was a lesson Coach Bell had taught me years before back in school. Anytime you lose your cool, brother, you're usually done for. The next thing I learned was to trust my own game. If anybody ever offered to 'fix' what was wrong with me, why, I was gonna run for the hills."

However, this episode also brought him an unexpected turn of good fortune. While he was counting his money behind the caddie shed, a well-dressed man walked up and congratulated Sam on his good showing, introducing himself. "My name is Fred Martin from the Greenbrier Hotel over at White Sulphur Springs in West Virginia. How would you like to be a full-fledged professional for me?"

According to Sam, he was momentarily at a loss for words, then asked the man if he was joking. The Greenbrier was as famous as the Homestead.

"Let's not waste time," Martin told him. "One of our pros is leaving and his job is open. We'll pay you forty-five dollars a month and room and board. Anything you can make teaching our guests is yours to keep. Do you want the job or not?"

They shook hands, and Sam gave his notice to Gleim the next day. Ingalls made no effort to keep him from moving on. Throughout his life, Sam possessed a strong sense of predestination not uncommon to the mountain people he descended from—and this moment only deepened that natural inclination. "I remember thinking that everything in my life was about to change, to really look up for once," he told a reporter decades later. "It was like a door suddenly opened up and I didn't waste no time gettin' through it."

By the end of the first week at the majestic Greenbrier, however, he nearly lost his job for driving the green on the 335-yard fifth hole of the Old White Course while a hotel guest was putting out. This happened to be Alva Bradley, who owned not only the Cleveland Indians baseball club, but also the Chesapeake & Ohio Railroad Company, which owned the Greenbrier itself. A portly despot known for his volcanic outbursts, Bradley ordered Martin to sack his new professional. It wasn't until a caddie confirmed what had happened that Bradley reluctantly agreed to play a round with the young man and witness his alleged power for himself. Sam let the shaft out and drove the fifth green a second time. Almost instantly, to hear Sam tell it, the two became good friends, and Bradley his work in progress. A short time later, Bradley broke 90 for the first time and tipped Sam a hundred dollars and told him to buy some new clubs. Instead, Sam bought a used tin-lizzie jalopy and a new check sports jacket.

"A thing that helped me in golf," he wrote years later in *The Education of a Golfer*, "was that every knock is a boost."

Like Ben Hogan, he learned early on that golf was pure survival of the fittest, and beating the other guy sometimes required every mental game and legal maneuver in the book. But unlike Byron and Ben, he had no kindly Ted Longworth or Marvin Leonard to influence his thinking and soften his perceptions of the motives of many who were drawn to the game, especially the high rollers and hucksters who were plentiful on the early tour and in the resort world and never far from any large amateur event.

Old friends of Sam's liked to tell the story of his first high-stakes match, which developed when a pair of wealthy sporting types staying at the Greenbrier offered to cover his expenses to come north and play T. Suffern "Tommy" Tailor, a Seminole member and old-money scion who would contend in several U.S. Amateur championships and play in the Masters but was far better known for the size of his wagers. Over thirty-six holes at the Meadow Brook Club on Long Island, Sam eked out a pair of victories that by some accounts earned him $10,000, to him an unimaginable sum. But according to Al Barkow, who describes the episode in detail in his biography of Sam, $50,000 and $100,000 were actually at stake in the two matches and the gullible Virginian was bilked out of a much larger payday. He also insists this took place before Sam left the Homestead, while other friends of Sam's maintain it happened not long after he arrived at the Greenbrier.

Whatever the truth of the matter—and Sam makes only oblique reference to Tailor and his big-money betting games in one of his autobiographies and a later book on the art of betting in golf—the undeclared windfall undoubtedly helped finance his early days on the tour, though his deep fear of the tax man or a more commonplace reluctance of rural folk to reveal their true assets for fear someone would seek favors or worse—an Old Testament fear of the stranger—dogged him and shaped his lifelong silence on the subject. Encounters like this, moreover, only deepened his natural resentment, verging on outright contempt, for the privileged classes who populated his early working life, and eventually made him wary of banks, financial advisors, even investment deals offered by close friends. The class chip on his shoulder even accounted for the pleasure he took in pricking the delicate sensibilities of snobby types—particularly wealthy condescending women—and his indifference to the criticism he received for behavior that endeared him to some and greatly offended others.

"Sam had all the charm in the world if he liked and trusted you—and not much concern for your feelings if he didn't," according to his long-time friend Lewis Keller.

His friend Bill Campbell, the amateur star and Princeton-educated

West Virginian Sam eventually adopted as his golfing protégé, once elaborated on this theme:

"As a result of the way he was taken advantage of early in golf, unlike Byron or even Ben, I don't think there was ever anyone in Sam's life he could model himself after and really admire—or learn to trust. Every young man needs a role model who shows him how to act and get along, but Sam never had that influence. He felt cheated and exploited by people around him from day one. My own theory is that's why he never saw much point in refining his behavior as his success and fame came to him. He really felt that money was about the only thing anybody in America really respected, so he made up his mind to make as much of it as possible. And that's pretty much the attitude he took with him to the early tour, which was no place for the fainthearted, and the wider world beyond these hills."

5

THE UNIVERSITY OF GOLF

HOGAN, THE YOUNGEST OF THE THREE and the hungriest, jumped out first. He was just seventeen.

It was a cold and unusually dreary day in February of 1930 when Ted Longworth gave Ben and Ralph Guldahl a lift to San Antonio's Brackenridge Park, a Tillinghast-designed municipal course with thin wheat-colored fairways and bare patches of mud. Both teenagers slapped down five dollars at the registration table of the Texas Open and officially declared themselves "professional tournament golfers," the only formality required in those days to make the leap from the amateur ranks. Though he was still "Bennie" to his family members, at the desk he tersely replied, "Ben Hogan," adopting the version of his name that his pretty, dark-haired girlfriend Valerie Fox preferred. In a sense, *Bennie Hogan* and his tragic past vanished forever on the spot.

A photograph of the two young men appeared in the *San Antonio Light*, each dressed in crisp plus fours but neither particularly happy—Guldahl because he was suffering serious misgivings about giving up his amateur status, Hogan because after beating most of the better players around Fort Worth and Dallas in money matches over the previous year, he was grittily determined to measure up against professionals like Bobby Cruickshank and Wild Bill Mehlhorn, the tournament's two favorites. Hagen and Sarazen—successful enough to pick and choose their tournaments, preferring sunnier and warmer climes in winter—were no-shows. Coming just four months after the Wall Street implosion, the fledgling tour of the Professional Golfers' Association, a loose alliance of tournaments that began in Los Angeles after the new year and wound up in the Carolinas in early March, would soon be in a fight for its very survival. The popularity of golf wasn't helped by Bobby Jones's official retirement from competition, which left an unfillable void in many minds. Jones was set to begin filming a series of short instructional films in Hollywood for Paramount Pictures, raking in ten times what he earned in one year as a sedate Atlanta lawyer; he was also being compensated handsomely for lending his expertise and name to a cutting-edge set of steel-shafted clubs the A. G. Spalding Company was hoping to soon bring to the market. But the game was measurably poorer for his absence.

On the chilly gray afternoon Ben Hogan made his professional debut, playing with thin-lipped Ray Mangrum of Dallas, Brackenridge's rain-soaked fairways were so indistinct they required stakes and work ropes for players to identify them. Ben went out in a respectable 38 but came home in 40, a score of 78 that ate him up inside; not only had the unfriendly Mangrum finished with 71, even gentle stoop-shouldered Ralph Guldahl, Ben's roommate for the event at a two-dollar-a-night boardinghouse, managed a 74. The next day, Hogan improved by three strokes—good enough to make the halfway cut—but did something mystifying, yet oddly revealing.

Without a hint of an explanation, he suddenly withdrew from the tournament and hitchhiked back to Fort Worth. "I found out the first day I shouldn't even be out there," he explained years later. When pressed for particulars, he allowed that his nerves had been so jumpy he'd found himself hooking shots out of play, something he'd worked hard to cure but apparently hadn't. Though he never addressed the subject directly, this was the first of the sudden withdrawals that plagued his early playing career and helped give rise to his reputation as a brooding loner, possibly even a quitter—though in fact just the opposite was true. "Right then and there," he said, "I decided if I couldn't handle the pressure and play any better than that, why, I had no right to be out there at all." From the beginning, in other words, he was an unforgiving perfectionist.

As the economic gloom deepened across the country, withdrawals weren't uncommon. Ben's eventual best friend on tour—and cheerful alter ego—Jimmy Demaret, would openly boast of pulling out of events where he didn't figure to make enough dough to cover his basic expenses. Only the first four or five top spots meant finishing in the money, and otherwise, Demaret reasoned, "there was no sense in paying for a hotel room and a half-starved caddie. Better to see what was waiting for me at the next stop."

The sportswriters and wire service men who covered these sparsely attended early tournaments never seemed to hold this against Demaret, as they certainly did his unlikely pal Ben Hogan, most likely because Demaret made friends wherever he went and carefully courted their approval with cocktails and thoughtful quotes guaranteed to make their jobs a little easier.

Ben's surprising withdrawal from the Texas Open, however, was driven by something beyond pragmatic economics. His inability to measure up unleashed a powerful wave of self-loathing, summoning forth the demons of personal inadequacy that first surrounded him on another gloomy February day just eight years before.

A week after his aborted start at Brackenridge, determined to try again, he took a train to Demaret's hometown of Houston and played even worse—77–76—in the city's open pro-am. This time he withdrew even before the cut line was determined, took a train home to Fort Worth and vowed to Valerie Fox, then a freshman at Texas Christian College, that he wouldn't show his face at a professional event again until he worked out his miserable nerves and tendency under pressure to hit a hook.

If anyone could appreciate his depth of despair, it was this painfully shy daughter of an itinerant movie projectionist named Claude Fox. By her own account, she met Ben the summer he turned fourteen and began carrying Marvin Leonard's golf clubs around Glen Garden. They were introduced, she claimed, at the Sunday school of the Morningside Baptist Church, which might well be true, though Hogan placed their meeting at Jennings Junior High the year before she moved on to Central High. Valerie was a year older and a grade ahead, an excellent student who had ambitions to someday be society editor for the *Star-Telegram*. He, on the other hand, was a poor student with a one-track mind. "Even before I went out with him I knew Ben was going to be a golfer," Valerie told a reporter decades later. "Everyone who knew him back that far knew this much about him. Golf and movies were all he ever talked about."

Her parents, Claude and Jesse Fox, liked him from the start, for all the reasons any parent approves of a potential suitor. He was polite, and always well dressed, and unfailingly on time when he came to call on their elder daughter, who in contrast to her younger sister,

Sarah, was something of a high-strung and emotionally fragile young woman. "I think my grandmother saw immediately how good Uncle Ben was for my aunt Valerie," says Sarah's daughter, Valerie Harriman. "He was strong and good-looking, and a take-charge kind of guy—not unlike her own father. Behind closed doors, Valerie could be hell on wheels if she didn't get her own way. But something about Uncle Ben seemed to calm her down."

The Fox girls were known around Fort Worth's Southside for their striking beauty and divergent personalities. Sarah was four years Valerie's junior, a natural extrovert, cheerful and unself-conscious, a spirited gal who relished her family's unapologetic Wild West past and would eventually blossom into one of the city's most popular hostesses. Valerie, by contrast, was extremely reserved and forever anxious about appearances, deeply insecure about her own prospects.

"For this reason my mother always said Uncle Ben and Aunt Valerie were perfect for each other, clearly destined to be together because they provided something vital the other needed," says Harriman. "She needed his strength of character and he needed someone to wholeheartedly believe in him through thick and thin. He provided her with a life she could never have found on her own, and she rewarded him with unwavering devotion and loyalty."

One trait they shared, she adds, was an almost pathological need to control everything around them, including the people closest to them. "Aunt Valerie's closest friend was my mother. My mother, on the other hand, possessed a real cowgirl spirit that I suspect embarrassed Aunt Val at times but made her very popular with lots of different kinds of people. She loved people and the social swirl of Dallas and Fort Worth, and could move through any circle. Uncle Ben loved that about her. They became great friends. She even became a good golfer. But his loyalty to Aunt Valerie was something entirely different. Both my grandmother and mother always said they fell in love the instant they met because each had a large void only the other could fill."

Though Ben publicly declined to comment in any depth on the long years that followed his first bitter forays in San Antonio and Houston that year, he later confided to friends that this only deepened his resolve. The expression commonly used by his mother and older brother, Royal—"Nothing divided by nothing is nothing"—reverberated in his head, driving him forward like a man who was afraid to look back and see who, or what, might be gaining on him.

Living in the small back bedroom of his mother's tiny frame house on East Allen Street, Ben at least had the satisfaction of his first head professional job at Oakhurst, a modest nine-hole public course—partially owned by Ted Longworth—between downtown and the banks of the Trinity River. "Not much of a job, with no real pay," Hogan recalled years later, noting that drought eventually took care of whatever was left of tiny Oakhurst by the time the Depression finished with it. There were few regular customers, but plenty of free afternoons to beat balls. "Practically all my revenue came from selling golf balls to one rich group of four businessmen, and by winning bets from them." By his account, these wealthy hackers made him perform like a trained seal at times—forcing him to play with only three clubs, or only while standing on one foot, demeaning and intolerable circumstances for a player with serious aspirations, though he was happy to clean out their pockets. His greatest excitement occurred, he explained, when two bank robbers holding "hog-legs" (long-barreled .45 pistols) held up the startled foursome as they teed off one Saturday morning, prompting Ben to sprint to his secondhand Hudson roadster (purchased with the $1,600 he'd recently won off the group) where he kept a .30-caliber rifle beneath the front seat for security purposes. He was prepared to give chase until his pigeons prevailed on him to let the police handle the matter.

To supplement his meager income from the course, Ben took a succession of nowhere jobs he refused to speak of to anyone save Marvin Leonard and a few Shady Oaks cronies decades later. For a while he mopped floors at a popular downtown restaurant and bell-hopped bags at the Blackstone Hotel, where he sometimes dealt poker at night. His facility with cards and natural affinity for numbers, an inherited family trait, eventually led to a brief stint as a stickman out at the Top of the Terrace, a notorious gambling joint off the main highway between Fort Worth and Dallas, and possibly a dealer's job at the notorious Green Oaks Inn, not far from the sanatorium where his father had been treated. When Royal found him a nine-to-five gig doing maintenance work for a local bank, that didn't last long because those banker's hours cut into his afternoon money matches at Z-Boaz, Katy Lake, and Glen Garden.

"These were not Ben's proudest years," recalled his longtime friend, oil man W. A. "Tex" Moncrief Jr. "He rarely spoke of the things he did to get by, though it was clear to many of us that he did what he had to do in order to save up enough to ask Valerie to marry him and—maybe most important of all—to take another shot at the tour. That was one helluva tough time, let me tell you. Ben would always tell you that. Any of the fellas who tried to make money at golf then said the same thing."

During the summer of 1931, Ted Longworth, who'd moved up from Glen Garden the spring before to the prosperous Texarkana Country Club in Arkansas, offered to take Ben and Ralph Guldahl along with him to an open tournament in St. Louis. Both enthusiastically agreed, but only Guldahl wound up in the money; Ben with nothing. The sting was mitigated slightly when Longworth invited them to accompany him out west for the start of the winter circuit. The three could split expenses, he proposed, and maybe even their earnings, a common practice in those days.

Ben had little or nothing to lose, but also nothing to finance his part of the bargain with. He first turned to Royal, who despite the economy was steadily making headway in the office supply trade and a name for himself in the local hierarchy of amateur golfers. When asked for a twenty-five-dollar grubstake, Bubber came through. Many years later, after he'd won the club championship at the Colonial Country Club almost more times than anyone could recall, Royal liked to entertain visiting reporters by telling them in no uncertain terms that he was considered, at least early on, the more promising player. "Someone in the family had to have an honest paying job," he would grimly assert, rattling the ice in his empty whiskey glass, and gazing over Colonial's immaculate, sun-splashed eighteenth green. "I'm just glad I could help him out when I did." For his part, though this brief trip west produced only empty pockets, Ben never failed to mention his brother's initial financial investment, nor the fact that Royal refused to take any money when he could finally afford to pay him back.

Ben also turned to Marvin Leonard for a starter loan. Despite the devastating effect the Depression was beginning to have on cattle prices and therefore on most of Fort Worth's banking and business communities, Leonard's department store was doing exceedingly well down on North Houston Street, now sprawling over an entire city block. Moreover, Leonard's interest in golf had become an almost all-consuming passion. During the summer of 1932, he served on the board of directors at Glen Garden and aggressively promoted the idea of installing bent grass putting greens, which struck some members as lunacy given Fort Worth's long and impossibly hot summers.

Not to be deterred, the genial businessman pointed out that better courses in the East all featured bent grass greens and offered to foot the cost of the experiment himself. The board agreed and the work began. By that autumn Glen Garden had the lushest greens in the state of Texas.

Eager to see a significant championship of some sort come to Fort Worth, Leonard proposed a similar renovation across town at the Rivercrest Country Club, where he was also a member in good standing. The board at Cowtown's leading private club, unconvinced that bent grass had a future here, or deterred by the expense in such perilous times, wasn't nearly as enthusiastic about turning their Bermuda greens over to him. "Marvin, if you like bent greens so damn much," the president reportedly told him, "why the hell don't you go build your own goddamn golf course!"

"Good idea," Leonard replied, and turned to the best courses in the West to gather both design ideas and insights for a true bent grass championship course in the Southwest. A short time later, displaying his willingness to think as big in golf as in his day job, he bought 157 acres of land along the winding Clear Creek branch of the Trinity, not far from the Forest Park subdivision where he and wife, Mary, resided. In 1934, he hired John Bredamus and Perry Maxwell of Oklahoma and asked each to submit five different plans for the course. Leonard liked options and wanted the very best results. Bredamus was known for his outstanding layouts in Houston and Galveston; Maxwell would soon design the spectacular Southern Hills layout up in Tulsa. Construction work on the Colonial Country Club—the name Leonard finally settled on—began the very next spring.

Three years earlier, he'd come through for Ben Hogan with a loan of fifty dollars that sent him west for the very first time, sharing a ride out to Pasadena with Jack Grout and a pro named Ralph Hutchinson. "I left here with seventy-five dollars in my pocket," Ben told Ken Venturi in a famous—and rare—TV interview in 1983. "Would you try that today?" After only three weeks he was out of money, supplementing his meager diet with oranges he picked off trees just off Sunset Boulevard in Los Angeles, and forced to wire home for more money. Leonard sent him another hundred dollars. A dip down to Mexico to play in the Agua Caliente Open, however, netted Ben $200 and a slight ray of hope. But the next two weeks, he came up empty again, and was almost broke. He limped back to the Texas Open, shot 75-80 and withdrew for a third time. Somehow he made it to New Orleans for the next event, where he also divided nothing by nothing.

"After New Orleans I wasn't in the money and I was broke," he explained to Venturi, his voice still quivering discernibly fifty years after the fact. "I had to come home."

The professional golf tour Ben was so eager to grab on to was nothing like it is today—or, for that matter, the Golden Age of just a few years before. The "tour" then, for one thing, operated only in the first five months of the year, limiting both public exposure and the players' prospective income. The winter events took players from the West Coast to Texas and Florida, and in the spring they moved toward the Carolinas. Then, for most of them, it was time to return to their club jobs.

Moreover, a perfect storm of circumstances combined to stall the game's growth in 1932 and even set it back, starting with how Wall Street's collapse rippled destructively through every segment of American life. During the first five years of the Great Depression, when a fourth of the workforce lost their jobs and national income dropped by nearly 65 percent, more than half the nation's golf courses either suspended play or shut down completely, while others reconstituted themselves from private to public. At one famous club on Long Island, a number of its wealthy members never bothered to return after the events of Black Tuesday, leaving their lockers full, their personal items uncollected.

Though he wasn't a professional, Bobby Jones was such a huge star that his retirement seemed historic, an unfillable void in the public imagination. But even as gate receipts declined and tournament directors scrambled to find any sort of sponsor, a dusty caravan of wily old pros and hungry-eyed newcomers continued to chase the game across the withered landscape like there was no tomorrow. The luckier ones augmented their winter quests with club pro positions and understanding members who didn't mind if they took a few weeks off before and after the holidays to make some money out west before opening up the club in the spring. Scattered among them were talented young amateurs who could no longer afford to play the game for the sheer competitive thrill, plus a number of far less savory sporting types—con men, trick shot artists, hustlers like the legendary "Titanic" Thompson, whose only principle was money, betting on virtually anything and raking in far more of it than any club or touring pro could dream of.

Fortunately, Walter Hagen still showed up from time to time to delight the noticeably smaller galleries with his brilliant shotmaking and sparkling repartee, though anyone who cared to look close enough could see his incomparable game had slipped a notch or two since he won the Open campaign at Deal in 1929; the hunger to win simply wasn't there anymore, nor perhaps the vaunted scrambling skills. Likewise, after displaying the promise of a human supernova, Gene Sarazen went off to hobnob with Hollywood types, purchased a dairy farm in Germantown, New York, and settled into the cozy life of a country squire as the Roaring Twenties slipped away like an echo from an empty dance hall.

Seemingly unaffected by the spreading financial panic, the 1930 Agua Caliente Open on the Mexican border in Tijuana offered a defiantly eye-popping purse of $25,000, the largest amount any tournament had ever offered, and enough to lure "Squire" Sarazen out of his comfortable rural life. He won the big payday and then launched a comeback in 1932 that culminated in victories at both the U.S. Open at Fresh Meadow and the British at Prince's, where he transported a secret weapon of his own invention—the sand wedge—beneath a topcoat in order to prevent the "gents from the R&A" from banning its use. But in the bleakest days of the Depression—roughly from 1931 to 1935, coinciding with Hogan's own darkest years—tournaments were fighting for survival, many simply folding while others halved their purses in order to develop creative ways of entertaining and boosting the morale of patrons who were constantly assured by their politicians that national recovery was "just around the corner." These included free medical check-ups or lunch with paid daily admission, raffles of used cars and idle farm equipment and livestock to raise money for local relief programs, even pie-eating contests and dance marathons. The Los Angeles Open lowered its $10,000 purse to $7,500 and then $5,000, which was typical of most events. Not surprisingly, the Agua Caliente Open was an early victim of hardening times, not long after Hogan won his first decent money as a pro there in 1932, and would probably have gone under had it not been for the hustle and creativity of Bob Harlow, an Exeter-educated son of a Massachusetts clergyman, who became the tour's first manager in 1931.

A veteran newsman, Harlow made his name as Walter Hagen's agent and personal manager, orchestrating exhibitions and public appearances that made the Haig one of the best-loved athletes of his time and reportedly a millionaire several times over despite his famously cheeky assertion "I never wished to be a millionaire. I only wanted to live like one." In desperation, an increasingly worried PGA Tournament Bureau hired Harlow to bolster shrinking galleries and stem defections from the winter circuit. By using his organizational skills and imposing regulations that reformed the lax manner in which some tournaments operated, he quickly gave the tour professional respectability and established the groundwork for a more autonomous organization.

To the chagrin of a few wildcatting pros who were out there for the easy money or to keep a step ahead of the law, he established rules governing personal behavior. In 1932, he began keeping records in an official tour book that exists to this day, detailing specific problems and solutions tailored to every event, including sponsors' opinions and covering everything from course conditions to crowd reactions.

Moreover, he arranged for short promotional films of upcoming tournaments to be shown at movie houses, and for banners to be lofted across main streets announcing the big-name golf stars who were about to arrive in town. "Bob saw pro golf primarily as a form of great public entertainment, and like all the great entertainers," said Paul Runyan, who joined the tour in 1931, becoming a Harlow client in the process, "he believed golfers had an obligation to put on a good show. I must have heard him say that a million times—'You boys are here to put on a good show for people.' But he wanted it done the right way, respecting the rules of the game, with class and sophistication."

Understanding the power of publicity and the challenge of looming deadlines, Harlow granted special pre-tournament interviews and radio visits with leading players, and adroitly recruited aging stars like Hagen and Sarazen to lure prospective sponsors to fund-raising affairs, flattery that prompted them to open their checkbooks. Among other things, he convinced the Golf Ball and Golf Club Manufacturers Association—later evolving into the National Golf Foundation—to help underwrite financially shaky tournaments in the Southwest and even reached into his own pocket to help guarantee their survival.

Among his many innovations, he introduced a voluntary marshal system, which encouraged stronger local participation in tournaments, enlisting scout troops to sell baked goods and admission tickets, or car dealerships to provide transportation for the players. In time, civic fathers lauded his tireless efforts to give their communities a much needed boost of pride, a good show, and a chance to showcase their town's can-do spirit in a time of great difficulty.

As a result of these and other deft orchestrations, though the number of events declined during his first two years at the helm, the tour's cumulative purses actually increased from $77,000 to $130,000, underscoring Harlow's belief that the eventual addition of a summer tour would make professional golf even more viable, a year-round proposition for stars like Hagen, Sarazen, and a handful of others who weren't locked into seasonal club jobs that required their presence from May to September. In 1932, the Tournament Bureau (composed of several disgruntled veteran players) declined to renew Harlow's contract, citing conflicts of interest that his list of famous clients presented. Harlow then became a principal architect of a new breakaway organization simply called the Professional Players Group, creating a template for the PGA Tour more than three decades before its official formation in 1968. This ambitious vision suggested that given proper promotion and player development, every tournament in the future could be comfortably sustained by a core of local sponsors of ten to twelve of the top players committed to play the entire circuit, creating both momentum and an ever-growing calvacade of stars who would, at least in theory, grow from season to season.

Not surprisingly, when it became clear that Harlow's idea appealed to most of the biggest names, he was rehired by the PGA Tournament Bureau and the incipient rebellion was quelled—or, more accurately, put off for another day. In the meantime, he'd won his point about the feasibility of a year-round tour, and by the end of 1935 had developed a roster of fourteen events that spanned the summer months and added nearly $60,000 in additional prize money, encouraging a new generation like Ben Hogan, Byron Nelson, and Sammy Snead to chase the game, even though they had to finish in the top five or six slots to make more than their basic expenses any given week.

For all Harlow's success in keeping the dream alive and improving pro golf's public profile, the vast majority of players still led a hand-to-mouth existence on the road. "It was one swayback town to the next," as Paul Runyan summed it up, "with everyone looking to catch a little lightning in a bottle."

He was, in fact, luckier than most. Members at his home club, the Metropolis Country Club in White Plains, New York, each put up $50 to stake Runyan and his wife to the winter circuit of 1931–32. In return, he would split any winnings evenly with his backers. With a wizardry that earned him the nickname "Little Poison" among his colleagues and eventually made him the most admired short-game teacher of his generation, he sent home $4,400 that first year on the circuit, and his admiring and appreciative members forswore their share of his earnings.

"It really was a vagabond's life in those days," he reflected one afternoon in the early 1990s. "I mean, most of the tournament sites were either in small towns or in the suburbs of major cities—so taking a train was pretty much out of the question, not to mention expensive. Everyone traveled by cars, which frequently broke down and were subject to weather and poor road conditions—and getting lost. Guys doubled up and shared hotels and some split their winnings until they banned the practice. It was all about surviving for another week. If a guy finished in the spinach one week, he might stay someplace pretty nice. If he didn't, it was whatever flea-infested rooming house he could find. There were fellas who actually rolled into town and went straight to the best hotel bar in town hoping to meet a divorcee who could provide a nice accommodation for the week.

"I remember Sarazen actually caused a dustup by railing against wives out on tour—claimed the life out on tour was no place for a married gal and too damn expensive. Gene claimed having your wife along only put unnecessary pressure on a fellow to win. That was easy for him to say—he was rich compared to the rest of us. Having my wife along never bothered me one bit. In fact, I welcomed having her with me. It was a lonely road and there weren't many Walter Hagens out there—but that didn't stop us all from trying to be the next Walter or Gene."

"Life on the early tour was nothing short of a paid education in survival of the fittest," the witty and urbane Harlow told a reporter about the time he founded *Golf World* magazine in 1947. "If you found a way to make it one week, well, you graduated to another week. And so it went. For a lot of those fellows, many of whom eventually became the tour's biggest stars, pro golf was like university education, a higher institution of hard knocks."

In the autumn of 1932, not long after he won the Rivercrest Invitational, Byron lost a part-time job he'd held at a Fort Worth bankers magazine and was trying to decide what his next move should be when a letter came from Ted Longworth informing him that the members of the Texarkana Country Club had put together an open tournament and were inviting players from four surrounding states, with a purse of $500. The assumption was that Byron would play as an amateur.

A week or so later, he boarded the Greyhound with his clubs, a small suitcase, and a couple of ham sandwiches his mother had made for him. "It was during that bus ride that I got to thinking about the prize money and realized there was no point in not playing for it," he explained. "By that time I'd played against many of the best players in the Southwest and I decided my chances of making some of that money were probably pretty good."

At the tournament's official registration table Byron asked what was required to play for money. "Just declare that you're a pro and put down five dollars," he was told, as Ben Hogan had been a year and half earlier in San Antonio. So he slapped down his money, finished third and collected seventy-five dollars. "That was more money in my hand than I'd ever seen before." Encouraged by his performance, he got back on the bus and went home and informed his parents that he planned to take a shot at the winter tour in California, specifically at four events played in suburban Los Angeles.

With the backing of friends who put up $500 to get him out west, and the reluctant blessing and prayers of his parents, Byron played decently but failed to make any money and was forced to wire his friends back in Fort Worth asking for more cash. They cabled back that they had none to send, so Byron was forced to scramble for a way home. Fortunately he learned about a Fort Worth businessman named Charlie Jones who was driving home from L.A. "I don't remember a whole lot about that ride except that I felt bad about running through that money and coming up empty-handed," he reminisced years later. "We talked about how different the golf courses were out in California. I also remember that Charlie Jones talked to me about the importance of making a business plan to make my goals clear. That stuck with me."

Better yet, a short time later, Ted Longworth sent another letter saying he was leaving Texarkana for a job at the Waverly Country Club in Portland, Oregon, and to urge him to apply for his old job. "You won't make much money—no salary, only what you make from the shop and giving lessons—but you will eat regular and it will give you more time to practice," his mentor wrote. In the first week of April, Byron acquired the position, which would pay roughly sixty dollars a month. "My parents were happy about it in one respect, because they knew by now I had golf in my soul," he wrote decades later. "They were sad to see me leave town, though, and told me to be a good pro, to take care of myself, to be good and to go to church."

As usual, he took his mama's advice to heart. After securing a room at a local couple's house for seven dollars a week, Byron found the Walnut Street Church of Christ, whose congregation included a large and active youth group. There he met a member who managed the local Ford dealership who gave him a good price on a new royal blue roadster. One Sunday at Bible Study class, he also met pretty Louise Shofner, whose father owned a grocery store. She'd been living in Houston with her aunt, learning to become a hairdresser. At a church picnic, Byron ate a piece of her angel food cake and got to know her. The next day, he invited her out to the movies; because she had a boyfriend, she politely demurred. He repeated the invitation the next day, receiving the same response. The next Sunday, he purposely planted himself beside her at Bible Study and made his pitch a third time; this time she agreed to let him take her to the movies, after he drove her home. They saw a Hollywood musical and went to the drugstore for an ice cream sundae. She had to be home no later than ten-thirty.

"I was twenty then, and she was seventeen," Byron recounts. "That was the first real date I ever had in my life, and once I met Louise, I never even thought about dating anyone else."

The best thing about the Texarkana Country Club was its golf course, a tightly wrought gem with heavily contoured greens and deep bunkers that rewarded a good shot and punished a poor one. Accuracy, in other words, was paramount. There was also a superb practice range where Byron spent every free moment he wasn't working or courting Louise. After about a year, a caddie named Miller Barber began shagging his balls and helping him find a groove with the steel-shafted Kroydon clubs he was playing by then. The caddie grew up to win eleven times on the PGA tour, including the 1968 Byron Nelson Classic.

Byron's search for the perfect swing was soon assisted by his growing friendship with Harvey Penick, gentle, cerebral assistant pro at the Austin Country Club, who'd thought a lot about how the newly introduced steel shafts might change the game. Unlike their hickory predecessors, steel shafts produced far less torque or twist, which meant the players didn't have to compensate for a bending shaft and thus it was easier to square up at impact. The two men—both future Hall of Famers, one as a champion, the other as a teacher—had numerous conversations during these years and it was probably Penick who convinced Byron that the new technology required a new swing altogether.

Byron was bound and determined to try to find it. When a supportive club member, J. K. Wadley, offered to finance Byron's return to the 1934 winter tour for half his earnings, he began working even harder on his game. "Hard as I practiced, I couldn't seem to put four good rounds together. But I knew if I wanted to make a living out on tour—which was really where you learned the most about the game in those days—I would have to get better." Without telling him, Louise had already spoken to her father about fronting him enough money to enter the Los Angeles tournament, where he once again failed to put together four good rounds and had to borrow money to go on to Phoenix, making only pocket change before arriving at Brackenridge Park in San Antonio for the Texas Open, the tour's oldest stop. By then he was $660 in the hole and had barely enough left to finish in San Antonio and compete the next week at Galveston. "After that, I decided I would just go home and go to work to pay off all I owed Louise's daddy."

Playing off rubber tee mats, Byron shot 66 to earn the first lead he'd ever held in a professional tournament, and played well enough in the closing rounds to place second, pocketing $440. At Galveston, another runner-up result gave him an additional $300, and he raced home in his roadster to pay back his future father-in-law. With the leftover $100, he bought Louise a half-carat diamond ring. Just over a year later, during which Byron gave lessons and played in a number of invitational events around the Southwest, the couple got married in her parents' living room.

After Christmas, with money they'd scrimped and saved, the newlyweds headed for California in the unheated roadster, Jack Grout hitching a ride with them and buying his share of the gas. They often drove all night. "Louise's feet and legs would get cold," Byron remembered. "Women didn't wear slacks hardly at all then, and always dressed nice, especially when traveling. But cars had no heaters in that day and time, so we heated bricks in the oven before we left home in Texarkana and wrapped them in paper. Then she put her feet on them and wrapped a lap robe around her."

He placed second at the Riverside Pro-Am, netting them $137. The next week at the San Francisco Matchplay Championship, he beat Lawson Little in the first round—"Honeymooner Beats Little" trumpeted a local headline, Byron's first serious notice by the press outside his home state—and lantern-jawed Vic Ghezzi in the second before losing in the quarterfinals to Harold "Jug" McSpaden, an amiable pro known to play miserably one day and brilliantly the next. The $150 Byron collected was enough to get them to Tijuana for the greatly reduced Agua Caliente event, where he tied for sixth place, made $257 and began a friendship with the winner, Henry Picard, a polite, clean-cut New Englander who was entering his fifth season as head professional at the Charleston Country Club. Like Byron, he'd grown up with parents who emphasized optimism and personal integrity. "You'll always be rated by the people you choose to be friends with," Henry Picard's father told him early in life, and that became the creed Henry lived by.

Five years his senior but likewise the product of a caddie yard, Picard also shared with Byron a fierce admiration of Bobby Jones's swing and an interest in teaching the game to others. During the summer of 1934, at the prestigious North and South Open at Pinehurst, the veteran Al Watrous advised Picard that his swing was perhaps a little too upright, and the younger man listened because Watrous was a respected teacher, two-time Ryder Cupper and head pro at the prestigious Oakland Hills Country Club in Bloomfield, Michigan; moreover, he'd taken Jones to the final hole at the 1926 Open Championship before surrendering the Claret Jug. After working with Watrous, Picard won the Pinehurst event, a tournament players loved competing in because this beautiful resort village in the longleaf pines—even in the depths of the Great Depression—was a place dedicated exclusively to the game of golf. The Tufts, who owned the resort, treated visiting players and their spouses like royalty, putting them up in the beautiful Carolina Hotel and providing their meals for free. Pinehurst also boasted the finest practice range in the country, nicknamed "Heartbreak Hill," which is where Watrous helped Picard with his swing.

In September, Picard played in his first Hershey Open in Pennsylvania and made a deep impression on its sponsors by shooting 67; chocolate magnate Milton Hershey promptly offered him a job at $5,000 per year, plus half of whatever he made giving lessons, with ample time off to play the winter tour. Picard enthusiastically signed on, picking up an extra $3,500 and free clubs—the same ones his hero Bobby Jones played—in an endorsement deal with Spalding.

Though no one could have imagined this at the time, these seemingly modest changes in the professional circumstances of a largely unknown club pro and an unknown pro would have a major impact on the modern game of golf.

Because of his solid if not scintillating play in the winter of 1935, Byron Nelson received a surprise invitation to Bobby Jones's new event in Augusta, Georgia.

The year before, at the inaugural Augusta National Invitation Tournament, a Pinkerton survey of cars parked on the grounds indicated their patrons came from thirty-eight states and Canada, all because they wanted to see Bobby Jones play golf again. They filled the city's two main hotels, the sprawling and elegant Bon Air Vanderbilt and the far more modest Richmond, plus every boardinghouse in town, and some slept in their cars. To no one's surprise, the press turnout was the largest anyone had seen since the host's triumphant Grand Slam; according to Western Union, reporters filed eighteen thousand more words than had been devoted the preceding summer to the U.S. Open. Contrary to Jones's express wishes, most of them referred to it as "The Masters Invitational."

Paired with Paul Runyan, 1933's leading money winner, Jones found his hands trembling before the opening round and shot an untidy 76. Though he steadied himself well enough to finish thirteenth in a field as strong as any national championship's held that year—notably missing only Gene Sarazen, who was fulfilling a commitment in South Africa that week—Jones later confided to his longtime friend and collaborator O. B. Keeler that he knew his competitive days were over. He was just thirty-two years old. The winner, Horton Smith, was a tall, boyishly handsome, exceedingly polite young man who went on to marry the daughter of one of Augusta National's founding members and play in the event until he was sixty-three.

If the first Masters had made an indelible impression on sports fans, garnering more coverage than any tournament that year, the second made an indelible mark on history. At the par-five fifteenth in the fourth round, needing three birdies in the final four holes to catch Craig Wood, who was already in the clubhouse with 282, Gene Sarazen boldly elected to go for the green in two, prompting the forty-one-year-old

Walter Hagen to shake his graying head with amusement. No more than a dozen spectators surrounded the water-skirted green, one of them Bobby Jones, who'd wandered out to watch this pairing—two thirds of the old triumvirate he had once commanded—come home. With his familiar lash that resembled a lurch, Sarazen struck a perfect four-wood that carried the water, skipped onto the green, and rolled softly into the cup for a double-eagle two. Sarazen finished in a tie with Wood and beat him by five strokes in the next day's playoff. Grantland Rice, among others, hailed Sarazen's miraculous "shot heard round the world" as something that gave the Depression-weary country a much needed lift—and certainly helped the struggling tournament, whose future was far from assured, stay afloat. But like the man who started it, Rice said, the Masters possessed a special magic.

Though Byron Nelson, owing to nerves and an erratic driver, finished ninth, his first Masters nevertheless proved life-changing. Impressed by how elegantly the young Texan played and comported himself, George Jacobus, the president of the PGA and head professional at the Ridgewood Country Club in New Jersey, pulled him aside and offered to hire him as his assistant, which Byron agreed to on the spot. "The job came with a little more money," he remembered, "but its real value to me was that it took Louise and me to a respected club in the East, where most of the tournament golf was played in those days. Also, because George was busy organizing events it gave me a unique insight to see how the tour was developing. Things were suddenly coming together for us." Battling a nervous stomach all week that caused him to skip a few meals, Byron still made sure to thank the host and crusty tournament chairman, Clifford Roberts, for inviting him to play. He also became friendly with Augusta's new head professional, Ed Dudley, learning that Henry Picard had been his silent benefactor in securing the summons to Augusta. "I wasn't a bit surprised to learn about that," Byron said many years later. "Henry was always quietly helping other fellows out that way. He was as generous a man as I ever knew in golf and I made sure I thanked him, too."

Before departing, very much in awe of these magnificent surroundings, Byron also confided to Dudley that he hoped to win the Masters "sometime in the next three years."

"I'm sure you will," the pro responded with a laugh.

What might seem dangerously close to a boast was, in fact, a pure and simple reflection of Byron's high regard for his host and the tournament he would come to admire above all others.

Later that summer he played in his first U.S. Open, at Oakmont, where the Nelsons rented an inexpensive room in a local parsonage. The night before the first round, over supper, Byron told Louise he planned to buy a new driver. A little later, while doing her needlepoint, she told him, "Byron, we've been married over a year. I haven't bought a dress or a new pair of shoes or anything for myself in all that time, but you've bought four new drivers, and you're not happy with any of them. It's one of two things. Either you don't know what kind of driver you want, or you don't know how to drive."

The truth stung. But the next morning he took his Spalding driver to the Oakmont pro shop and shaved some wood off the toe and heel to round off the face of the club, leaving a slight bulge, a design idea he'd been toying with since his discussions with Penick and Henry Picard; prior to this, driver faces were generally flat. His performance, alas, wasn't memorable—a disappointing thirty-second and miles out of the money, due to poor chipping and putting on Oakmont's fierce greens. One positive aspect, though, was the noticeably straighter drives, partly thanks to the bulge, a revolutionary concept Byron would pop- ularize and soon incorporate into MacGregor drivers, an innovation every club manufacturer quickly adopted.

Perhaps even more important, Louise's commonsense observations also led to an epiphany in his thinking. As he prepared for the winter tour in 1936, Byron was ready to invest precious money on a new set of clubs when Louise again intervened. "Byron, honey, why don't you quit kidding yourself? It just can't entirely be the clubs. Your trouble is *you*!"

"Louise had hit it right on the nose," he wrote years later in *Golfing Magazine.* "I had been afraid to admit this very truth to myself. But I couldn't argue against her. My immature and false sense of pride had prevented me from putting the finger on myself. I resolved to let the club makers worry about my clubs and to concern myself with my own use of the implements."

Right then and there, he decided he had to either abandon the tour or commence a comprehensive investigation of both himself and the game. He chose the latter, systematically analyzing the swings of the leading players, including "Lighthouse" Harry Cooper, Horton Smith, Ky Laffoon, Denny Shute, Paul Runyan, Gene Sarazen, Craig Wood, Walter Hagen, and his friend Henry Picard. "I studied all of them, try- ing to figure out what each swing had in common with the other. The time I wasted in trying to reshape clubs and in confused practice, I now put to purposeful experimentation." And whenever he grew frustrated by what would turn out to be a five-year quest to perfect his own swing, Louise assured him it was only a matter of time before it all came together.

The game of golf would never be the same.

Finally, the third card was turned over.

Late in the summer of 1936, flush with $75 from winning the West Virginia Open in a playoff, Sam Snead took the train to New York and briefly got lost in the crowds but managed his connection to Pennsylvania for the $5,000 Hershey Open. "Except for that crazy trip down to Miami the year before with Gleim in his rattling old Ford, where he refused to let me borrow his driver, I'd never been anywhere to speak of," he later recalled, carefully avoiding any mention of his mysterious outing on Long Island. "I looked at Hershey as a chance to see the big guns I'd been reading about in the fish wrappers, to see if I stood any chance up against 'em."

For years he told of walking up to the first tee, where four well-dressed players were starting a practice round, and asking if this was the course where the Hershey Open was being played. A short, soft-spoken man with kind eyes looked him over, smiling at the sight of the eight golf clubs in his scuffed-up canvas bag. "It is, kid," George Fazio told him. "Go change your shoes and you can play a round with us."

Following a miserable start—hitting two drives out of bounds and topping a third into the water in front of the tee—Sam settled down and, not counting the three mulligans granted on the first hole, finished with an eye-opening 67. When word spread about a "long-hitting hillbilly on the premises," the club's new head professional came out to have a look for himself. Henry Picard instantly saw something in Sam Snead he liked—a natural swing that was as graceful as wind in the fescue.

Coming off a terrific winter season—the leading money winner, he had five victories including big wins at Atlanta and the respected Metropolitan Open—Picard was proof that a club pro could satisfy his members and still have a glorious tournament career. And as a disciple of Alex Morrison, whose *A New Way to Better Golf* (1932) accommodated the advancing steel shaft technology by advocating principles radically different from those of Harry Vardon and the renowned English swing teacher Ernest Jones, "Pick" was also obsessed with the quest for the "modern golf swing."

Among other things, Morrison—the first teacher to use both still and motion photography to analyze his pupils' swings—proposed that the less flexible but more reliable steel shafts needed to be powered by the large muscles on the left side, specifically the left leg, hip, shoulder, and arm, with the left wrist "squaring up" at impact and accelerating through the shot's finish. He also advocated a natural "rolling of the feet" that encouraged a full release and delivered maximum power at impact. Finally, he stressed the importance of maintaining posture and balance to keep the swing that remained on plane and more upright than what was needed with the conventional hickory-shafted clubs. The story goes that Morrison once kept his weary protégé Henry Picard on the practice range for forty-three hours, hitting only seven-iron shots to begin to master these new moves.

Picard practiced so hard the summer of 1935 that his hands actually blistered and bled, though he soon saw his work deliver victories. And on this occasion, he encountered a swing that already incorporated many of these same ideas. "The first time I saw Sam Snead hit a ball from the fairway at Hershey," he recalled in the early 1990s, "I was taken aback. I thought that was perhaps the finest golf swing I'd ever seen, maybe even better than Jones's. It was so natural and fluid. The only flaw I saw was his footwork. Sam stayed back on his right foot a little more than he should have. And once I mentioned this to him, well, there was no stopping him. Sam became a true believer in the rolling action of the feet. He didn't quite realize it at the time, but he had it all."

Picard won his own tournament that September, and he gave Sam Snead some crucial nonswing advice. "In the tourney," he told him, "you'll be paired with Craig Wood. Wood represents Dunlop Tire and Rubber Company, one of the big ball-makers. I think he's considering you for Dunlop."

Sam shook his head, confused. "Considering me for what?"

"I mean, son, he may want to sign you up as a Dunlop representative. They'll pay you to play their clubs and balls."

"My God," Sam gasped, having only heard locker room talk of gravy trains like this.

"Now don't let Wood know I told you this," Pick went on, adding that Wood was also an influential member of the Ryder Cup team. "Just do all you can to impress him."

In the tournament, Sam routinely outdrove him, and Wood was as long as anybody out there. At one point, embarrassed to find his ball fifty yards behind the lanky Virginian, he demanded to know who his teacher was.

"I never had a lesson in my life," Snead told him flatly and truthfully.

"What's the best you've ever shot in a round?" Wood demanded.

"At the Greenbrier on the No. 1 course I had a 61 not long ago. But I three-putted the eighteenth hole."

Following Snead's fifth-place finish, Wood offered his "discovery" a deal worth $500 a year and two dozen balls a month, plus a new set of Dunlop clubs—simply to represent the company on tour.

"I was reaching for a pen before he stopped talking," Sam remembered. "My life savings at that time, if I hocked a few things, amounted to $300. With $800 I could risk going on the PGA circuit."

When Gene Sarazen first glimpsed Snead in the third round of this same Hershey Open, striking one three-hundred-yard drive after another and splitting his shirt at the seams in the process, the veteran walked back to the clubhouse and ordered a cocktail.

"I've just finished watching a kid who doesn't know the first thing about playing golf," he told another veteran. "But let me tell you something. I don't want to be around when he learns how."

6

SAM VERSUS THE WORLD

DURING THE 1936 PGA CHAMPIONSHIP, being played at Pinehurst No. 2, PGA president George Jacobus and executive board member Ed Dudley summoned Fred Corcoran from the scoreboard he was running to a private room for a meeting that had been arranged by Richard Tufts, who now ran the resort he'd inherited from his father, Leonard.

"Fred," Jacobus said, "I'll get right to the point. Would you be interested in taking over the job of tournament manager for the PGA?"

Bob Harlow, the thirty-one-year-old Corcoran learned, had once more been relieved of his duties, owing to conflict-of-interest complaints that had dogged him since day one on the job. Likewise, Horton Smith was being dumped as the players' representative on the committee in favor of Augusta head pro Ed Dudley.

The son of a Harvard Square tour guide and sports promoter who was credited with creating the first spectator program for a college football game, Fred Corcoran possessed his father's enterprising hustle as well as his upbeat Irish charm. While staging and handicapping golf events around the Boston area as secretary of the Massachusetts Golf Association, he'd innovated such practices as using different colored numbers on the scoreboard to indicate a player's status on the course, a practice soon adopted by tournaments everywhere.

Corcoran leapt at the opportunity to manage the tour and signed a one-year contract with the PGA on the spot, though he had no idea he was facing the resumption of the fierce behind-the-scenes war for control of the tournament circuit that had been simmering for years.

Upon arriving in Los Angeles, the winter tour's first stop in 1937, he was collared by the displaced Horton Smith and others who were steamed that the popular Harlow had been shown the door. "He went after me like a prosecuting attorney," Corcoran noted in his breezy memoir, *Unplayable Lies*, "digging at me with questions about my background and qualifications for the job that made me feel like I ought to go back to the gate and buy a ticket."

Even as he settled into his job, a petition was being circulated calling for his ouster—reflecting an abiding affection for Harlow and a growing contempt among lesser-known players for the PGA itself, considering it a cabal of club pros who wished to simply tighten control over those who competed on tour week to week. Meanwhile, in the absence of exciting new talent that might rekindle the public's interest, the game's longtime headliners Hagen and Sarazen now only made appearances at major tournaments, and relied on lucrative private exhibitions to finance their baronial lifestyles.

Not surprisingly, it was the cool, levelheaded Henry Picard who gave Corcoran the reassurance he needed to survive his turbulent first week on the job, as the conflict threatened to explode onto the pages of the nation's newspapers: "Fred, I don't care what they say. You just do a good job and you'll be okay with me. And that goes for the rest of the boys on this tour."

The next week in Oakland, Horton Smith orchestrated a meeting between disgruntled players and the press, hoping to force a Corcoran resignation. This gambit backfired when reporters made clear they had no interest in possibly damaging the turnout in Oakland by publicizing the rift, and again the rebellion fell short. As Corcoran later told his friends in Boston, "I survived for another day but I needed something good to happen to save my head from the Hottentots. I knew it was only a matter of time before they came back." His salvation came from an unlikely source. "Then something happened at Oakland that signaled the dawn of a new era in American golf—and took the pressure off me by focusing interest elsewhere," he wrote in his memoir. "Sam Snead suddenly exploded onto the sports pages. The rangy and picturesque boy from the [mountains] of Virginia popped in with 270 to win the tournament. It was the greatest thing that could have happened to golf—and to me."

The fuse of this sudden explosion was actually lit a month before when Sam made his second Miami Open and finished tenth, netting a paltry $108. This was where, on the range, 1931 British Open champ Tommy Armour pointed to a young player practicing diligently and asked Gene Sarazen, "Who is that kid over there with the crazy upright swing?"

"Name's Byron Nelson," Sarazen told him. "He's out of Texas. Nice kid. He won the Metropolitan last summer and placed third at the Western."

"Well, with that swing of his, he better go on back to Texas. He'll never make it out here, that's for sure," remarked Armour, who would soon be named the new head professional at the prestigious Boca Raton Club. Within a few years of this, the Silver Scot would completely revise his opinion of Byron Nelson's golf swing, calling it "the finest golf swing I have ever seen." But that was yet to come. At that same moment, Ben Hogan was back home in Texas, settling into a new job at the Nolan River Golf Club in tiny Cleburn, wondering if his professional golf career was finished before it ever got started.

After he played poorly in the next event, in Nassau, Bahamas, Sam himself questioned whether he had the means to keep following the caravan, but a chance conversation with Henry Picard and Craig Wood bolstered his confidence. "I asked Henry if he thought I was good enough to head for California for the tournaments out there and he told me I'd have to place one, two or three to even make my expenses. I was pretty downcast about that because Dunlop hadn't come through yet with the five hundred dollars they promised and I had only my puny earnings from Miami and some of the three hundred from finishing third at the Cascades Open. Then Wood said something that gave me a real boost. He told me I ought to give it a shot and if I ran out of dough, why, he'd help me get back home on his own nickel. Henry agreed to help out, too, and suggested I find someone to split traveling expenses with. That just made a world of difference to me."

Picard's confidence was justified when Sam met Johnny Bulla, a brainy Quaker minister's son from Burlington, North Carolina, a natural left-hander who grew up caddying and honing his game by playing right-handed against some of the best young players of the Carolinas. Bulla was Sam's junior by two years, but they shared a love of bass fishing and were kindred spirits. Their friendship blossomed quickly and only deepened as the years rolled on. Sam was soon calling Bulla "Boo Boo" for his tendency to blow important shots under pressure and moan about them later. Johnny Bulla, however, a dedicated reader of psychology and science magazines, believed he was on the verge of a major breakthrough, and he planned to be in Los Angeles when the winter tour started. He'd even already lined up a traveling partner—a homesick tight end from the University of North Carolina headed back to California to play football for USC. Bulla was only too happy to have Sam join them and divide expenses into thirds.

The three agreed to split oil and gas and lodging, and Sam volunteered that he had an uncle in L.A. who promised to put them up for the week. But when he proposed that he and Boo Boo split their tournament winnings, as well, his friend balked. "Don't mean any offense, Jackson," Bulla said, using the middle name he preferred, "but I don't see how I can come out on the better end of that deal." So off they went, staying in fleabag motels and living on roadside hamburgers. Every morning before they hit the road, the footballer made the golfers run a mile just to keep their legs limber. "Boo Boo hated that, but I wasn't that far from high school football myself so it didn't bother me much. That fella made all-American, too. But we had to squeeze nickels until the buffalo groaned," Sam remembered. And though Bulla had rejected Sam's offer to split earnings—one of worst decisions he ever made, he later admitted—he now suggested they have a standing five-dollar wager on every tournament, for a little extra motivation.

On the practice tee before the start in Los Angeles, Henry Picard offered to let Sam try out a new George Izett driver he'd spotted in his bag.

Made by a respected Philadelphia club maker, it weighed 14.5 ounces and had eight degrees of loft, an extra stiff shaft and a swing weight of E-5, basically unhittable by anyone short of a gorilla or a serious athlete. "The Dunlop driver I was using was so whippy I had a helluva time controlling my tee shots," Sam explained. "But this club was something else. The harder I swung, the straighter it went. That club gave me more control than I'd ever had in my life. Pick said I should just take it along and use it. My driving improved right then and there."

He insisted on buying it and paid Henry Picard $5.50 for the club that would make him the longest driver in the game, a club he used to win all of his major titles and, by Sam's account, more than a hundred tournaments. "That act of generosity by Henry Picard," he said, "could never be repaid because that wood was the single greatest discovery I ever made in golf and put me on the road to happy times."

Another bit of good fortune awaited him in L.A. During an impromptu quarter-a-hole putting contest with fellow pro Leo Walper, Sam borrowed his upright knockoff of Bobby Jones's famous "Calamity Jane" and nailed three long putts. Walper joked that he ought to buy it, and Sam had the money out of his pocket before Leo could change his mind. They made the exchange for $3.50. "You can't believe what those two clubs did for my confidence," Sam recalled years later. "Those are the two most important clubs in the bag by far, you know, and finding them when I did, first one then the other, was like I was supposed to win."

Sam had an unshakable faith in such signs. In L.A., he picked up $600 in winnings and another five bucks off Johnny Bulla, who made nothing in the tournament. To make matters worse, driving north to the next event at the Claremont Country Club in Oakland, Bulla cracked up his car and had to dole out $140 for repairs. "The way we figured it was one of us had to finish high in the money or we were finished," said Sam, who opened the tournament with a 69 but was annoyed that the scorer had spelled his name *Sneed*. "My gallery consisted of my caddie and an old man who kept hobbling after me, coughing and snapping his false teeth when I was putting," he said. After a third-round 69 tied him for the lead, the scorer finally spelled his name correctly—though few observers expected his luck to hold up.

Unaware that he'd taken the lead by the seventieth hole, a narrow "barrel" par-four where interlocking trees formed a canopy over the fairway, Sam became momentarily unnerved by the large gallery suddenly swarming around him and slugged his approach shot into the trees, dropping a stroke. After he recovered with a birdie at the home hole, he bolted for the locker room followed by a "mob" slapping him affectionately on the back.

A photographer wanted to take his picture but Sam superstitiously refused, believing this would ruin his chances of winning. He was heading for Bulla's jalopy when Fred Corcoran caught up to him. "Where are you going, Sam?" he said, having spotted something appealing in him and taken him to breakfast earlier in the week. "You've won this thing, son. The press is waiting to speak with you inside." The club's banquet hall had been turned into an impromptu press room and Sam was asked to stand on a table and field questions fired rapidly at him from all sides.

He looked, according to Corcoran, like a deer caught in headlights.

"The room was blue with cigar and cigarette smoke and Sam didn't like that," Fred recalled. "He was grumpy and uncomfortable. He wanted out." When a kneeling photographer flashed his photograph, a startled Sam leapt from the table and rushed for the parking lot, advising everybody to keep away from him. The photograph went out over the wires hours later and wound up in newspapers across the country under headlines like "Country Kid Takes Oakland Trophy" and "Reluctant Star Runs Away from Field."

Accustomed to being either ignored or condescended to by Country Club types, Sam was overwhelmed. But Corcoran recognized a promotional windfall when he spotted one, and scrambled to gather additional details from the colorful young Virginian as he fled the premises. Two days later down in Rancho Santa Fe, where singer and actor Bing Crosby was hosting his first annual "clambake," there was a protracted rain delay, during which Corcoran showed Sam his photograph in *The New York Times*. "Mr. Corcoran," Sam reportedly declared, "how come they got my picture in New York? I ain't never been there in my life."

This wasn't exactly true, of course, though both men mention some version of the exchange in their memoirs. Just about everything that happened to Sam Snead in those days was subject to artful exaggeration—by the press or the man himself or the gifted image maker who would soon become his business partner.

From Corcoran's standpoint, the timing simply couldn't possibly have been better. As the country was just beginning to lift its head from seven years of relentless bad news, the reading public craved stories about underdogs who rose from Nowheresville to succeed against all odds. While the undersized but big-hearted Seabiscuit was heading for the ultimate showdown against the presumed invincible War Admiral, Sam Snead seemed almost too good to be true, a poor rube from the backwoods who struck it rich in California, like a character from a Frank Capra film, a real-life Mr. Smith in golf spikes. Even his name possessed a magical, all-American simplicity—easy to remember, hard to forget.

The enterprising Corcoran quickly turned Sam's purported confusion about New York—which he'd passed through once, if not twice, before—to incalculable promotional advantage, feeding it to the idle pressmen at Rancho Santa Fe with various other enticing bits and pieces of his colorful Blue Ridge bio, somewhat indifferent to the purity of facts. He had "Slammin' Sammy Snead" loving to play golf barefoot and hunting possum whenever possible, and learning to play the game while dodging moonshiners in the hidden retreats, using no more than a hickory nut and a stout swamp maple limb for a ball and club.

It didn't stop there, either. When Sam mentioned to Jimmy Demaret that he'd made a practice green by sinking empty tomato cans in his family's backyard, the affable Texan quipped that he probably was planning to keep all his winnings there, too, a joke that grew more truthful with each passing year. Corcoran nimbly wove his natural frugality and mistrust of banks into Sam's rapidly evolving bio, because it resonated with millions of ordinary Americans who shared his beliefs. And the press ate up these folksy details and just about everything that Sam said, with his distinctive, wide-eyed drawl. Corcoran's hokey moniker—*Dan'l Boone with a driver*—seemed even more relevant when Sam captured the rain-shortened Crosby and pocketed $1,000 before heading up to San Francisco for the Matchplay Championship. Years later, of course, Sam would confide to friends and his first biographer that he resented being portrayed as an ignorant hayseed, but it played splendidly at the time, giving the tour a little sparkle when it needed it most—putting him on the road to wealth and fame.

"My hillbilly background provided sports writers with plenty of grist, and Corcoran kept them well supplied," Sam told writer George Mendoza in the 1970s. "I don't think I was ever totally the rube they made me out to be, but they loved to hear about how I'd spend my time between tours back up at Ashwood with my folks."

"No Hollywood scriptwriter could have invented Sam Snead; he was the real article," Corcoran wrote in his own memoirs. "He had the flavor and tang of authenticity, plus the magic that promoters dream about, that extra quality that brings people to the ticket window waving their money. Sponsors all along the line were wiring and phoning. They wanted assurance Snead would play in their tournament. And I promised them delivery of the new sensation."

Before the Houston tournament that closed out 1937's Western swing, at the suggestion of George Jacobus, Corcoran officially signed on to become Sam's manager and thus fanned the conflict-of-interest flames that cost Bob Harlow his job. Many fellow competitors, especially the lesser-known players, groused that Snead was suddenly given preferential treatment in the form of favorable tee times and other perks, including his pick of lucrative exhibition matches and endorsement deals. Indeed, before the year was out, though he didn't smoke or drink, Sam's name and likeness would grace Chesterfield cigarettes and National Bohemian beer, neither of which he consumed, not to mention Firestone tires and Gillette razors. He posed wearing Mexican sombreros and goofy straw hats, even put on overalls and had his picture taken pitching hay. The fact that he made no attempt to fraternize after hours with other players didn't boost his popularity with fellow players.

For their part, Jacobus and Corcoran were willing to overlook all this sniping and focus instead on exploiting this golden opportunity. For the first time in nearly a decade, professional golf had a bankable marquee player. And during the fifteen years Corcoran managed both the PGA Tournament Bureau and Sam Snead, the value of the former jumped from $120,000 to more than $1 million and the latter became a household word and a very wealthy man. (During this same time, Corcoran produced similar windfalls managing the likes of Ted Williams and "Babe" Didrikson Zaharias.)

"Sam Snead was a dream come true for golf," Corcoran confided to his former associates from the Massachusetts Golf Association. "But almost from the beginning it was Sam against the world. He didn't make many friends among the other pros and the reporters who got under his skin, but the gallery gobbled him up."

In 1937, Sam snagged five PGA victories, came in second place three times and third another five, earning $10,243 in official money (and close to twice that in side exhibitions and endorsement deals). The only man to win more, Lighthorse Harry Cooper, won seven tournaments and also took home the newly created Vardon Trophy for the lowest tournament stroke average, but bitterly complained that the hick kid he'd once beaten in a rain-soaked playoff back in 1935 at the West Virginia Open was commanding all the attention.

Byron Nelson got his first good look at this phenomenon in 1937 at the San Francisco Matchplay Championship, where he dispatched Sam three-and-two in the second round. "I'd heard a lot about Sam before I ever saw him swing a club," Byron recalled. "For one thing, he came in with a lot of momentum from Oakland. Reporters were following him everywhere he went. I had to play well to beat him though I don't remember much about our match. What I remember most was thinking what an absolutely wonderful golf swing he had. I'd never seen a better tempo. He was about my age yet he looked like he never worked at it at all." Ironically, Henry Picard, who'd helped them both find their footing on tour, then eliminated Byron from the championship.

For all the excitement surrounding the long hitter from the hills, Byron was considerably more advanced at that point in terms of experience. He'd played in over two dozen tournaments, collecting important wins at the New Jersey Open and the Metropolitan Open in 1936, earning about $1,800, which barely covered his and Louise's traveling expenses but certainly made him a player to watch.

Their difference of opinion regarding traditional club positions reveals a great deal more about their personalities and central ambitions. What Sam had in mind, despite his rough-hewn edges, was the living Hagen and Sarazen made off lucrative exhibitions, private matches, and endorsement deals, not giving lessons, keeping books, answering to the wishes of members, or running golf tournaments, and other club-related events. Though he maintained strong ties with the Greenbrier for decades, eventually becoming head professional and taking on some of these traditional duties, Sam's focus never wandered too far from the developing PGA Tour he, Byron, and Ben would come to dominate for almost twenty years.

Byron was far more conventional in his belief that a good performance on tour first of all pleased his club members back home and might possibly capture the attention of a more prestigious club down the road. Like his friend and mentor Henry Picard, he loved the analysis involved in teaching the game to others, regardless of their skill level. By now his dream was to catch on with a top Eastern club, and this came true in February of 1937 when, after George Jacobus recommended him, he signed a contract with the Reading Country Club in Pennsylvania that guaranteed him an annual base salary of $3,750 and whatever he could make by giving lessons and running the shop. "It meant," Byron remembered, "we would never have to borrow any more money from Louise's folks."

On a natural high from finally achieving one of his goals, just a week later he and Louise drove down to Augusta for the third Masters and splurged by checking into the pricey Bon Air instead of renting a modest room in a boardinghouse as they had just the year before.

His happy mood carrying over to the golf course, Byron opened with a sensational 66, his best score and a record by a Masters champion that would hold up for three years until Lloyd Mangrum bettered it by two strokes in the first round. Paired with wiry Paul Runyan during this brilliant opener, he hit every par-five in two, and the other greens in regulation. Runyan—who typically talked out loud to himself as he played—"C'mon, Pauly, hit the ball next time," or "Quit messing around"—said to the press after the round that he'd never seen such superior shotmaking. In a tournament where a few veterans still carried the odd hickory-shafted club in their bags, Byron's performance was a billboard announcing the accuracy of steel, a new swing, and even a new kind of player. Host Bobby Jones went out of his way to congratulate him.

Byron's first Masters title didn't come without a struggle. He shot 72-75 to lose his lead and in the final round found himself three strokes behind Ralph Guldahl at the turn. But his old friend put his tee shot into Rae's Creek at twelve and was forced to drop a ball and finish with a double-bogey five. Byron, who was watching from the tee, then went straight for the flagstick with a six-iron, leaving his ball just six feet from the cup, and drained the putt to suddenly tie him for the lead. After Guldahl stumbled again at the dangerous thirteenth, making a bogey six, Byron told himself that "the Lord hates a coward" and went for the green with his three-wood, his ball finishing just off the green, and chipped in for an eagle three. His 32 on the back nine gave him a two-shot margin and the title. There was no green jacket then, but Jones himself presented a beaming Byron the winner's gold medal.

"I still have that medal," he wrote years later, "and when my playing career was over, I looked back and realized that this was the most important victory of my career. It was the turning point, the moment when I realized I could be a tough competitor. Whenever someone asks me which was the most important win of all for me, I never hesitate. It was the 1937 Masters, the one that really gave me confidence in myself."

Before the couple headed north to his new job in Reading, "suddenly happy as a pair of honeymooners," according to Louise, Byron granted Atlanta newsman (and Jones writing partner) O. B. Keeler an interview in the players' locker room on the second floor of Augusta National's clubhouse. "Byron, I watched you play the back nine today," Keeler told him, "and it reminded me of a piece of poetry written by Lord Byron when Napoleon was defeated at the battle of Waterloo." Byron smiled and explained to Keeler that his mother was particularly fond of his poetry, which was why she gave her son the middle name of Byron.

The next day, he was surprised to see the Associated Press story headlined "Lord Byron Wins Masters."

The name stuck.

Though it doesn't show up in any record book, not long after Byron's dazzling Masters, Ben Hogan's luck began to change.

That spring, he and his extremely shy wife of two years moved into the twelve-story Forest Park apartment building where his mentor, Marvin Leonard, and wife, Mary, were living. This was considered one of Fort Worth's better addresses for upwardly mobile couples, though in the Hogans' case it was a *threesome* that included Valerie's effervescent kid sister, Sarah Fox, who was working for a top dress shop downtown and moved in to share expenses and cooking duties. "I'll let you in on a little family secret," Sarah's daughter, Valerie Harriman, once confided to a reporter. "My mother did most of the cooking and housekeeping at the apartment they shared because Aunt Val couldn't or wouldn't do it. This led to some amusing situations. Uncle Ben loved scrambled eggs for breakfast, and Aunt Val had no cooking skill whatsoever, so my mother would get up early and make Ben's eggs just the way he liked them—allowing Valerie to serve them to him. He and my mother became very close during that time, though I'm not sure he ever caught on about the scrambled eggs."

The toughest four-year stretch of Ben's professional life was just ending, a dark period that included his second failure to make it on tour, his poorly paid work at Oakhurst, and the roadhouse gambling jobs he rarely, if ever, spoke about. But then he found a decent job working as the head pro at the tiny Nolan River Golf Club in Cleburne, sixty miles south of Fort Worth, a job Claude Fox most likely orchestrated for his daughter's determined suitor. Though his salary was only $200 a month, Hogan augmented his work by giving lessons at three dollars an hour and living cheaply with his future in-laws, saving up every cent for a third assault on the tour. Meanwhile, on April 14, 1935, not long before Hogan decided to move back to Fort Worth for an office job his brother helped arrange at a petroleum company, he and Valerie got married by a Baptist minister in the front parlor of Claude and Jesse Fox's house in Cleburne. Curiously, the *Cleburne Times-Review* described the bridegroom as "a well-known golf professional from Fort Worth," making no mention of his brief but useful time in Cleburne, nor the fact that Royal and his wife, Margaret, were the only guests.

Ben skipped the '35 tour entirely, saving money and playing only money matches around Dallas–Fort Worth, most of which he easily won. By early the next summer, both his personal finances and his game appeared to be in better shape. He qualified for the U.S. Open at Baltusrol and asked Valerie to come along for moral support. The Hudson roadster was gone, replaced by a roomier secondhand Buick purchased, in part, because Byron and Louise Nelson had a similar car. Valerie detested travel and was prone to car sickness on any trip beyond twenty minutes, but consented to accompany Ben to New Jersey. "I had gone with Ben's mother to see him play an exhibition in Fort Worth," Valerie remembered. "That was all the golf I knew. But now that he was going to play in the U.S. Open, I was excited about traveling with him."

The first thing Ben did after getting settled in a motel two miles from Baltusrol's front gate was to phone Byron, who was at nearby Ridgewood Country Club. The two couples had dinner together, and the next day, while the men practiced, their wives took a ferry across the Hudson to New York City; it was Valerie's first glimpse of Manhattan. Arm in arm, they window-shopped for hours, Louise later told Grantland Rice, chatting up a storm. "Louise and Valerie liked each other right off," Byron said many years later. "I think that particular U.S. Open created a pretty good friendship between the girls and even a better bond between Ben and me. We traveled a lot together after that. Louise and Valerie were always the glue in the relationship."

Neither man distinguished himself on Baltusrol's difficult Tillinghast-designed Upper Course. Hogan shot 75-79, Nelson 79-74; both missed the thirty-six-hole cut. So after Tony Manero closed with a brilliant 67 to shatter the old Open scoring record by four strokes and capture his only national championship, the Hogans and Nelsons took another ferry for dinner. Despite the disappointing outcome, the week had some pluses as well, especially for Valerie. Tony Manero's wife, Agnes, a stylish and popular tour wife, had warmly befriended her and provided useful tips about the traveling life—which deeply impressed her and eased her fear of road travel. "Imagine," she wrote her mother, before the couple headed home to Texas, "I'm a friend of a U.S. Open champion's wife."

The following summer, Ben chose not to try to qualify for the 1937 Open. By now the Hogans had saved $1,450, and Ben was ready to attack the tour again. "It's now or never," he told Valerie before they loaded up the Buick and headed for Niagara Falls, Ontario, for the General Brock Open, where Hogan began keeping a little black book of both expenses and results for the first time, much like the one Byron had kept since the start of his career. Ben calculated that his odds of winning were improved at this tournament, in part because he was driving the ball more reliably, but also because many of the better players had returned home to attend to their regular club jobs. Jimmy Demaret, for one, who was growing close to Ben about this time, saw a new confidence as the two warmed up on the practice range in Ontario. "I've got the secret of this game now," Ben assured him. Demaret later wrote, "But if Ben found the secret at that time, he lost it again immediately. It was the same story, and a heartbreaking one, for the Hogans. Ben tied for eleventh in the General Brock, he came in ninth in the Shawnee Open, he placed ninth in the Glens Falls Open. And so it went."

In fact, though Ben's tendency to hook the ball in the heat of competition was still the main source of his undoing, the results of his efforts weren't quite as futile as Demaret suggested. Before Glens Falls, he'd snagged seventh place at the St. Paul Open, followed by an encouraging third at Lake Placid—netting $600, enough to keep going. Moreover, he won the long-drive contest over tour player Jimmy "Siege Cannon" Thomson, pocketing another $50. A local newspaper columnist wrote of Ben, "Now he's on the tournament trail and unless we are mistaken, that beautiful swing of Hogan's should really soon take him places." Valerie dutifully clipped the piece and pasted it into the new oversized scrapbook brought along for just such notices.

When the couple's travel-worn Buick rolled into the parking lot of the $5,000 Hershey Open, Ben's frustration was palpable. Henry Picard, the event's gracious host and eventual winner, spotted it right away. "I'd never seen a player work so hard as Ben Hogan and have so little to show for it," he recalled years later. "He reminded me of all the hard work I'd put in to get my game where it was, though in Ben's case you could see there was something beneath the surface that was driving him along. I was never quite sure what that was but I liked Ben. He kept to himself but he had an air of dignity that appealed to me. He wasn't afraid to work."

A touring professional needed to earn about $3,000 a year on the expanded year-round circuit to cover expenses. After six months on the road, the winnings noted in the Ben's black book amounted to just

$1,164. They went home to Fort Worth to discuss whether there was enough left in the kitty to risk heading for California for the start of the 1938 West Coast swing.

Not surprisingly, it was Picard who once again came to the rescue. A few days after Christmas, he and former Glen Garden assistant Jack Grout were having dinner at the Blackstone Hotel, where not so long ago Ben had dealt cards and even moonlighted as a bellhop, when they spotted the Hogans sitting at a corner table. They walked over to say a friendly hello, and discovered they were having a disagreement over the approaching winter tour. Valerie wanted Ben to go, but Ben disagreed, citing their depleted savings. "I want him to go," she told Picard and Grout in no uncertain terms. "I'll just stay home and find a job."

"In that case," Ben said, "I won't go. We both go or *nobody* goes."

"All right. Let's end this argument here and now," Picard calmly proposed. "Ben, take Valerie with you and go out west and play. If you need anything, come and see me. If you run out of money, I'll take care of you. You've got my word on that."

Ben stared at him for a long moment. Years later—when he fondly recounted the story to his members at the Scioto Golf Club, where he was tutoring young Jack Nicklaus—Jack Grout liked to say he could almost hear the battle being waged inside Hogan's proud and analytical brain. He wasn't the kind of man to accept charity from anyone, but Picard was one of the game's finest players and a model of everything Ben hungered to be—urbane, polished, a brilliant student of the swing, an unflappable and generous champion.

In a pure golf context, though neither man could fathom it at that moment, Henry was filling the same black void that Marvin Leonard had already addressed—an older, more accomplished man who recognized the decency and work ethic of a promising young player who simply needed someone to express confidence in him. In the end, Picard gave Ben something far more useful than money.

"Knowing that help was there helped me forget my troubles," Ben confided in a rare moment of self-revelation years later when his first book of instruction, *Power Golf*, appeared. "The support and confidence Henry expressed in me in the summer of 1937 meant all the difference in the world." The book, incidentally, was dedicated to Henry Picard.

So instead of giving up, the Hogans made a pact to head for California with their paltry savings and an emergency plan to sell the Buick, if necessary, and use the money for train fare home, at which point Ben would abandon his quest and find a better-paying club job or something in oil or finance.

In Los Angeles, he failed to finish in the money. Sam Snead won the second Crosby Clambake, where Ben placed eighth and earned seventy-five dollars, just enough to cover room and board for the week. A week later, at Pasadena, he made another sixty-seven dollars for tenth place; Henry Picard won, and Byron placed third, making $350.

On the drive up to Oakland, even Valerie's confidence in Ben began to waver. They had only $100 left—just enough to get home to Texas if they left right away.

"No, honey," Ben told her. "We made a deal to go as far as Oakland. If we don't make any money there, I'll sell the car and we'll go home, and I'll never mention golf to you again."

On the morning of the first round, he walked out to their car in the parking lot of their inexpensive hotel and found the rear end of their Buick resting on cinder blocks, thieves having made off with the tires. Reportedly he threw up his arms and marched back into the hotel, informing Valerie they were finished. "Nonsense, Ben," she told him. "We'll just find someone to give you a ride to the golf course and worry about the tires later." Afterward, in several interviews, Ben downplayed the incident, claiming he'd forgotten the precise details, undoubtedly in no rush to relive the most agonizing moment of his career, staring his darkest demon—abject failure at the one thing he believed he could succeed at—right in the face. As Valerie later explained to her sister, Byron and Louise happened to be staying in a hotel only a few blocks away, so a single phone call solved the immediate problem. Byron picked Ben up and drove off to the Sequoia Country Club while Valerie arranged to have the tires replaced. Days later, she told her sister, the new Masters champion offered Ben a loan. Though he declined, the gesture meant a great deal to Valerie, who suspected that it was Louise's idea.

Years later, Sam Snead recalled standing with some other young pros when they saw Ben outside the clubhouse, looking anguished and lost. If Sam's memory can be relied upon, this was the first time the two had the occasion to speak to each other.

"What happened, boy?" someone asked, and he pounded his fist against a brick wall, groaned, and declared, "I can't go another inch. I'm finished. Some son of a bitch stole the tires off my car." He then looked at Sam, the new darling of the press. "How bad can things get?"

"He was as close to tears as that little guy can get," Sam remembered.

Whatever Ben's particular motivation was that week—a fear of more nothing divided by nothing or a sheer desperation that focused his attention as never before—he placed sixth and won $285. "We thought we were rich," Valerie said.

"It was the biggest check I'd ever seen in my life," Ben told Ken Venturi in the famous 1983 TV interview, his voice catching at the memory of it. "And I'm quite sure it was the biggest check I'll ever see."

The modest windfall paid for new tires and carried them on to Sacramento, where he earned $350 for a solid third-place finish.

Several weeks later, seemingly out of the blue, the head professional of the Century Country Club, one of suburban New York's finer private clubs, offered Ben a position as the club's assistant professional. His pay would be $500 a month plus anything he could earn giving lessons. After learning that Henry Picard had wholeheartedly recommended him, Ben signed on enthusiastically.

Two months after that, Ben played in his first Masters. Like Byron before him, as he later told Sarah Fox, the moment he walked onto the grounds at Augusta National he felt a special affinity for the place. Perhaps, also like Byron, he was initially a little overwhelmed by the grandeur and significance of the club Bobby Jones had built. He finished in a tie for twentieth place, well out of the money, but expressed his deepest gratitude to Henry Picard, who won the title, beating the ever-present Ralph Guldahl by two strokes.

Of all the promising young pros refining their games with steel shafts that particular warm spring, Guldahl was by far the most polished—and ultimately perplexing. The affable, stoop-shouldered Texan—who began his pro career the same day as Ben in 1932—had progressed so rapidly he needed only a short birdie putt to beat the amateur Johnny Goodman by a stroke on the final hole of the 1933 U.S. Open at the North Shore Country Club. Instead he made bogey and finished second. Despite a personality so devoid of excitement and color that even natural promoters like Harlow and Corcoran were hard pressed to generate stories that made him seem interesting, his combination of finesse and power made him the leading threat of a new wave of Texas gunslingers that included Houston's Jimmy Demaret, Ray and Lloyd Mangrum, Byron Nelson, and Ben Hogan.

In 1935, following a forty-first-place finish at Oakmont, still just twenty-three years old but suddenly missing his putting touch, Guldahl fared poorly in other tournaments that year, and returned home to Dallas and informed his mother he was through with competitive golf. He tried selling cars, among other odd jobs, but eventually drifted back to a local nine-hole course and began working on his game again. After his young son, Buddy, developed a sinus problem, Guldahl moved his family to the dry California desert, where he played in a few events but won nothing of significance. While there, however, he met the movie executive Robert Woolsey and the actor Rex Bell and accepted their offer to stake him enough money to play in the inaugural True Temper Open in the spring of 1936, where he won $240 and followed up with an eighth-place finish at the U.S. Open. Just weeks later, his putting touch returned and he won the prestigious Western Open—considered a major title in those days—and finished the year with the best stroke average on tour, 71.65. After Guldahl's wild flurry of closing birdies cost him the Masters in 1937, he went on to beat heavily favored tour rookie Sam Snead by two strokes at the U.S. Open at Oakland Hills. After returning to form, he would win two more Western Opens in succession and defend his Open title by an impressive six-stroke margin at Cherry Hills in 1938.

"Though Sam and soon Byron were getting all the attention, Guldahl was the best player in the game," says Open historian Robert Sommers, "all because of a hundred-dollar stake by two men who had faith in him." Not surprisingly, his success attracted more Hollywood types, including the reclusive millionaire Howard Hughes, a fine golfer, who once phoned Guldahl before playing in a club event just to chat about bunker shots, downhill putts, and how to play in the wind. After Hughes won the tournament, a check for $10,000 turned up in the pro's mailbox.

Despite the noticeable improvements in Ben's 1937 performance, Guldahl was enjoying the kind of breakthrough success he could only dream about. When the Hogans rolled back into Fort Worth to visit his mother and spend the holidays with her parents down in Cleburne, their travel-worn Buick had an additional 3,600 miles on its odometer and bald tires.

Yet there was plenty to be happy about that Christmas. Back in September, once again fate and Henry Picard seemed to conspire to give Ben a much needed boost up. When the U.S. and British Open champion Tommy Armour broke a bone in his hand and announced he had to scratch from the Hershey Round Robin Four-Ball, a star-studded affair that included the tour's top sixteen money winners, Picard penciled in a pleasant but largely unknown named Vic Ghezzi into Armour's slot to partner with Ben Hogan. He also advised his boss Milton Hershey to pay close attention to the way Hogan conducted himself, both on and off the golf course.

"He's overdue to start winning tournaments," Picard told him, "and he's a self-made guy who lives clean and works harder than anybody out here." Hershey, both a Quaker and a self-made man himself who'd failed three times before he found the magic formula for making a fortune in chocolate, liked the sound of that and made a note to see how Hogan fared against the best players of the day. The bookies weren't impressed with the Hogan-Ghezzi pairing, however, ranking them dead last at the outset, the odds 200–1. But the pair startled everyone by firing a blistering 61 best-ball total in the opening round and continued the assault until they were fifty-three strokes under par for 126 holes of play. Only the team of short-game wizard Paul Runyan and the game's popular new star Sam Snead came close to matching them.

Despite Sam's success, Ben's shared triumph at the Hershey Four-Ball was quite possibly the most important win any player achieved that year, for it proved his relentless work ethic was beginning to pay off.

As Ben and his long-striding partner approached the final green of Mr. Hershey's tournament that September afternoon, their winners' checks all but in the bank, trailed by a gallery of some four thousand people, Ghezzi raked his fingers through his sun-streaked hair and waved to spectators. Ben, on the other hand, kept his head down, his handsome angular face devoid of emotion, his eyes sweeping over the surface of the final green as they approached—almost as if, on the threshold of what he'd dreamed about for so long, he half expected to discover it was only an illusion.

Earlier in the year, while still out west, he'd expressed his frustration to Valerie about his inability to close the deal coming down the stretch—admitting he still allowed his nerves or something in the gallery to distract him. She had stared at him with her sweet brown eyes and said in an almost childlike manner, "Well, Ben, maybe you just need to find a way to ignore the gallery completely and focus only on your next shot. Maybe you should concentrate harder and forget all of that." A simple piece of advice. Yet years later Ben credited his wife with giving him the key that unlocked his greatness. "Before she said it so plainly, I seemed to think about everything else out there except what I had to do at that very moment."

At Hershey, he had finally succeeded in doing what Valerie had suggested—blocking out the world at large, including many bitter disappointments both on and off the course, and concentrating on shot by shot. "If we'd lost," a relieved Vic Ghezzi afterward confided to Jimmy Demaret, "I'm quite certain he would have jumped out a window."

As it was, he pocketed $1,100 after making thirty-one birdies—six more than anyone else in the field. Milton Hershey was the first to congratulate the now broadly smiling Ben. "I heard from Henry that you were the man to watch this week," he said. "And Henry was sure right about that."

"Thank you, Mr. Hershey," he replied. "I'm glad I didn't let Henry down—or you, either."

Hershey patted him on the back. "Maybe we should stay in touch," he said.

"Yes sir. I'd like that."

In 1938, the year many social historians believe America finally began to emerge from the economic gloom that had defined the decade, Ben Hogan finished thirteenth on the tour's official money list with $4,794. His friendly Glen Garden rival and sometime traveling partner Byron Nelson, with two victories, made only slightly more. With eight victories that included the Canadian Open title, Sam Snead dominated the headlines and made Fred Corcoran smile, owing to the largest spectator turnouts in years.

But as Ben Hogan later described it, this was the turning point of his life.

7

BREAKTHROUGH AND HEARTBREAK

J UST AS THE TOUR FINALLY BEGAN to regain its footing in 1938, another kind of trouble loomed on the horizon—the danger of war in Europe.

This unspeakable possibility first made its presence known in the golf world during the sixth edition of Samuel Ryder's biennial gathering at Southport & Ainsdale Golf Club in Southport, England, in June of 1937, where both Sam Snead and Byron Nelson made their debuts as Ryder Cuppers. Two years before this, while serving as George Jacobus's assistant professional at the Ridgewood Country Club in New Jersey, Byron enjoyed the privilege of serving as one of the event's organizers and hosts, helping to select the wardrobes for both teams. This made an indelible impression on him. "It got me to thinking about getting to be a good enough player to make the team," he recalled decades later. "I wanted it as much for the clothing as anything else, but it gave me that much more motivation for working on my game." A strong American squad bolstered by Picard, Runyan, Wood, Sarazen, and aging captain Walter Hagen had little difficulty dispatching a respectable Great Britain and Ireland team, 9–3. When a deeply inspired Byron Nelson confided to several Ridgewood caddies that he planned to make his first Ryder Cup team in two years, however, they merely laughed at him.

From the beginning, an air of valediction hung over the Ryder Cup proceedings of 1937. For one thing, eligible to participate under the same rules of residency that had kept him from participating in three previous Ryder Cups, thirty-year-old Henry Cotton—widely acknowledged as the finest British player of his generation—returned from semiretirement in Belgium to lead a strong squad that had never lost the cup on home soil and included the winners of the last four Open Championships. With poor weather and gale-force winds predicted for the Lancashire coast in the late June event, the London oddsmakers gave the home pros a slight advantage.

Once again, the most popular American in Britain, Walter Hagen, now forty-five years old and suffering the effects of what even he jokingly called his "whiskey fingers," agreed for the sixth time to captain the U.S. side, though for the first time as a nonplaying participant. The first five of the ten-member squad had been determined early in the year and included the sentimental favorite Gene Sarazen; Denny Shute, former Open Championship winner and reigning PGA Champion; former PGA champion Johnny Revolta; two-time Masters champ Horton Smith; and Henry Picard, who'd won seven tournaments in 1935–36. The team featured three promising newcomers: Byron Nelson, the new Masters champ; the winner of that year's U.S. Open, Ralph Guldahl; and Sam Snead, a five-time winner on the tour who'd finished runner-up to Guldahl at Oakland Hills. Former team member Paul Runyan and others Hagen had overlooked in favor of Sam grumbled that Snead had no place on the team because he'd turned in an inaccurate scorecard that spring at Pinehurst and skipped at least two events where he was scheduled to play in favor of better-paying exhibitions. "If he can't find Pittsburgh or Thomasville, Georgia," sniped journeyman Jimmy Hines, "how can he possibly find his way to England?" Despite Sam's brilliant U.S. Open finish—the second lowest on record—the prevailing sentiment was that other veteran players were more deserving of the captain's picks, another case of Sam versus the world.

Just days before the team set sail for England, on June 16, the Haig made his final selections: Augusta pro Ed Dudley and Tony Manero. "If there's ever been a stronger team mounted from our side," he boasted to a reporter from the *New York Herald Tribune,* fully aware of the galvanizing effect this remark might have on his team's rookies, "I would challenge you to name it." Britain's redoubtable *Golf Monthly* seemed to concur, in the aftermath describing the Yankee Ryder Cuppers as "the greatest golfing force which has ever come to this country. A splendid spectacle of athletic youth."

The Americans, particularly rookies Snead and Nelson, performed well. On Tuesday morning Hagen sent Ed Dudley and Byron out to meet the home team's strongest pairing, Alf Padgham and Henry Cotton, in alternate-shot foursomes, and a headline in the local paper read "Hagen Leads Lambs to the Butcher." An inspired Byron drove his ball magnificently against Cotton all day, and put his ball inside the British star's on each of the par-three holes; he and Dudley stunned everyone except perhaps the wily Sir Walter by producing a relatively easy four-and-two victory, prompting a subsequent headline, "Lambs Bite Butcher." Then, in the singles, Sam demolished steady Dick Burton five-and-four, silencing his critics and sealing the match for the Americans, winning for the first time ever on British soil. For the other side, one of the few triumphant moments came in a nail-biting singles match between Byron and Dai Rees, the diminutive Welsh tiger who was three down after the raw, drizzly morning round but clawed his way back in a driving afternoon rainstorm to win three-and-one. With the cup already lost, he was nevertheless lofted onto the shoulders of his fans and carried triumphantly back to the clubhouse in the cold Lancashire rain. Byron later confided to Snead that he found this display of national pride deeply inspiring. Sam agreed, though true to his nature—and unfortunately within earshot of a sportswriter from the *Times* of London—he also noted that the only thing the Ryder Cup stirred in him was the desire to get the hell home as soon as possible. His complaints about English food and weather and golf courses, which Byron shared to some extent but chose not to give voice to, didn't go unnoticed—or forgotten.

The victory was banner-headlined in America, prompting President Franklin Roosevelt to cable Hagen and his young team that they were the "greatest golfers in the world and nothing less than heroes to the American people." During the concluding ceremony, the Haig, normally a flawless public speaker, grew so emotional—perhaps sensing this might be his final appearance at an event he'd come to cherish—that he mistakenly remarked, "I'm very proud and happy to be the captain of the first American team to win on home soil." The crowd chortled at this gaffe and he sheepishly raised four fingers to signify his four British Open Championship titles. "You'll forgive me, I'm sure," he clarified with a wistful smile, "for feeling so at home here in Britain."

No apology was necessary for the partisan crowd, who admired Sir Walter's lifelong classy showmanship, remembering his stylish efforts to democratize their clubhouses. Behind the bonhomie, however, lurked growing concerns about Nazi Germany, prompting many in the British golf establishment to question whether the Ryder Cup would even be played in 1939.

Immediately afterward, the American contingent headed to Carnoustie for the Open Championship and were greeted by more cold, drizzly weather that deepened Sam's gloom and uncharitable feelings but inspired Byron to a fifth-place finish that netted him $125. (Henry Cotton won.) The only downside was the cost. "Our boat tickets came to $1020," he wrote in *How I Played the Game*, "plus I'd lost weeks out of the shop [in Reading, at his new post] with the Ryder Cup and British, so you can see why we didn't play the British much back then," he explained. "The PGA did cover some expenses, but I lost $700–$800 out of my own pocket." Louise, however, found it "a delightful adventure, she made friends with the British wives and soaked up the local customs. But that was Louise, wherever she went she made it special. That made things easier for me."

By his own account, the rest of 1937 was a "whirlwind." Even as the reigning Masters champion settled into his new job in Reading's handsome Tudor-style clubhouse in Pennsylvania, happy to give lessons to every level of player, Henry Picard invited Byron to join him and Denny Shute on a late-autumn trip to Argentina to play a series of exhibition matches and the national open. At the season's close, the Nelsons shut the golf shop and house they rented from the local Studebaker dealer and headed south to Texarkana, where Louise would stay with her parents during the month he'd be in South America, and in the meantime he could practice to his heart's content, paying particular attention to his short game.

Byron was scarcely two years into what he later called his "five-year transformation plan" to construct the ideal swing for the new True Temper steel shafts he was using, but his conversations with superb ball strikers like Picard and Shute, combined with hours of trial-and-error experimentation, had already yielded some impressive hints of things to come. For one thing, he began standing closer to the ball and a little more upright, leading to a takeaway motion that was considerably less flat than the traditional swing plane of hickory-shafted masters. By experimenting with hip motion, he then "stumbled into the discovery that placed me on the right path to a solid, repeatable golf swing." Rather than begin his backswing by turning the hips and letting the swing take an inside-out path, as most veterans typically did simply to generate extra clubhead speed, Byron found that a slight lateral shift from left to right before the hips turned enabled him to take the club back on a one-piece motion that produced a straighter shot. This produced a modest "dip" that became in time Byron's distinguishing movement. Moreover, in contrast to the conventional technique of "rolling the wrists" during the takeaway and delivery of the clubhead at impact—the traditional pronation and supination used by every great player from Harry Vardon to Bobby Jones, a movement perfectly suited to the greater flex of hickory shafts—Byron discovered that keeping the back of his left hand "aimed" at the target well before impact and into the follow-through significantly enhanced his accuracy. He picked up these ideas from Henry Picard and to some extent Shute, himself an exceptional long-iron player, but they originated in the swing theories of Henry's mentor, Alex Morrison—key elements of the new steel-shafted era that would soon make Byron perhaps the most accurate ball striker of his day. A straighter left arm at the top of his backswing, he determined, also improved his accuracy.

In these early stages of Byron's rapidly evolving golf swing, his greatest weakness was chipping and putting, as he revealed with a disappointing tie for twentieth place at the 1937 U.S. Open at Oakland Hills outside Detroit, a beast of a course that required both pinpoint accuracy and length. The rookie sensation Sam Snead, by comparison, already excelled at both facets of the game and seemed to validate his popularity by tying the course record on the first day out with an impressive three-under 69. Forty-eight hours later Sam concluded his campaign on the difficult par-five seventy-second hole by reaching the green in two and sinking an eight-foot putt for eagle, a brilliant 283 finish, second lowest ever. When a revitalized Ralph Guldahl finished his day's work two hours later, carding a stunning 69 that lowered the record once again, Sam suffered the first of what would be a series of heartbreaking Open losses. During the presentation ceremony, as Guldahl, smiling lazily, held his trophy and $1,000 first-place check, Sam drew a laugh from the crowd by leaning forward to slyly peek into the trophy cup. Everyone knew it was simply a matter of time before he had one of his own.

Byron and Louise found life in Reading a genuine pleasure, and far more social than they'd expected. "The people there were initially a little reserved," Byron explained years later, "but after they got to know us, why, they invited us into their homes for parties and suppers and treated us more like members of the club. Louise made several of her finest friendships there, a regular bridge group, and I found it a wonderful place to teach and practice my own game."

After weeks in Argentina with his friends Picard and Shute, which handsomely compensated each man with $1,500 on top of expenses but made Byron so exhausted and homesick he was forever cured of wishing to go abroad, he was happy to get home to Texas for the holidays. Owing to that mental fatigue, made worse by a stomach that was sensitive to exotic foods, he made a hash of his debut at the 1938 Los Angeles Open, finishing forty-eighth, and wasn't really a factor until he reached the Thomasville Open in Georgia. There, he briefly recovered his form, edging out fellow Texan Lloyd Mangrum to win a rain-shortened fifty-four-hole event. Weeks later at Augusta, he mounted only a fair defense of his title and wound up in fifth place, but at least saw his good friend Henry Picard win his first Masters title.

The enduring memory he took away from this tournament—the first one where "The Masters" was commonly used by reporters and officials alike—was of playing the opening round with Bobby Jones, who shot 76 to Byron's 73. "It was the second biggest thrill of my career up till then," he said years later. "The only thing bigger was winning Mr. Jones's tournament."

There was also a rather poignant footnote that year. At the Bon Air Hotel, Augusta members conducted a rowdy Calcutta party, a wagering pool in which players and members were invited to "purchase" a player they believed would win the tournament, the most highly rated going first. Cliff Roberts explained to Byron that it was tradition that the reigning champion attend the festivities, so Byron went along. He didn't drink alcohol or gamble, but when no one bothered to "buy" Ben Hogan, he was moved to do so for $100. The next day, Ben approached Byron and asked if it was true he'd taken him in the Calcutta pool, and Byron confirmed that he had. "That's not something I normally do," he added cheerfully, "but in your case I thought that might be a pretty good bet."

Anytime a fan or reporter commented on how hard Byron practiced his game, he liked to point out others who worked even harder—notably Henry Picard and Ben Hogan. At that time, the vast majority of players never practiced unless they needed to work out a specific swing problem or wanted to test a new set of clubs. The idea of a daily, regulated practice session designed to reveal both strengths and weaknesses, and that included a range of shots from various kinds of lies, was a concept embraced by only a handful of pros who understood, as Ben once put it, that making practice shots identical to tournament shots "was the shortest route to success."

"Could I buy half an interest in myself?" Ben asked Byron that next day in Augusta.

"Of course," Byron told him, taking that as a healthy sign of Hogan's determination to make a good impression on Jones and Roberts.

Ben went away and came back a little later with the fifty bucks. Just a week before, he'd finished seventh at the inaugural Greater Greensboro Open in North Carolina, and was encouraged that his long hours on the range were beginning to pay off. But he opened his first Masters with a 75, blew to 78 in the third round, and finished with a baleful 301, in a tie for twenty-fifth place. He gathered his things and left town minutes after signing and turning in his card.

For Byron, another frustrating fifth came at the U.S. Open in June, where Ralph Guldahl successfully defended his title at Cherry Hills, high in the thin air of the Colorado Rockies. Weeks later, in the quarterfinals of the PGA Championship at Shawnee-on-Delaware, following a rest at home in Reading, Byron narrowly lost two-and-one to Pittsburgh pro Jimmy Hines in the quarterfinal, who in turn got demolished by Sam Snead in the semis, placing the lanky Virginian in the final for the Wanamaker Cup against diminutive Paul Runyan, who'd challenged Hagen's choice of Snead for the Ryder Cup team. To nobody's surprise, Sam was both the bookmakers' and the fans' clear choice.

"I don't think anyone but my wife gave me a chance to beat Sam that year," Runyan remembered with a wry smile. "He was on fire and the fan favorite by at least a two-to-one margin. I spent most of the match watching him put on a driving exhibition, outdriving me by at least seventy yards on most holes. Fortunately I had a few tricks up my sleeve." Even when using a four-wood to Sam's six-iron, Little Poison repeatedly placed his ball closer to the pin and holed a number of long birdie putts to win the PGA title in a romp, eight-and-seven, the widest winning margin in the championship's history up to that point, a humiliation that a visibly sulking Sam Snead never forgot.

For Ben, the stinging memory of his poor Masters showing was softened somewhat by his new post at the Century Club in Purchase, New

York, where the wealthy members provided the Hogans with a cozy cottage on the grounds and days off for excursions into Manhattan. Maybe best of all, Ben found himself routinely invited to play with fellow pros at the better known Metropolitan clubs like Winged Foot and Westchester. Owing to the demands of his new club job, he wasn't able to play a tour event between the Masters in early April and the Cleveland Open (where he finished fourteenth) the second week of August.

Though both Ben and Valerie were homesick for Fort Worth, and Ben was chafing to get back on the circuit, in many respects these were nevertheless pleasant days for the road-weary Hogans, especially Valerie. Ben had time to work on his game at the Century Club's splendid facilities and at least once that summer Valerie met Louise Nelson in the city for shopping and lunch. Ben's only real complaint was having to give lessons to his members. "Giving lessons to rich ladies isn't Ben's favorite thing," Valerie confidentially admitted to her sister. "He's working so hard on his game, and all he can think about is getting back out there on the tour."

Without question, 1938 belonged to Open champion Ralph Guldahl or Slammin' Sammy Snead, who not only successfully defended his Crosby Clambake earlier in the season but also won the inaugural Greater Greensboro Open and six other tournaments, including the Canadian Open. Moreover, finishing second six times and third three others, he was the tour's leading money winner that season, earning just shy of $19,000. "Sam's going to need to buy the tomato canning company just to have enough cans to bury his money," an ecstatic Fred Corcoran quipped to reporters. It was in Greensboro, during the opening two rounds at the Sedgefield Country Club, that John Derr got his first look at the "Virginia hillbilly everybody was talking about." In his twenties and new to town, Derr was the son of a rural North Carolina postman and a hustling college dropout who'd talked his way into various jobs as a stringer, reporting on Duke and Carolina football, and somehow had managed to wangle an invitation to the 1937 Masters, where he met Bobby Jones and hobnobbed with famous sportswriters Grantland Rice and O. B. Keeler. In the late winter of 1938, he was hired (for sixty dollars a week) as assistant sports editor at the *Daily News* in Greensboro, then the second largest city in North Carolina.

"I followed Sam for two rounds at the GGO to see if what everybody said about him was true. My first impression was that he had a golf swing of a serious athlete and, by golly, looked just about unbeatable. Folks were eager to get close to Sam—who was always uncomfortable in crowds—but someone introduced us and we seemed to connect right off the bat. From a reporter's perspective, I found him refreshingly candid. He would answer whatever you asked him, no evasions whatsoever, honest to the point of bluntness—though if he had a good audience he could spin a hell of a yarn, especially if there was a pretty woman anywhere around. Sam had a real weakness for a pretty gal, though I had no inkling of how much until I got to know him better."

Not long afterward, George Corcoran, Fred's younger brother and the head professional at the Greensboro Country Club, invited him to tag along with a friendly match he'd put together: Sam; Johnny Bulla; a pro from Danville, Virginia, named Al Smith; and the promising and fiery Clayton Heafner, who'd just made his own first foray to the touring circuit.

"Sam had pigeons up at the Greenbrier but no real competition to keep his game sharp between tournaments," Derr explains. "There wasn't a tournament every week in those days, sometimes weeks between events. So whenever there was a lull Sam would come down to Greensboro to fish with friends and play with Bulla. The deal presented to me was that I was free to come and watch them play but not write about anything I saw. That was fine by me."

More important to the young sportswriter was the opportunity to get close to the hottest player in the game. "Fred Corcoran understood ordinary people loved reading about Sam and at that instant he was exactly what the tour needed to get back the respectability it had lost during the Depression. Sam was happy to oblige. He loved an audience and played for the galleries—as long as they didn't try to get too close. By '38 people were coming out of their shells again, following baseball and horseracing and college football. Thanks to Sam, golf began to find its way back to the front pages, too, really for the first time since Jones left the game—all due largely to the Slammin' Sammy Snead image."

Even in a casual match, Derr noticed, Sam displayed an athlete's sensibility and a competitive edge. "He always attacked, never eased off. He also wouldn't play even a friendly match without something riding on it, at the minimum a five-dollar Nassau. With Bulla and Heafner and occasionally [tour player] Johnny Palmer it was never about the money, though. For Sam, it was about beating them."

During these "friendly" matches in Greensboro, if Bulla cut the corner of a dogleg, for example, Sam always did the same without a moment's hesitation and often needled his traveling partner whenever he outdrove him. "As most pros do, Sam was always looking for an edge, regardless of the risk involved. This quality would serve him well. He was basically fearless. But it would also cost him dearly. There were moments—as Ben Hogan liked to say about Sam—when a little mental caution would have gone a long way and probably served Sam better in the long run, but you couldn't tell Sam Snead that. He was on top of the world. He never took his foot off the accelerator."

The same was true on the highway.

Before the tour swung back east to Florida in March of 1939, he invited Derr to ride down with him in Bulla's new Buick Roadmaster sedan. "Sam loved to drive and he never worried much about posted speed limits, if there were any. The other thing he loved to do was talk, both on and off the golf course. He loved to tell stories and jokes, the raunchier the better. Because of his big personality, a common belief about Sam was that he never thought much about his golf swing, that it all just came naturally to him. In fact, Sam actually worked constantly on his swing, always trying to refine it. I'll never forget pulling into a gas station in the middle of nowhere with Sam and Bulla arguing about whether a good shot was hit on the third or the second groove of a middle iron, and whether a well-hit draw naturally goes farther than a well-hit fade.

"Next thing you know, why, even as the poor guy is pumping the gas into the car, the two of them have their clubs and are marching out into a field behind the gas station, arguing every step of the way. They must have hit balls back and forth for a full hour. Sam had just signed up to play Wilson golf balls, and Bulla played a thing called the Peau Doux, a ball that was sold exclusively through Walgreens Drugs stores for thirty-five cents apiece. They argued about that, too. Then we're all back in the car, happy as you please, barreling on to Georgia and Florida with the two of them still carrying on like a couple field scientists about the physics of the golf swing. Bulla was very much into that sort of thing, a highly analytical and scientific mind—and Sam just egged him on. They were quite the pair."

Sam's brilliant ball striking was in part due to his comfort with his new Wilson Staff clubs, a deal that came about in typical Snead fashion when, while having a casual driving contest with Ralph Guldahl on the practice range in Cleveland, Sam picked up one of Ralph's Wilson balls and was photographed holding it. Dunlop, his own sponsor, was incensed and offered him only $3,500 to re-sign at season's end. When I. B. Icely of Wilson Sporting Goods heard this, he tracked Sam down and offered him $5,000 on the spot. According to Sam, MacGregor offered him twice as much, but a hunch told him to sign with Wilson.

A venerable Chicago company established in 1913 to find creative uses for slaughterhouse by-products, Wilson Sporting Goods made surgical sutures and violin springs before manufacturing tennis rackets, catcher's mitts, and footballs endorsed by Knute Rockne; Wilson's stable of sports legends would eventually include Ted Williams, Babe Zaharias and Jack Kramer, the "Father of Modern Tennis." In the aftermath of Gene Sarazen's spectacular win at the 1932 British Open, the company created its fabled Sarazen signature R-9 sand wedge, selling fifty thousand of them in the first year alone. Sam signed with Wilson just weeks after the incident in Cleveland, forging a relationship that existed for the next half century. Down the road, Sam would reportedly receive a twenty-five-cents royalty off every ball Wilson sold, and they also sold more of his own signature Blue Ridge golf clubs—the first perimeter-weighted clubs of their kind, debuting the spring of 1939—than any other player's club maker did of his era.

As their records in early 1939 indicated, Sam's golf swing was slightly more advanced—or at least more productive—than Byron's and Ben's, if not as much as he himself believed. Veteran golf writer Al Barkow compared the sound Sam's irons made at impact to a Rolls-Royce door being slammed shut—"a rich sound, unmatched in his day, or perhaps any other. With a driver the sound was different; it had more of an explosive quality, the brisk but definite report of a rifle shot."

Early in his career, however, not unlike Byron but even more like Ben, Sam had such difficulty avoiding a low-running hook that he abandoned his driver and used a two-wood in competition, relying on his own superior athleticism to produce long drives. And he worked hard to build a repeatable swing tailored to his supremely athletic physiology. Contrary to another commonly held view, he was not double-jointed, merely blessed with unusually long muscles and superior joint flexibility, another Snead family trait. Once Picard placed the ultra-heavy Izett driver in his hands, according to Jack Burke Jr. and others, Sam Snead was destined to become the finest long driver of the ball ever.

But golf is nothing if not subjective. Within a very short period, other pros were saying exactly the same thing about Byron and Ben, each of them engaged in a similar quest to perfect the modern swing and edging ever closer as the 1939 tour got under way.

Perhaps because he really had begun playing the game barefoot, Sam's starting point was footwork and balance—factors many accomplished players overlooked and teachers rarely mentioned. "Footwork, balance, is everything to me because my life-long theory (and Ben Hogan agreed) is that the more you minimize hand, wrist, and arm action, the better," he wrote in his best instruction book, *The Education of a Golfer*. "I believe the body pivot launched by the feet is the *big* factor."

Beyond his considerable physical advantages, the key to Sam's unrivaled power and grace was a stance closed ten degrees to the target, a slight turn of his head to the right to place it in a position that could be held during the swing (a tidbit he claimed he'd copied from Bobby Jones and Walter Hagen), a gentle outward "kick" with his left knee to initiate the backswing, a slow and slightly more upright takeaway ("'Draw the bead easy, boy,' I tell myself, 'or there won't be turkey dinner tonight'") with his right elbow tucked close to his side, followed by a full turn balanced on the slight "roll" of the feet, and an unrushed downswing that appeared to "wait" for the body to catch up with the clubhead at impact. It was a model for the athletic swing of modern times, studied and copied by the players and teachers of generations to come.

On the mental side—by his own admission always his biggest challenge—as Sam addressed the ball, he attempted to clear his head of all distracting swing thoughts. "You don't think about how to swing the axe when you're splittin' wood," he once told a young reporter. "The same is true of a golf swing. Once you get ready to swing, you just let it go. The smoother you swing, brother, the easier the wood splits. Same thing with a golf swing." Yet owing to his innate musicality, he often hummed the "Tennessee Waltz" or some other four-beat popular tune not only to keep from dwelling dangerously on mechanics but also to establish his masterful tempo and rhythm. His position at impact, with his knees slightly bowed and nicely flexed, produced a slightly squatting posture that enabled him to accelerate naturally through the ball to a full finish.

As he adamantly insisted to Derr early in their evolving friendship, and anyone who ever asked about his incomparable swing, Sam never had a formal lesson from anyone, claiming everything he knew he'd picked up from watching the best players or experimenting on his own—though 1951 Masters runner-up Skee Riegel recalled something different from playing with him and Nelson Long, the Homestead pro, in 1939. As Riegel later told Al Barkow, "Long said that on a hole on the back nine he had Sam stop at the top of his backswing. He then pushed Sam's arms and hands high up over his right shoulder. He told Sam that was where the club needed to be. Sam had been swinging the club around his body, on a flatter plane, which he probably picked up from watching the [older] pros and others of that era."

At any rate, as 1939 dawned Sam's Rolls-Royce swing prompted the sportswriters once again to unanimously pick him as the man at that summer's U.S. Open at the Spring Mill Country Club outside Philadelphia. But as he struggled to regain his form out west, Byron Nelson began making headlines of his own with a second at the Crosby and a win at the rain-shortened Phoenix Open, where he beat runner-up Ben Hogan by an eye-opening eleven strokes.

Just six weeks later he rolled into Pinehurst, where the Tufts family's hospitality at the regal Carolina Hotel included black-tie dinners and French mineral water in their guest rooms—all on the house—made Pinehurst Louise Nelson's favorite stop on tour. The North and South Open was regarded as a major championship by the players, dating from 1902 and won by elite stars that included Walter Hagen, a three-time winner. Owing to the tournament's prestige and popularity, combined with a splendid Donald Ross golf course the designer constantly tweaked in search of perfection, writer Dan Jenkins once called it "the Masters before there was a Masters." Despite a shaky putting performance, Byron's superb iron play and 280 score was good enough that year to win the North and South by a margin of two strokes.

"That was a really important win for me," Byron reflected years later. "It gave me a nice boost of confidence just as my game was beginning to really come around. Everyone wanted to win in Pinehurst, in part because the course was so well respected but also because it was a wonderful tune-up for the Masters."

Something else nice happened to him at Pinehurst. Following a practice round with his friend Harold "Jug" McSpaden, he was introduced to a salesman for Field and Flint, maker of fine men's street shoes called Foot-Joys. Over dinner at the resort, Byron mentioned the deplorable construction of golf shoes—most of which, thin-soled and too narrow across the ball of the foot, hobbled players after only a few rounds of wear—and Byron wondered out loud if Field and Flint shouldn't go into the golf shoe business. Weeks later, he and Jug took a train to Boston to be fitted at the company's factory. Jug chose classic white bucks, Byron British tan wingtips, and fellow competitors were soon clamoring for their own custom-made shoes. For years thereafter, both men received a quarter royalty for every pair of Foot-Joys sold.

Days after his Pinehurst victory, Byron finished in tenth place in Greensboro, followed by a disappointing seventh at the Masters. Putting issues suddenly plagued him, so he decided to skip the next tournament in Asheville and head to Toledo, Ohio, for a job interview. "Even then," he relates in *How I Played the Game*, his folksy 1993 autobiography, "though I was playing well and winning money most of the time, I wasn't thinking about making a living on the tour. I needed that [club] job to survive." Through his old friend George Jacobus from Ridgewood and the PGA, he had an interview at the prestigious Inverness Club, another Donald Ross course, where Harry Vardon's heartbreaking collapse in 1920 had allowed his English traveling mate, Ted Ray, to capture the U.S. Open (and where the cathedral clock, courtesy of Walter Hagen, still stands in the club's foyer).

The other candidate for the job, ironically, was one William Ben Hogan. Both men, interviewing weeks apart, made good impressions on the Inverness committee. But something about Byron's cheerful mien and his stated affection for teaching the game to others struck the more powerful chord. Once again, Ben lost out to his old Glen Garden rival, a rejection he reportedly took hard and never spoke of again.

Weeks later, Byron signed a contract with Inverness that gave him a base salary of $3,000 a year plus all the profits from the club's popular pro shop. Moreover, just two weeks after his interview in Toledo, and only days before the start of the 1939 U.S. Open, he caught a train down to the Boca Raton Club in Florida where Scotsman Tommy Armour had orchestrated an equipment contract for him with MacGregor. After their brief meeting, Byron selected a new set of MacGregor Silver Scots, clubs he would play with for the next three seasons until MacGregor rolled out a top-of-the-line set with his elegant signature on them. A short time later, Ben would also sign on to play MacGregors—once again following Byron.

Sam's growing legions of fans, not to mention the official oddsmakers, however, considered him the favorite at Spring Mill, though some observers pointed out that his untidy performance at Cherry Hills the year before argued against his chances.

Designed by Bill Flynn, who worked on the construction crew at the Merion Golf Club under Hugh Wilson and later formed a design company with Philadelphia engineer Howard Toomey that created the new Cascades Course at Sam's beloved Homestead, Spring Mill lacked the physical drama of most Open sites and finished in a rather humdrum fashion with a pair of modest par-fours and a long uphill par-five of 555 yards, the only three-shotter on the course, for the championship.

Turned out in stylishly pleated gabardine slacks, and two-toned saddle shoes, and sporting the wide-brimmed white Fedora he adopted in 1937 to cover his increasing baldness, Sam drove the ball splendidly and opened with a record-breaking 68. His 71 in the second round gave him the halfway lead at 139.

His 73 during the morning round on Saturday left him a stroke behind Johnny Bulla and tied with Craig Wood, Denny Shute, and Clayton Heafner, whose 66 was the talk of the tournament to that point. Sam's Greensboro practice pals Heafner and Bulla fell apart in the final round, however, while he recaptured his form and played flawless golf until the seventy-first hole, where he made a careless bogey that unleashed the demons of doubt in his brain. He knew he was somewhere around the lead and perhaps even had it, but he wasn't certain. In those days there were no leaderboards, and his uncertainty would prove devastating.

Ahead of him by thirty minutes, finishing birdie-par for 68 and a total of 284, Byron could only wait and see if anyone could beat him. A par on the home hole would put Sam into the clubhouse with 283, he calculated, and possibly win him his first U.S. Open title, though Wood and Shute were playing behind him and roars from their galleries were filling him with anxiety. According to Sam, he asked playing partner Ed Dudley if he had any idea where things stood. Dudley, who hardly said a word to Sam all day, simply shook his head. The host professional, he also served as Bobby Jones's handpicked head pro down at Augusta National. A future president of the PGA of America, Dudley was well on his way up the establishment ladder. Not surprisingly, he was also close to Joe Dey Jr., who was the USGA's executive director, the man who oversaw pairing selections for the championship. Dey, like Jones, made no effort to hide his growing dislike of Snead, believing his crude jokes and public japery demeaned the gentleman's game they revered. To this day, Sam's biographer Al Barkow and many of his fans remain convinced beyond any doubt that his pairing with stiff and proper Ed Dudley—who was nine shots behind Sam at the start of the long double-round day—was orchestrated by Joe Dey to rattle him. At this time, tournament leaders were typically spaced out through the field as a means of spreading out the galleries. The practice of placing leaders at the back of the pack, in fact, didn't evolve until after the Second World War. Sam himself, who claimed to have a nose for chicanery dating from his very first tournament at the Homestead, was absolutely convinced of a conspiracy to hurt his chances.

"If I'd been playing with Bulla, Heafner or Wood," he said emphatically years later, "there's no doubt in my mind I would have won that Open. Dudley knew exactly where things stood because that was his job but he just played dumb as a plow mule. When someone told me I needed a birdie to win, that's what I decided to play for."

Whatever the truth of the matter, it was a disastrous decision. With his adrenaline surging, Sam lashed his tee shot into the left-hand rough, leaving his ball 275 yards from the green. Despite this, he opted to pull a brassie from his bag and go for it, figuring the worst that could happen was to come up short and have a short pitch, leaving birdie still well within reach.

Instead, he topped his ball and saw it scamper into a steep-shouldered fairway bunker on the left flank of the fairway, about 110 yards shy of the green. As Sam approached, his typically enthusiastic gallery fell deathly silent and he himself appeared ashen. The face of the bunker was five feet high. A wedge would easily have cleared it, though probably leaving him well short of the uphill green. He gambled on an eight-iron and took a ferocious swing. For an instant, in the explosion of sand, no one could see where his ball went, and then Sam realized his worst nightmare had come true: his ball had slammed into the wall and was embedded in some freshly laid sod near the top. He stood in disbelief for a long moment and then slowly shook his head. The Open—in his wheeling mind, at least—was now all but lost. He still believed he needed a four to win, but a tie was still possible. From an awkward stance, he tore through the sand and turf and sent his ball into another trap forty feet shy of the flag. Moments later, with his feet planted awkwardly outside of the bunker, he finally sent his fifth shot onto the green, rolling it forty feet past the hole—and three-putted from there for an unholy triple-bogey.

Stunned silence cloaked the huge gallery as the game's most popular player staggered off the green, his mind numb, his eyes fixed on the ground. "Women's eyes watered," notes USGA historian Bob Sommers. "Men patted him on the back. Other players turned away to save him embarrassment." Years later, Sam would claim he had only the vaguest recollection of this ghastly moment, and perhaps that's true. It was the most appalling collapse since Harry Vardon's horrific free fall over the closing nine at Inverness in 1920, a moment anyone would wish to forget, and second in the series of catastrophic Open failures that would haunt Sam Snead for life.

Eight-time Walker Cupper Bill Campbell, the West Virginia amateur who became something of Sam's protégé and a close friend as the years passed, often described a "darkness that fell like a November rain" on Sam at several critical times in his career. "There was a moodiness and fatalism in him that is often common to rural people," he told a writer from Golf Magazine. "I think it had to do with growing up in the woods, hunting and fishing on his own, being part of a natural world where life and death were all around and, in truth, he always felt most comfortable. The golf world, in some respects, was not a natural place for Sam. It was simply an arena where his talents made him a star. Sam delighted fans because he hid nothing. If his game was on, he conveyed his pleasure like no one else I ever saw. He loved to clown around and entertain people. He would roll his eyes, spin tales, talk up a storm. But there was always something in Sam that half expected things to eventually go badly. Country people learn to live by the seasons, you see, and know a storm will eventually come. Sam always had that feeling, I think, about the U.S. Open."

As the drama at Spring Mill played out, Craig Wood holed a birdie putt on the seventy-second hole to join Byron in the clubhouse at 284. Like Sam, Denny Shute needed a pair of pars to win outright, but bogeyed the seventeenth and made it a three-man playoff.

The next day, Shute faded quickly while Wood and Nelson, wearing the same kind of casual open-necked shirt that would soon become commonplace in golf, battled nip and tuck to the final green, where Wood's bold effort to reach the green in two knocked a spectator out cold. Regaining his composure, he chipped his third shot to within six feet of the cup. At that point he was a stroke ahead of Byron, who had his own birdie opportunity from inside eight feet.

As he addressed his ball, Byron said afterward, he suddenly remembered "all the times when we were playing as caddies at Glen Garden and we would say, 'This putt is for the U.S. Open.' Now I was really playing that dream out, and it steadied me enough that I sank my putt." Wood's effort stopped short, requiring a second play-off day.

For Byron, followed by many of his Reading members and good friend Jug McSpaden every step of the way, the highlight of that round came when he holed a one-iron shot for eagle on the fourth hole to take a three-shot lead, a margin that held up and gave Lord Byron Nelson his first, and only, U.S. Open Championship.

At week's end, the grateful members at Reading threw the Nelsons a party that was both a victory and farewell fete and presented Byron a gold watch inscribed "Byron Nelson, Winner U.S. Open 1939–40. Members of Reading Country Club." They also gave him a Winchester rifle for hunting, and a large silver bowl to Louise engraved with her name.

A few days later, Ben and Valerie Hogan spent a week with the Nelsons in Reading, during which "the girls spent time shopping and going to lunch with Louise's friends while Ben and I played golf." The couples were as close as they would ever be, and Byron saw an intensity in his friend's gray eyes that suggested Ben was getting close to something—either a breakthrough or a breakdown. Despite his miserable tie for sixty-second at the Open, he'd already recorded seven top-five finishes and two seconds for the year. "Ben never revealed much about his thinking," Byron recalled, "but I knew him well enough to know he had a resolve like never before to win. There were also changes in his swing that year, which told me he was working harder than ever and getting closer."

A week after the Hogans returned to their cottage in Purchase, Byron won the Massachusetts State Open by four shots over his pal Jug McSpaden. Then he went on to the Potmonok Club on Long Island for the PGA Championship. For the first and only time, his mother made the long trip from Texas to watch him play in a major. With his game clicking on all cylinders, he performed well, too—blitzing six players to reach the final against his good friend Henry Picard. Their match ended on the thirty-seventh hole when Picard rolled home a twenty-foot birdie putt to win his second major championship of the year. Byron took the next week off to prepare for the Western Open at Chicago's splendid Medinah No. 3.

Though the battle between Byron and Henry claimed the majority of press attention at Potmonok, a story with even larger implications unfolded a day before the first round on the practice tee, where Ben Hogan did something he had rarely if ever done before, confirming Byron's impressions about his state of mind. He asked Henry to watch his swing to see why he retained the maddening tendency to hook his drives when a tournament was hanging in the balance. Both his runner-up finishes that year had resulted from hooked drives and costly bogeys. Over the spring and summer, as he confided to Valerie just days before, he'd concluded that long straight drives were essential to winning any tournament, especially a major championship, and the way to "guarantee that win" was to "get so far ahead of everyone else [that] nobody can possibly catch me."

Picard deduced his technical problem pretty quickly. "Ben," he said, "in your case it's pretty simple. You'll never win until you learn to fade the ball." Using a five-iron, he shifted his grip to a more neutral or "weak" position on top of the club, then widened and opened his stance a touch. In a photograph taken of this interlude by a wire service photographer, the elegant, necktie-wearing Picard tilts forward to adjust his powerful left hand, while Ben's head remains bowed in an attitude of almost prayerful concentration—all of it adding up to the classic setup for a workable fade, the shot that would soon lead Ben from the wilderness into the land of milk and honey that Byron and Sam had already found.

Indeed, over the first thirty-six holes of this PGA, Ben fired a pair of impressive 69s, missing just three fairways, to take the qualifying honors with Ky Laffoon, Chuck Kocsis, and Dutch Harrison. Then he demolished Steve Zappe, a talented Springfield club pro, seven-and-six, and went on to face Paul Runyan in the third round. In their match, Ben's driving was peerless and often placed his approach shots well inside Runyan's. Using his famous metal-spooned putter, however, Little Poison rattled several long putts into the cup to claim the match.

"That sort of thing, repeated hole after hole," Ben confided to reporters, slumped and demoralized in the locker room afterward, "chokes the heart out of you. At least five times the gate was wide open for me, but Paul wouldn't let me through."

Also suddenly driving the ball straighter than he ever had before, Byron went on to win the Western Open the very next week, a tournament then regarded by many as a major championship. Next, he held the lead in the Hershey Open going into the final round but mysteriously lost his ball in the fifteenth fairway, congested with fans; this resulted in a two-stroke penalty and fourth-place finish. Ten days later, an anonymous letter showed up in his mailbox, with a note explaining that a young woman who knew nothing about golf had unthinkingly picked up Byron's ball and put it in her pocketbook. The letter also contained a money order for $300—the difference between third- and fourth-prize money.

By summer's end, Byron had replaced Sam as the new darling of the national sporting press, a gentlemanly counterbalance to the sometimes rough-edged Snead. "Regardless of how he played, Byron was always an approachable fellow, the soul of courtesy," John Derr observed. "He was such a contrast to Sam in almost every way. Sam was fun to watch, clearly the people's favorite, but Byron provided a class that reminded everyone of Bobby Jones. For that reason—especially coming after Sam's collapse at Spring Mill—I think Byron's rise to the national scene couldn't have been better timed. If Sam's success made golf popular again, Byron's elevated the game's stature in many sets of eyes."

Not surprisingly, the press also gave plenty of coverage to the episode of the lost ball and mysterious letter that concluded Byron Nelson's most rewarding year yet, in which he won a total of three "major" championships and more than $9,000 in purses. His stroke average of 70.02 also earned him his first Vardon Trophy. The happy Nelsons would celebrate by spending a month with Louise's parents in Texarkana, where Byron could practice and play every day to his heart's content with pro Don Murphy and other local friends, preparing for his new job at mighty Inverness and the start of the 1940 winter season out west.

All but lost in these unfolding events was Ben's strong performance at the PGA [where he was co-medalist] and impressive second-place finish at the Hershey tournament, where he closed by hitting every fairway on his final nine and was invited, with wife Valerie, to dine with Milton Hershey. This excellent showing also strengthened Ben's hopes that returning nonplaying captain Walter Hagen might make him a captain's pick for America's defense of the Ryder Cup, scheduled for early November down in Ponte Vedra, Florida. Byron and Sam had already qualified.

On September 3, however, when Nazi Germany invaded neighboring Poland, the storm clouds that had been gathering for years finally broke and Britain officially declared war on the Third Reich. Within days, a letter arrived from the chairman of the British PGA regrettably canceling the Ryder Cup until further notice.

It would be eight long years before the match resumed.

8

REDEMPTION

VALERIE HOGAN WAS WEARY of the road. "No, it's not too grand an experience living in suitcases and traveling 18,000 miles every winter," she told Arch Murray of the *New York Post* during the North and South Open of 1939. "It was a thrill at first but that's long since worn off," she said, describing how long days in a four-door sedan, drafty hotels, lumpy beds, and unpredictable diner food had begun to take their toll on her. The primary job of a "fairway wife," however, was to "hide her boredom and mental fatigue from her husband at all costs, to keep smiling and encouraging him no matter what anyone says. A golfing wife," she added, "has to be a combination of many things—nurse, masseur, comforter and whip-cracker—but most of all she has to be a psychologist. Your reactions to your husband's moods are vital."

Far more expansive than Ben had ever been with a reporter, perhaps because she'd once nurtured dreams of becoming a newspaper society editor herself, she explained to Murray that though she always preferred to await a tournament's outcome in the clubhouse—reading magazines or simply knitting socks for her husband—she could always instantly determine how her husband had performed by his body language on the final hole, where she typically joined him. If his pace was brisk and his head up, "his jaw thrusting forward, why, that means he has had a good round." Conversely, if his gait was slower and his gaze earthward "he's probably shot 75."

Toward the end of October, Murray checked in with the Hogans again and discovered that Valerie was "dreading closing up our snug little apartment" on the grounds of the Century Club and returning to the grind of hotels and highways for the 1940 tour, and that it was only the prospect of spending a month and a half "at home with family in Fort Worth" that made, if at all, the prospect tolerable. Ben, by contrast, was "bristling like a bulldog to get back at it, to attend a couple college football games and then head to Florida for the start of the winter season and the big swing out West."

"I think this year is going to be the vital one for me," Ben himself told Murray. "I have been knocking at the door too long now. I'm going to develop a finishing touch. I've had too many fellows in the trap, only to let them get away. That has to stop."

As a new decade dawned, marking the tenth anniversary of his efforts to outrun the gremlins of self-doubt, something was changing inside Ben Hogan, or perhaps just visibly hardening. Everything from his dress to his public demeanor reflected this. His clothing tastes, shaped by his fierce admiration of Marvin Leonard, ran to businessman conservative, well-tailored trousers that had both zippers and buttons to prevent accidental openings, sweaters in muted shades of gray or dark blue, with a traditional white or check flat cap that was his evolving signature and wore well in the wind—more of a uniform than a fashion statement, something he never had to think about.

Already known to be extremely reserved socially, and occasionally curt with reporters, he had now deepened his cowl of concentration even further, often giving the impression of icy aloofness. Beyond his considerable technical refinements, he allowed a few years later, he finally learned to win by blocking out everything but his game—gallery, his playing partners, small talk of any kind, even the weather and leaderboards. Chain-smoking Chesterfields, he would plod down the center of the fairway to avoid having to see or speak to any spectators, his gray eyes sweeping the terrain ahead for any potential advantage or peril. In effect, he willed himself into a trancelike state of absolute mental isolation perhaps only a Hindu holy man could appreciate. His closest friend on tour, Jimmy Demaret, observed that the way Ben Hogan studied golf courses and silently picked them apart reminded him of a bird of prey at work, a gray hawk on the hunt—an appellation that seemed to fit.

A writer from *The Saturday Evening Post* once asked Demaret, whose wardrobe preferences ran to eggplant-colored pantaloons, screaming argyles, and canary yellow plus fours, if his buttoned-up friend Ben Hogan ever said anything on the golf course.

"Oh sure," he breezily replied. "He likes to say, 'You're away.'"

"Seriously, Jimmy, Hogan seems so damn . . . unfriendly. How can you stand him?"

"Ben's not a bad egg at all—if he happens to notice you. It's not that he's unfriendly. He just prefers to play golf alone most of the time, even when he's your partner."

During the three weeks over the holidays that Ben and Valerie stayed with Royal and his wife, Margaret, Valerie filled her days by lunching and shopping with her sister, Sarah, while he went to the Colonial Country Club every morning for a couple hours of practice on the range, lunch with Marvin Leonard, and a round in the afternoon with him and Royal. During the years Ben had been away up north, and elsewhere, Leonard had spared no expense to make Colonial the premier golf course in Texas and waged a tireless campaign to attract a national championship, at one point tracking down USGA president Harold Pierce at his home outside Boston, keeping him on the line for half an hour with promises of unprecedented crowds, fabulous playing conditions, and incomparable Southern hospitality, not to mention a huge potential windfall for American golf's governing body. The USGA eventually submitted, designating Colonial as the first U.S. Open in the South for 1941. For years afterward, Marvin Leonard was ribbed by pals for making the most expensive long-distance phone call in Texas history.

The sight of a solitary Ben Hogan on the practice range at Colonial was becoming familiar to members. Tex Moncrief remembered asking him once why he spent an entire morning hitting nothing but wedges. Ben looked at him and tersely replied, "Because a good short pitch can almost always make up for a mistake." But his calculations didn't cease there. A year later, Moncrief spotted him hitting nothing but four-woods for an entire afternoon, pausing only for an occasional cigarette, Coke, or Hershey bar.

"Why four-woods, Ben?" the oil man asked him later in the bar. "You hit four-woods better than anyone in golf."

He told him, "I lost a tournament last summer up in Chicago due to a poor four-wood shot. I don't want that happening again."

"The message I took away from that was that he intended to leave no margin for failure of any kind," Moncrief recalled. "Ben didn't practice swings. He practiced shots. He wanted no shot to surprise him. He wanted them all, by God, to be perfect."

Before the season-opening Los Angeles Open, tour manager Fred Corcoran staged a long-drive contest inside the Los Angeles Coliseum, where Ben gave a preview of his new power, accuracy, and determination by placing second with a 255-yard blast that netted him $150, which he used to take Valerie out to the Brown Derby restaurant and a screening of *Gone With the Wind* that evening. When a Los Angeles reporter spotted the couple and asked Ben about how a slight 140-pound fellow who stood only five-foot-seven could hit a golf ball so unearthly far, Hogan merely looked at him and remarked that someday players his size would be hitting the ball over 350 yards. The reporter laughed, but Ben didn't. He wasn't joking at all. Byron Nelson, meanwhile, won the accuracy portion of Corcoran's contest, nailing three 225-yard drives directly between the goalposts.

Neither man did particularly well in the opener. Ben finished in a tie for eleventh, pocketing just seventy-five dollars, while Byron opened with a sloppy 75 and withdrew. A week later up in Oakland, Ben blazed to a second-place finish and Byron once again withdrew. At the San Francisco Matchplay, Byron briefly found his game and finished fifth. But the next week at Phoenix, he withdrew for the third time in four weeks.

In his memoirs, Byron confesses to being a little nervous early that year, happy about his new contract with the Inverness Club in Ohio but disappointed over medical tests that indicated he was sterile—probably as a result of the typhoid fever he'd suffered as a boy. Both Nelsons were eager to start a family, and Louise was immensely dismayed. Almost immediately, and encouraged by Valerie Hogan, she began to try to convince her husband that they should adopt a child. Byron wrestled with the issue for months before deciding that adopting was too "risky" and, given their nomadic lifestyle, probably not fair to any child. "If I had it to do all over," he told a reporter in 1994, "I probably would have adopted that child. Louise sure was eager to do it. It was one of the few things we disagreed on. I'll always regret she never got to be a mother. And I'm sure I would have enjoyed being a father."

The two-car caravan resumed. After Phoenix, the Nelsons in their new Studebaker President and the Hogans in their aging maroon Buick headed together down the highway for the Texas Open at Brackenridge Park in San Antonio. En route they always stopped at a place in Las Cruces, New Mexico, for homemade tamales. Plucky Louise and shy Valerie enjoyed staying together in inexpensive motels and eating in roadside diners because they had so much in common, including a desire for children. Valerie and Ben had discussed this as well, but he was firm about not wanting children in the foreseeable future. During their stop in 1940, however, the mood was considerably lighter, and the couples inquired about taking some of their favorite tamales home to Fort Worth with them, only to learn from the waitress that the tamales came from a can and were made by the Armour Meat Company of Fort Worth. "All four of us just looked at her," Byron recalled. "Then at each other. Somehow, those tamales had suddenly lost their appeal, and we never ordered them again."

Perhaps it was an omen of sorts, for something else began to change later that week.

Despite heavy downpours that turned Brackenridge's thin turf to muck, requiring the use of rubber tee mats, both Hogan and Nelson played brilliantly, each carding all four rounds in the 60s. As Ben waited out Byron's finish in the locker room, smoking a cigarette and rubbing liniment into an aching left hand, several players congratulated him on winning the Texas Open. Ben would have none of it, perhaps remembering what happened so long ago at the Glen Garden caddie tournament. "I hope he gets a 66 and wins, or takes a 68 and second so there will be no playoff," he told a reporter from the *San Antonio Express*, as if expecting the worst. Then he brightened a bit. "But if he wins, there's no one I'd rather lose to than Byron, for he's one of the best friends I'll ever have." Moments later, Byron birdied the seventy-second hole for 67, a record-tying 271 that left him all square with Ben.

Both men agreed to appear on a radio show in downtown San Antonio to generate local interest in their playoff. When asked about the quality of Ben's game—a pair of closing 66s had gotten him here—Byron smiled and replied, ever the ambassador, "Anytime you can tie or beat Ben, it's a feather in your cap, because he's such a fine player."

The two men were sitting side by side in the small studio. When the interviewer looked to Hogan for his response, an unsmiling Ben thought for a moment and said, "Byron's got a good game. But it would be a lot better if he would practice. He's too lazy to practice."

It was probably meant as a joke, a gentle poke in the ribs between old friends, though few outside the locker room knew Ben Hogan had a sense of humor. But the comment stung Byron, he admitted years later, partly because there was a grain of truth in it. He *didn't* practice nearly as much as Ben, without question, but not out of laziness. Rather, he'd completed his five-year transformation plan a bit earlier than expected, and his swing mechanics had evolved to a point where everything worked so beautifully and fluidly that some had begun calling him "The Robot." Tommy Armour was now on record as saying Byron's was the finest golf swing *ever*, and Gene Sarazen and Henry Picard agreed. His drives and long irons were by far the straightest and most accurate on tour, at moments machinelike in their precision, and his short game was fast approaching the level of Paul Runyan's. Only his inconsistent putting remained a problem. Otherwise, Byron saw absolutely no point in wearing himself out by practicing a swing that already displayed remarkable consistency. As he explained to Louise, too much practice might even compromise the great progress he'd made.

The other reason the remark bothered Byron was far more private in nature. From their early days together in Captain Kidd's caddie yard through their shared struggle to establish a toehold on the tour, Byron had always been the soul of encouragement, a friend reaching back to help another along. And though the two never spoke of it, he was one of the few people who knew something terrible had happened early in Ben's life, having heard whispers about Ben's father—a tragedy Valerie Hogan herself wouldn't learn of until she and Ben had been married almost a decade.

"I think Ben had some resentment about their early years together, due to Byron's early success," Sam Snead once told a writer in Hot Springs. "And I always heard that Ben really wanted that job up at Inverness that Byron got. Tournament golf will only magnify that sort of thing. Some fella you think is your best friend one day, well, you'd cut his throat and he yours the next day to have half a chance of winning a golf tournament. It's just the nature of the game. Nothing personal."

Maybe so. But in Ben's case, everything was personal. And something palpably began to cool in their relationship. While their wives would remain close until Louise's death in 1970, their own friendship would never be the same again.

The next day, Ben arrived two hours before their tee time and went through his comprehensive warm-up routine in his usual cocoon of unapproachable silence, pointing to shift a caddie equipped with a catcher's mitt and a bucket, a human target, around the range. Byron arrived an hour later, admitting that he hadn't slept very well. His stomach was acting up, as it often did in playoffs. Neither man, judging from their body language and expressions, appeared terribly happy.

The playoff, Ben's first as a professional, began at one o'clock on Monday, February 12, under low gray clouds, with an estimated two thousand spectators—having paid an extra $1.50 for admission—swaddled in wool overcoats and gray fedoras. They witnessed Ben leap ahead by one stroke only to fall back by the turn. By the fifteenth, he'd regained momentum and a one-stroke advantage, but here his tee shot landed in a muddy divot, and his approach came out heavy and landed in a small stream fronting the green. His bogey squared the match, then Byron struck a beautiful iron shot onto the sixteenth green and drained the birdie to go one-up. Both finished with workmanlike pars, leaving Ben at 71 and Byron at 70.

They took off their caps, and shook hands, and briefly posed together for a photograph, Byron looking more relieved than victorious, Ben smiling through his gritted teeth.

Asked what he planned to do next, Byron replied, "Drive home to Fort Worth and rest a bit." He added that several players from the canceled Ryder Cup team had a match against a group of top Texas pros at a charitable exhibition on Wednesday.

"How about you, Ben?"

"Houston," he replied tersely, then headed for the locker room to collect his things.

"You can't blame Ben," Byron commented to the reporters after he stalked away. "He's been close more than anyone lately."

One of them followed Ben to his car and discovered that some of Byron's equipment had been loaded into his trunk. He was taking extra shoes, balls, and clubs on to Houston for the Western Open, where Byron would collect them.

"That's awful decent of you, Ben. Not every guy would do that for the guy who just beat him out of an important tournament."

Ben gave him a withering look. Loyalty meant everything to Ben Hogan—and whatever else was true, he knew few souls on earth had befriended him as loyally as Byron Nelson had over the years. "Really?" he asked. Then he softened. "Well, we're friends." Another pause. "It's just a golf tournament. There will be others."

By mid-March, the PGA Tour seemed to belong exclusively to one James Newton Demaret, who'd dropped out of junior high to help his disabled house painter father support nine children and found his way to golf through humor and a hardscrabble Houston caddie yard. Two years older than Ben, Byron, and Sam, Jimmy didn't begin to find his game until 1938, at which point he began dressing like a human peacock and shooting the lights out. Johnny Bulla remarked that before Demaret came along the tour resembled an undertaker's convention, and Ben Hogan said devil-may-care Demaret was the most underrated player in history—his talent overshadowed by his showmanship, loud clothes, practical jokes, and reliable quotability. "This man played shots I haven't even dreamed of," Ben once said. "I learned them. But it was Jimmy who showed them to me first."

"Get out and live, you're dead a long time" was sunny Jimmy's prescription for the good life. Bing Crosby, a frequent playing partner, claimed Demaret was the funniest guy he ever knew who didn't have a script. "He was a wonderful guy," according to Sam Snead. "I never met anyone who didn't like Jimmy—except when he was beating you like a rug and making it look easy." Ben said the two met in Houston early in their careers and developed an almost instant rapport. Though their friendship struck some as wildly improbable—the dour tour loner who preferred shades of gray and the court jester whose bright pantaloons and friendly antics gave golf its most colorful star since Walter Hagen—they became an almost invincible four-ball team. In retrospect, it's not difficult to fathom why Ben was drawn to him. In many ways, Jimmy Demaret was a living and breathing personification of what he himself wished to be—Hennie Bogan.

After claiming a playoff win over Toney Penna at the Western Open in his hometown, "The Houston Hurricane" won in New Orleans and St. Petersburg to top the money list and bring his stunning early-season total to six victories in six tournaments. For the moment, he fascinated the press every bit as much as Sam Snead, curiously absent so far this year, was used to doing. After playing in the Seminole Golf Club's popular Latham Reed Amateur-Professional Tournament, a private pro-am where a winning player carted home at least 10 percent of a mammoth Calcutta pool, Demaret took a break from the action and returned home to play his trumpet and rest his game before the Masters, now only a month away.

Byron finished second in the opens at St. Petersburg and Thomasville,

Georgia, won several hundred dollars at his first Seminole Amateur-Professional, and then swung through Texarkana to pick up Louise, his game suddenly purring as smoothly as all eight cylinders of his sleek Studebaker President. By March 16, when they arrived in Pinehurst for the North and South Open and checked into Richard Tufts's elegant Carolina Hotel, the Hogans had been comfortably ensconced there nearly a week, Ben practicing for hours daily on Heartbreak Hill, and playing several practice rounds on No. 2, identifying preferred angles and danger spots on the course, leaving a trail of Chesterfield stubs in his wake. He had even lunched with Donald Ross, the course's famous designer and tournament host.

Though outwardly calm, Ben was desperate to break what he thought of as the ultimate contender's curse. Over the previous year he'd racked up no fewer than a dozen top-five finishes and half a dozen runner-ups. A popular story holds that he had only thirty-six dollars in his pocket and was so frustrated by his inability to punch through and finally win that he was on the verge of abandoning the tour. Perhaps, but his spirits were sufficiently high to place a long-distance phone call on the eve of the tournament to his friend Jimmy Demaret in Houston and waggishly thank him for staying home that week to attend to club business—proof, in fact, that he did possess a sense of humor.

Byron brought Ben an unexpected gift—a new MacGregor driver with a stronger True Temper steel shaft and fourteen ounces of swing weight. The moment Ben wrapped his oversized hands around the grip, he knew the club was ideal for him. Ironically, as an amused Byron revealed to friends a few months later, he brought *two* essentially identical drivers to Pinehurst and Ben had chosen the one that he himself liked—a familiar pattern in their relationship. At any rate, Ben took the new driver straight to Heartbreak Hill, pounded balls for hours, and over dinner that evening offered to buy it. True to form, Byron told him to save his money; the driver was his to keep.

John Derr, the new assistant sports editor for the *Greensboro Daily News*, drove down to watch his friend Snead play and arrived just in time to see Hogan—turned out in gray slacks, dark green sweater, white shirt, navy necktie, and signature white linen cap—tee off the next morning, splitting the fairway with a 270-yard blast. A seven-iron shot to twelve feet and a putt that banged the back of the cup yielded an opening birdie—setting a tone for what was to come. "I was there primarily to see how Sam did in the tournament," Derr recalls, "and the other buzz surrounded Byron. The crowds were there to see those two slug it out, but after I watched Ben play there was something about him that I couldn't take my eyes off. He betrayed absolutely no emotion but there was something about him that was like an animal let out of a cage. I'd never seen anything quite like it."

Ben holed a bunker shot on the eleventh and finished with an impressive 66, tying the competitive course record established one year before by Harry Cooper. "His precision was painstaking," notes Pinehurst historian Lee Pace. "On one putt of an inch, he went through all the footwork and positioning of a ten-footer." He didn't miss a single fairway and led by three over Paul Runyan. "There's something about this new driver that fits me like a glove," he said afterward in the locker room. "I tell you, I've never driven the ball better."

A second round of 67—again, he hit every fairway—widened his lead over Sam Snead and Johnny Revolta to seven. But the aging Gene Sarazen, an unapologetic fan of Byron's, had seen it all before. "He's never won before, and he won't win this time," he predicted. "Hogan's been out front before. But someone will catch him." When this filtered down to Ben, he vowed to prove him wrong. And as John Derr had noticed, there was something different about the tournament leader. Perhaps he'd finally fulfilled his own prescription for winning—to get so far out in front nobody could catch him. Perhaps the golf gods simply decreed it was time for all that humiliating failure and slavish dedication to perfection to at last pay off.

Whatever the case, on the final day, a chilly overcast Thursday, Ben under-clubbed several times in the morning round and stumbled to 74 but then redeemed himself in the afternoon with sterling iron play and putting that brought him home in 277, eleven under par, clipping two strokes off Vic Ghezzi's tournament record. Sam fired a brilliant closing 67 to finish second, Byron a workmanlike 70 for third—something that didn't escape John Derr's notice. "It was perfect symmetry and a glimpse of the immediate future," says Derr. "Though nobody could have appreciated the larger symbolism at that moment, the three greatest players of their age finishing one, two, three in a tournament many considered a notch below the U.S. Open in stature, in a place that made a rightful claim to be the Home of Golf in America. It still gives me goose bumps to think about."

As usual, Valerie Hogan joined her husband for the final walk up the eighteenth fairway. "Don't pinch me," she told Derr and others scribbling in their notebooks. "I'm afraid I'll wake up. Ben has been close so many times, only to see one fatal shot crumble all his hopes. He's never given up trying, though, even in his darkest hours."

The new North and South Open champion disappeared into the locker room to comb his hair and wash his hands and gather his wits, accepting the congratulations of Byron and Sam before appearing at the winner's ceremony, where he was presented with the trophy by Donald Ross himself and his earnings in crisp new fifty-dollar bills. Wary of carrying so much cash with him, he asked instead that a check be drawn and sent ahead to a bank in Greensboro.

On the porch of the resort later, Ben drank a glass of milk and talked to a group of reporters with surprising candor, explaining with visible relief, "I won one just in time. I had finished second and third so many times I was beginning to think I was an also-ran. I needed that win. They've kidded me about practicing so much. I'd go out there before a round and practice, and when I was through I'd practice some more. Well, they can kid me all they want because it finally paid off. I know it's what finally got me in the groove to win."

John Derr raced home though the chilly spring darkness to file his story for the morning edition of the *Daily News*. When the first copies of the paper came up from the composing room around midnight, he was horrified by the headline—"Hagen Wins Pinehurst North and South." He bolted downstairs to correct the mistake.

"What? It's not Hagen?" the foreman snarled at him above the din of the presses. "Well, who the *hell* is Hogan?"

In a matter of a days, the world would know the answer to that question.

Ben and Clayton Heafner fired matching first-round 69s to lead the Greater Greensboro Open, a tournament scheduled to finish with thirty-six holes on Easter Monday. But a spring snowstorm dumped three inches on the course on Easter itself, postponing play until Wednesday. "Let's ski it off," Sarazen blithely proposed. During the three-day delay, Ben stayed quietly out of sight at the O. Henry Hotel reading newspapers and putting on the carpet in his guest room, and playing bridge with Valerie, Byron, and Louise. His second-round 68 included three birdies and no bogeys, at which point the tournament shifted out to the elegant Ross-designed Sedgefield Country Club and he continued his assault on the field, posting 66-67 to finish at 270, a tournament record, nine shots ahead of Craig Wood. Byron finished third. "It was easy to see we couldn't catch that fellow, the way he is playing," Johnny Revolta remarked to reporters afterward. "You can't beat perfection." The Greensboro victory guaranteed nobody would ever confuse Ben Hogan and Walter Hagen again.

But redemption didn't stop there. Ben and Val's travel-worn Buick trailed Byron and Louise's Studebaker through a heavy fog to Asheville for the Land of the Sky Open, played over three mountain courses and ending at the lush Biltmore Forest Country Club where Bobby Jones honeymooned in 1925. After thirty-six holes, Ben and Lloyd Mangrum were one stroke back of Guldahl, with Byron just one back of them. The challenging Biltmore Forest course—another Ross gem—suited Ben's exacting eye in every respect. He later said it was among his favorite courses on tour. It didn't hurt that its elegant, wealthy, and refined membership treated him like he was one of their own. Not surprisingly, he closed with 69, which beat Guldahl by three strokes. In the clubhouse afterward, slightly chilled from his afternoon's work, he drank a cup of hot tea, posed for photographs with members, and told a man from the Asheville *Citizen*, "You wait and prepare so long for something like this to happen. I don't want it to end. Every time out I feel like I can win now." Byron, who finished seventh, made a point to congratulate his friend and urge him to keep it up. "Those wins couldn't have come at a more important moment for Ben," he recalled decades later. "Because they led up to the Masters, Pinehurst and Greensboro were tournaments everyone wanted to win, and Asheville was like icing on the cake. That Ben won all three in such a quick and decisive manner identified him as someone special, a player to watch."

In winning three tournaments over twelve days, Ben Hogan played 216 holes at thirty-four under par, a historic blitz none of his better-known rivals had accomplished. Prior to Masters week, the Hogans drove to Richmond so he could play an exhibition match at the venerable Country Club of Virginia, where he gave his first extensive interview. Choosing not to correct a reporter who asked about "growing up in Fort Worth," Ben explained how much his widowed, hardworking mother had sacrificed in order to buy him his first real set of golf clubs one Christmas. Beginning in Richmond, he doubled his exhibition fee from $250 to $500, and as a further indication of having arrived on Easy Street he agreed to do a national magazine ad for Bromo Seltzer.

By the time they reached Augusta, however, he was emotionally drained by his sudden success and all the resulting hoopla. Seemingly overnight, professional golf had a spectacular third new star, a workaholic nobody knew much about. Wherever Ben went, notebooks and microphones were poked in his face. He tried to be cordial and polite, mostly savoring the long-overdue recognition for all his hard work. In fact, he handled his explosive debut far better than Sam had his own "Sneadomania." He never fled in terror or shoved past overzealous fans, for instance—not yet, anyway. Besides, he'd had plenty of experience watching gracious winners like Picard and Byron perform in the spotlight. It was his turn now.

Madison Avenue was pursuing him as well, and a New York ad agency was eager to convince him to endorse certain brands of razor blades and beer. Though Ben personally preferred Schlitz, he signed a deal worth $3,000 with Rheingold. More tellingly perhaps, leading players who'd heretofore given him a fairly wide berth—Toney Penna, for example, or the increasingly imperious Gene Sarazen—now made it a point to speak and even chat up the hottest player in the game and welcome him to the winner's circle. The Squire's recent comments in Pinehurst still rankled him, of course, as did other swipes going back to his insistence that tour wives had no place on the circuit—a dig, Ben thought, about Valerie's steadfast presence—and his reflection on Ben's practice routines: "They exhaust me. With that swing of his, he won't last out here much longer." Still, he had finally risen above these absurd pronouncements by a man he'd admired early on and in some respects styled himself after.

His greatest opponent, however, his own self-doubt, had been soundly beaten. And though he would go on to become the top money winner for 1940, with $10,655 in earnings, capturing the popular Goodall Round Robin and finishing in the top five six more times before the season ended, succeeding Sam and Byron to win his first Vardon Trophy for the season's lowest scoring average, he perhaps paid too dear a price at the Masters, a victory he needed to draw even with Byron and keep pace with the emerging Texas mafia of Guldahl, Mangrum, and Demaret. Instead, he closed with a 74 and a disappointing ninth-place finish. The rested and red-hot Jimmy Demaret, to nobody's particular surprise, won the tournament by four shots over Lloyd Mangrum and five over hard-charging Byron. When Ben congratulated Jimmy in the locker room afterward, his colorful friend snapped open a cold beer and cheekily toasted him back, adding with a grin, "It was nice of you to take the week off and let me win one, Ben."

A very good thing came Ben's way that week, however, when Henry Picard pulled him aside and confidentially explained that he had just accepted the top job at Cleveland's prestigious Canterbury Country Club, doubling the $5,000 salary he'd been receiving at Hershey. The timing was perfect. Hershey was hosting the PGA Championship later that summer, and Picard was the reigning champion. "They're interested in either you or Snead as a replacement," he told Ben. "But I've told them you're the right pick. I think they'll listen to me."

As for Sam, he finished eighth in Augusta, one ahead of Ben, and pocketed just $200 for his trouble.

If Ben's excuse was simple exhaustion, Sam's problem was more complicated—an unexpected slump brought about by the strain of his giddy three-year ride to the top of the earnings list, and the challenge of living up to the fame and homespun personality that the media drummed to the public week after week. When in a good mood and performing well, he seemed to be a natural-born showman. But the truth was, he was as much of a loner as Ben—sharing an almost identical wariness of people in general and of big banks, smooth talkers, and in particular the inquisitive press. He, too, made his own travel arrangements, and allowed only manager Fred Corcoran to negotiate his lucrative commercial deals and exhibitions. "Nobody had helped Sam coming up," his longtime friend Lewis Keller says, "so Sam really wanted—or should I say trusted—nobody to help him. He preferred to do everything himself, from managing his money to driving to tournaments."

In a word, Sam was all too human. Beginning with his disappointment at the U.S. Open in 1937, followed by 1939's debacle, his larger-than-life personality appeared at times to vacillate between euphoria and gloom, depending on events. For example, in 1938—his sophomore season, when he seemed to win everything in sight—he was the picture of country charm and pure folk wisdom until Guldahl, his nemesis at Oakland Hills, eclipsed his brilliant closing 68 at Augusta and beat him by a stroke to win the '39 Masters, at which point Sam's mood blackened and he stormed past fans and reporters alike as he fled Magnolia Lane. He later apologized to Roberts and

Jones, but the display of poor sportsmanship left a lingering bad taste in both their mouths.

"Early in his career," says John Derr, "Sam became convinced he was up against a lot more than either Ben or Byron or anyone else out there faced—including a golf establishment he didn't think liked him much, players who were jealous of his quick success and genuine fame, and maybe even the Fates themselves. He made a few relatively minor mistakes attributable to youth and inexperience that were amplified by his brutally honest personality. Sam could never hide his emotions. Being a diplomat wasn't in his nature. If he was having a great time and enjoying himself, you absolutely knew it. If he was in a bad mood, stewing about a bad break or how he played, you knew that, too. In that respect Sam was the exact opposite of Ben, who locked up everything inside."

Critics pointed to his lack of grace following the eight-and-seven thrashing administered by Paul Runyan at the PGA Championship at Shawnee-on-Delaware in late '38, for instance, as well as his disqualification for marking a wrong scorecard at the North and South and a lackadaisical U.S. Open effort at Cherry Hills that offended sponsors and prompted some veteran players to question whether Walter Hagen should pick him for the '39 Ryder Cup. There was also his indulgence of lucrative private exhibitions, his continuing refusal to fraternize after hours, and, finally, his appalling self-destruction on the final hole that allowed Byron Nelson to win the '39 U.S. Open. That failure seemed to signal something more problematic than a mercurial personality: a tendency to choke when the stakes were highest.

To add salt to the wound, he met an attractive young woman out west and proposed marriage after the '38 season wound down. She briefly considered his offer before marrying a wealthy Arizona physician instead. This devastated Sam, according to his closest friends back home, which was directly reflected in his uneven play in 1939. He balmed his angst by helping himself to a string of attractive alternative candidates who showed up at sponsor parties and tournament shindigs, and increasingly on the course itself. "Oh, Sam led the league in pretty gals," uxorious Paul Runyan remembered with a quick laugh. "There always seemed to be one waiting for him wherever he went. They saw Sam as something between a star and Joe DiMaggio. And he could literally charm the pants off them."

It all added up to a young man struggling to reconcile his native instincts with the rigors of fame and constant exposure. Like most athletes, Sam loved performing well for the crowds. Success brought out his better side and fueled his natural sociability, elevating both his mood and charm. He'd horse around with players and fans alike, roll his eyes and make funny expressions for the photographers, happily sign autographs, and spin hilarious stories about characters back home that crackled with folksy wisdom. But let the round go sour or a hapless reporter question a particular shot or, worse, the state of his game, and Sam Snead went cold and wanted to get the hell away from the scrutiny, the pesky questions, the pressure of being golf's biggest draw.

At Toots Shor's in New York not long after America entered the Second World War, the story goes, Red Sox slugger Ted Williams—who'd just finished the season batting .406—was ribbing Sam about his sport being so much easier than baseball because a golf ball, instead of going eighty miles an hour, was hit while perfectly still, sometimes on a tee. "That may be," Sam drawled smoothly for the eavesdropping reporters, "but I have to play my foul balls." At one point, though, he pulled Williams aside and asked how he handled the high expectations and fickle judgments of the press, the pressure of fans, and his own growing fame. "Hell, Sam, they're just doing their jobs," Williams told him with a grin. "Some better than others. Just ignore 'em and go fishing."

"That easy, huh?"

"Hell no. But it works for me." Probably the best-known athletes in America at the time, they became good friends and regular fishing and hunting pals.

Following the disaster at Spring Mill, Sam went home to the Virginia hills, where he always found succor and perspective roaming the woods and streambeds of Bath County's rugged high country, an unexpectedly fortuitous move since this turned out to be his mother's final summer. Laura Snead died suddenly in early 1940, when her son was already taking a beating in the press. "After [almost] five years as a circuit pro," Sam recounts in his memoirs, "I'd won close to thirty opens, from San Diego to Miami, but not one national title. The papers called me a choke artist, a cheese champ, a 'mystery,' and a 'hex-haunted hillbilly.' One syndicated writer claimed I was Shoeless Joe Jackson of the links—Jackson never being quite able to edge Ty Cobb for the batting title."

"That stuff really began to get under my skin about 1940 and '41," he recalled in the '90s. "I went home to Virginia and started looking at land to buy, trying to put it all behind me. I went hunting and fishing and tried my damn best to ignore it. But it was always there. I couldn't pick up a paper without seeing something about myself, somebody saying this or that was wrong. Some of it was fair criticism, but it rattled me good, causing me to start pulling out whatever hair I had left in my head. My doctor told me he thought I might have myself a nervous breakdown."

"Sam doesn't kick away tournaments because he isn't trying," O. B. Keeler felt obliged to write in his syndicated newspaper column. "And he doesn't really choke up, the way some people claim. No one can say he isn't a money player with plenty of heart. His basic trouble is his failure to allow for trouble. He lacks imagination. Snead doesn't recognize the traps in front of the brook or the clump of trees in the dogleg. He doesn't consider the gamble involved when he blithely ignores them. He just steps up and socks the ball, and the next minute he's in a lie where a crowbar wouldn't help him."

Coming from Bobby Jones's Boswell, this analysis stung, too— mostly because it was absolutely, indisputably correct.

Under this kind of pressure, it's hardly surprising that 1940 was his weakest full year on tour, prompting some to speculate that Sam might simply be a flamboyant flash in the pan. After all, despite his finishing third to Byron and Ben at Pinehurst, he won only three tournament titles, all coming late in the season. But Sam had more on his mind than his deepest slump ever.

In early August 1940, the same year his mother died, Sam suddenly took the plunge and married Audrey Karnes, a large-boned country girl whose wit was as sharp as an ax bite. They'd more or less dated since junior high back in Hot Springs, and his longtime friends took his marriage to Audrey as evidence that he was seeking the comfort and stability of home, but tactfully waited for his mother to pass away before proposing. Reportedly Sam's mother was no fan of the Karnes clan, who managed a farm owned by Homestead president Fay Ingalls, Sam's old foil. Audrey, the family's youngest child, cooked for the farm's field hands and worked part-time as a maid at the resort. Graduating two years behind Sam, she'd been valedictorian of her class. A commonly told story, however, holds that Laura Snead feared that a strain of mental defectiveness ran through the Karnes family and might adversely affect any children they produced.

Her adamant objections only briefly delayed her youngest child's quest for marriage, children, and a stable home life to counterbalance his demanding public life. Days after their marriage at the Hot Springs Methodist church, refusing to reveal any honeymoon plans, Sam and Audrey climbed into his new Oldsmobile and headed for Niagara Falls, which was conveniently near the site of the Canadian Open. On their way there, the newlyweds got lost, drove in circles for half a day and spent their first night as man and wife in a cheap motel in Cumberland, Maryland. "We'll still get there in time," Sam assured her.

"What for?" Audrey tartly demanded. "For the falls or to see you tee off in the Open?"

It was a relevant question that revealed something about both their natures—the groom's restless desire to get back to the game he was expected to dominate, the bride's natural wariness of sharing her husband with countless strangers. Sam was so rushed and rattled by the time they reached Toronto that he appeared on the first tee wearing street shoes instead of golf spikes. The large gallery howled, assuming the country bumpkin was at it again. To make matters worse, the players ribbed him ruthlessly about having spent all his vital juices on husbanding. The press had a field day.

"If there'd been any way to leave," Sam later said, "I'd have taken it."

While Audrey raced back to their hotel for his shoes, he played the first three holes in his stocking feet, slipping several times. Once his spikes arrived, he was in and out of bunkers and stabbing at putts en route to a 72 that was under the circumstances fairly remarkable. According to the *Toronto Star*, "Shoeless Sam, the Bashful Bridegroom, the winner of the Canadian Open two years ago, is a 25–1 shot not to repeat, after arriving with a new wife and playing with all the pep of a sleepwalker." But he buckled down and played the last thirty-six holes nine under par to win, earning a small bit of redemption. "For once, the other fellows had nothing to say about it," he told Audrey.

The newlyweds immediately drove to Hershey for the 1940 PGA Championship, Henry Picard's finale as host professional. The early headlines, however, belonged to Walter Hagen, five times the champion, who found a bit of his old spark and advanced through the first two rounds of match play before being edged out 1-up by Jug McSpaden.

Ben, playing with his newfound confidence, easily pressed on to the quarterfinal, where Ralph Guldahl narrowly beat him. A significant consolation was that he was hired as Henry Picard's replacement. Sam had also interviewed for the post but later insisted he never really wanted it. Under the terms of Ben's new contract, he would be hand-somely compensated with a base salary of $10,000, and required only to make periodic appearances at the club—terms almost identical to Sam's arrangement with the Greenbrier, which had slightly upped his pay to keep him on the premises. He wasn't obliged to give lessons to members or run the shop, merely to represent the Hershey family's good name out on tour. This made Sam and Ben among the first to enjoy this kind of sweetheart deal, which over the next decade became commonplace on tour, as Vegas hotels and Florida resorts began sign-ing up celebrated professionals, hoping to feed off their success.

Sam, still hot under the collar from his honeymoon adventures, soundly defeated Jimmy Hines and Gene Sarazen, then thumped McSpaden five-and-four to reach the PGA final against none other than Byron Nelson.

Byron had spent most of the summer settling into his new job at Inverness, and had basically been out of action since the U.S. Open in June, when he placed a respectable fifth and Lawson Little nipped past the still dangerous Gene Sarazen in a playoff to claim the title. The caravan then brought him home to the Inverness Four-Ball, where he sentimentally teamed with Walter Hagen, who found the event so gru-eling he simply skipped playing the back nine in their last two rounds. "You can handle the boys," he assured the host pro, who as a kid had once lent him his cap to block the brutal Texas sun, and then headed back to the clubhouse for a toddy. Byron and his famous partner came in dead last, but Byron naturally savored the experience.

Unlike Sam and Ben, Byron viewed his club job as his main priority. Inverness had 350 golfing members who demanded the attentions of a full-time professional, and he was only too happy to provide it. He loved teaching players at any level, and believed a self-taught instruc-tor was the best kind. One of his first pupils there was a hotheaded, club-tossing teenager named Frank Stranahan, whose daddy ran the Champion Spark Plug Company; despite a shaky start in their relation-ship, Stranahan went on to become the world's leading amateur player for a time. Moreover, Byron enjoyed the give-and-take with members and viewed Inverness as his own version of Nirvana. Among other things, he innovated the practice of stocking Foot-Joy golf and street shoes in his shop, and convinced a member who owned an umbrella company to manufacture ones that could withstand the awful condi-tions golfers often played through. For several years, even after he was internationally famous, he visited leading department stores wherever he went, picking up $25 for every sales call he made plus a royalty from every golf umbrella or pair of Foot-Joy shoes that got sold.

Louise appreciated the settled life in Toledo even more than her husband did. Like Valerie Hogan, she was tired of life on the road. "I was very busy at Inverness and extremely happy," Byron recounts. "I did enough traveling during the winter in California and the Southeast that by the time the Masters was over, Louise and I were happy to get back to Toledo and spend the relatively cool summers there."

A month before the PGA at Hershey, he warmed up for the championship competing in a series of better-ball matches with his club's finest players. During this same interval he purchased a fifty-five-acre farm near Denton, Texas, not only to establish residency for tax purposes, but also to provide his parents and siblings with a comfortable place to live. His father was running a feed store in Handley and his younger brother, Charles, was preparing to follow their sister, Ellen, off to college. Byron picked up the tab on it all. Supporting the family who had always supported him was always high on his list of priorities.

He won several matches at Inverness, largely because his game didn't need much tuning up. When he reached Hershey, his drives were as straight and his irons as crisp and sharp as they had been earlier in the year. There was no trace of a layoff.

During his semifinal match against the tediously deliberate Ralph Guldahl, Byron—one of the quickest players ever—found himself struggling to stay patient and focused, but also a little unsteady on his feet. Beforehand, in the locker room, he'd thrown up his breakfast—a story that in time was broadly circulated and contributed to the idea that Byron, like his hero, Bobby Jones, was often queasy before a big match. In fact, such nervousness did increasingly assert itself with a churning acidity in the pit of his stomach.

The previous year he'd been runner-up, as his opponent, Sam, had been the year before, so in a sense 1940's PGA was a battle between two bridesmaids. Each had his ardent supporters on hand in Hershey, and over the first eighteen holes of their final match, Byron took a two-up lead. But Sam fought back in the afternoon to square things and take a one-up lead by the thirty-fourth hole. When Sam just missed his twenty-foot birdie attempt there, Byron made a two-footer to square things again with only two holes to play. On the next hole, a shortish par-four, Sam again put his approach inside twenty feet and Byron carved a magnificent wedge to within two feet again; Sam's putt lipped out, prompting a chorus of groans from his followers, and Byron coolly tapped in his birdie to take a one-up lead to the final hole, a long par-three.

Teeing up quickly, Byron made a smooth pass with a three-iron and finished ten feet from the cup. Sam, using the same club, pulled his shot slightly and watched his ball trickle off the green into a grassy collar. A few minutes later, his pitch came up short and he then narrowly missed his par effort, leaving Byron a careful two-putt for his first PGA Championship. At the presentation of the Wanamaker Cup, he reached over to offer a gracious hand to Sam, who shook and grinned. His left hand, however, firmly held the handle of the trophy he so desperately wanted to win. It was a telling moment—the first head-to-head outcome in a major that involved this great triumvirate.

A week later, just up the road in Scranton, Sam edged out Byron to capture the Anthracite Open.

Three months later, to close out the year, Byron fired three rounds in the 60s to beat Clayton Heafner by a stroke and won the Miami Open, where Ben Hogan finished third.

Days after Miami, a syndicated columnist from New York flew to Fort Worth to interview Ben in the members' grill at the Colonial Country Club, where Marvin Leonard's staff had already begun preparations to host the 1941 U.S. Open.

"How do you assess this year?" the columnist asked 1940's leading money winner, and Ben seemed more cordial and relaxed. He declined to talk about his past but had no problem addressing the season just ended. He complimented Byron and Sam and singled out his good friend Jimmy Demaret for particular praise. Excepting Sam, he explained, they'd all gone deer hunting in northern Texas only weeks before. The reporter later observed that he had a hard time picturing the three of them—the silent Ben, the genial Byron, and the outlandish Jimmy—together in the woods. Byron bagged a buck, however—and got socked with an eighty-dollar fine for not having a hunting license. "The year was very gratifying," Ben summed up, finishing his Coca-Cola. "But I've set my sights on winning major golf tournaments, and I still haven't done that." He thought for a moment and added, just so there was no confusion about the matter, "Until I manage to win a major tournament, I really won't be happy."

And with that, he excused himself and headed for perhaps the only place that made him truly happy—the practice range.

9

THE WAR WITHIN

G OOD PLAYERS WIN GOLF TOURNAMENTS, goes one of the game's simplest truths. Great players win major championships.

The North and South, the Western Open, the Metropolitan Open, and more and more the rapidly improving Masters were all considered just a notch below major status, titles any champion would be thrilled to claim. But they weren't the U.S. Open or the PGA crown, and with Britain now at war, the Open Championship, golf's oldest championship, was on hold and out of reach until further notice.

By the middle of 1941, the quality of American life itself was threatened by events that had already engulfed much of the world, and especially its closest ally. "There was kind of an eerie waiting that went on," Byron recalled. "Everyone knew it wouldn't be long until America joined the war against Germany, but we all tried to keep up normal life, so to speak, doing the things we'd always done." For Byron, who owned two major titles, and perhaps more urgently for Sam and Ben, who claimed none, this meant focusing their concentration more intensely than ever on winning a major championship before circumstances altered their opportunities. "Once Britain was in that thing," Sam remembered, "we all knew it was only a matter of time until even the tour got canceled. That put the hurry-up, let me tell you, in more than a few of us."

By the start of U.S. Open week at Marvin Leonard's magnificently groomed Colonial Golf Club in June of 1941, Sam had nearly fifty official and unofficial wins and had perhaps done more than any other single player to revive popular interest in the professional game. For him, winning a major championship would mean finally getting the monkey off his back and quieting the boo-birds of the press, some of whom openly doubted whether he could do so under pressure. Several influential sportswriters, most notably Grantland Rice, acknowledged the many positive effects of his yeoman popularity, but resented Sam's occasional crude antics and apparent indifference to their criticisms, not to mention his mercurial mood swings. Many were all too happy to question his resolve and knock his reputation down a peg or two.

For Byron Nelson, collecting another major championship trophy would simply burnish his already sterling reputation with the general public and the press, not to mention his past and present associations with Ridgewood, Reading, and Inverness, deepening friendships he carried with him wherever he went. From his point of view, winning a national championship was secondary to his reputation as a working golf club professional. The familiar duties and settled airs of club life were key components of Byron's personal happiness, in some ways the most enduring rewards of his career. As he confided to more than one friend, winning another major title would simply grant him the luxury of spending more time at home among friends and club members, doing what he loved best.

For Ben Hogan, finally, a major title would put even greater distance between himself and his carefully guarded childhood and the brutal years he'd spent struggling to master the game and coming up with little to show for it—nothing divided by nothing. "Ben's greatest struggle, I think, was always hidden pretty deep inside him," Byron remarked to a visitor to his ranch in the early '90s. "Almost from the day I first met him he was in a hurry to win something significant. And once he won, despite those unfortunate things—and maybe because of them—I don't believe there was anything that could possibly have stopped him."

Sam returned to action in 1941 with a rested body and a refortified attitude, quickly posting impressive wins at the Crosby Clambake, St. Petersburg, St. Augustine, and the North and South before turning his flashy new Cadillac into Magnolia Lane. On the downside, the new Mrs. Snead, a homebody at heart, found long-distance road travel and the social swirl on tour entirely to her disliking—the tedious hours on the road every week, the uncertainty of the food and lodgings, the boredom of waiting with gossipy spouses while Sam performed his magic on the course. Audrey didn't enjoy shopping or seeing the sights, and unlike her husband she wasn't a terribly stylish dresser, her tastes running to plain, sensible well-made dresses that could be bought off the rack cheaply at Sears. As natural as the mineral hills she'd grown up in—in this respect much like her husband—the former Valley High valedictorian and farmhand manager wasn't interested in social drinking or parties. Not surprisingly, almost from the beginning of their travels together, she made her displeasure known to Sam. The two sparred and argued, made up and moved on. "It was not a marriage made in heaven," notes Snead biographer Al Barkow. "It wasn't hell, either. It lived more or less in its anteroom—purgatory. It was a clash of fire and oil, of personalities that were, in some ways, too similar."

"Audrey and me had been arguin' since we were kids in the school yard," Sam once addressed the subject with a laugh. "But she sure didn't think much of life out on tour, that's for sure. I wasn't all that crazy about the travel, to tell the truth, though I do love drivin' a car just about anywhere I go. I got a big kick out of rollin' into a place where there was a big tournament, and bein' on the road helped me get my mind set around that, thinkin' about what I needed to do. But I think that's maybe why she didn't take to it at all. She wasn't really part of it. Audrey was a woman who had to have something to do—and at home there was always that." After months of mostly contentious travel, Audrey was homesick for Hot Springs and Sam was fed up with her refusal to go with the flow; they agreed she'd tend to things at home and think about starting a family while he took care of business on the road. As the East Coast portion of his schedule got going, Sam either went alone or invited his former traveling pals John Derr and Johnny Bulla along for the ride.

Byron, on the other hand, started slowly in 1941 and didn't really pick up his pace until just before the Masters, when at the Seminole Amateur-Professional Tournament he collected $803 for placing first and at least three times that amount in unofficial dough in the event's high-flying Calcutta. He also won at Greensboro by holding off the hard-charging reigning champion, Ben Hogan.

Of the three, Ben appeared to have the firmest resolve to win even as rumors circulated that the tour might suspend play as war loomed ever closer. In March, Roosevelt's Lend-Lease Act encouraged American companies to directly aid the besieged European democracies by selling, lending, or leasing critical war materials to the tune of $50 billion, the first step toward direct American involvement, and companies were already shifting to wartime mode, cutting back on consumer products in order to build reserves of rubber and steel. MacGregor, for instance, which Byron, Ben, and Jimmy Demaret represented on tour, had stopped manufacturing golf balls and clubs, converting its production floor in Dayton, Ohio, to making parachutes and aviation safety harnesses.

Almost overnight, there was a shortage of tournament-quality golf balls. For years Sam Snead loved to explain how, as the war effort deepened and material shortages led to rationing, he won several tournaments using the same golf ball for all four rounds; how he routinely scavenged lost balls from water hazards and often played with balls slightly out of round; how players sold or swapped excess equipment in the lobbies of their hotels. Another casualty of this period was the auto caravan that had defined the nomadic early tour. As gasoline and rubber grew noticeably scarce, many of the leading players, Hogan and Nelson among them, switched to traveling by train. Sam, however, stayed on the road.

In fourteen starts from January to June, Ben finished second six times and placed out of the top ten once. Teaming with his former critic Gene Sarazen, he lapped the field at the Miami Four-Ball and nearly defended his titles in Greensboro and Asheville. At the Masters, where he and Valerie dined with Bobby Jones for the first time, he had his best showing yet: fourth place. Byron, closing with a strong 70, finished second to Craig Wood, the likable Winged Foot pro and the first man to lead wire-to-wire. Wood, then thirty-nine, was perhaps the tournament's sentimental favorite, having been runner-up to Byron at the U.S. Open in 1939 and suffering an equally tough loss to Denny Shute at the British Open six years prior to that, losing both times in a playoff. It was also Craig Wood who was victimized by Sarazen's famous double-eagle blast at Augusta in 1935, losing that in the resulting playoff. The man who could most identify with losing a major in this manner, Sam Snead, opened with an untidy 73-75 and didn't find his footing until a final-round 69 left him tied with Vic Ghezzi.

Even under the threat of war—and maybe because of it—professional golf continued to enjoy growing public support. The Masters set new attendance records that spring, suggesting to some that Bobby Jones's boutique invitational had achieved "major" status. This continued a trend first seen in 1938, the year the governing USGA and PGA tour settled on a fourteen-club rule and more than sixty million rounds of golf were played, hundreds of public golf courses reopened, and more than half a million spectators turned out to watch some kind of golf tournament. Similar records were broken in 1940 and '41. With the reviving PGA Tour featuring twenty-one official events, purses totaled $185,500 (of which Sam Snead took home nearly $20,000) and tour manager Fred Corcoran required tournament sponsors to guarantee at least $5,000 for a 72-hole event. In the years immediately prior to the war, the Cleveland Open's $10,000 purse recalled the glory days of the late 1920s. At Augusta National, where not long before members were forced to pass the hat to keep the tournament alive, record gate receipts in 1941 confirmed not only that golf was on the upswing but also that Sam, Byron, and Ben were a primary reason why. Despite the loss of ten or so tournaments in 1939 and 1940 directly attributable to fuel and material rationing, professional golf bounced back in '41 with an increase in purses across the board.

During America's nervous early summer of 1941, as movie fans went to see Orson Welles's *Citizen Kane* and marveled at Joe DiMaggio's fifty-six-game hitting streak and the Nazi juggernaut rolled east into the Soviet Union, Byron and Ben were naturally considered the favorites for the U.S. Open in their own backyard at the Colonial Country Club in Fort Worth, followed closely by Sam, Jimmy Demaret, and Dallas native Lloyd Mangrum.

Despite a week of threatening weather, owing to Marvin Leonard's persuasive hustle and personal magnetism every civic club and organization in Fort Worth was involved in pre-tournament receptions and evening lawn parties. Hogan arrived home after a frustrating fourth-place finish at the Goodall Round Robin in New York (where at Toots Shor's he met Ted Williams, who when asked what shaking hands with Hogan was like tersely replied, "Bands of steel."). At Colonial, Ben stayed well out of sight, avoiding the hoopla and lunching with Royal (who was now reigning Colonial club champion, a title he held for many years) in the men's grill and working on his MacGregor Silver Scot irons in the workroom below the Colonial pro shop. Every afternoon following lunch, he and a caddie traipsed out to the ninth green for lengthy chipping and putting sessions, a privilege no other players enjoyed or even contemplated. Unlike many of the courses the tour played, Colonial boasted an expansive practice area, but the

Byron in his early twenties, probably not long after
he played in his first professional event

Well-mannered and waiting: early days
on the struggling PGA Tour

With Louise, not long after
their marriage in 1934

Mr. Golf's quest to perfect the swing coincided
with the arrival of steel shafts

Byron's famous "dip," at about the time of his first
major championship, the 1937 Masters

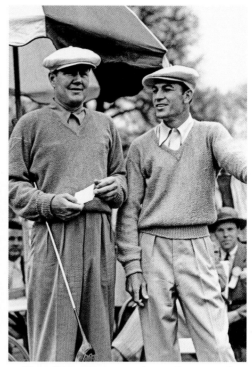

His second major title, the 1940
PGA Championship

Traveling partners early on, Byron and
Ben even shared tastes in clothing.

Friends and rivals: after Ben's breakthrough in 1940,
their relationship noticeably cooled.

Following the 1946 season, Byron became
a full-time farmer, part-time golfer.

A new life: Byron and Peggy
were married in 1984.

With his protégé Ken Venturi, the
1964 U.S. Open champion

The woodshop is where Byron felt
most at home in later years.

Augusta's longest running and most beloved starter

Hawk's growing preference for isolation reinforced a strengthening perception among his peers and tour scribes that Hogan did things his own damn way and didn't care what anyone thought about it.

With the press, Ben's growing image problems stemmed from a couple of well-publicized incidents in 1940 where he skipped town after winning a tournament, denying local reporters the opportunity to interview him and earning the wrath of both Fred Corcoran and the local sponsors, who needed every shred of good publicity their tournament could get. "Frankly, I was so excited to get to the next tournament and see what I could do, I just forgot to stick around for the interviews," Ben explained ineffectually. With a defensive edge that bordered at times on contempt and flat-out insincerity, he told one influential Midwestern columnist, "I sure didn't mean to offend anybody. But I have a job to do and that's winning golf tournaments." The only thing Ben really needed, his pal Demaret reminded those who were offended, was more hours of daylight for practice.

Rather than lingering to savor his long-pursued success and express his appreciation to admiring fans and sponsors, Ben appeared to grow even more oblivious to the protocols of gracious winning and even less tolerant of interviews of any kind. If a question annoyed or bothered him, for example, he simply ignored it or, even worse, fixed the reporter with a brief stare that wire-brushed him into silence. If it irked veteran reporters that his answers to legitimate questions were often miserly and curt, Ben was aggravated that many of them frequently took unreasonable liberties by carelessly misquoting his carefully parsed comments or taking them out of context. The end result, in any case, wasn't flattering. "He may be one of the best players in the game right now," a sports columnist for the powerful *Rocky Mountain News* complained after Ben collected his check and vacated the Denver tournament before anyone knew he was gone, "but he's certainly not making many friends where it counts—with reporters and fans."

In fairness to Ben, he appeared genuinely surprised by the vigor of the criticism provoked by what he considered unintended slights—and by doing what he believed was the only thing he was placed on this earth to do: win golf tournaments. In his ultra-pragmatic mind, moreover, winning merely helped make up for years of repeated failure, and underscored the fact that he needed to win everything he could before it all came to a screeching halt, for whatever reason. This kind of dark fatalism informed Ben's deep interior life and game much as it did his rival Snead's. "When Ben's around," Sam famously quipped about this time, "you can almost hear his watch ticking." As a world around them teetered on the edge of the abyss, both men were already fighting their own silent wars within.

Despite the large and enthusiastic crowds and lavish hospitality, the forty-fifth U.S. Open Championship failed to deliver the championship ending everyone hoped for. Fierce thunderstorms repeatedly halted play, flooding bunkers and greens and turning the fairways of Marvin Leonard's relatively young course into a quagmire, prompting one New York wag to cheekily label this the "Fort Worth Stockyards Invitational."

As crews fanned out under tumultuous skies and Leonard's watchful eye to squeegee greens and bail out sunken bunkers, the pros played cards and grumbled in the locker room. Convinced his game was rounding into top form right on schedule, Sam was eager to steal a national championship from under the noses of the Texas mafia in general and Ben and Byron in particular, only to tromp through the mud to a poorly managed opening-round 76, which he never recovered from, finishing in a tie for thirteenth in the final standings. Byron's campaign proved even more problematic. Staying with his parents on his new Denton spread north of town, shuttling into the tournament every morning by car and then encountering one rain delay after another, his tempo was hopelessly thrown off. He never found his comfort zone and finished in a tie for seventeenth place.

Of the three favorites, only Ben maintained anything close to his normal composure and focus. His sloppy second-round 77 came during the heaviest downpours but he finished the double-round finale with the lowest score for the 36-hole closing day at 68-70, a 289 total that put him in third behind Denny Shute and the eventual winner, Craig Wood—the only bright spot in an otherwise dismal week.

At least Wood's success made for a poignant and compelling conclusion. Days before the tournament started, he pulled a muscle and feared his ailing back wouldn't stand up to the pressure of an Open chase. A customized orthopedic back brace helped ease the searing pain but significantly constricted his golf swing. Only after Silver Scot Tommy Armour, fortified by nips from his hip flask, passionately urged him to carry on did Wood strap the brace back on and take his chances, expecting little or nothing in return. In fact, the pleasant New Yorker played masterfully, never missing a fairway over the final eighteen and finished at 284, giving the waterlogged fans of Fort Worth something to cheer about, and finally claiming a title that had eluded him for so long.

To anyone in search of a message, Wood's dogged persistence and triumph over adversity spoke volumes about what it takes to win major championships. U.S. Opens in particular are endurance contests where the plodding tortoise often fares better than the bolting hare. Every time Ben crept a little higher up the final leaderboard of a major, as he did at Colonial that year, his confidence in his own abilities grew exponentially. "The greatest thing Ben had to finally overcome," says Jackie Burke Jr., the Masters and PGA champ of 1956, who became a preferred practice partner and one of his closest friends on tour, "was the powerful insecurity he battled most of his life. There was no question he had all the shots by 1940—nobody was better prepared in that regard than Ben, frankly. But winning major championships requires a special kind of confidence few players ever acquire, and those who acquire it never seem to be able to keep it long. That's what finally made Ben so unique. Once it finally came together, once he finally got those big hands of his around it, once he found *that* kind of confidence, hell, he almost couldn't be beaten."

Byron addressed the elusive topic in a conversation with Al Barkow some years later. "Is there a psychology for winning? I don't understand the psychological function of the human mind sufficiently to answer that very well, except to say that winners are different. They're a different breed of cat. I think the reason is, they have an inner drive and are willing to give of themselves whatever it takes to win. It's a discipline that a lot of people are not willing to impose on themselves."

A poignant footnote to Marvin Leonard's one and only national Open underscores this point. Following the presentation of the trophy, during the drive back to his hotel in downtown Fort Worth with tour impresario Fred Corcoran, Wood found himself gazing out the window at a lighted driving range where patrons were beating balls into a clearing evening sky.

"Want to stop and hit a bucket?" Corcoran asked, giving a good Irish chuckle. "Just to keep the back loose?" He later explained that he'd been joking.

Wood needed only an instant. "Yeah," he said, "let's do that."

To the surprise and astonishment of the range's patrons, America's new national golf champion got out, paid his money, and hit a bucket of balls. Perhaps Wood appreciated how fortunate he'd been, trussed up in a corset, to claim a prize the three hottest players in the game were desperate to win. Or perhaps he sensed, as he later admitted to close friends at Winged Foot, how quickly the magic of success arrived and vanished in American sports, like moonlight on the water. Today's news wrapped tomorrow's fish, particularly in tournament golf.

In any event, classy Craig Wood had finally won the events he'd long dreamed of winning, the Masters and the U.S. Open, both in the same year. Maybe, as he hit shot after shot into the pleated evening sky over Fort Worth, prompting bursts of vigorous applause from the lucky hackers gathered around watching this extraordinary impromptu exhibition, he had a premonition that this would be his final moment in the light of victory. He would return to his job at Winged Foot a deeply grateful and satisfied man, winning only two more times before his game abandoned him for good.

As for Ben, if there was a message in his brilliant closing rounds of 68-70 in fitful conditions over one of the toughest Open courses, his score of 289 would actually have won three previous championships and seemed to suggest he now understood how to finish off a major with a cold killer's efficiency.

True to form, however, he took no consolation from his best Open showing to date. Within hours he was packing for a train ride up to the new Mahoning Valley Open in Ohio, where he took a third, then carried on to Toledo for Byron's Inverness Four-Ball, where he teamed with Jimmy Demaret to run the table. After losing to Byron two-and-one in the quarterfinal at the PGA—whereupon Vic Ghezzi subsequently beat Byron one-up in a taut thirty-eight-hole final to claim the Wanamaker Trophy—Ben went on a tear to conclude the season, winning in Chicago and at his own Hershey event, in total claiming second place at five of the six remaining tournaments to finish as the tour's leading money winner—with $18,734—and the game's most maddeningly elusive star.

After Fort Worth's Open, Byron went on a modest tear of his own, placing second at Mahoning Valley, and then winning George S. May's inaugural Tam O'Shanter Open outside Chicago, whose first prize was a tour-best $2,000 check. Before returning to Texarkana to spend the holidays with Louise's family, he captured opens in Ohio and Miami to earn $13,526 in official money.

That was just $650 more than Sam, yet because two of Byron's wins came at unofficial events he wound up as second-leading money winner, producing a final standing of Hogan, Snead, and Nelson, one, two, three, in the money race, a perfect snapshot of each man's psychological motivation. Sam likewise went on a post-Open run and collected victories at the Canadian and the Rochester Times Union opens followed by a blistering Henry Hurst Invitational, where he won by carding three rounds in the mid-60s.

That December, while tooling with his friend John Derr down to Miami's season-ending tournament in his Cadillac, Sam confided that he believed his game was poised to finally end his biggest hex. "Despite the fact that Ben and Byron were getting as much or even more attention than he was, Sam felt his game had finally matured to the point where something like a Spring Mill disaster could never happen again. He was ready to claim a major—but the question that haunted everybody, and maybe Sam most of all, would there even *be* another major championship anytime soon?"

An answer of sorts came during their drive. "It was a beautiful Sunday and we were going down a week early so Sam could practice and enjoy the warm weather, having a great time talking about everything from baseball to women," Derr recalls. "I think we were somewhere in Georgia and had stopped for gas. It was late in the afternoon. We had the radio on and suddenly the announcer was telling us that the Japanese had bombed Pearl Harbor. I couldn't believe it. I remember Sam just listening and shaking his head. All he said was something like, 'Them sorry sons-a-bitches.' It was all pretty solemn after that, very little bantering. We got down to Miami and everything had suddenly changed. It was all about business but the war was on everyone's mind. There was talk that the tour would shut down immediately. Nobody had a clue what might come next. Suddenly every shot, some guys figured, might be the last one in competition for a while. Sam was particularly concerned about that. He wanted that major championship more than anything and feared he'd been jinxed one more time—this time by the Japanese."

Byron blistered the Miami Lakes course with three rounds in the low 60s to win with a total of 269. Ben and Sam both had three rounds in the 60s, with Ben finishing at 274 and Sam one back of that, a one, two, three conclusion that seemed to splendidly summarize the state of professional golf.

Despite America's entry into the war, in 1942 the tour mounted twenty-one tournaments, with a collective purse of $116,000, before concluding in late summer at Byron's Inverness Four-Ball in Toledo. President Roosevelt, a lifelong fan of the game and a solid mid-handicapper player when younger, urged Fred Corcoran to keep professional golf going as a morale booster.

Ben played in twenty-one events, Byron in twenty, Sam in fourteen. The Hawk's private war for major acceptance began at the season-opening L.A. Open, where he carved a magnificent four-iron shot to the final hole and sank a clutch birdie putt to tie long-hitting Jimmy Thomson, and then beat him in the playoff, the first of his career and an excellent omen. Sam placed third, Byron sixth. The battlefield shifted to Oakland, where Byron cruised to a five-stroke victory. Next came San Francisco, where Ben and Byron dined with Francis Ouimet's pie-faced Brookline caddie, Eddie Lowery, who'd migrated to California and had done exceedingly well in the car business. Here Ben nailed down his second win despite the brief maddening return of a hook that had him aiming well right of most fairways, according to Byron; Sam finished second.

On they went to the Texas Open, where a weak putt on the final hole kept Sam out of the playoff between Ben and the eventual winner, Chick Harbert. The next week, at the rain-shortened New Orleans Open, Sam lost a playoff to Lloyd Mangrum, then went home to Hot Springs for a brief rest before driving to Florida and winning the St. Petersburg Open and St. Augustine Pro-Amateur back to back. In between he nearly won the fifth Seminole Amateur-Professional, an unofficial event that had golf's richest Calcutta; in 1939 the club gained unwanted national headlines for a wagering pool that topped $48,000. In Ben's second Seminole appearance, he became better acquainted with another invited guest, George Coleman, a future Oklahoma state champion he'd first met back at the lavish Agua Caliente in 1932 when both men had mostly lint in their pockets. Born to wealth the same year as Ben, Coleman had already made his first fortune in oil—an elegant, beautifully spoken man who would develop close friendships with both Byron and, especially, Ben, who fell under the spell of every-thing he saw at Seminole and grew to regard George Coleman as a brother. Founded with little fanfare by millionaire E. F. Hutton and his cronies in the snake-infested mangrove jungles of Juno Beach shortly before the stock market crashed in 1929, the club was ultra-discreet and dedicated to personal privacy, the ultimate sporting retreat for well-made men and their guests, offering a golf course widely hailed to be designer Donald Ross's finest work.

Its patrons numbered Pulitzers and Vanderbilts, wintering Holly-wood movie stars, barons of Wall Street and occasional British royalty, and its elegant pink-stucco clubhouse, designed by society architect Marion Wyeth, featured a swimming pool where some members origi-nally preferred to swim in the nude and—more important—a simple but magnificent wood-paneled locker room that would eventually become the envy of private clubs everywhere. Everything about the course pleased Ben's increasingly critical eye, especially the daunt-ing uphill sixth, a par-four that turned slightly left to right and whose sliver of a heavily bunkered green required a flawless approach shot. In time, Ben told his good friend Henry Picard—destined to become Seminole's sixth head professional in 1956—that it was his favorite hole in all of golf. Byron himself went on the record to call the place "Just about the finest club I have ever seen, full of very warm and friendly people." In the 1942 tournament, Ben finished third, three strokes behind Sam and four ahead of Byron.

Beginning the important Carolina swing and tuning up for the Masters, with dogwoods struggling to bloom along the fairways of Pinehurst No. 2, Ben and Byron opened the North and South Open Championship with sterling 69s, with Sam just a stroke behind. By the time four thousand spectators ringed the seventy-second green in a chilly spring twilight, to no one's particular surprise it was Hogan who had mounted a blistering ten-under assault during the final thirty-six to beat his top rivals, Snead and Nelson. One, two, three . . . again. A Charlotte sportswriter wondered if professional golf was a three-horse race, noting it was only a question of when—not if—the tour would cease operations.

Days later in Greensboro, former New York Yankee slugger Sam Byrd slipped past all three to win, though Ben claimed second place. At the next stop, the Land of the Sky tournament in Asheville, Ben made up for what he considered a poor finish at Greensboro by lapping the field at the posh Biltmore Forest Golf Club, another of his cherished Donald Ross courses, and winning for the third time in a row.

The Masters of 1942 would be last played before it, too, was shut down in a time of worldwide crisis—and surely among the most memorable. Ben, Sam, and Byron, the tour's leading money winners, were naturally the favorites. Many have even posited that this was the moment when the Masters, featuring the first live radio broadcast by NBC, achieved its major championship status. The bucolic setting in the lush grounds of a former horticultural nursery, and the sweet familiarity of a tournament guided and shaped by the enduring presence of Bobby Jones, attracted more and more national attention with the advent of every spring, especially from weary sportwriters slogging home from spring training baseball. "For many of us it was a genuine reprieve from our regular duties covering baseball," John Derr says, "and a chance to rub elbows with the royalty of golf. Cliff Roberts made sure the reporters were treated like patrons, a strategy few other tournament directors picked up on until well after the war. I don't know if '42 was the year it became a major event in most minds, but it was surely well along that road in a hurry. That's why nobody wanted to see golf stop."

And this year, like a gift from the gods meant to carry for the war's duration, the Masters provided a championship for the ages, a nip-and-tuck scrimmage between Byron and Ben that saw the latter take on twenty-eight putts in the second round, amid a wild and swirling wind that shredded virtually every other score in the field. "Best managing I ever did out there," he calmly explained in the locker room. "I mean manipulating the ball, allowing for wind and roll. You had to do that in that wind." Despite Ben's impressive 68, Byron led him by three strokes as they headed into the weekend play. Sam opened with a sloppy 78, complained of a bad back and never recovered enough to figure better than seventh. As the *Augusta Chronicle* reported, in the strange final round Byron seemed to have only bad luck and Ben nothing but good luck. Yet Byron arrived at the final two holes of regulation needing just two pars to beat Ben, who twenty minutes before had coolly dropped a six-footer to narrow the lead to a stroke and posted 280.

A weak approach shot at seventeen, however, left Byron buried in the bunker with a fried-egg lie that cost him a bogey on the swift and grainy Bermuda green. He now needed a birdie on eighteen to win. Unfortunately, attempting to steer his drive close to the inside of the dogleg to give himself a better angle at the steep uphill final green, he pushed his ball into the trees on the right and found it sitting atop a heavy clump of grass and pine needles. Gripping down on a five-iron, he miraculously hooked a shot through a narrow gap and somehow coaxed it onto the putting surface, ending fifteen feet from the cup. Minutes later, his birdie attempt lipped out, producing a sharp gasp of disappointment from the crush of spectators wedged around the green. Byron tapped in for par, removed his cap and smiled, clearly showing the stress of the day. The Monday playoff would begin at two-thirty, patrons learned.

That night at the Bon Air Vanderbilt, Byron slept fitfully, waking several times to a stomach that was in knots, producing several bouts of vomiting. The following morning, Ben knocked on his door and, discovering his old friend and rival in a pale and unsteady state, offered to postpone their match. Byron thanked him but declined. Later that summer, he confided to close friends at Inverness that just like Bobby Jones, his stomach sometimes caused him distress before a critical match. His hero's cure was a steaming bath and several fingers of good corn whiskey, preferably well-aged bourbon, whereas Byron opted for a bland chicken sandwich and a cup of warm tea, hoping to keep that down until his nerves settled. More than nerves were on edge, however. During the train ride from Asheville to Augusta with Louise and his good friend Jug McSpaden, the two men calculated that by banking $100,000 in winnings each could live comfortably off the interest and never have to tour again. Still harboring secret hopes that Byron might change his mind about adopting a child, Louise made no attempt to mask her growing disaffection for life on the road, reserving travel now primarily for major events like the Masters and the U.S. Open. Though Byron owned the ranch where his parents lived in Texas, the couple constantly talked about finding a place all their own and putting down more permanent roots. Louise favored a certain neighborhood in Dallas; Byron, who was thirty years old that spring, and approaching the end of his prime by the standards of any other sport, pictured a spread out in the country near his folks in Denton. Ever since childhood, he'd dreamed of owning a ranch.

The fatigue many had perceived in Byron's gait and facial expressions was largely psychological. In the heat of competition, he rarely smiled, prompting some to conclude that, as it had with Jones, tournament golf was becoming a great burden to bear. And in fact, his

happiest days were spent teaching at Inverness, performing exhibitions, interacting with members, and playing challenge matches with
friends and promising young players. The tension of a major championship only exacerbated his nervous stomach and made him privately
yearn for a simpler life, the sooner the better.

Testifying to the significance of this playoff for the coveted Masters medallion of 1942—the signature green jacket wouldn't be introduced until 1949 (the year Sam captured his first Masters)—at least
twenty-five touring pros hung around to see Hogan and Nelson decide
the matter, among fifteen hundred spectators who skipped work to follow the action. "Here for all intents and purposes were the two best
players in the game," Henry Picard explained years later, "and I don't
know anyone who wanted to miss it except perhaps Sam Snead. I don't
recall seeing Sam there. I suspect he cleared out fast. He didn't need to
be reminded what the three of them were chasing."

From the outset, Byron played like a man who'd been throwing up
all night. He opened with a towering slice into the pines that required
him to poke the ball back into the fairway with a putter held in his
left hand, resulting in a double-bogey against Ben's par-four. Several
times he paused and blew his nose. But on the par-five second hole, he
struck a rousing low-iron shot onto the green and just missed making
eagle. Both men birdied. After five holes, however, he found himself
three down.

Among his many graces, Byron Nelson always possessed an almost
magical talent for escaping disaster. On the par-three sixth, he laid his
tee shot ten feet from the cup and smoothly rolled home the birdie as
Ben missed left and made bogey, losing two strokes of his lead. Then,
on the long par-five eighth, Byron unleashed a 280-yard drive and
carved a spectacular three-iron shot to six feet, canning his second
eagle opportunity to take the lead by one. On the downhill tenth, Ben
missed the green and made bogey to go two down. At the par-three
twelve, in the verdant heart of "Amen Corner," Byron nearly holed a
seven-iron and tapped in for a birdie that placed him three up with six
to play.

But Ben, who'd never beaten him in a playoff, refused to give up. Ban-
ishing all thoughts of Glen Garden and the Texas Open from his mind,
he kept coming like a trained killer, silent, methodical, his bright gray
raptor's eyes seeing only the beautiful green battlefield ahead of him.
He drained a clutch fifteen-footer at the fourteenth to cut Byron's lead

by a third. On fifteen he made another birdie while Byron three-putted for par. The lead had shrunk to one.

Ben had the honor at sixteen but pushed his tee shot into the right-side bunker, staring at it disbelievingly for several seconds. Byron then struck one of the finest clutch shots of all time, dropping his ball thirty inches from the cup. He missed the short sloping putt but Ben made bogey from the sand. The lead was now back to two.

That's how they arrived at the final green, greeted by a rising tsunami of appreciative applause from a gallery that included their contemporaries and a large contingent of young men already in uniform. Both had left their approach shots in the deep bunker fronting the green, and both played fine explosion shots to eight feet. Byron putted first, his ball stopping just shy of the cup, and he tapped in for bogey. Ben took only a moment before rolling his par putt home, cutting the final margin, once again, to a single shot: Ben 70, Byron 69.

They removed their identical flat linen caps, made by the same Times Square hatter, smiled cordially and shook hands. All over again, Ben was the soul of gracious in defeat. Up the slope in the applauding gallery, their wives exchanged long, tearful hugs, Louise knowing all too well how painful this was for Valerie. It was Glen Garden and the Texas Open writ larger than ever.

A few minutes later, Alfred Bourne, the head of the Singer Sewing Machine Company and a prominent Augusta member, playfully signed the winner's check for $1,500 on the champion's back. Someone in the press reminded Byron that, prior to the match, he'd promised to reveal his secret to playing Augusta National—assuming he won.

"Always shoot for greens," he said, visibly relieved to have it over with. "Try and avoid the bunkers. And never go for a dangerous flag position." This was his own version of "course strategy."

"How do you think you did today against Ben?" he was also asked. Byron took a moment to answer.

"Except for the first hole," he said gently, perhaps attempting to soften the blow for his long-suffering friend and rival, "I think that was the finest round I ever shot."

For Sam and Ben, redemption of a kind came within weeks.

A week before the start of the PGA Championship at the Seaview Country Club outside Atlantic City, New Jersey, Sam drove to Norfolk to enlist in the navy. "My thinking there was that they might station me right there, close to home, where I knew a good number of folks and some of the better golf courses," he laughingly explained years later. "But I guess that was pretty naive thinking."

At the time, he told several recruiting officers, including, he claimed, an admiral who turned up to have their photos made with him, "The PGA Championship is next week up in New Jersey. They're planning to cancel play until this thing is over and I'd like one more shot at a title. Will that be a problem?"

"Oh, we'll give you a pass for that, don't you worry," one of them assured him. "You just go ahead and sign."

Something, however, told Sam to wait. "I thought about my wife, Audrey, and about the three thousand dollar purse and the two thousand dollar bonus from Wilson [if he won], and I decided the rest of the boys could handle Tojo all right for just one more week." He asked if his induction could be delayed a week, and the brass reluctantly agreed. It turned out to be perhaps the wisest—and most challenging—decision of his playing career.

Though other top stars were signing up to serve as well, the most competitive field of the year began grueling match play in the final week of May on the relatively short but demandingly tight composite course that drew from Seaview's Bay and Pines eighteens, layouts to which Donald Ross, Howard Toomey, and William Flynn had all contributed design work.

En route to the thirty-six finale, Sam beat Vic Ghezzi, red-hot Sam Byrd, an aging Willie Goggin, PGA president Ed Dudley, and ever-dangerous Jimmy Demaret, who playfully advised Sam *not* to wear his sailor's cap in his match against Corporal Jim Turnesa, who was on leave from the army's nearby Fort Dix and had brought along a throng of seven thousand GIs to cheer him along. "This crowd isn't exactly pulling for you," Dudley had remarked to Sam earlier in the tournament. The hostility, Sam later learned, stemmed from a rumor circulating that he'd attempted to dodge his enlistment—and that it was the navy only doubled the offense, hence Demaret's joke.

Turnesa is quite a story himself, one of the seven sons born to Vitale and Anna Turnesa, who'd immigrated from Naples, Italy, to Elmford, New York, in 1904. All the boys became prolific golfers, creating perhaps the game's most storied family dynasty. Phil, Frank, and Doug became outstanding teaching professionals. Joe, Mike, and Jim

migrated from the amateur ranks to the tour in the 1940s and early
'50s, between them winning dozens of events, reaching the final of
every major championship, having played on both the Walker Cup
and Ryder Cup teams. With help from his older brothers, the youngest
Turnesa, Willie, attended the College of the Holy Cross and went on
to have an amateur career that rivaled Bobby Jones's. Upon hearing
that he'd won the U.S. Amateur at Oakmont in 1938, the story goes, the
patriarch Vitale supposedly declared, "Why shouldn't he win? All he
does is play golf!"

Jim, short and trim and unusually quiet by nature, the second
youngest, born the same year as Sam, reached the final by eliminating
Dutch Harrison and Jug McSpaden, and then the country's two hottest
players, Ben and Byron—all of which produced an avalanche of sports
headlines from just up the Hudson that immediately transformed Jim
Turnesa into a star and poster boy for the American GI.

On the eighth hole of their Saturday double-round match, Turnesa
dropped a fifteen-foot birdie putt and Sam missed his. On the thirteenth, he drained a thirty-five-footer that electrified the troops, then
followed up by holing a sensational bunker blast on the sixteenth that
set them off even more explosively. Sam appeared shaken, in part
because on several holes friendly soldiers kicked Turnesa's wayward
drives back into the fairway, but also because the openly partisan gallery raised such a ruckus and razzed Sam so fiercely that at one point
Dudley had to step in and request them to calm down or risk being
"invited" to leave the grounds. Turnesa himself attempted to quiet the
crowd, and afterward Sam quickly pointed out that Turnesa was a true
gentleman throughout.

After twenty-three holes, however, Sam was three down and
struggling to maintain his composure. A twelve-foot par save on the
next hole, which Turnesa bogeyed, narrowed the lead to two. By the
twenty-eighth hole, Sam had drawn dead even and noticed Jim taking several extra waggles, a subtle sign he was beginning to feel the
pressure of the moment. After missing the green at the thirtieth hole,
Turnesa missed an easy par putt to give Sam the lead, producing a chorus of boos and grumbles. A short time later, on the short thirty-fifth
hole of play, suddenly "feeling as confident and loose as I ever felt in
a finish," Sam struck a beautiful seven-iron shot that flew 160 yards
and dropped into the cup to close out the championship like a bolt of
lightning.

He stood for a moment in the buttery late-afternoon light, a broad smile spreading across his handsome features. He reflected that upon winning his first major championship—the most important title of his career, he always claimed—he uncharacteristically heard neither the cheers nor the catcalls from the gallery. "It ended so damn fast," he quipped, "I almost forgot to notice."

At the presentation ceremony, he congratulated the game's newest star and wished him well. Six years later, Turnesa would finish second to Ben Hogan in the same major championship, then finally claim it himself in 1952, a lovely story of one man's persistence.

But for now it was Sam Snead's golden moment, his long-awaited redemption. He playfully kissed the Wanamaker Trophy and held it up to a large ovation from a crowd including many soldiers whose minds were apparently changed by the strength of this dazzling finish by golf's most colorful star, and they weren't the only detractors his victory finally silenced. For once, the press couldn't heap enough praise on his impressive come-from-behind win in enemy territory.

On Sunday morning, Sam woke up the new PGA champion and would remain so for the war's duration. "I never had a better feeling in my life," he remembered. "The only thing that brought it down some was the fact that golf was pretty much done for the time being. None of us had any idea when it might come back—or even if it would."

On Monday morning, he drove back to Norfolk and signed his enlistment form, officially making him a seaman first class in the Special Services of the United States Navy.

Sam—deep in the rigors of basic training, though treated as something of a VIP—wasn't granted a furlough for the Hale America National Open that was held three weeks later outside Chicago at the pretty Ridgemoor Country Club. The tournament was a one-time affair, co-sponsored by the Chicago District Golf Association and the USGA, meant to serve as a fund-raiser for the Navy Relief Society and the United Service Organization, and designed to heighten public enthusiasm for buying war bonds. Millions of fans failed to grasp that it was a replacement event for the officially suspended U.S. Open Championship.

To help drive home the point that all Americans needed to chip in and do their part, newly commissioned Captain Robert Tyre Jones Jr., fresh from intelligence training in Harrisburg, Pennsylvania, showed up in his new Army Air Corps uniform to play a practice round with Ben Hogan. Because of a painful varicose vein condition, Jones had actually been classified 4-F—meaning he was physically unfit for service—but argued persuasively that a legendary sportsman in uniform might do wonders for recruitment. Following his practice round, he remarked to PGA president Ed Dudley and Charlie Bartlett of the *Chicago Tribune*, "I have never seen anyone who works as hard at this game as Ben Hogan does. He is remarkable and an inspiration."

In a well-publicized pre-tournament charity event, Ben allowed his red-hot Spalding putter to be auctioned off, netting $1,500 for navy relief. The gesture was seen as one of tremendous generosity and patriotism—though it maybe wasn't as altruistic as it appeared on first glance. Back home in Fort Worth, he'd been trying out a new center-shafted model whose head was made from a melted-down doorknob. On the threshold of enlisting himself, he had already decided this would be the putter to carry him into postwar tournament action, if and when the tour resumed.

After opening with a mediocre 72, he shellacked the field with 62-69-68 to cakewalk to the tournament's title, winning $1,200 in war bonds and a "victory" medallion nearly identical to the bronze medal presented by the USGA to its national Open winners. For the record, Byron played well, too, finishing seven strokes back in fourth place.

In the locker room afterward, Ben appeared uncharacteristically happy and approachable—almost as if he believed he'd actually won the U.S. Open. Reporters discovered that he, in fact, believed exactly that—that he'd finally won a major. When asked if he considered this his major breakthrough, Ben blinked hard at the questioner and replied without hesitation, "Yes. I think given the quality of this field it's a major championship." Whereupon he gave a wintry little smile and added, "At least I feel that way. Don't know about you boys."

The reporters laughed. Most of them, it turned out, didn't share Ben's opinion of the Hale America Open and its ersatz bronze medal, and neither did the blue sports coats of the USGA. For many weeks, however, a gentlemanly debate was waged in the pages of America's newspapers. Ben's own growing ranks of fans were multiplying, and many of them regarded the Hale America as a legitimate major, and wrote letters to the USGA demanding that it be recognized as such. But in the end, the win counted only as a standard tour victory.

In early August, after many of his contemporaries had signed up to serve in some capacity or another, Ben was unable to let go of the reins and finished fourth in the Canadian Open, and then won the Rochester Open on his way back to Fort Worth. This pushed him to the top of the money list for 1942, a $13,143 total that just edged out Byron Nelson and Sam Snead—a powerful glimpse of the postwar world to come.

10

Mr. Golf

Sixteen million Americans, about 13 percent of the nation's population, answered the call of duty in the Second World War, and more than half were enlistments. Despite President Roosevelt's hope that golf could boost morale on the home front, the PGA mounted only three official events in 1943—in part because gas rationing and other shortages meant almost nobody was traveling more than a few miles by car, but also because in some cases there were scarcely enough quality players to fill out a competitive field. Ten days after the attack on Pearl Harbor, the Office of Price Administration issued an order reducing production of new golf balls by 80 percent, and within days a similar order halted club manufacturing entirely.

Despite the War Commission's message urging Americans to get out and play golf, roughly a third of the nation's courses and clubs shut down for the duration. Those clubs that remained open did so with skeletal maintenance crews that allowed grass to fill bunkers and narrowed fairways and removed rough entirely to reduce the need for mowing. Some shortened their course to nine holes and used the rest for victory gardens. Wykagyl Golf Club in New York, for instance, plowed up two holes to provide home gardens for its sixty members. At nearby Westchester Country Club, divers were hired to collect golf balls from the ponds, and an Atlanta country club actually drained its ponds, netting sixteen thousand balls for reprocessing. These foundlings generally performed at only 70 percent of their initial capabilities, though scientists at DuPont soon developed a synthetic rubber substitute that made them more reliable (a material still used in the golf balls of today).

Bobby Jones had been among the first to sign up after he and Clifford Roberts jointly decided to close Augusta National immediately after the 1942 Masters, hiring a wartime caretaker to raise turkeys and look after the two hundred head of steers purchased to graze on its idle fairways. The tour's leading names followed suit. Long-hitting Jimmy Thomson went to the coast guard, and Henry Ransom the merchant marine. Lawson Little, the son of an army colonel, became a navy officer. Snead, Jimmy Demaret, Herman Keiser, and a young Lew Worsham also joined the navy. Lloyd Mangrum, Dutch Harrison, Clayton Heafner, Jim Ferrier, Horton Smith, and Vic Ghezzi signed up for the army. Most of these pros wound up staying stateside, stationed at bases where they essentially played golf with top military brass, though Herman Keiser spent thirty-six months at sea and Ghezzi, Smith, Heafner, and Lloyd Mangrum all served overseas. At the Battle of the Bulge, Mangrum sustained a serious leg wound and was awarded a pair of Purple Hearts. Jones himself went ashore with the intelligence unit of the Ninth Army Air Corps on D-Day-plus-one and hunkered down through several nights of enemy shelling.

William B. Hogan reported for active duty in the Army Air Forces on March 25, 1943. Valerie drove him to the Tarrant County Courthouse, where inductees were put on a bus bound for basic training outside Fort Worth. The night before, Ben presented her a star sapphire ring. "I don't know when I'll be able to give you another gift," he said, "so I want to give you this before I go." She slipped the ring on her finger and never took it off again.

He requested she leave before his bus arrived. It was only a short ride out to the recently renamed Tarrant Field.

"I don't want to leave," she insisted. "I want to stay until the bus pulls away."

"I want you to leave," he repeated, displaying his usual mineral resolve.

Years later, she recalled, "I realized he didn't want to tell me goodbye with the bus there." So she left.

Lacking a high school diploma, Ben was assigned the rank of private. His decision to join the air forces was a curiously Hoganesque one. He was terrified of flying, but later confided to close Shady Oaks friends that, true to form, there was a strong element of calculated pragmatism to his choice. Texas and Oklahoma were home to most of the top flight training camps, enhancing his chances of staying closer to home. Beyond this—and far more psychologically rooted—Ben fancied learning to fly in order to conquer yet another fear. "His whole life up till then had been about confronting his fears and beating them to a pulp," explained a regular lunch companion for more than three decades. "For Ben, learning to fly an airplane was all about taking control of that fear and beating it down. I'm not the least bit surprised he chose the air force."

Ben himself said as much when he told a reporter from Dallas, "I've never really flown very much, and I'm eager to see what flying is all about. A number of golfers have taken to flying between tournaments. Perhaps, if I become a pilot, I might also."

After basic training—during which he used money from his own pocket to purchase cleaning solutions for his unit's barracks—he was shipped to Officer Candidate School in Miami. "I'm eager and willing to do whatever the Army needs me to do," he told the *Star-Telegram*. "And I'm pretty sure that doesn't mean playing much tournament golf. From now on, I think most of my golf is going to be played only on Sundays."

In November of 1943, Valerie proudly pinned the new gold bars of a second lieutenant's rank on her husband's shoulder, and the newly designated squadron leader complained that his unit had not yet managed to win the weekly marching pennant. "He really worked his men," she told a reporter back home some years later. "One of them was Mark Payne, the architect who years later would design our Fort Worth home. Mark later told me, 'Ben was the toughest officer we had. He nearly killed us.' Finally Ben's squadron won the marching pennant. He was so happy, and so typical. Golf or marching, he had to win something."

Assigned to a newly formed Civilian Pilot Training Program designed to pump out interim instructors who could teach basic techniques to younger combat pilots, Ben was shipped off to air bases in Texas, Arkansas, and Louisiana for his own flight training, ultimately winding up at the Spartan School of Aerodynamics in Tulsa. In an article published not long after he arrived, the *Tulsa World* announced that "Hogan Gives Up Golf" yet noted that he'd already played in at least two dozen Red Cross exhibitions, helping to raise much needed money for other service-related charities as well. During one of these matches at prestigious Southern Hills—a Perry Maxwell design that would eventually host three U.S. Opens—a lean and smiling Lieutenant Ben Hogan assured reporters that he felt confident he would soon be "sent overseas to join the action."

"I frankly think Ben enjoyed being out of the tournament world for a time," reflected Tex Moncrief, his longtime friend from the Rivercrest Country Club and Colonial. "It was a good time for him to step back and think about how far he'd come and what he might do when things swung back into action. I also think he really did want to go abroad and serve the way Bob Jones and others did. Ben had the heart of a lion, and in that regard he really was fearless. I'm sure he would have served with distinction over there."

But owing to his age and fame—thirty was old for a combat pilot, and his status as a celebrity made him a figure much in demand among golf-loving generals—that was simply not in the cards. By early 1944, experienced combat pilots were being furloughed in droves, and Lieutenant Hogan's talents as a pilot, whatever their level of proficiency, were no longer needed. Like others in his situation, he was sent home and allowed to put on civilian clothes and lead a fairly normal life. The Hogans found a pretty garden apartment out on Camp Bowie Boulevard and Ben worked on his game at Colonial and nearby Ridglea Country Club, played friendly matches with brother, Royal, and even ventured off to special "victory" tournaments in Dallas and Chicago, where he hobnobbed with Bob Hope and Bing Crosby to raise funds for the USO, counting the days until Germany and Japan were defeated and another kind of warfare was resumed.

Seaman First Class Sam Snead had pretty much the same wartime experience, only in navy-issue fatigues. Following basic training at Norfolk, he was scheduled to be shipped to Pensacola to teach gunnery techniques to budding pilots. Instead, owing to his fame and proximity to Washington, the brass kept him in Norfolk playing with admirals and visiting dignitaries and teaching the game to pilots, also putting on the occasional charity exhibition. He spent the concluding months of his service in La Jolla, California, playing golf with surgeons and high-ranking officers on some of Southern California's better layouts. "I got to play plenty of golf in the service," he later told biographer George Mendoza. "No question I was lucky, being able to continue doing what I do best while those other boys were out there giving their lives. I'm very grateful for it."

He added, "Winning the 1942 PGA seemed to prove to the world— and to me—that I'd managed to learn something during those years.

And as my tour of duty came to an end, I was rubbing my hands. Once I got back on the tour, I felt sure it was going to be Katy-bar-the-door. I felt alive again."

Byron Nelson was turned down for military service. The culprit was a previously undiagnosed blood-clotting problem the press broadly interpreted as a form of hemophilia. Days after his rejection in early 1943, PGA president Ed Dudley invited him to contribute to the cause by participating in a series of exhibition matches for the Red Cross and USO being arranged by Fred Corcoran. His pal Jug McSpaden, also rejected because of a sinus condition, had already signed up. Byron enthusiastically agreed and the two of them—dubbed the "Gold Dust Twins" by a Midwestern newspaperman—did 110 exhibitions, criss-crossing the nation on troop trains and military aircraft dozens of times between late 1942 and early 1944. Along the way, they visited wounded soldiers in military hospitals, gave lessons at special reha-bilitation camps, and toured with Hope and Crosby at USO shows, often getting swarmed by fans seeking autographs. "Bing sang 'White Christmas' just about wherever we went and Bob entertained every-one with his one-liner jokes," Byron fondly recalled. "It was a lot of fun, looking back, traveling with the troops and my best friend Jug, who later named his son after me. Louise stayed with her parents in Texarkana for most of this time, or with her sister Delle in Fort Worth, and that turned out to be the only real hardship for me. I really missed her. But Jug and I felt we were making a real contribution." To be sure, the Gold Dust Twins helped raise thousands for the war effort—but also kept golf in the public eye at a time when it could easily have dis-appeared from sight.

Byron played in the only three events the PGA mounted that year, placing third at George S. May's All-American Open at the Tam O'Shanter Club in Chicago, picking up $900 in war bonds, and nar-rowly failing to defend a title he'd won annually since 1941. May would have a significant, if unlikely, impact on the revival of the game imme-diately following the war. A short, potbellied former Bible salesman and self-made millionaire, he'd purchased equity shares in the run-down Tam O'Shanter Club throughout the Depression; he then acted on longtime *Chicago Tribune* reporter Charlie Bartlett's suggestion that he seek to host the struggling Chicago Open in 1940, and thus began an eighteen-year run of tournaments that not only broke barriers in terms of purses but also provided a stage for returning stars that attracted thousands of curious newcomers and introduced several critical innovations, including live television coverage. But that was yet to come.

Initially May launched a pair of tournaments called the All-American that ran concurrently with one division for amateurs and another for professionals, with the $2,000 first-place prize being the largest payout in 1941. Two years later, he added another for female pros and announced a new tournament ambitiously called the World Championship. Displaying a marketing moxie perhaps only a P. T. Barnum or Marvin Leonard could fully appreciate, he turned his tournament grounds into a Romanesque carnival of popular delights by hiring airplanes to drop free tickets to his tournaments in the city's financial district and engaging strolling musicians, jugglers, and magicians to entertain the huge crowds that resulted. May is credited with being the first to erect major grandstands at finishing holes, and became a tireless promoter of the women's game, welcomed minority patrons into his galleries, treated visiting reporters to lavish accommodations, and aggressively wooed foreign players to his ever-expanding events. He also retained local club professionals, trick shot artists, and comedians to mount entertaining clinics for newcomers who understood little or nothing about golf, thus broadening its appeal.

Without question, at a moment when tournament golf hovered on the brink of cultural irrelevance, May's colorful exertions kept the sport visible with a host of stunts including his propensity to personally open his events wearing his signature Hawaiian shirts and introducing players to delighted crowds by encouraging them to predict their final scores in advance—offering to pay up to $100 for every stroke under their prediction if they, in turn, would pay him fifty dollars for every stroke over.

Many of them took the bait, and May's lavish Roman spectacles became a highlight of the war-reduced tour. One of his more controversial moves was to insist that players wear nametags so fans could easily identify them. Several balked at what they regarded as a humiliating distraction, and one William Ben Hogan famously dug in his heels and simply refused to submit. When he captured his first World Open in 1947, May retaliated by shaving three grand off the eye-popping $10,000 first-place check. Ben responded by snubbing the tournament for the next seven years. By then May no longer required pros to wear identifying nametags, replacing that with a system that had all caddies wearing numbers—a practice that became commonplace on tour.

"Going to a tournament at Tam was like Christmas morning and a major sporting event all rolled into one," remembers Paul Gerlacher, a Chicagoan whose father took him to his first All-American in 1943 and soon found himself manning a booth selling Cokes and cold beer during his high school and college days. "For anyone who liked golf or was even mildly interested in the game, May's tournaments became something thousands looked forward to. They were more than just golf tournaments, and I'm convinced a lot of people took up the game because of them."

Reporter John Derr could only read about the colorful goings-on at Tam O'Shanter from the Associated Press news wire in a radio broadcast booth in Calcutta, India, where he did a daily half hour news roundup for American troops stationed in the China-India-Burma Theater. Initially trained to serve as a radio mechanic on B-17s in the Far East, the enterprising Carolinian—during a long boat trip around Cape Horn—met a VIP who remembered him from covering a Duke-Army football game before the war and invited him to join the staff of theater commander Lieutenant General Joseph Stilwell. Derr soon found himself interviewing no less than Mahatma Gandhi and reading the latest home-front news and sports on his evening broadcast. He stayed abroad for thirty-three months.

During this interval, he received letters from Sam Snead and Johnny Bulla, filling him in on their eagerness to get back into competition and their worries about the tour's future.

"Sam was particularly worried about this," Derr remembers. "Of course, it was just his luck to have finally broken through and won the PGA just as the party shut down, so to speak. That played right into his private fears about being hexed by fate, and I think he was chomping at the bit to get back out there and prove something to everyone, especially himself, that his one major championship was no fluke. The problem was, nobody knew for sure what kind of golf tour would resume when peace broke out—or even if it would. I think that thought ate him alive, especially to see what Byron was doing in 1944."

In 1944, mostly through some persuasive hustling and arm-bending by Corcoran and Dudley, the PGA Tour managed twenty-three events including a PGA Championship, though the Masters and U.S. Open remained dormant and most of the marquee names were unavailable. Standing in for them were aging stars like Paul Runyan, Lawson Little, Craig Wood, Johnny Revolta, and Henry Picard, players whose splendid careers would basically ebb during the hiatus. Fortunately there was Lord Byron Nelson, who was over par only three times in his twenty-one events, collecting ten wins, six second places, and a record $37,000 in war bonds—twice as much as anyone had ever earned in a single season—and winning the Associated Press's coveted Athlete of the Year Award in a romp. Byron's only disappointment was losing in the PGA final.

Late in the summer, as he consulted with Cliff Roberts on how quickly the devastated turf at Augusta could be put back into tournament condition, Bob Jones was asked to assess Byron's terrific year in light of Ben's and Sam's conspicuous absence. Saint Bobby minced no words.

"It is my belief that Nelson is one of the greatest golfers the game has ever known," he said. "He has that rarest of all qualities—consistency. Byron rarely has a bad day or a bad round. He has more finesse than any of the others. You remember that I told you Ben Hogan was the hardest worker I've ever seen on any golf course. He was the hardest worker I've seen in any sport. I've also felt that Sammy Snead was the greatest stylist I've ever seen. By stylist I mean the accomplishment of results with the least amount of effort. Snead has always been a fine artist. But it's Nelson they all must watch and fear."

The public supported Jones's opinion, frequently turning out in record numbers to watch Byron as well as Jug McSpaden and other "old-timers." At George May's All-American—which Byron won easily, claiming $10,000 in war bonds and his sixth title of the year—the crowds were so large and enthusiastic that extra transportation and police were put on. Just a week earlier, no doubt encouraged by accounts of the Allied successes following D-Day, record galleries turned out to watch the unknown Bob Hamilton nip him one-up in the final of the PGA Championship at pretty Manito Golf and Country Club in Spokane.

Even better for the casual fan, Sam Snead was released from duty early in the autumn and quickly jumped in to make up for lost time. He was barely out of his navy issue and into his favorite two-toned golf shoes and newly adopted banded straw hat before he lapped the field at Portland and scored a second win at San Francisco a week later. "Byron's been having all the fun since some of us were away," he told a group of reporters in high spirits before crossing the bay to Oakland, the city where Sneadomania began in 1937. "But a few of us would like to cut in on some of his action. They say Ben will be back any day now, too." He had a disappointing tie for eighth in the Oakland Open, barely covering his expenses for the week, but then bounced back by winning the Richmond Open, collecting $1,600 in war bonds. His winning Wilson golf ball was auctioned off to the highest bidder, netting $1,000 for charity. Buoyed by his immediate success, Sam proposed a two-man match with Byron, who responded that he would be happy to meet him "anywhere, anytime, over thirty-six or seventy-two holes, match or medal play." Tour impresario Fred Corcoran immediately got to work on the logistics, aiming to stage the greatest challenge match since Gene Sarazen played his hero, Walter Hagen, for the hyperventilated Championship of the World in 1922. Within weeks, he set the date for May 26–27, and the venues, Fresh Meadow in Flushing, New York, and Essex County Country Club in West Orange, New Jersey.

Back home with Louise and his parents in Denton, America's newest Athlete of the Year settled in briefly to enjoy the holidays and take stock of his game and financial situation. Byron had covered his own traveling expenses while touring for the USO and Red Cross, so despite his record-setting earnings that year he incurred a significant loss that forced him to redeem the war bonds he'd won before they reached maturity, taking a loss.

The significance of this wasn't lost on him. Before the Masters was suspended in the spring of 1942, he had dinner and a life-changing conversation with Cliff Roberts, who bluntly advised him to find a career outside tournament golf. "You'll wear out long before you ever make any serious money at this game," Byron remembered him saying in no ambiguous terms. "I suggest you think about other opportunities that will provide a reliable income and not grind you to pieces." Roberts knew a great deal about his financial situation because after his U.S. Open breakthrough in 1939, Byron had called on Cliff at his Wall Street brokerage and asked if he could invest some of his winnings. "I'll do it on two conditions," Roberts told him flatly. "The first is that you send me a regular contribution to your account. The second is that you never ask me what I do with that money." Byron agreed to the terms.

Years later, Byron recalled that even then Roberts believed it wouldn't be long before the top tournaments were carried live on radio, and perhaps even television, assuming that nascent medium ever amounted to anything. (RCA's David Sarnoff had introduced the first commercial television set at the 1939 World's Fair, and by 1944 more than 100,000 American homes had early models.) Their conversation in the 1942 Masters simply underscored these points.

"Cliff believed I ought to get into a business of some kind with a future, invest my money in something solid, and maybe even consider broadcasting golf in some form or another down the road. He thought my background as a club pro and a top tour player and the fact that I enjoyed people might lead me to something else in golf, though my mind was really elsewhere by that point."

Specifically, it was down on the farm in Texas. When he spent time at the modest spread he'd provided for his parents in Denton, tending his father's small herd of cows and doing simple chores, Byron was powerfully reminded of his own boyhood dream of someday owning enough land to graze a couple hundred head of beef cattle. He was almost thirty-three years old, in his athletic prime yet aged beyond his years from more than a decade of chasing the game across the continent. Privately he yearned for the slower life he and Louise always talked about, with Sunday mornings that were free to attend church instead of giving golf lessons or competing, a permanent home with real neighbors and an actual mailing address. Though he rarely spoke of this, dating from the life-and-death struggle that defined his boyhood Byron's faith was central to everything he did on and off the golf course, yet the practice of that faith necessarily took a backseat to the demands of his public life. He prayed every day, sometimes several times, and those prayers included a petition to find a more meaningful life of service to others. At moments, he actually considered using his fame to become a missionary and spread the Gospel of Jesus Christ through a world ravaged by war. Like Bob Jones before him, the pressure of tournament golf frequently twisted his fragile stomach into knots so painful that he and Louise both worried about potentially dire consequences.

"One of the first things I learned about Byron when we got to be friendly after the war," remembers John Derr, who returned from the Far East in early 1945, got married, and signed on to work for CBS Radio as a sports broadcaster, "was the quiet fear he had that his upset stomach in tournaments might lead to a bleeding ulcer. Given his unusual blood condition, which wasn't quite that of hemophilia but something close enough to it, I think that possibility genuinely concerned him and Louise both. The pressure on Byron was immense. Sam and Ben were really gunning for him every time they played, and the press trumped up that rivalry every chance it got. The other two thrived on that kind of competitive grind, but I think it took its toll on Byron. I have no doubt that's why he was in a rush to wind up his playing career as the tour resumed. He told me this several times over the years."

To be sure, the social life Byron and Louise enjoyed in Ohio offset some of this psychic ache for a more settled life, but even sedately beautiful Inverness presented pressures of its own. The historic club where Harry Vardon bid adieu to America in 1920 and Gene Sarazen played in his first Open now boasted more than five hundred members who demanded more attention than Byron was able to provide. When former board president Cloyd Haas let slip that several members had privately complained that his extended absences and his financial success on tour seemed to reflect his different priorities, he took this to heart and contemplated resigning. He would greatly miss the steady annual salary—estimated at around $20,000, not counting the revenues from the pro shop—but the reliable stream of income he'd developed working as a roving vice president for Haas-Jordan, selling golf umbrellas and Foot-Joy shoes for Field and Flint, helped spur his feeling that he was ready to move on.

"I had pretty well made up my mind by the end of 1944 that it was time to resign my club position," he later explained. "I had been a club pro for over a decade and enjoyed my work in every respect. But I felt it was time to do something different and the members at Inverness, many of whom remain my very good friends, were very understanding about that fact." After the summer golf season wound down, he resigned his post at Inverness, whose members gave him and Louise a lavish and emotional farewell dinner before they headed home to Texas for the winter. For years thereafter, as an honorary Inverness member, Byron returned annually to play with his friends at the club.

"Leaving Inverness made it possible for me to enjoy for the first time the freedom the pros in the sixties later knew," he summed up in his 1993 autobiography, "of being able to play in as many tournaments as you wanted and concentrate solely on your game, with few distractions and worries. It was another part of what made the year to follow as memorable as it was."

In his famous little black book, the log of his tournament earnings and observations he'd faithfully kept since 1935, Byron noted two areas of his game that needed improvement for 1945: "1) I wasn't concentrating as well as I could, and 2) my chipping wasn't as good as it needed to be."

By January of 1945 Paris had been liberated and the Allies had the Wehrmacht on the run in Belgium. With the Japanese suffering a string of defeats in the Pacific, strategic war planners were already working on a massive air and sea assault on the home islands in hopes of ending the war, a bold strategy that would undoubtedly cost countless American lives. For this reason, coverage of the tour's newly expanded roster of thirty-six tournaments received only moderate notice at the start of the year, opening with the revived Los Angeles Open at the Riviera Country Club.

"We think the open this year will resolve into a battle between Slammin' Sammy Snead, late of Uncle Sam's navy, and Lord Byron Nelson, the Toledo sharpshooter recently named athlete of the year," wrote the *Los Angeles Times* on January 3. "And of this pair we have a leaning toward Snead, come rain—oops, inclement weather, or shine."

The winter rains held off but dense fog rolled over the daunting course, designed by George C. Thomas Jr. in 1927, halfway through the third round, halting play with Jug McSpaden, Sam, and Byron clustered near the top of the leaderboard. In the morning, followed every step of the way by his pipe-smoking friend Bing Crosby, Byron finished that round at one under par and then shot even par to finish the tournament, apparently headed to yet another playoff with his Gold Dust pal, Jug.

On the treacherous eighteenth hole, however, playing just behind the leaders, following a burst of birdies that tied him for the lead, Sam struck a gorgeous four-iron to five feet and drained the birdie putt to win by a stroke, his third victory in five starts since returning from service, conveying the message that golf's most colorful attraction now really understood how to close the deal. Byron immediately set off on the 375-mile road trip to Phoenix. Sam, according to a gossipy report in *Variety*, nursing a slipped vertebra in his lower back, booked a table for six at the Brown Derby in Beverly Hills but never showed up because he was already on the road to Phoenix in his Cadillac, eager to resume the hunt. Lieutenant Hogan, officially still in army fatigues, could only watch Sam's rampage and grind his teeth.

Under cloudless skies and ideal temperatures in Phoenix, Byron's second-round 65 included seven birdies and gave him the halfway lead. "If you can't shoot good golf on a day like this," he remarked to reporters coming off, "you might as well give up." His closest contenders were reigning PGA champ Bob Hamilton and recently discharged veteran Herman Barron, five strokes back. Byron then finished with 72-69 to breeze to his first title of the year. Blaming his sore back, the hero of week one finished fifteen strokes behind the man he was gunning for.

The caravan trundled on to Tucson's El Rio Golf Club where Byron had set the course record of 63 in an exhibition match in mid-1943. He posted four rounds in the 60s but finished second to Ray Mangrum, Lloyd's older brother. A week later with neither Sam nor Ben in the field at the Texas Open in San Antonio, it was ex-Yankee outfielder Sam Byrd who nipped Byron by a stroke and claimed the prize. Sam Snead skipped the following Corpus Christi Open to rest his ailing back, too, though this saw the return of Jimmy Demaret, who used a week's furlough shortly before officially mustering out of the navy to make his debut. In the third round, Byron shot a scintillating 63 to pull away from a pack that included Byrd, amateur Freddie Haas, and Craig Wood. Demaret, twirling his irons and dressed in bold peacock colors like the showman of old, mounted a strong bid with matching 68s in the middle rounds but still found himself eight strokes behind Nelson in the concluding double thirty-six-hole finish on Sunday, February 4.

It was Byron's thirty-third birthday. Following a light breakfast of buttered toast and warm tea, he carved a 65 out of the relatively short course in the morning and concluded with a workmanlike even-par 70 in the afternoon, chipping and putting brilliantly in the breezy gusts off the Gulf of Mexico to claim the $1,000 war bond and his second win of the young year, tying the tournament's scoring record. Jug finished fourth while Demaret's 66 put him in sixth. Owing to Byron's unwavering steadiness and accuracy an Associated Press reporter playfully labeled him "Golf's automaton." Years later, Byron confided to a writer that during this period his irons were so accurate he occasionally had to guard against losing concentration and becoming a little bored. "My swing was so familiar to me I rarely had to make an adjustment for the same reason I didn't have to practice so much," he explained. "To some of the reporters I suppose this seemed a little monotonous at times. But fortunately I had a major goal in my mind that helped keep me focused."

Unknown to anyone save Louise, Byron was on a dual quest to earn enough money to purchase his dream ranch outright—she was willing to go along with the plan, he said, as long as they didn't incur any debt—and to leave an indelible mark on the game in the form of the lowest tournament scoring average. "At the time, the [tournament] scoring record was 264 held by Craig Wood and a few others," he wrote in his memoirs. "I also wanted to be the leading money winner again. So you see, I had a whole collection of goals I wanted to reach, and every good shot I hit supported them all."

The following week in New Orleans, competing against a strong field that included Snead and several U.S. Open winners, Byron beat Jug by five shots in an eighteen-hole playoff to claim his third win, Sam finishing fourth. The next event, the Gulfport Open, required only a seventy-five-mile drive to the historic Great Southern Golf Club. Overlooking the Gulf of Mexico, the short 6,200-yard Donald Ross course is Mississippi's oldest, the birthplace of Ole Miss golf, dating from 1908, eccentrically bisected by a railroad track that once brought wealthy Yankee snowbirds to the sunny coast. Here, Sam Snead needed only a par on the final hole to win the tournament but missed the green, and then—as Bobby Jones had in the 1925 U.S. Open—called a penalty stroke on himself after his ball moved at address. The resulting bogey left him tied with Byron Nelson, who closed with a blistering 66.

On the final hole of the following day's playoff, after Byron's uncharacteristically poor approach to the green, Sam had a five-foot putt to win—but missed. They went back to the first hole in a sudden-death, whereupon Byron drove his ball into an irrigation ditch, took a drop and eventually made bogey. And when Sam stroked his third shot within a foot of the cup, Byron conceded the match—a technical violation, as it happened. Under the rules of stroke play, everything must be putted out. Even so, it ended in a one-shot victory for Sam.

At Pensacola, where hundreds of rowdy uniformed navy men turned out to cheer on their fellow sailor, Sam picked apart the course and won with 267 while Byron closed with a 65 to place second again. Seven days later, Sam bettered his winning margin by a stroke at the Jacksonville Open, where Byron wound up nine shots back, in sixth. Moreover, he'd never enjoyed much success at the popular Miami

International Four-Ball, where a revitalized Sam received the lion's share of press coverage. Complicating the scenario from Byron's perspective, the event marked the brief return of Lieutenant William Ben Hogan to tournament action, who'd mustered out six weeks earlier and had been polishing his game ruthlessly at Colonial during the Gulf Coast swing of the tour, watching Sam and Byron collect all the hardware and headlines.

Ben teamed with his friend Ed Dudley but lost four-and-three to Byron and Jug McSpaden in the second round. The Gold Dust Twins then polished off Henry Picard and Johnny Revolta three-and-two before demolishing Sam Byrd and Denny Shute eight-and-six in the final, a romp that placed them twenty-one strokes clear of the field for the tournament and set the tone for the onslaught to come. Demoralized, Ben went home to Fort Worth to knock some more rust off his game and play several lucrative one-day exhibitions, while his rivals carried their running feud on to the Carolinas, growing the galleries with every stop.

The week after American troops successfully crossed the Rhine into Nazi Germany, the next battleground on tour came at Charlotte's Myers Park Country Club, another Ross gem, and a featured attraction at one of the nation's first planned residential communities. En route, Sam, Byron, and Jug stopped off for a Red Cross exhibition at the beautiful Palmetto Golf Club in Aiken, South Carolina, where Sam fired a course-record 63 and became—after winning three in a row, and six since returning to golf—the 2–1 favorite at the Charlotte Open.

After seventy-two holes, Byron and Sam were tied at 272, requiring another eighteen-hole playoff. In this one, they reached the final hole, a 220-yard uphill par-three, with Sam up by a stroke. He played a one-iron to the lower front half of the heavily bunkered, two-tiered green, leaving himself a monstrous putt of over ninety feet. "I was getting a little tired of having Sam beat me," Byron later recounted, "and I thought, 'There's a chance he might three-putt from there.'" So Byron put back his own butter knife and took out a three-wood and hit a splendid shot to within twenty feet on the upper tier. Sure enough, Sam three-putted and Byron made his par, forcing a second eighteen-hole playoff.

"I was steamed at myself for leaving that first putt short," Sam remembered decades later. "There's no damn doubt in my mind that missing the chance to shut him out left the door wide open and gave

Byron a helluva boost in confidence, explaining the tear he went on after that." Even more troubling, the next morning's *Charlotte Observer* suggested that Sam intentionally three-putted so he could get a share of additional gate receipts for a second playoff round—exactly the sort of rumor that damaged his public image among the game's governing elites. "Nothing could have been further from our minds," Byron said in his defense. "I know I was trying my hardest to make that birdie putt on the eighteenth hole and you could see how put out Sam was with his bogey."

After reading the assertion in the paper, Snead blew his stack and began packing up to hit the road to Greensboro, where he won the inaugural event in 1938 and was so popular and accomplished it would eventually be nicknamed "Snead's Alley." All week he'd been annoyed by the gallery's seeming hostility to him, and the scandalous suggestion in the paper merely confirmed that someone had it out for him. Only a lot of smooth talking over breakfast by Fred Corcoran and Byron convinced him to ignore the story and complete the playoff. The reporter who wrote it later published an apology.

Several misinformed hecklers nevertheless populated the considerably smaller gallery, but Sam appeared to put the fracas behind him by taking the lead on the opening hole with a birdie. Yet once it became apparent that most of the spectators were openly rooting for Byron—whoops went up when a couple of Sam's shots flew wide of their targets—he increasingly showed irritation and discomfort as the match progressed, twice driving into the woods on the closing holes. Byron, conversely, was supremely calm throughout, curling a thirty-foot birdie putt on the final hole as the gallery erupted, shooting 69 to Sam's 73.

"From there on," Byron said, "I just kept going and playing well and it seemed everything was going my way." A poignant footnote to this pivotal tournament was Henry Picard's surprising announcement after a first-round 75 that Charlotte would be his last tournament on the PGA Tour, ending an illustrious career that included twenty-six wins, two major championships, and a pair of winning Ryder Cup appearances—not to mention the seismic influence he had on the three budding stars of his era, shaping their swings, minds, and fortunes. Gentle and classy as always, he told reporters that he would teach golf "to promising youngsters" for the rest of his days. The moment certainly didn't go unnoticed by Byron Nelson, even as his remarkable turnaround against Sam commenced a string of victories unrivaled in golf.

At Greensboro's Starmount Country Club, in the heart of Snead Country, ten thousand spectators, the largest gallery of the year, turned out in warm spring sunlight to watch Byron's beloved Spalding blade putter scorch the greens for a 271 that shattered the course record by eight strokes, earning him his sixth win of 1945. Sam hobbled home in sixth place, complaining again of an aching back. "Byron Nelson remains lord of golf!" crowed Smith Barrier of the *Greensboro Daily News,* one of the regional and national reporters the sponsoring Jaycees had treated to free meals and an improved press tent, an innovation that reflected the sport's sudden revitalization. Then they followed the pros to Durham's beautiful Hope Valley Golf Club, another Donald Ross masterpiece. A robust Easter Sunday crowd of three thousand trailed Byron, Sam, and Toney Penna and saw a scowling Sam falter badly with his putter. Byron, on the other hand, displaying an other-worldly accuracy, missed only two greens and made five birdies in the afternoon, shooting a course record 65 to lock up his fourth win in a row, equaling Ben Hogan's sweep of the Tar Heel State in 1940.

In Atlanta seven days later, a front-page story in the *Atlanta Constitution*—just below an account of the U.S. Army tightening the noose around Berlin, heralding the approaching end of the war in Europe—told a nearly identical story: another win, and a record-shattering score, 263, for the courtly Texan who always broke into a gracious smile after finishing a round. This title held extra luster because the Masters was still under wraps and Atlanta was Bobby Jones's hometown—he came out to cheer Byron on, in fact—and also because the event raised thousands of dollars to provide portable iron lungs for kids with polio. The runner-up, Sam Byrd, was twelve shots back, and poor Sam Snead finished in sixth place, a full eighteen. In the clubhouse, Louise Nelson apologized for the nasty head cold she shared with her victorious husband, and then revealed to the Asso-ciated Press's Ruth Ingram that she and Byron hoped to use Byron's winnings from the year to buy a cattle ranch and retire. "Well, boys," Byron was quoted as quipping when he sunk a birdie putt, "there comes another cow."

"Byron Nelson," Sam Byrd told reporters in the Capital City Club's locker room after his final round, "is playing the most consistent golf of any player in history. The way he's going, why, none of us may catch him this year."

Five wins in a row—a new PGA tournament record—netted Byron headlines in every newspaper in the country and an offer from Wheaties to put his picture on their cereal box, which in the past had used the likenesses of Babe Ruth, Lou Gehrig, Joe DiMaggio, and Ted Williams to promote the "Breakfast of Champions." They paid Byron $200 plus all the cereal he could eat—most of which he wound up giving away.

Atlanta marked the official end of the tour's winter season, and during this eight-week break the pros who held club positions returned home to stock and reopen their shops for the summer. Free of these duties for the first time in a dozen years, Byron embarked on a series of well-paying one-day exhibitions in Mobile, Montgomery, Memphis, and St. Louis that led him to his father's farm in Denton, where he began scouting around and found a large parcel of appealing pastureland near tiny Roanoke, Texas.

The break hadn't come a moment too soon, because he was feeling the stress of being under constant scrutiny by the press as the excitement surrounding his streak grew week to week. Unlike Ben, who had no interest whatsoever in promoting the tour, or even Sam, who had the fame and personality to do so but was notoriously unpredictable with his off-color stories and sudden mood swings, Byron felt obliged to serve as a field ambassador for a game that was struggling to gain back the popularity and respect it had enjoyed not so long ago. That is, beyond his stated hopes for a retired life on a cattle ranch, he felt pressured to keep playing and winning for the good of golf.

Wherever the Nelsons showed up that year, tournament sponsors clamored to have him speak at banquets and civic luncheons, and Fred Corcoran arranged radio appearances that meant they usually had to arrive a day or two early. Byron obliged them all, partly because he had a deep, genuine interest in the game's health and was by nature grateful for his good fortune, and partly because the larger the gate receipts, the closer he edged to fulfilling his dreams in Texas. "You see, golf in that day and time was so small and needed help so badly that when we'd get into town for a tournament we had to go to the Kiwanis Club, the Lions Club, all the types of clubs to promote the tournament," he told Al Barkow years later for Barkow's oral history of the tour, *Gettin' to the Dance Floor.* "And because of the streak, all they wanted was me."

Four days after the Atlanta Open, President Roosevelt passed away at his winter retreat in Warm Springs, Georgia. For millions of ordinary Americans, this felt like the death of a beloved parent, or at least a national hero—the avuncular, patrician figure who'd guided the country through its darkest days of economic depression and the costliest war in human history. Byron Nelson understood this impact on the national pysche better, perhaps, than most public figures. From the day near rock bottom of hard times in early 1933 when—just weeks before Roosevelt was sworn in—he boarded a Greyhound bus in Fort Worth with little more than his mother's prayers and thirty-five dollars in his pocket to ride up to Texarkana for his first professional tournament, to his electrifying fifth straight win in Bobby Jones's hometown that made him a star whose name was known by virtually every sports fan, he had witnessed both the terrible struggles of ordinary Americans and the country's determination to shake them off and get back on its feet.

With industry still operating on wartime production schedules and the economy deeply mired in debt, there was no guarantee that when peace broke out and millions of soldiers returned to civilian life they would even find jobs. In fact, one influential economic board warned that depression might resume if companies didn't find a way to retool for peacetime and start hiring in a hurry.

In May of 1945, during the tour's brief hiatus, the government's War Production Board lifted the ban on manufacturing that covered goods like golf balls and equipment, and courses from Bangor, Maine, to Bakersfield, California, began getting their fairways back into shape. In some ways, Fred Corcoran's cooked-up "World Championship" match between Slammin' Sammy Snead and Lord Byron Nelson couldn't have occurred at a better moment. New York City, after all, was still enjoying the afterglow of an exultant V-E Day celebration when Byron and Sam teed it up in front of an estimated eight thousand spectators at the Tillinghast-designed Fresh Meadow Club in nearby Flushing.

Sam bolted to a three-stroke lead after the first eighteen holes, but Byron closed the gap on the second loop and only lost, 143–144, when he missed a long birdie putt on the thirty-sixth hole. The next day at New Jersey's Essex Country Club, this time in a match-play format, Byron seized a commanding six-up lead by hole thirteen and held on to win the match four-and-three. Because his overall total of 272 was lower than Sam's 276, most commentators declared him the winner.

The gallery, eager to see "the streak" continue in any form, seemed to unanimously support this view. In a celebration broadly interpreted as a polite swipe at Snead, Grantland Rice was inspired to write a poem in honor of Byron's wonderfully consistent swing.

Would I trade all my slicing arcs and all my hooking swerves
For Byron Nelson's perfect play?
You bet your shirt I would!

Despite the tournament lull, owing to Byron's daily practice back home in Texas, that swing was in great shape when he opened the Montreal Open on June 10 with another 63 before a gallery of some 25,000 at the Islemere Golf Club—then went on to forge a new record for tournament play in Canada at twenty under par, ten strokes better than the runner-up, Jug McSpaden.

Seven days later, at the Llanerch Country Club in suburban Philadelphia, he and Jug raced to the finish of the Philadelphia Inquirer Invitational, Byron edging out Jug out by two strokes to extend his streak to seven and boost his official earnings for the year to $27,000. "The phlegmatic Nelson was so overjoyed at his victory," Harry Robert reported in the *Evening Bulletin*, "he took two swigs of beer from McSpaden's bottle, the rarest occurrence in the world for him."

Beginning with his first appearance at the Western Open in 1933, Byron had never managed to win anything in Chicago. But he made amends for that at the Chicago Victory Open the next week by beating perennial long-drive champ Jimmy Thomson in the pre-tournament driving contest and—despite a suddenly flaring backache that nearly caused him to withdraw before Sunday's thirty-six-hole finale—finished seven strokes ahead of McSpaden and Ky Laffoon for his eighth victory in a row.

His loss to unknown Bob Hamilton in the 1944 PGA Championship still weighed heavily on his mind. Facing a brutal format that required two qualifying rounds followed by four individual matches of thirty-six holes each to reach the final, Byron arranged this year to have osteopathic massages every evening just prior to and throughout the major championship at the Moraine County Club in Dayton, Ohio, admitting to a local reporter at the start of the week that he felt like he was "100 years old." His desire to compete was heightened by the fact that he knew the course well and that, with the U.S. Open and Masters still in suspension, this was the year's only major. It didn't hurt that Ben Hogan and Jimmy Demaret, still in uniform, were unable to play, or that Sam Snead fractured a bone in his arm in a pickup softball game back in Hot Springs during the two-month break. Another motivating factor was that Byron had reached the PGA final four times in his career and only once, in 1942, had came away holding the Wanamaker Trophy. In his mind, his record in this championship was one of missed opportunities and frustration. It was now or never.

Fortunately, because he was runner-up in 1944, he wasn't obliged to play in the qualifying rounds; curiously, he chose to do so anyway, most likely to see how the course was playing under competition—and to pick up an extra $250 for being low qualifier. "More cattle feed money," he joked to Louise that evening after his extensive back massage. After dispatching the aging Gene Sarazen four-and-three with relative ease, he survived a close match with Mike Turnesa, needing two birdies and an eagle over the closing holes to win 1-up and advance to the quarterfinal against Denny Shute, the former British Open champ, whom he beat three-and-two on the strength of flawless driving and a suddenly hot putter. The magic carried over against Claude Harmon, the future Winged Foot head pro who would go on to capture the 1948 Masters, send a number of great teaching pros into the game, and sire a famous clan of teachers himself. In a match delayed by rainy weather, Byron overcame a shaky start to take a three-hole lead by the halfway mark, and went on to win with relative ease, five-and-four. The final was against Sam Byrd, who'd been eating Byron's dust all year. In the morning, Byrd finished with four straight birdies to take a two-hole lead to lunch, then went up by three early in the afternoon, by all appearances cruising to victory. Ignoring the tender soreness in his lower back, and remembering his vow to concentrate on chipping and putting, however, Byron hung tough and won three holes in a row when Byrd's putting stroke suddenly went cold. Byron also had some lucky breaks when errant approach shots struck spectators and dropped close to greens, allowing him to save par with clutch chips. After he drained a lengthy birdie putt on the twenty-ninth hole, Byrd all but threw in the towel.

After he'd retreated to the locker to comb his hair and put on a sports jacket for the trophy presentation, a somewhat pale Byron admitted to reporters this was "the toughest tournament I ever won." Flanked by Ed Dudley and Fred Corcoran, he smiled at the record gallery assembled. In all, 38,752 people had turned out to see if Byron could extend the magical streak. For the first time ever, the PGA deployed ropes to keep spectators confined to designated viewing areas. After the presentation, Byron took his sixteen-year-old caddie, local high schooler George Gould, into the Moraine pro shop and paid him $150.

In the days after the PGA, owing to his unprecedented domination of the game, the Associated Press began referring to him as "Mr. Golf," and *Life* magazine, read weekly by an estimated one out of every six Americans, proclaimed that he was the greatest golfer ever because he'd perfected the golf swing and wished to "quit and become a gentleman farmer," which only confirmed his humility and grace as a champion.

He'd now won nine in a row, but paid a heavy toll to beat what he privately considered his PGA "jinx." Byron's back ached so fiercely he was forced to withdraw from the St. Paul Open before play started and pay a visit to the Mayo Clinic for special osteopathic treatments. Over several days he took extended heat massages and rested.

His friend Charlie Bartlett, the *Chicago Tribune*'s evangelistic golf writer, had spent years convincing his editors that professional golf wasn't a "sissy sport" and deserved a place on the front page of the sports section; later he helped organize the Golf Writers Association of America. But the following week he couldn't have been more pleased with the outcome of George May's All-American Open. "Surprise!" Charlie told his devoted readers on the morning of July 31. "John Byron Nelson, the man who even the gaffers of the Vardon-Hagen-Jones era now admit is the greatest golfer who ever swung a club, yesterday won his fourth and richest All-American Open championship in five years with a 72 hole score of 269 at the Tam O'Shanter Country Club."

Byron finished at nineteen strokes under par, scoring 30 on his final nine, and eleven strokes ahead of his closest competitor, an intensely silent Ben Hogan, freshly released from military service. In the locker room afterward, a young reporter brazenly asked Ben how it felt to be back in action.

"Fine," he chastely replied, pulling off his new custom-made British shoes that contained an extra spike for traction. "But I've had just about enough of all this Mr. Golf business." For the moment at least, overshadowed by Byron's historic run, he and Sam Snead—who finished in a tie for fifteenth and fled the scene—were reduced to tournament footnotes.

Sam's gloom deepened days later when he posted a miserable 296 at the Canadian Open, where he was a two-time champion. Ben skipped the tournament and went home to practice at Colonial, stopping en route to do a pair of lucrative exhibitions. Meanwhile, despite the loss of a dozen pounds owing to stress and injury, Byron fired an even-par 280 over Toronto's recently lengthened Thornhill Golf Club to boost his streak to eleven. After battling swing problems for two rounds, Byron made further headlines by admitting his fatigue to reporters and officially announcing his intention to retire from professional golf within the next two years. The story made front-page headlines nationally in many of the same editions that carried news of the atomic bomb being dropped on Hiroshima, which instantly killed nearly a hundred thousand people.

Heading to the Memphis Open, Byron stopped off in Spring Lake, New Jersey, for an unofficial thirty-six-hole benefit to raise money for a nine-hole golf course for disabled veterans; the event raked in $6,000 for the charity and Byron won it, pocketing $1,500. Still, he admitted to O. B. Keeler that he was nearing the point of physical and psychological exhaustion. "It would almost be a relief not to win," he ruefully confided, and Keeler told him Jones sometimes had felt the same way.

New Orleans insurance broker Freddie Haas, the amateur who battled Snead earlier in the season at his hometown event, provided the relief Byron craved at the Memphis Invitational, playing the difficult Chickasaw Country Club course brilliantly to end the streak at eleven. As it happened, Byron's historic run ended hours after the Japanese surrendered and World War Two officially ended, setting off national celebrations and, in the lobby of Memphis's famed Peabody Hotel, a drunken week-long party.

But it didn't end there. Seven days later, with Sam and Ben back in hot pursuit, Byron lapped the field by ten strokes to claim the Knoxville Invitational. Only days later, at the Nashville Open, finding his own form, Ben opened with a 64 en route to a stunning 265, four strokes better than Byron's second-place 269. Sam found his game and won at Dallas the next week—then repeated it at Tulsa, claiming his sixth win for 1945 but feeling all but forgotten in the hoopla attending Nelson.

Then it was out to Spokane, Washington, for the reformulated Esmeralda Open, where Mr. Golf beat Jug McSpaden by six, Sam and

Ben by eight, and captured his sixteenth official win for the year. Sam, who'd shot a course record 63 during the event, joked to reporters that he hoped Byron—who spent hours signing autographs for servicemen and -women—might soon "decide to enlist."

Much to the delight of America's golf-starved, war-weary golf fans, Nelson, Hogan, and Snead were suddenly engaged in a battle royale for the dominant position in golf. During the tournament seasons of 1945 and '46, for instance, Byron's final two years on tour, with PGA fields again at full strength with veterans and several promising new-comers, Byron would collect twenty-five victories, Ben sixteen, and Sam twelve—better than 70 percent of the tournaments played dur-ing this interval—and collectively finish second twenty-two times, an unrivaled period of domination by any trio of golfers.

The timing couldn't have been better. Corresponding to this jug-gernaut, several scoring records fell and gallery turnouts steadily increased, giving professional golf exactly the postwar boost it needed, bringing both stress and relief to tournament manager Fred Corco-ran, who behind the scenes survived yet another nasty power struggle between the governing home pros of the PGA and touring profession-als who desired more autonomy, leaving the tour's future hanging in the balance. In late 1944, Corcoran's contract came up for renewal and key figures on both sides of the dispute demanded his ouster, some citing the paucity of tournaments during the war as a reason to give him the boot while others complained that his handling of business affairs for stars like Ted Williams, Babe Zaharias, and Stan Musial dis-tracted from his duties of managing the tour. Looking for any excuse to claim his head, a third faction even objected to his close friendship with the likes of Bing Crosby and Bob Hope and Byron Nelson, rela-tionships that developed during the scores of charity exhibitions that raised hundreds of thousands of dollars for the Red Cross and other wartime organizations.

"It was mostly subterfuge," Corcoran said many years later. "Every-one was eager to get back to business and each side wanted their own man and I was once again caught in the middle. The truth was, many of the tour players had done their time away in the service and were eager to make up for lost revenue, and in no mood to be told by anyone—least of all the PGA establishment—how to run their affairs." At one point Corcoran considered an offer to leave the tour and work as the road secretary for the Boston Red Sox, but eventually signed a new contract with the tour that paid him a base salary of $7,500 plus expenses to take on a greater role in promoting the reemerging tour.

The highlight of Ben's return to the tour during Byron's most triumphant year in 1945, in any case, came at the Portland Open just days after Byron's win at the Esmeralda, where he put together four extraordinary rounds (65-69-63-64) to shoot an unearthly 261 that clipped three strokes off Byron's seventy-two-hole scoring record—even sweeter because Ben bested Byron by a yawning fourteen-stoke margin. When a grinning Jimmy Demaret congratulated him on this new record, Ben merely grimaced and remarked, "I guess that takes care of this Mr. Golf business."

"There now was not much love lost between Nelson and Hogan," according to Gene Gregston, who knew both men fairly well and wrote the earliest biography of Ben. "Their rivalry was too close for the close friendship to survive. Nelson backers said Ben in action and word showed he resented the success Nelson had attained in the war years. Hogan backers explained that he was too combative to be a buddy to the man who stood between him and his goal."

"The way I remember this time," Sam Snead recalled years later, "was the tension both Ben and Byron seemed to play under every week. I felt some of it too, but the truth of it was, in my case, I was just so happy to be back in the game I figured it was only a matter of time before I started winning my share. Ben seemed to be still fightin' that war we'd just won."

Two weeks after Portland, Byron shattered Ben's mark with a 259 and won the Seattle Open by thirteen strokes. "I was so embarrassed at having Hogan beat me by fourteen," he admitted, notably saying *Hogan* instead of *Ben*, "that I might not have played as well at Seattle if I'd only been three shots back at Portland." When asked how long he calculated his 259 might stand, he mused, "You don't know in this game. The record could be broken next week. Or maybe not forever." In fact, the record stood for a decade, until Mike Souchak shot 257 at the Texas Open.

Two weeks after Seattle, Ben won the Richmond Invitational in Virginia, then drove his new Buick down to Pinehurst hoping to add another North and South trophy to his hardware collection. This was a tournament all three men thoroughly enjoyed playing; Ben (who won it three times) because Pinehurst was his first solo win; Sam (also three) because the friendly galleries often contained neighbors and friends from nearby Greensboro; Byron (who won once) because of his high personal regard for Richard Tufts and everything Pinehurst symbolized. But with November now upon them and Byron utterly exhausted, he phoned Dick Tufts and apologized for being unable to appear, explaining that he needed to go home and rest his back.

Unfortunately, neither of his rivals seized this golden opportunity. Ben's dodgy putter left him in third place behind winner Cary Middlecoff, and Sam finished a disappointing ninth.

Byron and Jug McSpaden went hunting for two weeks in Idaho, where he "completely forgot golf and forbade any talk of it." Afterward, he rendezvoused with Louise in Denton and turned up to speak at the Rotary Club for "Byron Nelson Day" in Fort Worth. The proud Rotarians presented the Nelsons with a pair of Tennessee walking horses named Linda and Rex. "While Rex turned out to be a bit difficult to handle," notes John Camponiotte in his fine book about Byron's streak, "Linda was gentle and cooperative, and the Nelsons kept her for years."

Ben, meanwhile, went on a small tear, making his intentions for the future clear by winning the new Orlando Open. Before he and Valerie turned toward home themselves, he finished sixth at the Miami Open.

As the gods of bittersweet irony would have it, just two weeks before the tour's official Christmas break, he and Byron ended their historic year at the inaugural Glen Garden Invitational, where they'd both been introduced to the game and, in a playoff that now seemed a distant lifetime ago, one of them won his first tournament ever, and the other suffered his first stinging defeat.

Perhaps the Ghost of Christmas Past was too much in evidence. Driving to a Wednesday practice round, Byron's new Studebaker President skidded on an icy bridge and overturned. Both he and Louise escaped injury, though they had groceries and a carton of eggs splattered all over the car. Valerie Hogan took Louise into Fort Worth to shop and have lunch and take in the festive Christmas window displays at the Leonard Bros. department store. Byron joked with proud Glen Garden members about having egg all over his face.

Beyond the unusually cold temperatures that had spectators cloaked in wool overcoats and hats, both he and Ben later conceded that there was something distinctly uncomfortable about what should have been a nostalgic return to their youthful stomping grounds. Ben in particular played poorly over the modest little course where they'd learned the game as boys. His 287 was good enough only for sixth place.

Byron won again, of course—by a fourteen-stroke margin over a strong field that had showed up in large part out of respect for the two of them, though it didn't include Sam, who chose to take a few weeks off in the relative warmth of Florida. The victory increased Byron's unprecedented winnings to $62,437.62, not counting an additional $12,000 in exhibition fees paid mostly in war bonds.

Even as he prepared to leave the game, winning his eighteenth official tournament of the year was a firm reminder to the world at large, and maybe to his erstwhile friend and greatest rival, that Byron Nelson was—at least for the moment—still Mr. Golf.

11

An Unexpected Open

OR A MAN SERIOUSLY contemplating retirement, and possibly because of it, following a brief holiday break with his folks in Denton, Byron started 1946 pretty much where he left off by winning the first two events, in L.A. and San Francisco, by impressive margins. At Riviera, a tournament he'd always set his hope to capture, he was five strokes better than Ben's second-place 289. Days later, at the San Francisco Golf Club, his 283 bested him by ten strokes, and Ben finished third. Sam, meanwhile, had difficulty getting started, tying for tenth and sixteenth respectively. "If Slammin' Sammy finds his putting stroke anytime soon," wrote a columnist for the San Francisco *Examiner*, apparently anticipating the most intense three-man rivalry since Hagen, Sarazen, and Jones, "golf could enjoy its greatest year ever." But this was just the beginning of Sam's fabled putting woes, which for years would cost him dearly.

These were optimistic, almost euphoric times, with postwar America standing alone in terms of economic power and prestige—at the "summit of the world," as an admiring Winston Churchill put it. Despite concerns about rampant inflation, both farms and factories were quickly answering growing consumer demand using technologies refined in wartime to boost the country's workforce to nearly full capacity, fueled by a sudden national enthusiasm both for work and play. And when Secretary of State George Marshall's plan to rebuild war-torn Europe with $13 billion in guaranteed loans and aid took shape beginning in 1947, signifying America's position as the leader of a new world order, ordinary pleasures, especially spectator sports, were once more available to the masses. In 1946, both major league baseball and the National Football League significantly expanded their offerings, lowering admission prices to lure fans back out to the field. Not to be left behind in the stampede for things at once familiar and dear, the PGA presented its most ambitious roster ever: twenty-five open fields, plus half a dozen invitational tournaments stretching from January to December, offering a record amount of prize money that topped $410,000.

Perhaps no single sporting event symbolized these elevated hopes more than the revival of the Masters. By the end of March, Byron had claimed a victory in New Orleans and Ben had matched him by winning at Phoenix, San Antonio's all-important Texas Open, and Petersburg. Meanwhile, hungry youngsters like Arkansas's Tommy Bolt and four-time Tennessee amateur champion Cary Middlecoff were rising to the challenge. So Bobby Jones's personal championship was perhaps in even better shape than ever. Clifford Roberts had overseen his own Marshall Plan at Augusta National by using a small army of laborers to restore the course to peak condition in the fourteen months prior to reopening. Moreover, an unexpected gift from a member just before the war had funded a much needed overhaul of the clubhouse, providing modest accommodations in the "Crow's Nest." In the fall of 1945, when the still closed club's membership surged to a new high of 130, a generous gift from Edward Barber of the Barber Steamship Lines in the form of a $100,000 loan at extremely favorable interest rates enabled Roberts to go on a building binge that added a golf shop, residential suites, and kitchen and formal dining room to the original clubhouse, not to mention the first of a series of residential cottages or "cabins," as Roberts insisted they be called. The first cabin went to founder Bobby Jones.

In feverish anticipation of watching their tournament being revived, Augusta's members voted to boost their purse to $10,000. Cliff Roberts, however, was worried about the inadequacy of spectator housing. The small but loved Richmond Hotel was showing its age, and the popular, sprawling Bon Air had fallen out of the Vanderbilt chain and never recovered its footing. In a letter to the town fathers, Roberts hinted that the tournament's future itself might be in doubt if additional accommodations weren't soon developed—a move that led to the construction of several small hotels and the first appearance of postwar "motor hotels" along adjacent Washington Avenue.

Another concern had to do with popular Calcutta auctions that were dutifully covered by the *Augusta Chronicle.* "Betting was still big, and still acceptable, in 1946," Curt Sampson noted in *The Masters: Golf, Money, and Power in Augusta, Georgia.* "Bookies patrolled hotel lobbies as well as the golf course, never neglecting their best clients, the golfers themselves."

For his part, ironically, Roberts early on had consented to the club's own wagering fete in hopes of fostering bonhomie among members, but privately disdained betting of any kind as "simple banditry." Upon reopening in 1946, he began a diligent if unpopular campaign to halt the club's involvement in Calcuttas once and for all, especially in light of the Bon Air's growing reputation for hosting known big-time gamblers. Increasingly obsessed with shaping the Masters's image as that of an elite gathering of the game's finest players and movers and shakers, golf's classiest invitational, he expanded the club's infrastructure by creating patron stands and improved access and parking, and instituted policies aimed at discouraging betting pools and the common practice of purse splitting. It would take him, in fact, until 1952—when Ben Hogan first proposed the idea of a Champions Dinner, and newspapers across the country began to write about poorly regulated Calcuttas rife with fraud—to shut down Augusta National's auction, though the Bon Air's Calcutta roared merrily along for many years thereafter.

"Cliff came out of the war years determined to make the Masters the premier event in golf, maybe all of sports itself, to attract the right kind of people and do whatever it took, leaving no detail unattended to, in order to make the Masters the hottest ticket in golf," says John Derr, who covered his first Masters for CBS Radio that spring. "He understood better than most what golf symbolized to a nation that had just somehow beaten back the two most powerful military powers in history—a gracious, civilized game where one who played by the rules and won had something in common with the great Bobby Jones. He set out deliberately to cultivate that image, whatever it took."

A conservative Wall Street banker, Roberts was also enough of an armchair psychologist to understand that the Masters had a chance to become something unique, an event that made every ticket holder, or "patrons," as he called them, feel privileged and unique, almost like members of the club. At the time, fabled tournaments like the North and South, Western Open, and even the long-running L.A. Open, long considered "major" championships a notch or two below the U.S. Open and PGA in terms of importance, were struggling to regain the premier status they'd enjoyed before the war. Roberts saw an opportunity to fill a cultural vacuum by making the Masters the best-run, most admired championship in the game—and thus, at least in theory, the most desired ticket.

If Chicago's George May attempted to make his tournament a circus maximus of sensational commercial entertainments catering to every fancy imaginable, Roberts aimed to make his the golf equivalent of a Carnegie Hall recital with limited seating reserved for the most discerning followers of the game. This unapologetic approach would take at least a decade and the arrival of a charismatic young pro named Arnold Daniel Palmer to come to full flowering, but the foundation of the tournament's major stature was unquestionably laid by the intense rivalry between Ben, Byron, and Sam.

Plainspoken Tommy Bolt, who turned pro in 1946 and drove his red jalopy up to Augusta from his Shreveport club job just to watch "Hogan, Nelson and Snead, the three by-God best players who ever lived bar none," put it in simpler terms. "The last damn thing Cliff wanted was a bunch of sorry big-time crooks getting into Augusta's pot of glory, that magical place where everyone felt like an important *somebody*—if only for a few days each year."

Ironically, the Masters revival in 1946 would best be remembered for exactly the kind of press Roberts hoped to avoid when a dark horse who spent much of his service time toiling in the same Norfolk navy yard as Sam Snead rose up out of nowhere to beat Ben Hogan, the favorite, and later made unflattering remarks against the tournament's founders. Sallow-faced, long-legged Herman Keiser— sometimes called the "Missouri Mortician," owing to his generally downcast demeanor—emerged from a group of early leaders that initially included all three of the favorites to take a commanding seven-stroke lead by the halfway mark, only to see his lead vaporize under Ben's withering Sunday afternoon charge that brought him to the seventy-second hole needing only a two-foot downhill putt to win. The greens were rolling so firmly, he later remarked, that they almost sounded crisp.

Finishing forty minutes ahead of him, Herm Keiser had retreated to the clubhouse, unable to watch the finish, partly because he was stewing over a host of perceived injustices he claimed began when he was assigned a lame caddie who couldn't keep up on the hilly course, and continued when he nearly missed his third-round starting time because someone neglected to notify him in advance that it had been changed. Larger than these distractions, however, was his sensational accusation that a Bon Air bookie had informed him that two prominent Augusta National members had each placed an eye-popping $50,000 wager on Hogan to win, implying that Keiser should carefully weigh the merits of *not* beating a man the club powers favored to win.

He maintained for years that it was all part of a plot in which Roberts and Jones himself conspired to get the monkey off Ben Hogan's hardworking back and boost him to the title. Among other indignities he was subjected to, Keiser claimed that Grantland Rice, a known Hogan cheerleader, moseyed out to the course at a critical moment in round three to warn him about slow play, obviously trying to rattle him. Keiser's charges were eventually deemed groundless, though it was no secret Bob Jones harbored unusually strong affection for both Ben and Byron. Hogan's doggedness and formal dignity appealed greatly to him, and about this time he was asked by a wire service reporter which golfer he would choose to hit the proverbial one shot "to win all the tea in China." Jones thought for only a second before replying, "That's not hard for me to answer—Hogan. Hogan had the intangible assets—the spiritual."

Likewise, he deeply appreciated Byron's wondrous consistency and the ambassadorial grace under fire he brought to every situation, not to mention the revitalizing effect his historic run in '45 had on popular interest in both golf and the Masters. These elements were at the heart of his fraternal love for Byron. Golf courses and clubs nationwide reported a nearly 50 percent surge in membership applications and actual play during the first two years following the war. Moreover, Byron would happily tell anyone who asked that his 1937 Masters title was the most meaningful victory of his career—even more important than the U.S. Open in 1939 or his two subsequent PGA Championships.

Curiously, almost from the moment he first set foot on Augusta National, on the other hand, Sam Snead, despite his supreme physical gifts and broad popularity, never attained the lasting affection of either Jones or Roberts. Neither, for that matter, did the fourth best player of the day, Jimmy Demaret, whose witty repartee and clubhouse pranks provoked a scolding letter of rebuke from Saint Bobby himself. Sam's early breaches of Masters protocol famously included an incident where he removed his shoes and socks and played a nine-hole practice round in his bare feet simply to make a point about the importance of footwork, which netted a swift and angry response from Gene Sarazen, the locker room's self-appointed chief of protocol, who took the matter directly to Jones and came back with an unambiguous threat of future banishment if anything of that nature happened again. Sam let the incident roll off his back.

But even before play resumed in 1946, it was Sam's salty language and colorful storytelling—specifically his jokes that got bluer as his audience grew—and his casually indiscreet attitude toward women, that soured the affections of his hosts. Sam always attributed the technique of turning his head slightly at address and fixing his left eye on the ball directly to Jones, a move that enabled him to drive the ball so solidly—and that Jack Nicklaus would in time emulate. And Jones in turn was lavish in his praise of Sam's unrivaled natural abilities. But by 1946, none of that was enough to overcome his growing conviction that Snead was an uncouth rube with a gift from the gods. His raw language and lack of discretion at moments were simply too much to bear, especially for a man presiding over America's most elite shrine of golf.

In any case, with the Masters on the verge of attaining the lofty stature that Jones and Roberts had been trying to achieve for more than a decade, the last thing either man wanted was any sort of scandal.

Moreover, Herman Keiser's final complaint that being paired with Byron Nelson—eight shots back at the start of Sunday's final round—somehow placed him at a disadvantage simply doesn't wash. Masters officials, like most others in those days, typically based pairings on the popularity of certain players. It would be several more years before final pairings were arrived at by fifty-four-hole scores, and putting Keiser with the decade's hottest golfer could hardly have been a disadvantage. In fact, in 1948, after an ailing Bob Jones "officially retired" and gave up the largely ceremonial tradition of playing the fourth round with the tournament leaders, Byron Nelson took over that task at his personal request and brought the eventual winner home on at least four different occasions.

For all the external drama, the internal seesaw battle emerging between a weary and withdrawing Byron and a hungrier-than-ever Ben Hogan in the end came down to the Hawk's two-foot putt on the seventy-second hole. Nobody in golf was better from ten feet and in than Ben. Taking the familiar tripod stance he'd developed in early

1940, he gently nudged his ball with his beloved brass doorknob putter and heard a cascade of gasps as his par putt grazed the edge of the
cup and rolled to a stop four feet below the hole. He stood staring icily
at the traitorous ball as the huge throng around the green shifted and
whispered and attempted to settle down. A few moments later, after
taking even more time to assess his bogey putt, he saw that one lip out
as well—making Herman Keiser the first postwar Masters champion.

In the clubhouse, it was the genial Henry Picard, already retired
from active competition, who delivered the good news to the wan and
agonizing Keiser. "Congratulations, Herman," he said, slapping him
robustly on the back. "The little man took the choke. Those were the
three worst putts I've ever seen him hit."

These stark echoes of the past, the effect of this failure yet again
to close the deal, followed Ben home, where he spent the next month
in solid seclusion at Colonial working on his game—a pivotal turning point, or so he later claimed. "I left the tour and went home to
Fort Worth about as desperate as a man could be," he recounted in
his famous 1955 *Life* magazine cover story in which he supposedly
revealed the "secret" of his success to the public. "I sat and thought
for three or four days. I did not pick up a club, although I wanted to in
the worst way. One night while laying awake in bed I began thinking
about a technique for hitting a golf ball that was so old it was almost
new."

Ben's revelation involved pronation, an old Scottish technique from
the age of hickory clubs in which players "rolled" their hands upon
takeaway, permitting the face of the club to open at the top—an archaic
system largely discounted by most modern teachers of the game, who
warned it could provoke hooks. Ben coyly explained that "two further
adjustments" rendered his swing "hook-proof," noting they were "so
delicate that no one would ever think of looking for them—and I certainly was not going to tell anyone where to look." Over the following decades, as teachers and players alike attempted to deconstruct
his swing and learn his alleged secret—generating an avalanche of
speculative articles and books all claiming to decipher his Archime-
dean swing perfection—Ben himself revealed nothing further, and his
Shady Oaks cronies chortled at what they considered a brilliant exploi-
tation of his growing mystique. Who, after all, was going to challenge

the greatest shotmaker the game ever produced? Moreover, they noted, the estimated $50,000 from *Life* came exactly when his fledgling equipment company needed a serious infusion of cash.

Perhaps Tommy Bolt, one of a group of younger players Hogan took a shine to, came closest to summing up his friend's complex and unique form of genius. "You got the feeling that everything was his real so-called secret. By that I mean, piece by piece, nothing too small was considered and either used or discarded. And once he took it and learned and refined it, brother, it was *his*. Nobody did it better than Hogan, and that's the bottom line."

Even Herb Wind—who ghostwrote the famous "Secret" article for *Life* and collaborated on his groundbreaking 1957 instruction book, *Five Lessons,* the best-selling instruction book in history—didn't believe there was anything particularly "secret" about this so-called discovery. He pointed out that Ben merely placed his left thumb down the center of the shaft and locked his left wrist as it came through the ball at impact, avoiding a rollover effect that would create a hook. "There wasn't anything revolutionary about what Ben learned about this," he said years later. "Most good players knew these principles as well as he did. But Ben Hogan was all about *evolution*—specifically his own. The more he worked at these principles the better he got. I often think, to this day, Ben Hogan's *real* secret was the difficulty of his life, the effect his long climb to the top had on his mind, his spirit. He *thought* through every detail every second he was out there. His mind never drifted. That was his real secret. Life made him, in time, fearless and almost invincible—and down the road, though he never saw it coming, a golf immortal."

In *Life,* Ben claimed he took his new secret straight back to the tour and proved it successful by winning George May's All-American Open, though in fact he finished fourth, and complained so sharply about being asked to wear an identifying number on his back, which he ultimately refused to do, he declined to return for many years. The sustaining highlights on the heels of his devastating Masters loss were back-to-back wins at Marvin Leonard's Colonial Invitational and the still mighty Western Open. Two weeks after the latter, however, he missed a four-footer on the final hole at the U.S. Open—at Canterbury, in Cleveland—that left him a stroke out of a playoff with Byron, Lloyd Mangrum, and Vic Ghezzi. But he rebounded quickly, claiming five more wins in nine starts that made him the joint favorite with Byron for the PGA Championship, scheduled for the end of August at the Portland Country Club in Oregon.

Byron's playoff at Canterbury exhausted whatever enthusiasm he had left for the highest levels of competition. "I was really tired by that point and though I'd really hoped to get another U.S. Open title before I left," he explained years later, "my focus just wasn't the same as it had been. I was too busy thinking about ranchland back home in Texas," he added. "I think that's perhaps why just about everything went wrong that could."

On the weekend, with some twelve thousand spectators swarming unchecked over the course, largely indifferent to the marshals who haplessly tried to contain them behind hastily strung yellow ropes, players and caddies had to shove through galleries and hit their shots through alleys of unruly fans—perhaps costing Byron his last best hope for a second national championship. After he played his second shot on the par-five thirteenth hole in the third round, for instance, the excited crowds rushed ahead and closed around his ball. His caddie, young Eddie Martin, struggling to maneuver his heavy leather bag through them, lost his balance and stumbled onto Byron's ball, resulting in a penalty stroke. Even so, he fashioned a 69 and after fifty-four holes held a one-stroke lead over Ghezzi and Mangrum, Ben just another stroke back. Sam putted atrociously, blew to a 74, and was never a factor—the U.S. Open jinx again blooming evilly in his mind.

In the final round, on the seventy-second hole, Byron needed only a par-four to claim his second title. But he uncharacteristically smother-hooked his drive into ankle-deep rough twenty yards off the fairway, and had to use an eight-iron to get back into play, leaving his second shot thirty yards shy of the green. The fatigue was visible in the slackened face, as O. B. Keeler described it, "of a man who simply wanted to go home and put away his clubs for a while, maybe forever."

"You could see the strain showing on Byron's face all right," USGA rules official Ike Grainger agreed. "At the seventy-first hole, the long par-three, he hit his approach shot right into a lady spectator's hat, for instance, and had to have a ruling, which cost him a lot of waiting and loss of concentration. He made bogey. That's where I believe he actually let the Open slip."

Byron's desperate twelve-foot putt for par on the final hole just grazed the cup, leaving him tied with Ghezzi and Mangrum. A few minutes later, Ben and Herman Barron reached the final green and had medium-long birdie putts to win outright, but they both made weak attempts and missed maddeningly short par putts. Ben shook Barron's hand and stalked to the locker room without saying a word to anyone.

The next morning, all three men shot 72 in their eighteen-hole play-off, forcing another round in the afternoon, when whatever strength Byron had by the seventeenth hole vaporized when he missed a short par putt and—again, uncharacteristically—slammed the putter into his bag in pure frustration and disgust. "I was so angry with myself for the terrible chip that preceded that putt," he remembered. "Because that cost me my last chance at the Open. I knew at the moment I would never have that opportunity again."

In the end, the four thousand spectators who stuck with the marathon beneath blackening skies that periodically spit cool rain and rumbled with distant thunder saw dual Purple Heart recipient Lloyd Mangrum, the most underrated player of his time, according to Byron, tap in a short putt for 72 to beat Barron by a stroke and Byron by two. The three men shook hands, and Byron offered a weak smile that almost looked, upon reflection, relieved.

He would never play in another U.S. Open. But at least he had something wonderful to go home to.

A few weeks earlier, he had paid $55,000 cash for 630 acres of ranch-land just west of tiny Roanoke's sleepy main street junction, the contribution coming from his work on *Winning Golf*, an instruction book with Minneapolis sportswriter Otis Dypwick. By the time sequence photos were being called for by publisher A. S. Barnes in late summer, Byron was busy painting fences on his dream ranch, and splotches of red paint are visible in the photographs. The first among his rivals to produce a how-to book, he was uncommonly proud of it. And it netted him some decent money, too, a neat quarter from every copy sold. By Christmas that year *Winning Golf* had sold 130,000 copies, the equivalent of a *New York Times* best-seller.

PGA boss Ed Dudley personally assigned archrivals Byron and Ben to separate brackets in the championship that summer in Portland, hoping to produce another great duel in the year's last major. Unfortunately, this wasn't to be: Byron's heart simply wasn't in it. With rumors circulating that he hoped to win the Wanamaker Trophy and then announce his official retirement, in the quarterfinal he was upended by Ed "Porky" Oliver on the final hole of play. (Sam and Mangrum, for the record, were booted out in the first round of match play.)

At that point, the Nelsons headed home and began moving to the somewhat ramshackle ranch house they'd just been given the keys to in Roanoke, leaving the retirement announcement for another day. Tellingly, they needed only two carloads to accomplish the task. After enduring fifteen years of cramped rental houses and drafty hotel rooms, the couple finally had a home. "We had no furniture of our own because we had rented furnished homes the entire time I was on the tour," Byron explained. They borrowed a stove and refrigerator from Louise's sister, Delle, whose husband was still away in the service, and made a few other modest purchases. "When everything was settled, we found we had $2500 to live on," Byron later wrote, "which we figured we could make last six months."

He was careful to add, "I don't recall a happier moment in my life."

After demolishing a pair of largely unknown club pros en route to the PGA's thirty-six-hole semifinal match against his good friend and four-ball partner Demaret, Ben appeared to be a man on a holy mission, posting an unearthly sequence of nines—33-32-31—and steamrolling Jimmy ten-and-nine. Demaret took off his yellow tam and playfully fanned his pal as they shook hands and headed back to the clubhouse to await the verdict on Ben's opponent in the final. One AP reporter compared the victory to the night Joe Louis showed no mercy in knocking out John Henry Lewis, the heavyweight champion's one-eyed and elderly best friend, while others chided Hogan for humiliating his best friend so ruthlessly, though Demaret shrugged off all such talk. When asked, "What was the turning point in the match with Ben?" Jimmy simply gave a broad grin and quipped, "I'd say about ten o'clock, when the match began." The room broke up. Lawton Carver of the Independent News Service, however, soberly concluded, "Hogan is the most ruthless, most cold-blooded and least compassionate of golf foemen. He doesn't merely want to beat you. He wants to trample you underfoot."

That turned out to be the truth, given what happened to Porky

Oliver, a friendly ape of a man who dressed almost as clownishly as Demaret, and entered their thirty-six-hole finale with the imagined momentum of having just beaten the game's leading figure going in his favor. Oliver was a streak putter known for patches of brilliant play that could leave opponents gasping for air. Five years earlier, for instance, at the Western Open, Ben had finished the tournament with a three-shot lead and assumed he'd won, only to see Porky blaze home with a record-breaking 28 to beat him by a stroke.

In Portland, the game's heaviest and lightest competitors (220 pounds versus 137) put on a great show. At the lunch break, Oliver's red-hot putter had him three up and many assumed Ben would choke as he had at Augusta back in the spring. The Hogans retreated to a quiet corner of the clubhouse dining room, where Ben ordered only unbuttered toast, chicken broth, and a glass of ginger ale, which he believed thinned his blood, improved the feel in his fingers, and eased his pesky sinuses, which sometimes flared up during a rainy summer. Before their final eighteen, he dressed head to foot in corporate gray and spent a silent forty-five minutes rapping putts by himself at a remote corner of the practice green, his jaw set like a boxer's awaiting the final-round bell.

Amid fluttering breezes, the knockout began when Ben went out in 30 and leap-frogged over Oliver by two with nine to play. He opened the final nine with three birdies in five holes, four of which he won, and ended the match on the thirty-second hole with yet another birdie. After starting the afternoon round three down, he'd made eight birdies in fourteen holes to win six-and-four, one of the strongest finishes recorded in a PGA final.

At the presentation of the Wanamaker Trophy, his necktie knotted immaculately and every hair on his head neatly water-combed, Ben Hogan finally let out his best movie-star smile.

He'd finally won a major championship.

Beside him, wearing an open-necked shirt under a wrinkled two-tone travel jacket, pleasant Porky Oliver cupped a Pall Mall and grinned sheepishly as the flashbulbs exploded and Ben chose his words carefully.

"It's impossible to explain how much this means to me," he began, halting for several seconds to self-edit whatever was coming next, a quintessential Hogan trait that allowed no room for a misunderstanding. Being misquoted or seeing his words taken out of context by lazy or inexperienced reporters infuriated him. Then he cleared his throat, smiled again, and simply added, "So I'll just say thank you to the PGA and my wife, Valerie."

That appeared to be *that*—though his eyes did widen as he glanced around the press room until he spotted her, standing demurely in the back next to Bob Hudson, the Oregon fruit baron who would just weeks later cover the travel expenses for the British Ryder Cup team and lavishly host them here at the Portland Country Club. As usual, Valerie Hogan looked stylishly turned out, wearing a late-summer corsage of red roses pinned to the lapel of her light tweed jacket. She simply smiled back at him, too shy to reply, blushing adorably.

After reluctantly agreeing to take a few questions, Ben suddenly excused himself and inexplicably left the interview room, prompting a veteran reporter to grumble out loud, "Vintage Ben, another rebuff by golf's frigid midget," prompting ripples of nervous laughter. When Ben returned a few moments later, massaging his eyes, he didn't bother sharing the reason for his abrupt departure because Ben Hogan never felt the need to explain himself to anyone, least of all the press.

In fact, he'd left to take a phone call from Fort Worth, his mother wanting to tell her youngest child how very proud she and Royal and Princess were of him.

Behind the scenes, in the days leading up to Portland, Ben had played a very different role in a dispute that had been simmering for years and now threatened to become a large and nasty public debate. With 2,168 dues-paying members, the vast majority of whom were working club professionals who never got anywhere near a professional tournament, the PGA of America functioned pretty much as a grassroots organization that relied upon its constituent members to give lessons, peddle golf equipment, run amateur events, and serve their club members in whatever social capacity was needed, effectively acting as the Johnny Appleseeds for the old Scottish game in the New World. It was the strong conviction of the PGA establishment that this approach was the one that would broaden golf's appeal as the postwar years unfolded.

However, to the independent contractors whose livelihood, or most of it, came from tournament purses, it was their success, covered in the nation's newspapers and shown in movie-house newsreels, that heightened golf's visibility and attracted newcomers. As far back as the middle 1930s, Gene Sarazen vilified anonymous club pros who slipped away from their day jobs to plunk down an entry fee and compete in a sanctioned PGA tournament, often filling up fields and sometimes depriving their touring rivals of a spot, only to disappear again as invisibly as they came. He dismissed them as "pay and play pros, guys who take the dough from a serious player's pockets and will never be seen again," adding that the only real measure of a player's abilities to compete and draw crowds was how a man performed week to week on tour.

Though only a small percentage enjoyed comfortable affiliation deals that Squire Sarazen had hashed out with a host of clubs, or that Ben enjoyed with Milton Hershey and Sam had with the Greenbrier, many dedicated touring pros believed that breaking away and forming their own management organization was inevitable. Part of Byron's personal conflict related to his own powerful ambivalence—or simple guilt—about serving two masters at once. His internal struggle to reconcile his natural love of teaching as a club professional and his proven ability to compete at the highest level and earn the kind of money that could fulfill his boyhood dreams of owning a ranch was ultimately what drove him from the game.

"In the end," veteran touring pro Paul Runyan said, "Byron might have been the only guy who managed to do both jobs better than anyone. But he paid a big emotional price. Byron felt obligated to just about everybody who wanted a piece of him. That ranch saved his life."

Fred Corcoran's skillful management of players and tournaments through the late '30s and early '40s did much to forestall any outright revolt, but as both hopes and the economy revived in 1946, the issue resurfaced in locker room grumbles that something had to give. The regular tour players wanted their independence, and some were prepared to walk in order to prove it. The PGA wanted to maintain control for a variety of reasons, most of which were related to the money earned by sanctioning accredited tournaments. Days before the pros arrived in Portland for the championship, Ben was chosen to represent them in closed-door meetings with the PGA's board of directors, reprising his sometimes critical hero Gene Sarazen's role in arguing for more autonomy. "Among the top playing pros," wrote PGA historian Herb Graffis, "Sarazen and Hogan are, on the record, the coldest, toughest, most defiant proponents of the policy that tournament golf is a problem whose answers are worked out by clubs, balls, and the scorecard, instead of being a playground for the welfare state."

No breakthroughs, however, were announced in the initial negotiations, merely the news that in November Hogan and the board would convene again to continue their discussion at the board's final meeting in Chicago. Perfectly true to form, buttoned up in his gray cashmere sweater—the very symbol of a corporate man at leisure—the players' negotiator refused to entertain any further public discussion on the matter.

As the summer wound down, many reporters believed the Hogan-Nelson duel that failed to materialize at the PGA in Portland might, ironically, take place at George May's grandiose World Championship in the first week of September, a somewhat meaningless and unofficial two-day moneyfest that was the spiritual antecedent of the big-money, season-ending TV extravaganzas that came to define the game's silly season three decades later. But owing to his revulsion of May's antics—having actually been docked half his earnings for refusing to wear a demeaning number at the All-American earlier in the season—Ben skipped it altogether.

Yet news of the most sensational kind was made at Tam O'Shanter that week when Byron chose this unlikely spot to announce that he was retiring from tournament golf. Though he'd been dropping hints for more than a year, many insiders chose to believe this was just talk, given how brilliantly he was playing and winning. Nothing else made sense. Byron was only thirty-four, realistically at the peak of his game, coming off a streak unlike any in the history of the game. But he had made up his mind.

"From this point onward," he told Charlie Bartlett of the *Tribune*, creating front-page headlines on the eve of the tournament, "I'll only play a few times a year, at the Masters and Texas PGA events mainly." He didn't elaborate on this stunning decision or explain in any depth that owning a ranch and being a homebody would grant him the kind of stable life he'd been craving for years. Eerily presaging the future he'd now charted out, he finished two strokes behind Sam in May's two-day, winner-take-all golf extravaganza. The winner, aping as usual for the photographers, took home the $10,000 first-prize check, while everyone else merely earned traveling expenses for the week.

Within days, Byron was off in the mountains of Idaho elk hunting with a Seattle businessman and Jug McSpaden, telling tales and eating grub by a campfire. Looking down the sights of his rifle at a large bull elk, he squeezed off a shot and saw its knees buckle. "Truthfully," he allowed decades later, "I always felt a little bad about killing animals in the wild. But that turned out to be a wonderful trip in many ways." He had the elk's head mounted and shipped to his father-in-law, Pop Shofner, who hung it on a post in his grocery store and left it there for many years.

Byron's final tournament of the year was the newly renamed Fort Worth Open, where as defending champion he felt obliged to play. Uninspired, he finished seventh. Tellingly, neither Sam nor Ben bothered to show up.

"What a relief to have it all over with," Byron said later. "I packed up my clubs and sent them to MacGregor and told them to keep them till I asked for them, which was going to be a long time. That way, if someone asked me to play even a casual round of golf, I could just tell them I didn't have my clubs, and that would get me off the hook."

And what of Sam? In a year understandably defined by the media's fascination with the storybook rivalry between the departing Byron and the ascendant Ben, Sam was hardly a forgotten man. Despite his growing problems with the flatstick, he managed to collect a respectable six victories, highlighted by a third Miami Open and a second title at Greensboro, both of which were upstaged by an unexpected title he never saw coming, and one of the biggest plums of all—the Open Championship at St. Andrews.

Eight weeks before taking George May's loot in Chicago, he had a meeting there with I. B. Icely, the president of Wilson Sporting Goods, to discuss the latest version of his premium Blue Ridge irons and a line of Sam Snead wedges the company planned to roll out early in 1947. Sam was already playing a custom Wilson golf ball, and in the years ahead would receive a princely royalty off every sale using his name or image. Over the next thirty-five years, Wilson also counted LPGA founders Patty Berg and Babe Didrikson, Walter Hagen, and a promising Pennsylvanian named Arnold Palmer among its playing staff. The company would produce no fewer than four different lines of Sam Snead clubs, sustaining one of the longest player representation deals in any sport.

Icely had been talking to wily old Hagen, four-time Open champion and honorary Anglophile, who convinced him that Snead needed to be the first postwar American to win a Claret Jug. With the golf's oldest and most venerated championship resuming at St. Andrews after a six-year break, a win by the most colorful American in the game—not to mention the closest in spirit and personality to the Haig himself—would amount, he argued, to a public relations windfall for both Sam and Wilson.

Sam initially rebuffed the idea. "I still had memories of the bad food and the sorry accommodations from the Ryder Cup in 1937," he explained years later without a whit of hesitation. "And when I learned they were putting up something like only six hundred dollars, why, I said no way to that. That wouldn't even cover my expenses." Sam's opinion was best summarized by this acid comment: "Anytime you're playing golf outside the United States, hell, it's just camping out."

He also protested that his putting was, at least for the moment, in terrible shape. He could handle the thirty-footers all right, he said, but every time he stood over a three-footer "it's like a rattlesnake lifts its head out of the cup." Moreover, the firm and quirky British courses—typically less manicured than their American counterparts, producing unpredictable bounces and situations—simply didn't suit his game. Undeterred, Icely replied that the greens at St. Andrews were "big as a barnyard" and that Walter Hagen had graciously offered to give him some putting tips and advice on playing links-style courses. Then he sweetened the deal by promising to pay his travel expenses. Reluctantly, Sam agreed to go.

Things went unpromisingly from the start. The sum of Sir Walter's putting advice was that he should strike the ball above the equator in order to impart more topspin, ostensibly producing a truer roll. Sam rejected this notion based on his own conversations with Hogan, who maintained that too much topspin prevented the ball from "dying" near the cup, a theory he'd picked up from watching Jones putt. Since Ben was then widely regarded as the finest putter in the game, Sam was quick to trust his ideas. "Using Hagen's method," he later wrote, "I'd seen many a ball go half in and flip out. And I'd topped far too many putts, also."

Then, before taking off from New York's Idlewild Airport, the distinctive three-tailed Lockheed Constellation sprang a fuel leak and suffered an engine fire, prompting a hasty runway evacuation of the smoke-filled plane. Sam, shaken by the episode and forever susceptible to a cosmic reading of events, perceived it as a sign of awful things to come. Only the thought of facing down both Hagen and Icely got him back on the plane. Upon reaching London, a city still in the throes of postwar reconstruction, he found that the hotel Wilson had booked for him was still undergoing renovations and hadn't reopened yet. He spent the entire afternoon and evening carting his large leather golf bag around Mayfair and Kensington Road, looking for a suitable hotel or guesthouse, before giving up and making for Paddington Station, where he spent the "miserable night cussing my bad luck" on a bench waiting for a morning train to Edinburgh.

Transferring to the smaller train that linked Edinburgh to St. Andrews, Sam was pleased to discover his fellow American Lawson Little ensconced in a cramped first-class compartment with a tweedy British gentleman. He joined them and fell into conversation, offering his usual blunt perspective on a range of subjects, starting with his belief that British food was even worse now than it was before the war. At one point, as the dreamy spires of St. Andrews appeared on the horizon, Sam glanced out the window and casually remarked, "Well, boys, what do you make of that? Looks like an old abandoned golf course."

"That, sir," his British traveling companion declared with visible indignation, "is the Old Course at St. Andrews, the most famous golf course on earth. That building beyond it is the Royal and Ancient Golf Club."

"Well, how about that?" Sam came back, unimpressed. "Looks more like a pasture back home than a golf course."

Within hours, his comments found their way to the sports pages of Britain's dailies, featuring him as a Twainian rube abroad. "Snead, a rural American type," sniffed the *Scotsman on Sunday*, "would think the Leaning Tower of Pisa a structure about to totter and crash at his feet." A columnist for the *Evening Standard* wondered why arguably the most popular player in his own country had even bothered to come so far if he found "The Home of Golf so unsuited to his tastes. Perhaps a pasture back home in Virginia would suffice."

The mutual disaffection deepened when Sam was unable to secure a decent caddie, and in fact he had four different ones over his days of practice rounds and the tournament itself. The first whistled whenever he putted and was sent packing the moment they finished. His successor, a young man in Royal Navy pants, couldn't read distances worth a lick, and Sam—who unlike Ben relied heavily on a caddie's judgment—came up woefully short on several approach shots. He was let go in favor of a veteran caddie recommended by the head porter at Rusack's Marine Hotel, where Sam was staying.

"Old Scotty," he was assured, was the finest looper in the Auld Grey Toon, as good as they came at reading the Old Course's quirks. They played a final practice round and, indeed, Sam's nerves not only settled a bit but he also began to see what Bob Jones meant by his remark that every time one played the Old Course, one's admiration of it deepened. Unfortunately, on the eve of the championship, Old Scotty vanished into his favorite pub and got arrested for public drunkenness, requiring Sam to hire a fourth caddie, little more than a teenage bag carrier, just minutes before he teed off.

Somehow, through all of this, providence smiled on him. Tee to green he was never in better command of his game, playing the most intelligent golf of his career, outdriving a strong field that in addition to Little included the great Henry Cotton, South African Bobby Locke, Welshman Dai Rees, and even his old Carolina traveling pal Johnny Bulla by an average of thirty yards. More important, he admitted later, his respect for the Old Course's countless subtleties began to appeal to the natural shotmaker in him; the need to improvise and imaginatively create things on the spot was an instinctive talent Sam possessed in much greater depth than either Byron or Ben.

On the vast double greens, for instance, using a slightly heavier blade putter than his normal one, he devised a strategy of lagging his ball to within a three-foot circumference rather than trying to hole every long putt. After fifty-four holes, with a sharp wind increasing off the Firth, he found himself sharing in a three-way tie for the lead with Rees, Locke, and Bulla. "Sam had the golf in him to win," as Herbert Warren Wind noted. "The only question was how Sam, who had never won a big championship at medal play after his ordeal at Spring Mill, would bear up to the crucial eighteen holes."

He was the last man to go out, thus bearing the additional pressure of knowing what score he'd have to beat in order to win. On the outward leg, indeed, he suffered two costly three-putts and missed yet another maddening two-footer at the ninth for an easy birdie. "Putting in that wind," he said later, "was a guess." On making the turn, however, he learned from a marshal armed with a military walkie-talkie that the others were having even more difficulty in the high winds, their scores ballooning. At ten, he drained a slow-rolling downhiller for a birdie, and on twelve rolled home a timely second birdie from thirty feet. On the fourteenth tee, a Scotsman stuck his whiskers in his face and declared, "You can shoot sixes from here on in, laddie, and win."

After Spring Mill, Sam was taking nothing for granted. He played cautiously wide of infamous "Hell Bunker" and made birdie on the hole but three-putted on sixteen green for bogey. Coming off the green, facing the notorious "Road Hole," he spotted Richards Vidmer, the former *New York Times* columnist who was covering the Open for the *Herald Tribune*, and asked for an update on scores. Rees and Bulla, he learned, were still close. But the others had fallen back. "A pair of sixes on the last two will get you in with a tie," Vidmer told him. "But a six-five finish will win it."

Sam still wasn't convinced. Following a conservative drive to the left-hand side of the dangerous, half-hidden fairway, his smooth nine-iron approach shot was batted to the right by a sudden, brisk cross-breeze, settling in a swale off the putting surface. Though one of the finest chippers ever, he cautiously opted to lag putt—having absorbed one of the cardinal lessons of Old Course mastery. Rewarded for his decision to keep his ball on the ground, he watched it climb the slope and curl lazily toward the hole, given an extra roll or two by the wind itself—and then disappear into the cup. The most appreciative golf fans on earth hailed the least popular figure in the field with a robust volley of cheers. Brilliance on the Road Hole forgave a multitude of sins, including intemperate and uninformed remarks.

Sam finished with an easy par that gave him a four-stroke victory in golf's oldest championship. He removed his hat and shook hands all around, smiling like a man who'd been promoted from the mail room to the office of the chairman of the board.

For years to come, he would tell anyone who'd listen that his surprising birdie on seventeen—rightly considered the toughest hole to birdie in all of championship golf—won him the Claret Jug, though in fact he had the championship well in hand by then. Some British writers actually take a much different view of his finish. "His victory at St. Andrews in the first championship after the war was remarkable rather for the failure of Locke and the others, including Cotton and Rees, to stay the course, rather than for Snead's exceptional play," reflected an otherwise admiring Pat Ward-Thomas in the *Manchester*

Guardian. "This was not surprising as the British were unaccustomed to the pressure of tournament golf after six years without any, and there may have been something in Cotton's claim that the lack of good food undermined their stamina." Even Sam might have concurred with this last point.

Regardless, indisputably, his 290 eclipsed all four of Walter Hagen's victories, two of Bob Jones's three winning scores, and also bested Tommy Armour's when he carted home the Auld Mug. More to the point, Sam had won his first medal-play major championship under extremely adverse conditions by playing the most astute golf of his career, and though the paltry financial benefit prompted him to decide on the spot that he would likely not return to defend his title, which made him few friends in the Home of Golf, he went to his grave spinning tales about that magical week on the Auld Sod and rightly giving himself some credit for helping to revive American interest in the Open.

One of his favorite moments came as he was leaving the presentation of the Claret Jug, when his errant caddie Scotty reappeared from the crowd and begged to have the winning ball as a keepsake, a memento of their special time together. "I'll always treasure it," Scotty growled affectionately, wiping an eye as Sam handed it over.

"Damned if he didn't take that ball and sell it within the hour," Sam loved to say, shaking his head and laughing, then admitting that he might well have done the same thing himself under the circumstances. "He made fifty pounds off that ball—more than I made for winning the Open."

12

Then There Were Two

W ith Byron Nelson now a full-time rancher, Sam Snead approached 1947 believing that only Ben Hogan stood between him and domination of the PGA Tour. Sam had already concluded that Ben was the premier ball striker of their day and perhaps all time. "Nobody was ever better at eliminating mistakes from a golf swing than Hogan, and knowing exactly which shot to hit when it was needed," he once said. "That's what set him apart from the rest. He intimidated the pants off most of the other guys out there because he never gave up ground. But he brought out the best in me. My record shows that. Anytime I played head to head with Ben, why, I felt there was something special on it."

Ironically, Ben told friends he felt Sam was the premier ball striker of all time, lacking only in the decision-making department. "If I'd caddied for Sam," he once told friends at Shady Oaks, "no one else would have been in the record book."

Coming off a season-ending win at the Miami Open in early December, Sam believed he'd finally worked things out with a balky putting stroke that had cost him half a dozen tournaments that year alone. But his optimism proved premature. At the start of the '47 season in Los Angeles, a pair of 69s broke the event's thirty-six-hole scoring mark but an old nemesis suddenly returned, the jerky putting stroke he labeled "the yips," producing one of the largest scoring free falls in years. "I broke down completely. . . . The yips took me then and tore me apart," he recounts in *The Education of a Golfer*. "The rest of my game was never better but on the carpet I was a zombie. Over the ball, I felt like someone else's hands held the putter. All control was gone. No such thing as a straight line to any cup existed." He finished tied twenty-fifth in a tournament he'd won just two years before.

A week later in the relatively cloistered privacy of the Monterey Peninsula, he desperately experimented with a variety of grips and techniques on putts: cross-handed, reverse grips, stiff-armed, even putting one-handed as Joe Turnesa suggested. He saw slight improvement but finished third in the Crosby Clambake and was happy to climb aboard another Constellation for a flight to Africa for a series of exhibition matches against the gnomish and knickered Arthur D'Arcy "Bobby" Locke, who'd tied for second in the Open Sam, won at St. Andrews, and brassily proposed a $10,000 challenge match over a series of courses on his home turf. Fred Corcoran was happy to oblige, and the South African Tourism Board and a diamond company put up the funds.

After their first nine holes at Locke's home club near Johannesburg, Sam had his host five down. "I thought I'd run him right out of Africa," he remembered, "but then he went to work, and after thirty-six holes he had me eight down with seven holes to play."

It was the height of irony, perhaps, that the particular genius of Old Baggy Pants—as Sam liked to call him—was Locke's brilliant and wildly unconventional putting stroke, which required him to grip his putter high and lightly and take the putter head back sharply on the inside path, then hood the face at impact, producing a distinctive "hooking" spin on the putt, a technique he claimed he'd picked up from a dipsomaniacal Englishman while serving in the South African Air Force in Egypt during the war. In doing so, Locke violated every commonly accepted principle of putting. He had a closed stance, "swayed like a Bloomer Girl" instead of staying still, and claimed to be able to hook or, conversely, fade any putt into the hole by manipulating the putter head with his hands, meant to neutralize the effect of the grainy Bermuda greens of the warm-weather courses where he grew up playing. Moreover, he could read a green superbly, and went on to capture four Open Championships of his own. And he certainly made a true believer out of Sam, whom he blitzed in twelve of their sixteen matches over three weeks. At the Bulawayo Club in Rhodesia, a large gray monkey sauntered onto the green and leaned against the flagstick as Sam struck a short approach shot. "Here, buster," the Slammer quipped, trying to hand him his putter, "you can do better than me."

Before they parted company, the genial Locke asked his victim if he thought he might make some money on the American tour. "With that putter of yours," Sam said with his usual candor, "you could get rich." In his estimation, the only putter equal to him was Ben Hogan and his sidekick Demaret.

Sam's frank appraisal led to unexpected grief back home when, within weeks, Locke was winning tournaments right and left on American soil, pocketing more than $27,000 with his unconventional putting stroke during his first five months in America. Despite his late start in 1947, he finished in second place on the PGA money list behind Demaret, and in the fifty-nine events he played over the next two and a half years, he won eleven times and finished in the top three in more than half of the other events, leaving his American competitors increasingly resentful. In 1949, ostensibly because of his alleged failure to fulfill several playing commitments, the tour took the unusual step of banning Locke from the American circuit. Claude Harmon, the Winged Foot pro and '48 Masters champion, came closest to identifying the real motivation when he candidly told an Augusta reporter, "Locke was simply too good. They had to ban him." Not until 1951 did the tour yield to complaints of unfairness in the American press and rescind the decision. But by this point the colorful Locke, who favored long-sleeve shirts and four-in-hand ties, had collected two Open titles en route to seventy-two international career wins that established him as the world's first truly international golf star, and certainly the patriarch of a distinguished line of South Africans from Gary Player to Ernie Els and Retief Goosen, among others.

Sam's African adventure only deepened his gloom and marked the beginning of a classic "dark night of the soul" in which he actually stopped competing for several months. He went hunting and fishing, dug up boulders in the new pasture, and worked in the barn at the handsome new home, Old Snead Links, that he and Audrey built in a lovely vale just south of the village of Hot Springs. "I was a walking nervous breakdown," he said. "Hanging up my clubs, I swore I'd never play like a dog in public again. . . . Six years of good putting during which I'd won forty tournaments followed by three years of yips made no sense. Off by myself on the Old White Course at the Greenbrier, I started experimenting all over again."

Over the next three months, he ventured out to play in just one event, the Masters, where Byron Nelson, to nobody's particular surprise, came out of retirement to finish in a tie for second with his former pupil, Frank Stranahan. Demaret claimed the title with a sensational seven-under total, and Sam finished with a wretched tie for twenty-second place. A week before the U.S. Open, however, he registered modest improvement at the National Capital Open in Washington, a tie for fourth, using a heavier blade putter with no offset, making several key adjustments that included a "comfortable wider stance" over the ball, more arm motion to improve his smoothness and a takeaway that emphasized keeping the putter low and encouraged the left hand to "lead" through the putt—a technique more reminiscent of Ben Hogan's than Bobby Locke's.

As the national championship commenced at the relatively short and benign St. Louis Country Club in Clayton, Missouri, he was rolling the ball noticeably better, opening with a workmanlike one-over 72 and trailing a group of largely unknown players except for Locke at 68 and Hogan at 70. The book on Sam was that in this event he started like a thoroughbred but finished like a nag, as symbolized by his infamous Spring Mill disaster and a final-round collapse in 1940 when he led going into the final round at Canterbury and could have won with a mere 72. Instead he produced the worst concluding round of his Open career, a horrific 81 that seemed to validate his Open jinx in many minds, worst of all his own.

This time, however, Sam played like a champion to the seventy-second hole and beyond. With Hogan and Locke having blown their chances by ballooning to 75 and 74 respectively in the second round, he cobbled together three solid rounds of 70 and faced a fifteen-foot birdie putt on the final hole to tie relatively unheralded Lew Worsham. The supposed "hillbilly choke artist" calmly holed the putt to force an eighteen-hole playoff. "The crowd roared. Sam smiled, and Worsham walked over and shook his hand," recounts U.S. Open historian Bob Sommers. "It was as courageous a putt as any man ever holed." Perhaps his greatest demon had finally been vanquished.

Indeed, over the first fifteen holes the next day, Sam displayed the same power and control that won the Open at St. Andrews while Worsham, a wry and likable twenty-nine-year-old fellow Virginian, was in and out of the rough, scrambling to make pars and keep up. "With three holes to play Lew was two down and it looked like Sam finally had his Open. I think the gallery was really with him at that point, wanting to see him get this jinx thing behind him," remembers Bill Campbell, the recent Princeton graduate Sam had befriended back when they played together in a pro-am at the Greenbrier in 1936. Just fifteen when they met, Campbell would go on to play in thirty-nine U.S. Amateur Championships—winning in 1964—and anchor eight Walker Cup teams, serve two terms as president of the USGA, and become captain of the Royal and Ancient Golf Club of St. Andrews. The unlikely rapport between Sam and this worldly, Ivy League paragon of amateur golf ripened over time into one of the game's most enduring friendships.

On the sixteenth hole, Worsham rolled in a clutch twenty-foot birdie putt to halve Sam's lead. Owing to nerves, both men hit poor second shots to the par-four seventeenth green. Worsham hooked his to the adjoining eighteenth fairway and Sam's cut shot left fell short in deep rough. Worsham got his third onto the green but Sam punched his ball over the green into the rough, then chipped to within six feet of the cup. He missed his putt and Worsham holed his and the pair headed to the home hole all square.

For a change in an Open playoff, the estimated five thousand spectators closely trailing both players were treated to one of the most dramatic finishes in history. Sam struck a gorgeous approach shot to the semiblind eighteenth green that left him twenty feet to negotiate for birdie. Worsham's ball skipped across the putting surface and ran off the back edge, stopping just shy of the thick collar. Wasting little time, however, he chipped a low runner that caught an edge of the cup and stopped two and a half feet past the hole.

With the title in his grasp, Sam calmly stepped up to his ball and rolled it gently down the slope, his only miscalculation being the speed of the putt. His ball stopped short about the same distance away as Worsham's, only on the upper slope.

"I knew Sam's body English and personality well enough to know he was zeroed in on that final putt," recalls Bill Campbell, who was planted on the back portion of the green, as close to the action as he could get. "That's why he went straight up to it and prepared to putt. Sam had one of the best eyes for distances ever—a hunter's eye, you could say. He knew he was away. That's why what happened next rattled him so deeply."

As he took his stance, Worsham suddenly called out, "Wait a minute, Sam. Are you sure you're away?"

Sam glanced up, scowled slightly, backed off a few paces and shook his head, convinced he was being gamed—himself being a walking encyclopedia on little things that could unnerve an opponent at a critical moment. He was certain he had the honor, and his mind began to bubble with anger.

Ike Grainger, the wiry chairman of the USGA rules committee, was summoned to determine who was entitled to putt first. "Somehow the story got started that there was a long delay and a lot of confusion over the issue," he recalled to a reporter in the mid-1990s. "But that wasn't the case at all. Sam was visibly upset and told me he was obviously away and wanted to putt. I made him wait. He walked off a few yards to wait for a tape measuring device brought by our assistant on the scene."

One can clearly read Sam's feelings in a remarkable photograph taken as Worsham and the two USGA officials bend over to measure the two putts. His feet are crossed, his right hand planted on a hip as he leans gently on his putter with his left, radiating an expression of incomprehensible disgust.

"I was so mad I could have spit," Sam recalled decades later. "But I knew that was exactly what Lew had hoped would happen, I'd be rattled. We both knew what was going on and I just failed to get my mind settled in time to recover my composure."

Grainger's ruling confirmed what Sam already knew. He was 30.5 inches away as opposed to Worsham's 29.5. Shaking his head, he took his stance again, inhaling and exhaling to try to regain his focus and make the smooth left-hand finish that had served him so splendidly all week. It wasn't an easy putt, downhill with a significant left to right break, exactly the kind Sam detested. As he leaned over the ball, only the drone of a plane far overhead could be heard. He stroked the putt smoothly but too gently to hold its line. The gallery groaned as his ball missed the cup and stopped two inches away. Worsham, on the other hand, wasted no time in replacing his marked ball and firmly rolling his short uphill putt into the back of the cup to become the 1947 U.S. Open champion.

"Sam looked like he'd been shot through the heart," Bill Campbell recalls. "I didn't want to go over and speak to him because I knew he was in absolute agony. I followed him up to the clubhouse and we spoke a little later. By then he was pretty well composed. But coming on the heels of his other Open troubles, that one proved the most devastating. It only confirmed his worst fears about a jinx."

After a week of farm work back home, he was in Detroit for the

PGA Championship, still brooding about the incident, when Ben Hogan—who'd finished tied for sixth at St. Louis—walked over in the Plum Hollow Country Club locker room to say hello. "I was always grateful to Ben for that," Sam remembered. "He knew what it meant to me more than anybody else because he'd been there."

According to Bill Campbell, "If Sam had won either of the Opens he blew on the final hole I'm convinced his life would have been, in some ways, quite different. There's no telling how much more he would have won. He would have had the respect he so desperately hungered for most of his career, especially playing in the shadows of Hogan and Nelson. He once told me a day never passed when he failed to think about that missed putt at St. Louis."

Curiously, according to Campbell, Sam never held a grudge against Worsham. In fact, at season's end, they went deer hunting together. "Sam always blamed himself for not keeping his composure that day," he adds. "But what happened in St. Louis, I'm convinced, ruined the Open forever for Sam, and sent him into a very deep slump that could have ended his playing career."

Indeed, Sam finished 1947 with no victories and only slightly more than $9,000 in official earnings, less than he'd won his first year on the tour a decade before. The following year was even more nightmarish, with a host of unimaginably bad finishes—a woeful tie for thirtieth at the Crosby and another for forty-third at St. Petersburg, a tournament he'd won twice. He played seventeen events and won just once, slipping past a modest field in the rain-delayed Texas Open in early February to finish a distant eighteenth on the money list, earning a paltry $6,980 for the year. Compounding his frustrations—and touching his greatest fear of all, common to many rural survivors of the Great Depression, the unvoiced terror of going flat broke—were whispers that his endorsement contracts with Gillette razors and Havoline Oil were in jeopardy. Only Wilson Golf and the Greenbrier reaffirmed their commitments to a suddenly struggling superstar. The company's new mid-range clubs bearing his distinctive signature were, after all, the best-selling off-the-rack sets among the estimated one million golfers who took up the game that year.

One man's misfortune, goes an ancient Chinese proverb, is another's golden temple. And so it appeared to be with the remaining active

members of the American Triumvirate. Following his PGA triumph in
'46, Ben won four of his seven tournaments, including another North
and South Open, concluding the year with thirteen victories and
$43,212, the most tour prize money any professional golfer had ever
made in a single year. Perhaps more significantly, exactly three months
after hoisting his first Wanamaker Trophy the game's most dominant
player appeared behind closed doors at Chicago's stolid Bismarck
Hotel, dressed like a successful Wall Street banker in a summer-weight
worsted gray suit, and resumed his case for more self-governance and
greater autonomy on the tour. "There's a big need for young blood,"
he argued in an article written exclusively for Detroit's *Free Press* that
went out over the national wires to four hundred newspapers before
the meetings. "It's wide open for those who can make the grade but
that need isn't being filled."

As he bluntly put it to the PGA's executive committee, if the touring
pros' growing resentment and their desire to handle their own affairs
and determine their own fate wasn't soon addressed, promising prospects would either stay put in the amateur ranks or opt for safer club
jobs. In order to give professional golf a suitable platform to create new
stars that would, he argued, "stimulate interest and grow the game,"
the tour's players needed—in fact demanded—their own governing
organization. "If you don't do this," he soberly warned, "you're likely
to soon have one hell of a civil war on your hands."

The PGA board listened to his assessment with clenched teeth, and
one of them later remarked that Hogan left the room the most "loathed
man in golf." His remarks sounded more like a manifesto than a discussion, but if anyone had the power to call down the long-threatened
rebellion, it was Ben Hogan. So the committee reluctantly voted to create a Tournament Bureau run strictly by the players themselves, essentially independent of direct PGA influence. It was further proposed
that Fred Corcoran continue merely as the tour's promotion director,
a clear demotion owing to his close business ties with Sam Snead,
though everyone agreed that he was unrivaled at lining up sponsors
and generating commercial perks and lucrative exhibitions.

In a fascinating footnote to these negotiations, the genial Corcoran
tore up his old contract with the PGA and accepted this diminished
role in exchange for a new contract that granted him exclusive TV and
radio rights on all tour events. With his marketer's genius, he saw the
advent of commercial television as a potential windfall for profes-

sional golf in general and himself in particular. Introduced in 1939 but derailed by the war, the first TV sets reached the consumer marketplace in 1946, and the far-sighted Corcoran understood that this exciting new medium could make Snead, Hogan, and their colleagues (not to mention his other star clients) even wealthier and household names across the country.

In this sweetheart deal, he retained a full third of any profits that derived from broadcast rights for the next three years. "That was the most valuable document I ever held in my hand," he lamented years later. "Today that contract would be worth millions. But I was a little ahead of my time." Among other things, he described calling on Tom Gallery, the sports director of the National Broadcasting Company in late 1948, and offering him exclusive rights to PGA golf for television. Since the early '40s the network had limited coverage of the U.S. Open, the Masters, and the PGA Championship through its radio network, competing for this privilege with rival CBS Sports—soon to be headed by John Derr, who shared Corcoran's belief that TV would soon become a factor in the broadcast mix. "All he [Gallery] had to do was sign up and NBC would have owned television golf," Corcoran said. Instead, Gallery told him, "Listen, Fred. Golf is just not a TV sport. Don't bother me anymore."

Derr and Corcoran weren't the only ones who saw a future in televising golf. In the fall of 1945, Cliff Roberts sent a memorandum to Augusta National's club manager, James Searle, expressing interest in the emerging medium. Moreover, when upstart CBS Sports declined to renew its radio contract with the Masters—having failed to strike an exclusive deal—Roberts signed a new contract with NBC that gave NBC the option on television as well. "As late as two months before the 1947 Masters," according to Masters historian David Owens, "Roberts believed they might do so." But Gallery showed no interest, convinced that the logistics of covering a tournament with unpredictable lighting and stationary cameras were unfeasible. That same summer at the U.S. Open where Sam Snead's heart was broken again, a St. Louis TV station broadcast the final hole of the fourth round—a first in television history. Little came of it, however.

It wasn't until six years later—or three years *after* Corcoran's new contract ran out—that another visionary, Chicago's George S. May, decided to give the medium another shot by broadcasting live coverage of the final hole of his World Championship at Tam O'Shanter, a drama that remained in doubt until the tournament's final shot. Once more Lew Worsham was at center stage, needing to get down in two from the fairway in order to tie journeyman Chandler Harper, who was already perched on the clubhouse terrace enjoying a gimlet cocktail. A single wide-angle lens secured on top of the grandstand (another May innovation) enabled the viewing audience to see Worsham punch a wedge from a hundred yards, his ball disappearing into the cup for an eagle. Unable to contain his excitement, Jimmy Demaret, who was commentating for radio and television, blurted out, "The son of a bitch holed it!" What in time would be called the "shot seen round the world" stunningly illustrated the medium's dramatic potential, though regular coverage was still three years in the future.

Coming on the heels of his first major championship, Ben's successful negotiations with the PGA of America in late 1946 serve as an effective birth date for modern professional golf, establishing a working blueprint that would lead to formal separation and a fully independent PGA Tour two decades later. In the meantime, just six days into the new year, Hogan blitzed the field to win his second L.A. Open, wasting little time while his rivals jockeyed for influence in the new self-governing tour and haggled with Corcoran over such minutiae as caddie fees and entry fees. During a dispute over the higher exhibition fees Corcoran set for marquee names—a charge he didn't deny—Johnny Bulla confronted Corcoran and sucker-punched him in the gut, followed by an equally irate Dick Metz, who poked him in the nose. "I felt like I was under siege all over again," Corcoran explained to a reporter decades later. "No one really knew what this new independence would mean to the players, or how it would essentially work. So everybody wanted in on the decisions, fearing they'd be short-changed. Eventually it settled down when the boys realized Hogan was a bigger threat to their livelihoods than either me or the PGA of America."

As Sam disappeared to deal with the worst slump of his career, Ben put together a strong year by anyone's standards except perhaps his own, winning nine tournaments (two unofficial) and more than $30,000, good enough for second spot on the money list behind his pal Jimmy Demaret, who also captured his second Masters. The real surprise of 1947 came on the eve of the U.S. Open in June, when nationally syndicated sports columnist Oscar Fraley broke some startling news:

"Ben Hogan, the miniature Irishman who ranks with the all-time golfing giants, has just about reached the point today where he is ready
to retire. Hogan, like many of his illustrious predecessors, is deathly
tired of the competitive fairways and greens. Others who reached that
breaking point where they actually hated the game were Byron Nelson and Henry Picard—and they didn't hang around long afterwards."
Declining to name his sources, Fraley concluded, "The bantam Benny
is hanging on because he wants one more crack at the U.S. Open and
wants to try and defend his PGA title. After those two are over he
is expected to say adieu, even though he won't admit it now." Weeks
before, Fraley and others had begun writing the same thing about Sam
Snead, noting that his age—thirty-five, relatively old for athletes of any
other sport—and ailing putter might finally be pushing him to the
front porch for good.

True to form, Ben made no effort to either confirm or deny Fraley's
claims—though his sixth-place finish in St. Louis did little to challenge
them. Just a week later, in a rare back-to-back staging of major championships, both Ben and Sam seemed to confirm Fraley's clairvoyance,
with the former free-falling to a tie for thirty-third at the PGA Championship at Plum Hollow, and the latter struggling home in seventeenth
place.

Only the dazzling performance at the 1947 Ryder Cup at Oregon's
rain-swept Portland Country Club in early November briefly stanched
the rampant speculation about the game's biggest stars. Under a new
points system that allowed each team's captain to make two additional
selections, Ben invited Byron to play and the American side demolished the visiting Brits 11–1, the largest rout in Ryder Cup history, small
consolation being that host millionaire and Oregon fruit baron Bob
Hudson picked up the entire traveling tab for the distinguished visitors. In the Saturday foursomes, Sam and Lloyd Mangrum, Ben and
Jimmy Demaret, and Byron and Herman Barron won with relative ease,
while on Sunday, secretly nursing a severely sore back, Ben sat out and
watched Sam destroy Henry Cotton and Byron polish off Arthur Lees
in single matches that sealed the lopsided triumph.

During the Christmas break, Ben saw a specialist in Fort Worth and
took heating treatments for his lower back and the mysterious pains
radiating through his shoulders and neck; a battery of tests deter-

mined there was nothing wrong beyond the draining effects of fatigue and stress on his well-traveled thirty-five-year-old body. His physician prescribed daily aspirin, an improved diet, and plenty of rest and relaxation, advising him to take up a new hobby.

Ben Hogan was not a hobby kind of guy. For two decades every molecule of his being had been dedicated to putting him through the refiner's fire, transforming himself from a West Texas nobody into the most efficient killing machine in golf. Telling him to find a new hobby was like asking Fred Astaire take up square-dancing for fun, or Humphrey Bogart to try community theater. Even so, he accepted Jimmy Demaret's invitation to go deer hunting in Arkansas, where for three nights they sat under the stars by a fire and shared views on a variety of subjects, including the touchy one of retirement. Time was also knocking on Jimmy the Showman's door. For years, he'd implied that Ben, Byron, and Sam were his venerable seniors—when, in fact, he was actually two years older. Taking full advantage of his recent breakthrough and domination of the money list, however, he was already pondering a second career in radio, and possibly television, and was eager to start his own golf club back home in Houston.

"You know, Jimmy," Ben surprised him by saying on their drive back to Texas, "I feel better than I have in years. This break has been just the thing."

According to Demaret, they'd spotted several trophy-sized whitetails, but unlike Byron in the Bitterroots two autumns before, neither man had the desire to fire a shot.

Two weeks later, in vivid contrast to the gloomy, unapproachable figure who failed to make any headway at the U.S. Open and the PGA Championship the previous summer, a visibly relaxed and beaming Ben Hogan showed up at the Riviera Country Club in Pacific Palisades three days before the start of the L.A. Open. Being in Tinseltown, where he and Val dined with the likes of Katharine Hepburn and his pal Bing Crosby, always elevated Ben's spirits, a poignant echo of his childhood fascination with Hollywood stardom. As more than one reporter noted, whatever had been chewing at him for most of 1947 appeared to be gone. He granted several relaxed interviews and made self-deprecating jokes about his back and Oscar Fraley's fortune-telling skills.

Few if any sportswriters had a clue about what made Ben Hogan tick. Like Sam, he was actually a friendly and highly sentimental man whose life was governed by a strong code of honor, though he carefully entombed this part of his nature behind an impenetrable wall of hard work, accomplishment, and an unshakable fear of revealing any more than was necessary about his past. His hard shell and curt responses were merely about self-preservation. Hennie Bogan, on the other hand, had a soft spot for stray animals and a natural compassion for anyone who'd been dealt a raw hand. He sometimes clipped newspaper stories about people facing undeserved setbacks and tragedies, piling them neatly in his office desk drawer, and he always exhibited great personal warmth and almost fanatical devotion to his wife and her family and a handful of intimate friends that included Marvin Leonard, Bing Crosby, and oil man George Coleman, whom he met on tour in the early 1930s and later became Oklahoma Amateur champion.

Two other factors gave Ben's spirits a lift that week at Riviera. One was the publication of *Power Golf,* an instructional book that would soon follow Byron Nelson's book onto the best-seller lists. In gratitude to the man who'd helped him unlock the mystery of his own golf swing, Ben dedicated it to Henry Picard. As this remarkable year unfolded, the fact that his book outsold Byron's gave Ben untold satisfaction.

The other positive was Riviera itself. Ben had grown to love just about everything about this tight and challenging course with its small, firm, and fast greens and sticky kikuyu grass rough. It's where he began the 1947 season with a convincing victory, and he naturally hoped to defend his title. Unlike most of his colleagues, Ben generally played his best golf on the most difficult layouts, which made his unsuccessful U.S. Open performances doubly frustrating. Not counting his controversial 1942 Hale America Open victory, which he considered the national championship under a different name, in seven appearances before 1948 he had never finished higher than tied for third—rather pathetic for a man now regarded as the best player in the world. In June, however, the Open was scheduled to return to sweet Riviera, which made the L.A. Open feel a little like a glorious warm-up session, reflected by Ben's four beautiful rounds of 68-70-70-67 for a record-breaking 275, a mark that would stand for another quarter century.

When asked about his sterling play, he attributed it to the fast greens and superb conditions, then added that Riviera would be a "very different place" for the national championship, playing at least six to eight strokes tougher. Before heading to Bing's Clambake, while signing books at Bullock's department store in downtown Los Angeles, he confided to a sports columnist, "I think a score of 282 to 284 will win the Open," a distinctive Hogan ploy to make a demanding course seem even more intimidating to any would-be rivals. As usual, what he didn't say was more important than what he revealed. As he confided to Valerie afterward, the more psychologically intimidated other players were by the prospect of Riviera in June—and, not coincidentally, by his mastery of it—the fewer of them he would have to beat.

At this point in his career, not unlike Byron and Sam at their peaks, Ben calculated that there were generally only a handful of players he needed to worry about in a major championship, so the harder the course played, the better his chances. In years to come, employing a variation of this form of psychological warfare, he made a point of granting select interviews following his practice rounds at major championships and expressing mild surprise at the relatively easy conditions. This immediately panicked the sponsoring organization into sending out maintenance crews to double-cut and roll the greens to make them lethally fast, to heavily water the rough and let it grow longer and thicker, to plan tougher pin placements and strengthen all the course's defenses—all of which, generally speaking, benefited one little gray man far more than anyone else in the field.

On the Monday morning he and Valerie checked out of the swanky Beverly Wilshire Hotel, he saw a headline that declared him the "Man to Beat" at the upcoming U.S. Open. Riviera, meanwhile, had a new nickname. The press was already calling it "Hogan's Alley."

By April, however, Ben's game was inexplicably faltering. In six tournaments after the L.A. Open, he won only at Crosby's unofficial celebrity pro-am. Moreover, in the twelfth staging of the Masters, Claude Harmon, who now divided his year as a club pro at Winged Foot and Seminole, shot a brilliant 279 that tied the tournament record and beat one of the most formidable fields assembled in the pines. Hard-charging but painfully deliberate Cary Middlecoff finished second, perhaps heralding a change in the guard. Ben finished sixth, and Sam fifteenth, prompting fresh buzz about retirement in both cases. Notably, this would be Bobby Jones's final appearance as a competitor, owing to a mysterious pain and stiffness in his neck and spine.

A rare flip-flop in the schedule had the PGA Championship being played at the Norwood Country Club in St. Louis in late May that year, and Harmon once again made headlines by surviving an epic forty-two-hole duel with Sam to reach the quarterfinal. Joining them there were Hogan, Demaret, and Mike Turnesa, a delightful thirty-nine-year-old White Plains head pro whose younger brother, Jim, lost to Sam Snead at Seaview in 1942. After eliminating Harmon on the thirty-seventh hole of their match, Turnesa advanced to the finals against Ben, who beat his friend Jimmy Demaret two-and-one shortly after his birthday and quickly retreated to his downtown St. Louis hotel to rest his legs from the marathon finish, declining all requests for interviews. Some in the press expressed dismay that the finale wouldn't pit Hogan against the reigning Masters champ, since they were known to practice together down at Seminole in the winter. On offer, instead, as one Midwestern columnist put it, was Cinderella against golf's most "methodical killing machine."

Turnesa, who rarely played professional tournaments of any kind, playfully quipped to reporters, "I've got to wash out some socks tonight. Didn't plan on staying this long, fellas."

Most of them saw this as a walk in the park for the "Garbo of Golf," as a rebuffed sportswriter from St. Louis called Ben on the eve of the final. Indeed, Ben's brilliant 65 in the morning round put him four-up by the halfway mark, a lead he easily held through the third nine holes of their match, at which point he clipped off three successive birdies to end the ordeal and claim his second PGA Championship by a yawning seven-and-six margin. An army jeep picked up the two exhausted competitors on the thirtieth hole and drove them back to the clubhouse. Both looked relieved that it was over.

The only real surprise came at the presentation of the Wanamaker Trophy. "I know you all think I'm the great stone face," Ben began, after complimenting Turnesa's courage and pluck, "but this is a competitive game. I know the other fella doesn't expect any quarter from me—and I don't give it."

Thus far, vintage Hogan. But then came this unexpected glimpse of Hennie Bogan, the man within:

"You probably think I'm happy over winning this tournament, but I'm not. I hate to beat these men. They have to go back to their clubs and tell how they were beaten. The physical ordeal of the PGA just takes too much out of a man." He paused, looking around the room, then added, "I just don't want to put myself through that anymore."

Reporters exchanged glances, wondering if this could be the anticipated retirement announcement. But true to form, he left them hanging and headed straight for a train home to Fort Worth.

Having played in twenty-seven PGA Championship matches over
seventeen years, some 718 holes of intensely competitive golf that
included twelve qualifying rounds and produced two trophies, and a
winning average of 81 percent, Ben not only wanted to go home and
rest up for the U.S. Open at "Hogan's Alley," now less than a month
away, he also wanted a change in the grinding match-play format, the
last tournament of this kind, or else he might simply skip the championship altogether, having nothing further to prove to anyone.

By the time his train reached the Texas & Pacific Railway station in
Fort Worth, the national press wires were humming with such headlines as "Hogan Hates Winning—Gives PGA Shove" and "Bantam Ben
to Quit PGA Forever." Surprised by the negative backlash, believing
that his remarks had simply once again been distorted by the media,
Ben attempted to clarify his position in his hometown newspaper, telling the *Star-Telegram*, "I still think the tournament is too long, but they
can't do anything about it. But I may try again next year."

This halfhearted walk-back convinced nobody. Most insiders
expected Ben Hogan would never show up anywhere near a PGA
Championship again.

And they were right.

He played in only one tournament between the PGA and the
Open—his hometown Colonial, now called the Colonial National Invi-
tational, where he finished tied for second with Skip Alexander. Sam
returned to Virginia in this same period and didn't play competitively
except for a couple of scheduled corporate outings at the Greenbrier.
The rest of his time was spent practicing, working in his barn at Snead
Links, and fishing with friends. He also made at least one trip up to
New York City, to appear on Arthur Godfrey's national morning radio
show and to dine with friends at Jack Dempsey's on Eighth Avenue.
"Outwardly Sam was Sam," remembers his friend John Derr, who
worked on Godfrey's show before moving over to CBS Sports full-time.
"He loved spinning stories and being with people he knew and trusted.
Strangers always made him uncomfortable. But at this moment, his
worst year as a professional, I know for a fact he was worrying about

his future, trying everything to find his putting stroke again. Hogan seemed to be on a holy mission and Byron was making noises of going into broadcasting. Demaret seemed to be having the time of his life, playing his best golf ever. But the clock was ticking for all of them."

"It was a difficult time for Sam," confirms his friend Bill Campbell, who won George May's Tam O'Shanter Amateur Championship that same summer. "I think Sam feared his game might really be on the downslide. Approaching forty is when the putting stroke begins to leave most people. Tee to green Sam was as good as ever, maybe even more effective. But the yips—a term he popularized—were driving him crazy. Most reporters associate Hogan with tireless practice. But Sam practiced in those days nearly as long as Ben did, especially with the Open approaching. That was the one he wanted most."

Amid a sudden controversy about the depth of grooves in club-faces, the USGA forced more than forty players—including Hogan and Demaret, both of whom showed up a week early to practice together—to moderately alter their irons before the start of the U.S. Open of 1948. On the eve of the first round, Ben agreed to be inter-viewed by several handpicked sportswriters in his plush suite at the Beverly Wilshire and was asked about the grooves dispute and his thoughts about how golf could be improved.

"The rules and equipment are fine," he declared, "the only thing golfers need is more daylight. There isn't enough time during the day to practice and play, to key one's game up to where it should be."

The reporters laughed; Ben didn't.

"You're not joking," one of them said.

"No, I'm not," he replied, as Valerie sat there primly on a brocaded couch, hands folded in her lap.

After the interview, a man from the *Los Angeles Times* asked if a pho-tographer could get a picture of Ben and Valerie together. Very few pho-tographs were ever taken of the couple in public, and none whatsoever that reflected the fruits of Ben's recent success, largely because Valerie had a growing aversion to publicity that rivaled her husband's—no small irony in a woman whose college ambition was to be society edi-tor for the Fort Worth *Star-Telegram*.

"I don't see why not," a surprisingly relaxed Ben Hogan agreed, pick-ing up the wedge he'd used to show what alterations had been made, and walking over to stand beside his silent wife. She glanced up ador-ingly at him; he smiled affectionately down at her. The photograph went out over the wires and appeared in hundreds of newspapers on the morning the U.S. Open got under way.

"Sam is running out of time and hair," one columnist concluded in his cheeky handicapping of the top dozen contenders. "And there's maybe only one man in the field who's as hungry as he is to win this thing—Hogan."

Sam, who had a history of fast starts, began by putting like the Snead of old, crafting a pair of sterling 69s that established a new thirty-six-hole championship record and propelled him to a one-shot lead over Hogan and Locke, and two shots over Jim Turnesa, whose silken swing tempo rivaled his own. Three shots back were Jimmy Demaret and Sam's nemesis of the year before, Lew Worsham.

With the excruciating thirty-six-hole Saturday finale looming, most observers believed it was a three-man race between Ben, Sam, and Jimmy. The fourth player who might have figured in that mix was, in fact, tagging along in the gallery, taking pictures for his own scrapbook with a new camera. Byron Nelson was just a friendly, familiar face in the crowd—wearing a smile wire to wire, as some wag pointed out, for the first time ever at a U.S. Open.

Sam made his statement early on Saturday, dropping a fourteen-foot putt on the first hole for an eagle, then followed this with a gutsy birdie on the difficult second that sent an electric charge through the record gallery of seventeen thousand that roamed over Riviera's scruffy, eucalyptus-shaded ridges. Weeks later, reflecting on what happened next, Sam confided to a reporter than he "foolishly felt like I had the thing well in hand" at that moment—opening the door to disaster.

As the yips began to creep into his stroke, he struck half a dozen brilliant approach shots only to three-putt, several times from short distances, missing at least two easy birdies and finishing with a disappointing 73. After the lunch break, which he spent most of on the practice green trying to smooth out his stroke and calm his mind, he went out and battled the same jumpy nerves, never gaining traction and struggling home in 72. As putts failed to drop and sudden cheers rose from other holes, he later said, it made him heartsick to notice fans peeling off to go watch the other leaders. "It's like they can smell when you're losing it," he later said. "It can make you feel like a true has-been out there."

Hogan and Demaret, on the other hand, were a fans' delight, creating a two-man road show of matching 68s in the morning loop that provided Ben with a two-stroke cushion over the field and his best opportunity yet to claim the championship. Playing half an hour ahead of him in the afternoon's final round, however, Jimmy caught fire and rolled home a succession of birdies between the seventh and twelfth holes, grinning and twirling his clubs as he went four under for the stretch and seemed to seize the momentum. At thirteen, he struck a gorgeous eight-iron to four feet but missed the short birdie attempt that would have drawn him into a tie with his friend. As shadows began to crowd Riviera's narrow fairways, he failed to mount a charge but parred his way home to an impressive 278 total that lopped three strokes off the old Open mark set by Ralph Guldahl at Oakland Hills in 1937—or as Sam Snead like to put it, "the first one that got away."

Unfortunately, Demaret's record lasted only about thirty minutes. Despite a three-putt hiccup on the sixty-ninth hole, Ben completed his business as coldly, methodically, and implacably as any U.S. Open champion ever had, finishing with a 276 that further bested Guldahl's mark by five. The victory meant far more than the $2,000 first-place prize money, and Ben Hogan, beaming like a Hollywood matinee idol, removed his signature flat linen cap and acknowledged the wildly applauding masses in the natural amphitheater around Riviera's famous eighteenth green. Then he hurried on to the scorers' table to methodically total up his card and sign it, eager to leave nothing to chance or error, then vanished into the bowels of the locker room to water-comb his sleek black hair, already showing traces of gray at the temples. Finally he climbed the carpeted stairs to the members' lounge where Valerie kissed him on the cheek and they briefly embraced, their usual post-victory ritual. In this instance, the club's kitchen staff appeared in the doorway to applaud the new National Open winner and a young boy walked over and politely asked for his autograph. Ben smiled and obliged, carefully signing his name on the cover of a program like a man whose signature was worth millions.

Indeed, this title was worth even more than the estimated $100,000 it would produce in the form of commercial endorsement opportunities and future paid appearances. His standard exhibition price instantly jumped to $1,500. Like Byron, Ben had a lawyer go over all his business details but personally negotiated his own appearance fees and commercial opportunities. Unlike Sam—who allowed Fred Corcoran to exploit his homespun image in a stream of commercial opportunities—a model of the modern player-agent relationship to come—Ben didn't want anybody to influence his public image or make money off his success. Within days back home in Fort Worth he was fielding calls from representatives for Milton Berle, Jack Benny, and Perry Como, all eager for the Garbo of Golf to drop in as a guest on their shows. He did, too.

Still, the deepest satisfaction of this championship was that it proved he'd finally reached the summit of the game, following perhaps the longest, most arduous climb any athlete ever made from the grim anonymity of a childhood shot through the heart.

In a summer that saw the mighty Citation win the Triple Crown, Babe Ruth die of cancer, and Joe Lewis knock out Jersey Joe Walcott, Bantam Ben Hogan became a poster boy for America's undersized underdogs, the loser turned champion by dint of relentless self-improvement, commanding the biggest headlines of them all, closing in on his own brand of immortality. He was no thoroughbred or icon who'd enjoyed the limelight from the moment he stepped into the arena, just a tough little cuss pushing forty whose heart and will to win, after years of bitter failure, had far more in common with Seabiscuit than Citation.

And he wasn't done yet.

Over the next seven weeks, Ben captured five straight titles, including Byron's Inverness Invitational and the Western Open, prompting Hogan cheerleader Grantland Rice to point out—as Ben and Val barnstormed the upper West—that neither Byron nor Sam had won more golf tournaments in a shorter period, forty-nine victories since 1940. "Who can possibly stop Ben Hogan?" he wondered.

Between the Western and Denver events, they began house hunting in the Westover Hills district of northwest Fort Worth, a neighborhood home to many of the city's cultural elites. Ben also special-ordered a new Cadillac sedan that featured a state-of-the-art, two-piece tinted windshield, tailfins inspired by Lockheed's famous P-38 fighter, and a purring Hydramatic transmission that was the talk of the automotive industry, a $3,000 dream car for the American road.

During the same week, Babe Didrikson Zaharias, reflecting on Ben's long climb from rural obscurity to worldwide fame, wrote in her nationally syndicated column, "Hi Ya," that "If some bright person in Hollywood can find time to find the forest through the trees, he will make a movie of the life of Ben Hogan."

In mid-October, after Ben claimed a final win—his tenth for the season—at California's Glendale Open, by shooting a course record 64 in the final round, the Hogans boarded a train home. The win gave him a third Vardon Trophy and the money title for 1948, $35,812 in official and unofficial tournament earnings. That same week, Hogan's publisher, A. S. Barnes, announced that sales of *Power Golf* had surged through the roof, more than 25,000 copies.

On a cool, overcast Sunday evening after Thanksgiving, 1,500 of Fort Worth's finest stood in a long reception line at Marvin Leonard's Colonial Country Club to greet and congratulate the new undisputed king of golf—even as rumors continued to circulate, not hurt by his own cautiously dropped hints, that Bantam Ben was preparing to say goodbye. "Don't believe everything you read in the papers," he told a reporter from Dallas. "In fact, don't believe it unless you see it with your own eyes or I tell you about it."

All of Ben's family was present that magical night at Colonial: his mother, Royal and his wife, Margaret, and their two children, also Valerie's sister, Sarah Fox, and her precocious ten-year-old daughter, Valerie. A new Hogan friend was there, as well. Granville Walker was the spellbinding preacher from the nearby University Christian Church near the TCU campus, a man Ben greatly admired. Unknown to even some of Ben's closest friends, he frequently slipped into a rear pew of the church during the eleven o'clock worship service and exited before the final procession just to listen to Granville's powerful sermons. Meanwhile, Marvin Leonard had proudly displayed Ben Hogan's medals and trophies in the club's foyer for everyone to admire.

Underscoring the evening's happy mood and sense of homecoming, the Hogans then drove to their beautiful new home on Valley Ridge Road, a pretty, two-story colonial set beneath mature live oaks in one of Forth Worth's finest neighborhoods. Valerie Hogan spent weeks getting the place ready and hiring a pair of African-American maids she insisted on dressing in the style of French servants. The dominant color scheme throughout the house was white. "Aunt Valerie loved everything French," says her niece, Valerie Harriman. "And in her book everything that was French and elegant was white."

As the couple motored the short distance home that night in the luxurious Cadillac, Ben could be forgiven for believing he'd achieved the American dream. On paper, owing to the flood of deals and income wisely invested by George Coleman and others he trusted, he was close to being a millionaire. He was already thinking about what he might do in a world after competitive golf—possibly design his own golf clubs or even a course of his own where he could practice and play to his heart's content in privacy. Colonial, after all, had become Fort Worth's Hogan's Alley, already something of a shrine where fans and curiosity seekers turned up regularly hoping to catch a glimpse of the man himself.

In short, Ben Hogan was finally on top of the world, without doubt the greatest golfer of his time.

"Nobody goes through life without something happening to them," he told his friends that night at Colonial, eerily presaging events to come. "You just have to take those things as they come along, and go ahead with life," he declared, smiling over at his adoring wife.

For the moment, at least, not even someone as prescient as he was could have imagined what within days would come barreling at him through the fog.

13

HOLLYWOOD COMEBACK

W HETHER BY SHEER COINCIDENCE or providence, Sam Snead's
luck suddenly changed four days after Ben Hogan nearly died
on a foggy highway in the Pecos River Valley of West Texas.

After finishing a dispiriting twentieth at the Tucson Open, while
packing up his gear at the El Rio Golf and Country Club, site of the Tucson Open, the fifth official event of the 1949 season, won by a surging
Lloyd Mangrum, Sam found an unexpected gift in his locker: a putter.

"Nobody in the locker room knew who put it there," he recalled,
"so I took another look. It wasn't new or fancy. It was a stiff-shafted,
brass-headed, straight-faced, center-shafted job which hefted nicely in
my hand. I judged it to weigh about sixteen ounces, or slightly heavier
than anything I'd been using."

He took it along with him without any thoughts of using it, though
in a matter of a few weeks this simple putter would rekindle his game
and change his life.

Meanwhile, like everyone else on tour, Sam's mind was focused
on a hospital room in El Paso, where his friend and rival Ben Hogan
lay heavily sedated and clinging to life following a devastating collision with a Greyhound bus that took place shortly after sunrise on the
morning of February 2 as the couple headed for home on winding U.S.
Highway 80. Perhaps one man would have noted the poignant irony
of the accident's timing. Had he survived, it would have been Chester
Hogan's sixty-seventh birthday.

On the heels of a slow start at the year's first event, a surprising
eleventh-place finish on the same Riviera course he'd dominated

just months before, Ben easily captured the Crosby Clambake, then accompanied his host and friend to his ranch in Nevada where he'd impressed Bing with his ease and handling of horses. Eight days later, at the Long Beach Open, he beat another good friend, Jimmy Demaret, in a playoff, a favor Demaret returned the following week at Phoenix, where Jimmy beat Ben in a playoff. Over a beer after the tournament, Demaret playfully proposed a "rubber match down in Tucson." "No, Jimmy," Ben replied, "Val and I want to get back to Fort Worth. No sense having a house if we don't live in it." He added that a decorator had finished her work and declared the place ready to host a first dinner party.

As usual, Jimmy gave his best-ball partner the needle. "What's the matter, Ben? I beat you and you have to run home and practice for a month?"

Ben smiled. Over the previous twenty-three days, he'd put almost three thousand miles on his new Cadillac sedan and played in four tour events, given two free public clinics and endured half a dozen sit-down interviews with the press about his uncertain career plans, revealing little or nothing newsworthy. He'd also taken time off to discuss the first of several instructional films, won two tournaments and collected enough prize money—$5,800—to take the early lead in earnings. At the start of this Western juggernaut, only a few days into the new year, his smiling, angularly handsome face had even graced the cover of *Time* magazine, with the story inside, "Little Ice Water," charting his phenomenal rise from obscurity to a national championship. "If you can't outplay them," went the featured quote on the cover, in the chaste idiom of pure Hoganspeak, "outwork them."

In truth, Ben was growing weary much as Byron had before him. The pressure to win every week, the fusillade of prying questions from reporters, the struggle to ignore being portrayed by several nationally syndicated columnists as a coldhearted SOB who routinely snubbed fans and offended sponsors, not to mention the relentless mental fatigue that came with days of road travel and unfamiliar hotel rooms—all of it added up to the near breaking point. Among other decisions he'd reached but shared with no one but Valerie, he'd already made up his mind not to return to action until the Masters in April. After that, he planned to halve his playing schedule in order to preserve his strength for the U.S. Open, scheduled for Chicago's Medinah Country Club in early June.

"It's the traveling," Ben told Jimmy rather prophetically in Phoenix, almost like a man who sensed his days were numbered. "I want to die an old man, not a young one."

Perhaps our words, as the poet Homer said, tempt the Fates. Roughly halfway between Phoenix and Fort Worth, the Hogans stopped to spend the night at the El Capitan Motel in Van Horn, Texas, where they'd first stayed with Byron and Louise back in the days when they traveled together. The modest motel was clean and comfortable and served a robust breakfast of bacon and eggs, Ben's favorite meal. Valerie skipped eating that morning because she often had a queasy stomach at the start of the day.

The morning was clear but cold, with fingers of ground fog obscuring the highway east of town. They got an early start around 7:45, and within ten minutes Ben detected a skin of ice on the highway and slowed to thirty miles per hour. About forty minutes later, as they approached a small bridge spanning a dry culvert and wreathed by fog, he suddenly saw *two* sets of headlights just an eighth of a mile ahead. Closing fast upon them in their lane was Greyhound Bus 548 with thirty-eight sleepy passengers aboard and substitute driver Alvin Logan behind the wheel, desperate to make up time lost to bad weather between Dallas and El Paso. Seizing his chance to pass a lumbering freight hauler he'd been trapped behind for miles, Logan, as he admitted to authorities later, had gunned the ten-ton vehicle's massive General Motors Super V-12 Coach engine and drew even with the truck as they both approached the short bridge.

"Honey," Valerie recalled her husband saying quietly, reaching over to touch his wife's knee, "I think he's going to hit us."

She opened her mouth to scream, but no sound came out. Everything happened too quickly. Prevented from veering off either side of the highway by steel guardrails, Ben instantly made a calculation that probably saved their lives, steering the Cadillac to the narrow right-hand shoulder, grazing the guardrail and then, in an instant before impact, hurling himself across the seat to shield his wife. Witnesses reported that the driver's side of the car took the brunt of the collision, crumpling that side of the passenger compartment like a concertina, shattering the distinctive grillwork and blowing out the curvilinear windshield. In the span of two seconds or less—about the time it takes an average golfer to swing a club—the car's five-hundred-pound engine was propelled through the protective firewall into the lower half of Ben's body, while the steering column was driven straight through the driver's side seat, the rim of the steering wheel smashing his left shoulder, fracturing the collarbone. A split second later, the left side of his face struck the collapsing dashboard and he fell unconscious into Valerie's lap. Something struck her, too, above the left eye, and she briefly lost consciousness. An instant later, in a shower of sparks, the 3,900-pound car ricocheted off the Greyhound and skidded sideways for a hundred or so feet before slipping backward down the incline into the dry wash, engulfed in steam and smoke.

The crystal of the new Bulova wristwatch Valerie had given Ben for Christmas was shattered, freezing the moment of calamity at exactly 8:30.

More than ninety minutes passed before an ambulance arrived from El Paso's Hotel Dieu Hospital, the Inn of God. By then he had been freed from the tangled mass of metal that pinned his legs against the car seat. The first doctor on the scene, an osteopath from Van Horn, found the bus passengers walking around in a daze and Hogan stretched out under a blanket on the rear seat of another motorist's car. Wreckage was strewn everywhere. According to Valerie, Ben drifted in and out of consciousness five or six times during the interminable wait for help, at first insisting that the men who helped pry him loose attend to his wife instead, later asking if Valerie had managed to save his golf clubs, in each instance growing grayer and colder—clearly slipping into circulatory shock.

A brief initial bulletin, apparently based on sketchy information conveyed by an excited witness who'd rushed to a pay phone in Van Horn, first broke around lunchtime back east, reporting that golf champion Ben Hogan had been killed in an automobile accident near El Paso, which was what Demaret and Snead heard as they were playing in the pro-am in Tucson. "There are moments when golf seems kind of irrelevant," Sam remembered decades later. "And that was sure one of them for me. When we first heard that Ben had died, hell, none of us could believe it. Nobody wanted to play, either. We all just sat around the locker room waiting to hear more news. I called home to speak to Audrey. I also went off by myself and said a little prayer, hopin' ol' Ben was as tough as we all thought he was."

Taking matters in his own hands, Demaret called an administrator he knew in the Texas Highway Patrol in Houston, hoping to get the full story, but was asked to leave a call-back number. "I hung up and stood there dumbly looking at the wall in front of me," he recalled. "Then the fellow called me back and said, 'Yes, Hogan was in an accident. But he's alive. He's at the Hotel Dieu in El Paso.' It felt good, damned good, to know Ben was alive."

A short time later, the Associated Press followed up with a report that said both Hogans had survived and were at an El Paso hospital where Ben was being treated for three broken ribs, severe chest injuries, and a broken back. This diagnosis was, in fact, slightly more encouraging than the actual one. Ben had also suffered a double-ring fracture of the pelvis, a broken left ankle, and several deep cuts and contusions around his left eye. By the time his brother and Valerie's sister reached his bedside later that day, his left eye was covered by a large gauze bandage and he was sleeping under heavy sedation.

Rancher Byron Nelson heard the news on his car radio just before noon as he was driving to Denton to meet with an expert in the poultry business, having decided to add several thousand laying hens and possibly even a sideline in turkeys to his 250 head of Hereford cattle. He immediately turned around and sped home to tell Louise, who'd already been told about it by a mutual friend and was desperately trying to find Byron. "The first thing we did was say a prayer for Ben and Valerie," he remembered. "And then I called Marvin Leonard to see what he had heard. By then we knew Royal Hogan and Valerie's sister were on their way to El Paso and that Ben was likely to pull through." The first sprays of flowers to arrive at the Hotel Dieu came from the Nelsons, soon followed by others from Demaret, the Sneads, and Fred Corcoran.

Later that day, still wearing the same clothes she'd put on in Van Horn, Valerie displayed a bruised face and a mildly sprained left arm, plus various nicks and cuts from flying bits of glass. As she sat with Royal and Sarah in Ben's quiet hospital room, she glanced over at her sister and said wearily, "If Ben hadn't put himself in front of me, you know, I would not be here." A nurse checking on Ben's feeding tube heard this remark and smiled and asked if she could do anything to make Valerie more comfortable. A little later, she conveyed this comment to one of the dozen or more reporters gathered in the waiting room for updates. For the next two days, Valerie left her husband's side for only a few minutes at a time, and she ate little or nothing. That first night, she slept in an armchair next to his bed.

The following day, more and more bouquets arrived. So did Herman Keiser and Dutch Harrison, the first colleagues to lay eyes on the patient, who surprised the former by asking him to check on the whereabouts and condition of his golf clubs. "That told me Ben was feeling better," Keiser told reporters. "Though he looked pretty bad."

Later that same day, Hogan's doctors asked him if he felt like speaking with the press. "I have nothing to say," Ben replied, sounding remarkably like his old self.

As evening fell, though, and new X-rays were taken and plaster casts were fitted to his mangled legs, Valerie gave her account of Ben's actions in the vital seconds before the bus hit them, and her account—bolstered by the first horrific photographs of their mangled Cadillac, and even one of her ashen husband strapped to a gurney as he was rushed into the hospital—appeared in hundreds of newspapers the next morning.

The combination of these startling images and intimate details of the crash coming just weeks after *Time*'s unflattering cover portrayal of a cold-natured and ruthless athlete produced an extraordinary transformation.

"There's absolutely no question that accident and the stories that came out about it completely changed the image most people had of Ben Hogan," Tommy Bolt later reflected. "Up till then he'd been seen as a cold and unsympathetic character who didn't give a damn about anybody but himself. People respected him for the way the little guy played golf, but they sure as hell didn't love him the way they loved Byron and Sam and Jimmy. Some of us who were lucky enough to see a more private side of Ben soon saw a very different guy. He helped some of us young bucks out there get started—gave us advice, even offered to lend us dough if things got tough—though he never wanted any of that known. I guess he feared people would mistake such kindness as weakness. But that car accident changed everything—even Ben himself."

Only a day later, reflecting on the avalanche of get-well cards, cables, and letters that filled a dozen cardboard boxes in the hospital's mailroom, Valerie confided to the Fort Worth *Star-Telegram*, "If there's one good thing out of this accident, it's been that Ben realizes how many good friends he has everywhere. People have been wonderful." She paused and smiled, then added, "I guess you don't know these things until something like this happens."

Heroes are created, in large part, by displaying their human vulnerability. Prior to what happened on Highway 80, Ben Hogan symbolized what an unflagging work ethic could do for the proverbial underdog, but he was hardly a hero in the classic sense of the word. Suddenly, however, by lurching to save his wife—something every husband and ordinary Joe would like to picture himself doing without a moment's hesitation—he now took on a mythic status. In the mere two seconds it took Ben to try to save the only girl who ever truly believed in him, he became a national hero.

To this day some critics doubt the sincerity of his hospital room epiphany, but the hospital staff reported seeing their famous patient sitting up in bed for hours reading intimate messages from total strangers, prompting him to shake his head and sometimes grow visibly emotional. A local secretary was hired to record names and addresses so Ben could personally write these well-wishers back, which indeed over time he did. "If I ever get out of here," he reportedly told Valerie the day his doctors reported to the press that he was making an unexpectedly speedy recovery, "I'm going to be more aware of people—and their kindnesses to me."

Ben's closest friends insist the accident only stimulated his deep-seated compassion for any honest hardworking soul who was struggling to rise above misfortune, as if another's tale of adversity simply reminded him of his own lifelong trauma over his father's suicide. Whatever else is true, it's indisputable that Ben's close brush with violent death served to loosen his affections for friends and family, certain fans and even a few reporters. In the aftermath, he deepened the rituals of practice he found so comforting and strengthened his exercise of his faith. Following long months of recovery at home, for instance, he began showing up at Granville Walker's Sunday morning services on a more regular basis.

"To a man who stared death in the face the way Ben did," observed Ken Venturi, whose stellar career benefited mightily from his close friendships with both him and Byron, "battling to win a golf tournament and deal with all the distractions that go with it was suddenly nothing. That wreck made Ben pause and appreciate life a bit more, no doubt about it. But in the long run, it also only made him even more fearless in competition."

But all of that was yet to come.

Four days after Valentine's Day, the secret anniversary of his father's suicide, while preparing to go home to his new house in west Fort

Worth, Ben felt a sharp pain in his chest and urgent X-rays revealed that blood clots were moving toward his lungs and heart, floating time bombs in his circulatory system. All talk of a speedy recovery was moot. Less than twenty-four hours later, as the staff struggled to thin his blood and halt the advance of the killer clots, his condition grew critical, his blood pressure plummeting and his pulse erratic. After consulting with the Mayo Clinic in Minnesota, his doctors contacted a renowned Tulane University specialist named Alton Ochsner to discuss an extremely risky procedure that involved tying off the vena cava artery, which carries blood from the heart and lungs to the legs and pelvic region. Though Ochsner was a pioneer in vascular surgery—credited, in fact, with introducing blood transfusions to the United States—this radically invasive surgery required that a large incision be made through the abdominal wall in order to reach a large vein about the diameter of a half dollar, whereupon it would be cut and tied off "like closing a faucet." In theory, he explained to Valerie and Royal Hogan over the phone, the procedure was relatively simple; in practice, there was little or no guarantee the patient wouldn't bleed to death.

It was perhaps their only hope, however. Royal Hogan arranged to have Ochsner flown to El Paso. Hours later, as the risky surgery was under way, the Associated Press alerted its seventeen hundred subscribers, sending out a sixteen-paragraph obituary, "intended for use in the event of his death."

Two hours later, a weary but smiling Ochsner told Valerie the surgery had been successful. With surprisingly little bleeding, the artery was now secured. Furthermore, he predicted her husband would begin to recover in about a week's time and possibly be "up and around with limited mobility in several months." On the downside, he advised her that Ben's long-term mobility would also be greatly diminished—perhaps even his ability to walk a golf course. When Royal bluntly asked Ochsner when or if his brother might ever be able to play competitively again, the famous surgeon shook his head and reportedly replied, "I just don't know. Only time will tell."

Sam Snead loved the Greensboro fans because they treated him like a native son. He had fishing buddies in the galleries of the Gate City and enjoyed a productive relationship with a gifted Pinehurst caddie named Jimmy Stead who appeared to understand his complicated game even better than he himself. According to Sam, they met when Sam won the North and South Open at Pinehurst in 1941 and Stead regularly drove two hours up the road from the Sandhills whenever he played in the Greater Greensboro Open, an event that alternated between two fine old clubs.

It was there, inside the Starmount Country Club's locker room, that he solved the mystery of the brass-headed putter he'd found in Tucson, which belonged to a popular Chicago club pro named Stan Kertes. How it wound up in his locker was never determined, though both men agreed a locker room attendant probably mistakenly put it there. When Sam confessed that he liked the putter's heft and had in fact been practicing with it for several weeks, Kertes invited him to keep it. "See if it brings you any luck," he said, and Sam decided to give it a shot.

He drained putts from every direction and length to tie Lloyd Mangrum for first place and then beat him in a playoff, 69 to 71. Sam's "hometown" galleries were ecstatic.

A few days later, on the eve of the Masters, he took a lesson from Vic Ghezzi that helped him visualize shorter putts and smooth out his yips on shorter distances. He also began to "blot out the world" in his mind over critical putts, something he'd long heard Hogan talking about. With Jimmy Stead on his bag and a hot flatstick in his hands, he put together a pair of brilliant closing 67s in a biting spring wind to capture the season's first major, including eight birdies in the final eighteen, winning the first of his three Masters titles. Not at all surprising to seasoned patrons, one of his victims was Byron Nelson, who returned as promised and gamely gave chase but finished ten strokes back.

For Sam, this breakthrough marked the beginning of the greatest run of his career, during which he won twenty of forty-two events.

Three weeks after his stunning display in Augusta, where he donned the first green jacket, armed with his magical new putter and comforting Jimmy Stead on the bag, Sam sauntered past Jackie Burke Jr. and Jimmy Demaret to reach the semifinal of the PGA Championship in his own backyard, Richmond's lush Hermitage Country Club. In the final match, he trailed fellow Southerner Johnny Palmer until the twenty-second hole, where a monstrous birdie putt tumbled into the cup and vaulted him into the lead. He closed Palmer out on the thirty-fourth hole and then put on a new houndstooth sports jacket and beautifully knotted silk tie for the presentation of his second

Wanamaker Trophy. He was the first man in history to win both the Masters and the PGA in the same year. "The only difference in Snead is that he's getting hump-backed from picking balls out of the can," Demaret quipped.

A fortnight later at the U.S. Open at Medinah, where, even without Jimmy Stead along to help, Sam played solid golf through seventy holes and reached the penultimate green tied with pleasant Cary Middlecoff, a recent graduate of the University of Tennessee Dental College. Facing a lengthy chip shot from the fringe just off the green, however, Sam opted to lag putt and rolled his ball eight feet past the cup. Then, after taking an unusually long time over the ball, clearly attempting to clear his mind of past Open disasters, he grazed the hole and finished a thin stroke out of a playoff, tied with Clayton Heafner for second place, a runner-up for the maddening third time.

Undeterred by the jinx, and eager to make hay while Hogan remained on the sidelines, Sam responded by winning three of his next six tournaments including the Western Open, finishing no worse than third place, to claim the money title, his second Vardon Trophy, and Player of the Year honors for 1949.

"Given that I'd been largely written off as dead by many of the scribes," he was moved to remember some years later, "that was the most satisfying year I'd ever had up till then. It takes a lot out of a fella to reach the top of the heap the way Ben and Byron and I all did. Nobody gets to stay there long. But as Ben and I both proved, it's a helluva lot harder to climb back up there once you've tumbled off because you know what it takes out of you to get back."

His friends spent years trying to decide if his mysterious putter or Ben Hogan's absence was the key that revitalized Sam Snead's ailing game, though most agreed it was undoubtedly a combination of both and the steadying presence of Jimmy Stead. Sam himself was quick to point out that he was destined to earn more than $100,000 with Kertes's putter, establishing a postwar record for tournament wins that would endure for several decades.

By his own estimation, he didn't yip another putt until late 1952, when an assistant at the Greenbrier leaned on his beloved putter and snapped it off at the hosel, sending Sam into conniptions. As he later said, he recovered well enough to "nearly convince myself my putting problems were cured for the time being"—only to see the dreaded yips return with a vengeance in 1960.

Chester Hogan and his son Ben in happier times, 1913

Ben turned professional in 1932, failing on his
first attempts to make it on tour.

He married Valerie Fox in
the spring of 1935.

Jimmy Demaret was probably Ben's best friend on tour—
and the player he felt was most underrated.

Ben and Byron remained close up
to the start of Wold War II.

After Ben won the Los Angeles Open and the U.S. Open at Riviera
in 1948, the press dubbed the course "Hogan's Alley."

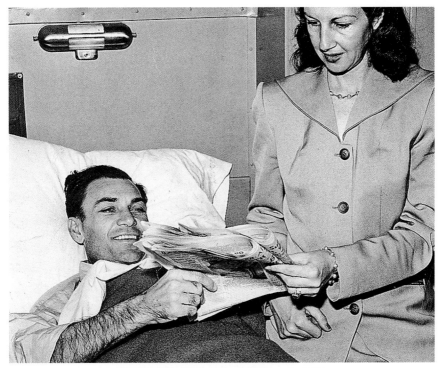

The nearly fatal car crash in early 1949
made him a truly mythic figure.

The most famous photograph in golf: Ben's immortal pose
at Merion, en route to winning the 1950 U.S. Open

Sam won his second green jacket in 1952, as Ben did in
1953—setting up a playoff for the ages in 1954.

After winning the British Open in 1953, Ben was given a ticker tape parade in New York City. Bobby Jones was the only other golfer so honored, in 1926 and 1930.

Ben fans Jack Fleck's red-hot putter following his surprising U.S. Open victory at Olympic in 1955.

With his wife, Valerie, at Shady Oaks, where Ben spent his happiest
hours after withdrawing from public view around 1970

When word leaked out that Ben Hogan had quietly registered for the Los Angeles Open of 1950, the tournament instantly became one of the most anticipated events in modern sports. Ticket sales soared above the ten thousand mark within days, and Riviera's staff was besieged by requests for press credentials from as far away as Spain and Germany, with newspapers from Pinehurst to Pasadena hailing the second coming of an American hero, a brave little man who'd returned from death's doorstep.

This breathless anticipation was understandable. With a predictable and impenetrable curtain of silence cinched around the pretty colonial house on Valley Ridge Road in Fort Worth, the public and press knew little or nothing about Hogan's convalescence. By late spring of 1949, however, Ben began taking short morning walks around his house with the help of a cane, trying to strengthen the atrophied muscles in his severely damaged legs, which now relied on smaller veins to carry blood to his lower extremities, every step producing sharp pains. On April 5, he put a topcoat over his pajamas, a fedora on his head, and hobbled slowly around his yard. The next afternoon he ventured a little farther to inspect the plant beds Valerie's yardman installed over the winter. Ben chatted with him, and Valerie detected a noticeable improvement in his mood over the days and weeks that followed. Ben's interest in gardening was marginal, but even so, he sometimes surprised and impressed Colonial golfing partners by his knowledge of certain plants, using their proper Latin names.

At the end of April, he returned from a comprehensive checkup with Dr. Ochsner in New Orleans buoyed by his optimistic suggestion that by midsummer he might even be able to walk a golf course, albeit with heavily bandaged legs. Hoping for the best, weeks later he filed for a spot in the field of the U.S. Open at Medinah though by early June his uncooperative legs couldn't carry him farther than a few blocks around leafy Westover Hills. He was reportedly so depressed about not being able to defend his national open title that he skipped the radio broadcast and subsequent TV highlights of Sam Snead's most recent gallant failure to win the Open.

By August, however, Ben was hitting wedge shots and putting at the Colonial course on a daily basis, using a golf cart to get around, a new development largely popularized by the far-thinking George S.

May. Still, during these brief outings, his legs continued to swell and, at month's end, a sharp recurring pain in his right knee was diagnosed as a torn cartilage by Ochsner, who recommended surgery. Ben slept on it before rejecting any further surgery, fearing that would only slow his recuperation, opting instead for stronger bandaging and a single aspirin for the pain.

In September, the public had its first view in nine months of a somewhat gaunt Ben Hogan, who was strong enough to serve as nonplaying captain and travel with his American Ryder Cup team to the Ganton Golf Club (Harry Vardon's old club) on board the *Queen Elizabeth*. During a rough crossing, Henry Longhurst of the *Times* and Leonard Crawley of the *Daily Telegraph* had lengthy conversations with him, and both thought he seemed noticeably more approachable and pleasant. Among other things, Hogan assured them that he would eventually claim another championship. "Longhurst and I looked at one another," Crawley later wrote, "and when Hogan left us, we said in the same breath, 'How pathetic.'"

Any suspicion that Ben had gone soft was quickly dispelled by the assault he orchestrated on British golf. At Ganton, he ran his team as he had as a second lieutenant drilling raw recruits for war, imposed strict meetings and curfews, and practice sessions before every match. He also insisted that his players eat every meal together. With rationing still in effect across England, the fact that he brought along a cache of fresh eggs and butter, half a dozen Virginia hams, thirty pounds of smoked bacon, and six hundred pounds of iced-down prime Texas sirloin beef to feed his squad produced howls of indignation on Fleet Street.

The insult grew when Ben ordered his charges to go easy on the time-honored traditions of drinking in the pub and fraternizing at night. "Hey, Hawk," Demaret asked at one point, "we training for golf or for the army?" A prominent London editorialist wondered if Captain Hogan planned to "post a sentry guard by the door" to guard his "splendid rations." Feathers were only slightly smoothed when Ben, sensing his team's growing discomfort, eased his iron rules a bit and, on the eve of the first matches, shared his larder with the home team. "How gracious," sniffed one Fleet Streeter. "Hogan has offered us what Americans like to call their 'leftovers.'"

Motivated by the perceived snubs or sheer pride or the memory of the shellacking administered by the Yanks just two years before—all three factors, most likely—Arthur Lees and Dick Burton upset the "unbeatable" team of Mangrum and Snead in their opening Foursomes match, striking a positive note for the hosts, who by the final days of Singles needed just three and one half points to return Sam Ryder's venerable cup. With a giddy British press all but declaring victory, however, Ben delivered a tongue-lashing that sent the Americans out like a winter gale off the North Sea. "It was tough words from a tough little man who'd been through hell," Sam remembered. "We listened pretty good, I reckon. Nobody wanted to be the one who lost that damn cup." Playing with quiet fierceness and resolve, they dominated the day's matches and retained the cup, 7–5, carrying it home aboard the *Queen Mary* to a robust New York reception.

The Ben Hogan who showed up at Riviera between Christmas and New Year's to practice for the 1950 Los Angeles Open was, in many respects, very different from the "Little Ice Water" depicted in *Time* magazine.

Though he'd managed to put on some weight, he still looked haggard and was ten to fifteen pounds shy of his normal playing weight of 140. As a favor to Valerie and his doctor, he'd agreed to address his cigarette habit of three and a half packs a day, and by the time he appeared for his first official practice round in eleven months, with a portable shooting stick seat like those used at steeplechase races, he'd more or less ditched cigarettes, at least for the moment. But like the Hogan of old, he had yet to officially confirm that he would play in the tournament.

His choice of practice partners that morning was also no accident. One was George Fazio, the smooth-swinging Pennsylvania pro whose easy style and graceful manner Ben found greatly appealing, whereas the other was Sidney Lanfield, a portly high-handicapper with an ungainly, abbreviated punch-swing. Ben loathed playing with hackers of any sort, but Lanfield had a special dispensation. On the morning the Hogans checked into their usual suite at the Beverly Wilshire, a reporter asked him if there was any truth to an item in Louella Parsons's popular gossip column that a movie script was being written about his remarkable life and heroic comeback.

As usual, Ben refused to comment, but in fact a script had already been written for Twentieth Century Fox, and a director selected, to whom he'd been introduced years earlier by Bing Crosby: Sidney Lanfield. Moreover, a dozen leading actors had already been screen-tested for the lead role. Ben's first choice was rangy, stoic Gary Cooper. Lanfield, however, had settled upon young Glenn Ford.

In this initial outing, having played his first complete round since the accident only a month before, supported by adhesive bandages swaddling both legs, Ben walked slowly through an impressive 33 on the front nine, coming home in 36—sending a seismic charge through the press room. Afterward, he appeared far more relaxed and generous with his time, answering questions from a large contingent of reporters, even pausing for photographs with tam-wearing Billy Seanor, twelve, the tournament's cute Mascot Trophy winner.

"Say, Ben, that 69 is quite a score," one of them said. "You really tore up the place out there."

He gave a wintry half smile. "I did a lot better than I expected. But my legs bothered me."

"Still, you'll play . . ."

"Tough to say."

As he'd complained to Fazio halfway through the round, his legs were killing him. But he indeed finished better than he'd expected to, faced his brief press inquisition with surprising ease, then went straight back to the Wilshire for a warm bath with Epsom salts, and an aspirin and ginger ale, followed by a soothing Ben-Gay rubdown and rest—in theory still undecided about playing. Valerie strenuously argued against it. But by now he'd more or less made up his mind to play. This was, after all, *Hogan's* Alley.

On New Year's Day, following one of rest and seclusion, he declined an invitation to watch undefeated Cal and Ohio State in the Rose Bowl, and played an afternoon round at Riviera with only his caddie for company, shooting 70. The next day, he played a third round with Demaret, former PGA champion Bob Hamilton, and reigning Open champion Cary Middlecoff. They had a ten-dollar Nassau going, and several times between holes on the second nine Ben had to stop and rest on his portable stool for several minutes, admitting that his legs were feeling the strain. Middlecoff suggested knocking off, but he refused and hobbled home with a 75, telling reporters he was "satisfied" with his game. Following another day of rest, he put together a fourth round of 67 that hardly went unnoticed; his aggregate score of 281 was three strokes better than Lloyd Mangrum had won with the year before. Finally, following a fifth round of 68, Ben ended the suspense and announced he would compete.

Meanwhile, the hottest player in the game had arrived, playing only a single practice round with Mangrum and Herm Keiser. Sam shot 67 and gave a lazy catfish smile when told about Hogan's decision to play. "If he keeps them legs under him," Sam drawled to the reporters, "Ben'll be damn hard to beat out there. As you know, Ben loves this place."

And with that, he climbed into a rental car to take Audrey and actor Randolph Scott to dinner at the Brown Derby.

The city announced it was adding a dozen buses out to the Pacific Palisades course to accommodate spectators, a record-breaking crowd of nine thousand passing through the gates for the first round, most of them following Ben and Sam. Despite handheld signs prohibiting cameras, the click of shutters was constant, and on the first fairway a visibly annoyed Ben exchanged sharp words with a small group of foreign press photographers. Perhaps because of this problem, Ben's opening round of 73 was no thing of beauty. "Ben is a walking miracle," Middlecoff gushed to one of Lanfield's roving writers, hired to gather extra bits for the script. "He couldn't possibly be on his game after that long layoff. If he wins this thing, believe me, it won't be with his game," Cary added. "It will be with his heart." This gem was dutifully jotted down.

In Saturday's second round, Ben finally settled down and shot a 69 that could have been at least two strokes better had a pair of putts not lipped out, while Sam opened with 71-72. A biblical downpour washed away Sunday's scheduled third round, however, flooding barrancas and forcing the tournament rules committee to scrap every round after only fifty-seven players managed to reach the safety of the clubhouse and seventeen others, including Ben, were forced to pick up their balls. Out in the tumult on the course, Snead and Demaret picked up their balls and headed for the clubhouse even before play was officially suspended, risking disqualification, and Ben eventually found himself stranded by a raging creek on the eleventh fairway, hands on hips, glaring at the swollen waters like an Old Testament prophet. After briefly waiting for a tournament official to assess the situation, he, too, set off with a slow hobble to the clubhouse beneath his umbrella, grim-faced and puffing a Chesterfield, a blessing, as it turned out. His total after just nine holes was an untidy three-over 39 and his fingers felt a creeping numbness. The greatest misfortune of the day belonged to former Pasadena glove salesman Jerry Barber, whose ten-stroke lead was wiped away by officials.

After a soak in Epsom salts, an early dinner with friends from back home in Texas and a good night's sleep, however, Ben seemed refreshed and proved it by bagging three birdies in the first seven holes of the replayed third round, recording a 69 that put him within two strokes of Barber's lead, as the citizens of Hogan's Alley roared their approval. Five strokes back and all but forgotten was the oddsmakers' favorite, Sam Snead.

"I'm plenty tired. I'm not even sure these old stems can go another eighteen," Ben confided to a crush of reporters in the locker room. But the next day, tapping into a reservoir of adrenaline and mental strength perhaps only he possessed, he finished his first tournament back with a third round of 69—a 280 total that seized the tournament lead. Coming off the famous eighteenth green, surrounded by worshipful fans packed into Riviera's natural amphitheater, he tipped his flat linen cap to the sustained and thunderous cheer. "The second coming of Lazarus," a Mutual Network radio commentator declared over the din. "Why, I wouldn't have believed it if I hadn't seen it with my own eyes!" Lanfield's secret battalion of scriptwriters couldn't have written a better Hollywood ending.

At that moment, with Barber and Demaret having fallen back, the only player with a reasonable chance to catch Ben was his archrival, Sam Snead, who was three under after fourteen holes and needed two birdies in the final four holes simply to tie. After failing at fifteen and sixteen to get them, Sam turned to his playing partner, Jack Burke Jr., and quipped, "Guess I've got to knock a couple in the hole to catch the little man." A clutch ten-footer for his fourth birdie in six holes at the next hole drew him one shy of the lead, but he suddenly faced one of the most daunting finishing holes in golf, Riviera's difficult 445-yard, par-four eighteenth, a hole that yielded precious few birdies.

"I had no doubt in my mind that I could catch Ben," Sam recalled years later. "My hands were just itchin' for the next chance to putt. That old putter of mine was magic that day."

On the final green, following a brilliant six-iron approach that left him a fifteen-footer for birdie, the vast gallery fell to hushed silence, and Sam took his good sweet time assessing the putt from various angles. "For three full minutes I quartered the green," he explained, "looking for major and minor breaks, estimating the speed needed and inspecting the turf around the cup."

As he stood over his ball, a limb in the large eucalyptus tree just below the green snapped, sending a zealous fan tumbling into the bushes. "I'm all right, I'm all right!" he hollered, leaping to his feet, and everyone laughed.

A year or two earlier, Sam would have blown his stack, but now he was playing the finest golf of his life. In fact, the producers of Ben's movie hoped to convince him to play himself in the forthcoming biopic. Yet in this instance he rewrote the script by smiling and briefly backing off to take a final read on his putt. Finally, he calmly stepped up and smoothly stroked the ball, rolling it into the center of the cup to force a playoff.

"The sound that went up at that moment was pretty amazing," Middlecoff remembered. "Half of it was Sam's fans cheering like crazy, the other half—or maybe more—belonged to Ben's fans, groaning and cursing."

Pandemonium erupted on the hillside as rain-loosened sod gave way and spectators tumbled onto the green. Several rushed to swarm and congratulate Sam, who grimaced and shoved a few out of the way in order to reach Jackie Burke and shake hands. Sam quickly checked, signed, and submitted his card to officials and fled into the safety of the locker room where he found his rival already showered and dressed, sitting with Middlecoff and Fazio, smoking one of his forbidden Chesterfields.

"I figured you would make that putt, Sam," Ben told him with an icy little smile, dreading the very idea of an additional round.

"Well, Ben, I can't miss 'em all," Sam said with a grin.

A few minutes later, a knot of reporters gathered around Ben as he draped his topcoat over his arm. "I wish Sam had won it out there," he told them. "I don't feel bad about Sam tying me. I just don't want to play another round. I'd rather Sam had won."

Someone asked, a bit inconsequentially, if he planned on driving himself and Valerie up to the Crosby after the playoff. Media access would be more restricted there and he could relax a little more with his friends Crosby, Coleman, and Eddie Lowery, the San Francisco car dealer, before the tournament got under way on Wednesday.

"I don't drive anywhere but home anymore, fellas," Ben explained, excusing himself and heading up the stairs to where Valerie was waiting for him in the foyer. Left by himself to face a barrage of questions, Sam swigged a Coke and was only too happy to hold forth, having finally finished off an important tournament as well as he knew he could—with a scintillating 66.

One major wire service went slightly overboard that evening in describing the next act as the "Golf Match of the Century," an echo of Hagen's ballyhooed matches against his triumvirate rivals, Sarazen and Jones. But the gods clearly had something else in mind after dense Pacific rains swept in overnight and flooded the course a second time. The playoff was postponed for a week, dampening the Hollywood ending Lanfield and the media hoped to record.

To complicate matters, by the time Ben reached foggy Monterey, he had a nasty head cold. And by the time he finished up the three days of play with his partner, Bing, who ironically gave him an engraved cigarette lighter, a late Christmas gift, his miserable 223 left him in a tie for nineteenth place. Naturally, Sam won the affair for the second time in his career. Boarding the train back to Los Angeles, craving a smoke, Ben's only comfort was provided by his lawyers back in Texas, whose settlement with the Greyhound Bus Company granted him $25,000 a year for life. Even if he never swung a club in competition again, he was financially secure.

Neither man distinguished himself in their predictably anti-climactic playoff encounter, which only 2,091 fans paid sixty cents to witness on an overcast and cool Monday afternoon following Bing's Clambake. Sam managed an uninspired 72, while Ben, swaddled in two cotton sweaters, hobbling badly and repeatedly pausing to blow his nose, scored a wretched 76. They scarcely spoke but shook hands afterward, displaying all the enthusiasm of longshoremen who'd been forced to work on a national holiday. They split the modest gate receipts—pocketing an additional $500 apiece—and parted ways. Hogan made no excuses. "I've obviously got more work to do," he told reporters before vanishing into a hired car. Sam lingered a little while longer, making little jokes, savoring as best he could another victory over his greatest rival.

Following a six-day rest at Dallas friend Pollard Simons's house in Palm Springs, Ben arrived at the Phoenix tournament and found the event this year renamed the Ben Hogan Open in his honor. He limped to a twentieth-place finish, smoking like a chimney again, and thanked the generous fans of Phoenix for turning out in such large numbers. Within minutes he and Valerie were headed to the train station and home. Sam, continuing his tear, placed second.

By the start of Masters week in April, Sam's red-hot putter had carried him to record-breaking wins at Texas, Miami, and Greensboro. Ben looked rested and much better, too, fresh from two weeks of practice at the ultra-private Seminole Golf Club with his friends George Coleman and Paul Shields, a Wall Street banker and a close friend of Cliff Roberts's. Coleman would eventually join and be elected president of the cloistered seaside club where Ben and Valerie now made their annual late-winter retreat from the Texas cold, hobnobbing with the likes of the Duke of Windsor and Wallis Simpson and Chris Dunphy, a colorful former Hollywood agent who ran the club like a genial Irish despot, arranging daily matches between millionaire members that often ran into staggering sums. His friendships with Ben, Sam, and Byron meant all three became regulars at the unofficial Seminole Amateur-Professional where as much as $150,000 exchanged hands in its famous Calcutta, played out of sight of the celebrity-hungry press and agents for an even more interested Internal Revenue Service. Not until agents posing as caterers were able to penetrate the Pinkerton security force that Dunphy hired to keep unwelcome guests off the property—and jot down the names and winnings of players they could present with tax bills—did the full scope of Seminole's invitational become known. While other well-publicized Calcuttas began running afoul of authorities about this time, Seminole's beautifully run event—independent of the personal tax issues it generated—never had a whisper of scandal due to Dunphy's imposing presence.

In March of 1950, just days before the Hogans set off for Augusta, Dunphy even managed to convince Ben to commit to the new Spring Golf Festival he helped orchestrate at Sam's Greenbrier in early May. As Dunphy knew, the thought of taking one back from Sam the way the Slammer had taken the L.A. Open in Hogan's Alley was simply too attractive to resist. Ben showed up at the Bon Air in Augusta looking tanned and unusually relaxed. Chatting with reporters, he explained he was working on a new "strategy of course management," a phrase that quickly became attached to the growing Hogan mystique. Asked about this strategy, Tommy Bolt quipped, "New words for the same old Ben. He hits balls wherever he wants. We should just aim for his divots."

Ben's opening round was a disappointment, however, with his stamina giving out early in the round due to the course's hilly terrain and a putter that never got on track. He finished the Masters with an embarrassing 76 and a total of 288 that left him five strokes behind the winner, Jimmy Demaret, who claimed his third title and first green jacket—a tradition that had begun just one year before. Sam finished one stroke better than Ben, tying for third at 286, his putter giving him trouble, as well.

A month later, however, with the Duke of Windsor and Chris Dunphy in the gallery, Ben evened the score by putting the lights out at the Greenbrier's famed Old White Course, recording eye-popping rounds of 64-64-65-66 for a breathtaking 259 that equaled Byron's historic 1945 mark and lifted the trophy of the inaugural Spring Festival right out from under Sam's slightly out-of-joint nose. The closest competitor was, of course, Sam himself, who finished second but ten strokes back. "If Ben's gonna putt like this," he quipped at the gala dinner following the tournament, "I'd just as soon he'd go on back to Fort Worth and take it easy for the rest of the year."

That spring, over lunch at Colonial, Ben heard from his mentor, Marvin Leonard, that he was thinking of building a private members golf retreat somewhere in California, and had even inquired into purchasing the Pebble Beach Golf Links but found the $20 million asking price too rich for his groceryman's blood. This conversation, however, would eventually lead to a discussion about building a course somewhere in the city's prosperous western suburbs. During this same luncheon, Ben aired his dissatisfaction with MacGregor, his longtime equipment provider. "They can't seem to make a club to suit my specifications," he complained to Leonard. Ever the entrepreneur, Leonard wondered if this meant he was contemplating a company of his own that would compete with the club-making titans of Wilson, MacGregor, and Spalding. The idea seemed almost incomprehensible. The big three had factories, after all, not to mention great distribution in pro shops across the country and generations of expertise in club manufacturing.

"It's something I'm looking into," Ben confirmed. "I don't give a damn about their histories. I'll make clubs better than they do, for anybody who wants to play golf the way it ought to be played."

After the Greenbrier event, Sam successfully defended his Western Open title at Brentwood Golf Club in Los Angeles, his sixth victory of the year, and then moseyed down to Fort Worth and shot a pair of nimble 66s to snatch the Colonial Invitational trophy from under Ben, who tied for third and wryly remarked that he wished Sam would consider taking the rest of the year off to hunt and fish back home in the hills.

The good-natured public banter hid an almost palpable desperation in each man to beat the other, and this now came to a head as the year's largest prize hove into view.

The fiftieth United States Open, the golden anniversary of golf's second oldest championship, was scheduled for the Merion Golf Club, the Hugh Wilson gem outside Philadelphia where Jones captured the U.S. Amateur in 1930 to complete his fabled Grand Slam and where Ben had played miserably in his first national championship back in 1934.

Sam had his own sizable issues, of course, namely his Open jinx.

But he also had a plan to keep the great Jimmy Stead on his bag here: several of his Merion admirers had arranged for Stead to slip quietly into the pool of Open caddies. Unfortunately, however, the USGA disallowed this move and Sam was forced to pick a caddie from the registered pool, which reinforced his growing belief that he'd been singled out by executive director Joe Dey for treatment that diminished his chances of winning the prize he most coveted. Several USGA officials, including at least two former presidents, would ultimately agree with Sam's interpretation.

By Open standards, Merion was short—just 6,700 yards—but a target shooter's dream with narrow alleys of fairway and small greens fringed by thick, unyielding rough and strategic bunkering that recalled its spiritual antecedents, the great heather courses of Britain. Ben's planning, as usual, was meticulous. Playing alone, hitting three shots on every hole in the practice rounds in welcome June warmth, he determined that his seven-iron was pointless, and replaced it with a one-iron, a move that proved critical as events unfolded.

Ben's two-over 72 in the opening round left him eight strokes behind Lee Mackey, an obscure Alabama pro whose 64 tied the eighteen-hole Open record. Sam, still stewing over what he considered roughshod treatment by Dey and company, opened with 73 and declined to comment when a Philadelphia reporter asked him about the flap over Jimmy Stead.

The next day, as often happens to unknowns who briefly catch lightning by the tail, Mackey shot himself out of contention with a woeful 81, and a scowling Sam came home with 75. The halfway lead was shared by Dutch Harrison, Jim Ferrier, and Johnny Bulla. Young Julius Boros, a darkly handsome accountant from Connecticut playing in his first national championship, held the lead. Ben, whose improved 69 placed him in fifth place, was being chauffeured from the grounds

to the luxurious Barclay Hotel on Rittenhouse Square by Frank Sullivan, a crusty lawyer who worked for the publishers of his best-selling
Power Golf, when he suddenly asked him to pull over so he could throw
up. A little while later, following his soak in Epsom salts and a glass
of ginger ale, he confided to Valerie and Sullivan over an early dinner
that he wasn't sure his ailing legs would hold up to the thirty-six holes
he faced the next day.

Saturday dawned beautiful and warm, and Ben's early-morning
prep was precisely the same as it had been since Los Angeles—a warm
bath followed by stringent leg massages with Ben-Gay, followed by
an extensive bandaging routine from ankle to crotch, and an aspirin
washed down with a glass of orange juice and a splash of ginger ale.
After this two-hour ritual came a thirty-minute drive to the club in
suburban Ardmore. Because of the Merion's limited practice facilities,
he reduced his customary warm-up period and spent more time putting on the practice green.

The contenders all played cautiously that morning. Ben's 72 inched
him forward into a tie for second with Middlecoff and Johnny Palmer,
two strokes behind Lloyd Mangrum at 211.

After having a bowl of chicken broth for lunch on the terrace with
Valerie, he trudged through an outward nine in 37 strokes, suffering
such acute pain that he often stopped to rest and even clasp his legs
as he ascended the steeper slopes. But the other leaders, fighting their
own wars of Open attrition, all gave up ground in the first nine of the
afternoon round—allowing Ben to hobble to the top of the scoreboard.

After he lashed his drive at the twelfth hole, his legs spasmed so
badly that he was forced to grab a spectator's arm. "I thought for sure
he was going to collapse," Middlecoff, his playing partner, later told
a reporter. But he didn't. Despite several more severe leg cramps, he
arrived at the last hole having squandered a three-stroke lead over the
previous six, needing to make par to tie Mangrum and Fazio, already
in the clubhouse with 287.

Following a perfect drive to the heart of the home fairway, he was
pinching a Chesterfield when he spotted Fred Corcoran and the pro
Jimmy Hines in the gallery and asked them for the low number. Hines
said it was him at 286. But Corcoran corrected him.

"No. It's 287. Fazio."

"And Mangrum," someone else chipped in.

Hogan studied the uphill green for a long moment. The very thought of a Sunday playoff made him queasy.

As Sam said more than once, nobody ever knew which club to hit at any given moment better than Ben Hogan. Without much hesitation, choosing wisdom over valor, he opted for a one-iron instead of his four-wood and executed a beautifully balanced swing that was captured by *Life*'s Hy Peskin in a photograph destined to become the most famous golf shot in history, in more ways than one.

Ben's ball finished on the left side of the green, forty feet from the cup, and the gallery standing ten-deep in places exploded. After looking over the putt from three different angles, he firmly rapped it four feet past the hole, producing a wave of anxious murmurs. Moments later, taking much less time than usual, he stepped up and stroked the ball into the left side of the cup, igniting another monstrous cheer that followed him off the course.

As he departed the grounds in Sullivan's car, stone-faced and silent, Valerie Hogan was convinced her husband was finished, had no more strength left in him. "I had given up on him being able to play in the playoff," she confided to sportswriter Dave Anderson decades later. "But I couldn't tell him that."

From the spectator's standpoint, as events proved time and again, U.S. Open playoffs are almost always a disappointing anticlimax. In this instance, starting a little later than normal owing to Pennsylvania's Sunday blue laws, Hogan and Mangrum finished Merion's first nine in 39 strokes, Fazio two better. On the back side, however, with five holes left to play, obviously weary but appearing to draw strength from some other dimension, Ben Hogan caught up to his competitors and began to pull away.

Fazio's nerves caused him to overshoot several greens and make bogey; Mangrum's indecisive approach shots resulted in similarly wasted strokes. When Lloyd was assessed with a one-stroke penalty by referee Ike Grainger for illegally marking his ball for a second time on the sixteenth green, Ben went to the penultimate hole with a three-shot lead. Summoning something for the ages, he sealed this extraordinary victory with a long uphill birdie putt that sent what was believed to be the largest gallery to ever witness a U.S. Open playoff into a joyous frenzy.

Seated on the terrace, Valerie Hogan listened to the roar, sipped her iced tea, and began to cry. "I knew then that Ben had won it," she allowed later.

It was, at last, the Hollywood ending that just about everyone had hoped for.

Perhaps the only man unhappier than Lloyd Mangrum or George Fazio was Sam Snead, who concluded the championship with a baleful 74 and hit the road for Hot Springs without saying a word to anyone. Despite his brilliant finish to the year—four more victories that gave him a total of eleven, a new postwar record—he was narrowly defeated for Player of the Year honors by a man who won only one official event in 1950.

"In some ways," Sam conceded many years later, "that was the toughest thing I ever had to swallow. I'd had the greatest year of my career—better than anyone had had since Byron Nelson's run—and Ben got all the honors." He paused and added, "For a while, I seriously considered hanging it up. I couldn't do any better than I'd done. Once I got home to Virginia and thought about it some more, though, I decided to keep on going. But between you and me, the tour was never quite the same for me after that."

14

IMMORTALITY

Byron Nelson was happy to be out of competitive golf.

During the period Ben was recovering from his injuries and Sam was reveling in his rediscovered putting touch, Byron and Louise invested $20,000 in state-of-the-art chicken houses and grew their cattle herd of prize Herefords to nearly three hundred head. On the first night they spent at the modest house at Fairway Ranch, as Byron named his spread one mile west of Roanoke, Texas, the couple slept on the floor. But as Byron set about repairing the roof and updating the insulation, Louise went on a shopping expedition to Fort Worth that quickly made the place the kind of home she had always wanted—cozy, warm, filled with family pictures and the paintings of the Old West that Byron would eventually begin collecting. Maybe most important of all, they became active in a Church of Christ in Roanoke, substituting a routine of numbing car travel and tee times for the sweet familiarity of Wednesday evening Bible classes and Sunday morning services. "I don't miss much about being on tour," Byron told *The Dallas Morning News* less than a month after arriving home for good. "I'll be playing most of my golf with friends from now on—if I can ever find the time."

Byron made good on his promise to Louise to hang up his clubs for a lengthy spell, playing only a few casual rounds during his first year out. An exception was the 1947 Masters, where he finished tied for second behind Jimmy Demaret, and could easily have won but for a couple of putts that didn't fall.

His success there surprised nobody. "Because of the simplicity of his swing," said his friend Eddie Merrins, Bel-Air's head professional,

"Byron had the kind of game he could park like a fine automobile. There weren't a lot of moving parts and the engine was beautifully tuned. That's why he could leave the game for whole periods of time, then come back and play outstandingly well with only a little practice. In this regard, he was more like Sam Snead than Ben Hogan."

But the game wasn't entirely forgotten by the man many had already begun to regard as the father of the modern golf swing. In the summer of 1949, as his instructional book continued to rack up sales, his longtime friend Eddie Lowery persuaded him to appear on Ed Sullivan's Sunday night show for five straight weeks, where, among other things, he hit plastic golf balls into a thrilled and gasping audience. He made a thousand dollars each time—or roughly a year's worth of cattle feed, to his way of thinking. He also found enough time from the daily demands of ranching to play well in Bing's popular celebrity pro-am, the Masters, and the Goodall Round Robin. Over the next two years, he substituted the Colonial Invitational for the Goodall and nearly won it in 1951.

For years Sam loved to recall how Ben was motoring through some hill town en route to the Greenbrier Pro-Am in early May of 1951 when he glanced up and saw that his newly released Hollywood blockbuster was playing in the theater—*Follow the Sun,* starring . . . Sam Snead.

This anecdote speaks volumes about the ongoing rivalry between them, which reached its peak during these years. But the film was released that spring to uniformly lukewarm reviews, with phlegmatic Glenn Ford and Anne Baxter playing the title roles of Ben and Valerie, featuring brief cameo appearances by Sam, Jimmy Demaret, and Cary Middlecoff. Ben, who had script approval and also served as a technical advisor, had become so obsessed with having himself portrayed accurately, he personally gave lessons to the actor, a high-handicapper who never sufficiently mastered Ben's incomparable swing. Given Ben's intransigence about authenticity, Sidney Lanfield agreed to have a special mask created that enabled him to stand in for Ford in key action shots, a strange reversal of roles. Lanfield later confided to associates that he'd never been so happy to wrap up a film because Hogan, he said, was more difficult to work with than any temperamental Hollywood starlet.

Sam's memory of that marquee, however, was off by at least a year and maybe two. The Greenbrier Pro-Am wasn't played in 1951; the nonofficial tournament took a one-year break before it resumed in

1952—won, naturally, by Sam in record-setting style—and thereafter briefly became the the Greenbrier Invitational and eventually the Sam Snead Festival. Still, considering how slowly Hollywood films found their way to the hinterlands, it could easily have been in 1952 or 1953, when Ben played in the popular event for the first time since his car accident. If Ben *did* in fact see a marquee with his movie and Sam's name on it, this probably didn't happen while he was driving down unknown roads in West Virginia. After the crash, Hogan was mildly skittish about driving anywhere outside of the familiar Dallas–Fort Worth area. As a rule, he and Valerie took sleeper trains or flew to wherever he chose to appear.

Whatever the fact of this matter, perhaps even more revealing of Sam's state of mind—still simmering from his sloppy eighth-place finish at the '51 Masters where Ben, after ten solid days of solitary practice on the course with a caddie, finally won his first title before the largest gallery in the event's history—was that he turned up just over a month later for the elegant pre-tournament champions dinner on Ben's turf at the Colonial Country Club with a woman who was not his wife. This didn't go down well at all with his hosts, especially since he was the event's defending champion.

"Someone called her a professional debutante," recalled Marvin Leonard's witty daughter, Marty, "and my father and the other members were deeply embarrassed and insulted. Some thought it was a personal dig at Ben. Whatever it was, because of it, the committee refused to invite him back for the next year. That was something to have to tell to a reigning tournament champion—you can't come back because of your behavior. But Sam was doing a lot of things like that in those days, I'm afraid. He seemed oblivious to what people thought of him."

He finished in a tie for nineteenth place and left town immediately and never returned to Colonial.

Sam's professional summary for 1951 reflected his own weariness with the nomadic life on tour, and also the hard feelings that were building up between himself and the golf establishment at large, particularly with certain USGA types and Bob Jones of Augusta National, largely the result of stunts like the one he pulled at Leonard's Colonial fete. He entered just fourteen events that year, and won only twice, though he did rack up his fifth major in a manner that left no doubt about his talent and desire. In early July, submitting once more to the Darwinist ordeal of the PGA Championship—a road too rough for either Ben or Byron—he reached the thirty-six-hole final against Walter Burkemo, a Detroit club pro and Purple Heart survivor of the Battle of the Bulge at mighty Oakmont Country Club outside Pittsburgh, demolishing him seven-and-six. Burkemo, who returned to claim this title just two years later before returning to the far less grueling club life, described Sam's play that week as that of a "man who was out to prove something."

Whether this was some kind of statement to the ruling elites or just a very good week that caused him to reconsider giving up the grind, Sam finished his paltry year with yet another Miami Open title, his fourth in a decade. Fortunately for him, money was no longer a primary concern. His contract with the Greenbrier—where he oversaw the introduction of electric riding carts and earned income for their use by hotel guests—and his ongoing winter association with the Boca Raton Club paid him better than anyone else on tour, almost forty grand a year between the two. Moreover, his exhibition fees topped the rest, as much as a thousand for a day's outing.

Back home in the jagged hills of Bath County, life was considerably more problematic, a source of constant worry and irritation. His eight-year-old namesake, Sam Snead Jr., "Jackie," was a pleasant kid born with severely crossed eyes that required several surgeries to correct and made him a natural target for ridicule in a community where all Sneads were resented for their physical prowess and material success. The bullying problem was compounded by Sam's frequent absences.

"Probably for the first fifteen years of my life," Jack Snead confirms, "I wasn't in a rush to tell anyone that I was Sam Snead's son. You know how kids pick on anyone who is different, especially one who has crossed eyes. I heard all the awful things kids could say, which only made it worse when they learned who my father was. Dad was often gone in those days. My mother was one strong lady, but who wants your mama sticking up for you?"

During the first week of April in 1952, Sam came out of seclusion to claim his second Masters convincingly, displaying the kind of intelligent shotmaking that recalled his brilliant British Open course management (to borrow Ben's term) six years before at St. Andrews, battling a week of wild winds and tempestuous spring weather to win his second green jacket with a two-under total that beat Jack Burke Jr. by four strokes and Ben and Julius Boros by seven. Within the month, he won his own Greenbrier Pro-Am with a record 264 and took the Palm Beach Round Robin seven days after that, whereupon he went home for the birth of his second child, born on his own fortieth birthday no less, one Terrance Dillon Snead, whom his parents simply called Terry.

From the beginning, there were complications. Sam and Audrey spent years insisting Terry had been born perfectly normal, but then had contracted a virus and fever that greatly diminished his mental state. Two decades later the symptoms would be instantly recognized as some variation of severe autism or Down syndrome, an impairment brought about by the presence of a twenty-first chromosome that affects roughly one in every one thousand newborns in this country and causes mild to moderate retardation.

Without question, Sam's closest friends and associates would agree in time that having a son who would require lifelong care and steadfast attention dealt his superstitious psyche a major blow, yet Sam remained devoted to Terry for the rest of his days, often traveling great distances just to see his son for a few moments at various institutions where he stayed. "Sam's devotion to Terry was very real," says his friend Bill Campbell. "Family and friends meant more to Sam than he sometimes let on. The golf world wasn't his natural home—these hills were. He had a decency and kindness that really flowered when he was back home in the place that made him."

Following his heroic comeback year and miraculous U.S. Open win at Merion, Ben appeared in public only four times in 1951. But those four weeks of work would deepen the gathering mystique of a damaged man who could apparently summon greatness at will. "If anything," Tommy Bolt once told a writer in Florida, "that wreck made Ben an even more dangerous critter. He saved everything inside for the titles he wanted most and the rest of the time he just practiced, practiced, practiced."

From its inception in 1895, the United States Open was designed to be golf's sternest test, the game's version of an Olympic marathon. In 1951, it returned to suburban Detroit and the Oakland Hills Country Club where in 1937 Ralph Guldahl deprived the red-hot rookie Slammin' Sammy Snead of his first national championship.

Embarrassed by how Guldahl, Snead, and others had manhandled their Donald Ross gem, the members subsequently hired English-born

Robert Trent Jones to update the course to modern standards. Known for his risk-reward philosophy, multiple platform tees, and the concept of signature holes, the designer actually shortened it by one hundred or so yards, cinched the fairways like a Victorian corset to reduce preferred lines to frighteningly narrow aisles, sharpened angles and installed large "flashed-up" bunkering at strategic points, ditched two fairly humdrum par-fives entirely and shifted and shrank putting surfaces into even smaller targets requiring pinpoint accuracy. "While no one denied [the revised] Oakland Hills was good," Open historian Bob Sommers remembered, "they questioned if it was great." The players, almost to the last qualifier, howled about its stentorian difficulty from the first day of practice. More than two dozen complained personally to the USGA's Joe Dey.

Ben and Sam weren't among them, though after several practice rounds the former artfully let slip to reporters that the course was "probably too hard for most players in the field," effectively halving the number he regarded as a threat, soberly adding that the changes were "completely ridiculous." The only player whose driving prowess and touch around greens the new Oakland Hills really favored, Ben cagily declared, was Snead. When Sam heard this, he winced, owing to a deeply held superstition that anytime anyone complimented him on his game—especially a rival—it fell apart.

On the eve of play, Ben seemed to soften his appraisal by predicting that Guldahl's course record of 281 might actually fall that week, prompting a worried USGA committee to hastily convene and decide to skip a final mowing of the rough and, in fact, water it more heavily, causing Sam to smile lazily, shake his head, and point out that this really only benefited one man in the field—Hogan.

Ben had a history of successfully picking final winning scores. And from the outset, he looked to be both a prophet and a contender. As he'd predicted, Sam followed his usual Open pattern by shooting 71 and charging to the front of the pack. Ben struggled around the course—generally having to lay up shy of Jones's new arsenal of bunkers that now required longer shots from everyone—with a 75 that left him in a large group clustered near the top. "The stupidest round of golf I've ever played," was all he had to say on the matter, then falling silent in the locker room.

Following an opening day in which no one managed to break par, grumbling reached a new crescendo among the 144 qualifiers. After following Sam and Demaret during their final warm-up round, watching them miss targets and three-putting, even wily old Walter Hagen felt compelled to wipe a hand over his gleaming pate and declare Oakland Hills the toughest Open layout he'd ever seen. "This course is playing the players instead of the players playing the course," he drolly remarked. "It really *is* a monster"—a phrase that stuck.

Majors are generally won by those who refuse to give up ground, and Sam himself fell victim to the Monster in the second round, blowing to a 78 largely due to three-putting and chipping poorly from the deep and clingy rough, falling into a large cluster that included Ben and Lloyd Mangrum. For his part, Ben played steady golf through the steambath heat that eased the strain on his legs, finding a strategic rhythm in the process, resulting in a respectable 73, leaving him five shots off the pace being set by Bobby Locke, the ever-beaming South African who'd returned from exile, with his billowing plus fours, old-style neckties, and incomparable wristy putting stroke.

Fourteen players lay between Ben and Sam and the title both craved with every fiber of their being. "But I'd have to be a Houdini now," the former said on the eve of Saturday's taxing double rounds. He noted that veterans Demaret and Locke were atop the leaderboard and that neither typically gave up ground. They were joined by Clayton Heafner and Julius Boros, relative youngsters who seemed oddly impervious to the Monster's meanness. "It would take 140 to get to the lead," Ben soberly concluded, "and how can anyone shoot 140 on *that* course?"

Not surprisingly, a new record single-day gate of eighteen thousand spectators turned out on a hot, cloudless Saturday to see if either of the sentimental favorites could somehow catch the leaders and claim the championship. Ben began his run quickly, birdieing three of his first five holes and completing the opening nine in 32 strokes, sending tremors of excitement through the galleries, many of whom began drifting away from the leaders to follow the two players who had a scent of immortality about them.

They weren't disappointed. Ben, lighting a fresh Chesterfield off the end of the one dying in his hand, completed his morning round in 71 strokes, the second-best round of the tournament, and was right back in the thick of things. Sam played well, too, finishing with a 72 that could easily have been three strokes better. But he later admitted that when he heard a fan excitedly remark to a companion, "Sammy's hot but he always seems to find a way to blow it," he felt his gut churn with the old anxiety.

During the break, Sam had a light lunch in a quiet corner of the club dining room with Fred Corcoran and then disappeared into the locker room, where he sat marking several new Wilson Staff golf balls and gathering his thoughts on how to subdue his Open jinx. Tommy Bolt remembers pausing to speak to Sam when Ben suddenly walked past and stopped, coming off the tournament's fifty-fourth hole with his head down. The two men greeted each other cordially, according to Bolt, who was being thoroughly humbled by Oakland Hills (he would finish in twenty-ninth place), and chatted for a few moments about "everything, it seemed, but what a mean sumbitch that golf course was out yonder. I remember thinking to myself, 'Here's probably the two best damn players who ever lived, fellas who could beat this beast if anyone could, and by God they're talking about their laundry or Ike's golf game or some such thing.' I have to say, that made one helluva impression on me. They were like two old prizefighters who knew what they had to do, but neither of 'em wanted to talk about it."

Ben did, however—and right on the first tee, no less.

"I'm going to burn it up," he advised his referee, Ike Grainger, the same USGA official who'd made the pivotal decision penalizing Lloyd Mangrum's double-marked ball at Merion, a ruling that punctuated Ben's heroic comeback. But a costly bogey on the long par-three third was only balanced by a birdie on seven, for an even-par 35 on the front nine, hardly the run he'd been counting on. He heard that others were rapidly falling back, except for hard-charging Bobby Locke and Clayton Heafner, Sam's old Greensboro practice partner, who held a two-stroke lead. On the brutally long and narrow tenth, Ben lashed a drive of 265 yards and then rifled a two-iron to within four feet of the cup, producing a volcanic eruption from the gallery around the green. He picked up the birdie, then followed it on thirteen with a fifteen-foot side-hiller that tumbled gently into the heart of the cup for a second birdie. "It was my best shot of the tournament," he allowed afterward. "It went exactly as I played it, every inch of the way."

Sam, playing a couple of groups ahead of him, wasn't having much luck, though almost anyone could have predicted this fate. He lipped out several excellent birdie attempts and struggled to find his chipping touch in the Monster's sticky rough. In this instance, a final round of 69 would only have lifted him to a second- or third-place finish. Ben, meanwhile, closing in on Heafner, played fifteen with a three-wood rather than a driver, which had left him in the fairway rough that morning, and nearly holed out a six-iron on the fly, running home the three-footer for birdie. At sixteen he made an equally brilliant approach to four feet, but singed the hole and stared at it with glacial contempt for several seconds before tapping in for par. After a surgical two-iron and two putts gave him par at seventeen, he came to the seventy-second hole needing one more par to cinch the victory.

With his adrenaline pumping and a slight summer breeze at his back, after taking a little more time than usual he uncorked one of the longest and most accurate final drives he ever hit in championship play, his ball carrying the bunkered ridge of the dogleg, an extremely gutsy play for the game's most conservative tactician. A roar went up from the gallery once again standing ten-deep around the final hole. Minutes later, he carved a six-iron boldly straight at the pin and left his ball fifteen feet above the cup.

He finished a cigarette on his trudge up to the green, thumbing it away and merely touching his famous white linen cap as the vast crowd greeted him with a thunderous and sustained ovation that grew into a lusty cheer. They quickly fell silent as he stalked the green sizing up the putt, and took his familiar slightly crabbed tripod stance over the ball. The putter eased back and came forward, his ball trickling down the hard, heat-scorched green, gathering speed until it clattered into the cup. There was an instant of silence followed by even wilder cheers on all sides.

One of them came from Bill Campbell, Sam's young West Virginia protégé who'd trekked back after his cause was lost to follow Hogan in. "The way Ben played those three closing holes illustrated something wonderful about Hogan, something that became his hallmark—namely that he could always hit exactly the shot that was needed at that moment. Great champions can all do that, of course, though I never saw anyone better at that than Ben."

Ben's final birdie gave him a 67, the second-lowest finishing round ever by an Open contender, and a 287 total that came nowhere near Guldahl's mark but was historic nonetheless. His back-nine 32 was by far the most satisfying of his career, making him national champion for the third time. "There have been other great finishes since then," declared U.S. Open historian Bob Sommers. "Arnold Palmer's slashing 65 at Cherry Hills in 1960, the 65 by Jack Nicklaus at Baltusrol in 1967, Johnny Miller's 63 at Oakmont in 1973, and the two 68s Cary Middlecoff put together at Inverness in 1957—but none compared to this one."

As irony would have it, Robert Trent Jones's wife, Ione, was among the first to shake the winner's hand after he'd come off and filed his card. "Ben," she told him, extending her hand, "I'm so proud of you. You must be very pleased with the way you played."

He accepted her hand and stared at her. "Mrs. Jones," he calmly said, "if your husband had to play the courses he designs for a living, I'm afraid you'd be in a breadline."

In the locker room, smiling cautiously as he sipped a cold beer and the pain in his legs receded, he sounded more conciliatory to the crush of reporters bending over him. "Under the circumstances, it was the greatest round I have played. To be honest, I didn't think I could do it. My friends said last night that I might win with a pair of 69s. It seemed too much on this course. It's the hardest course I've ever played."

Twenty minutes later, with his thinning hair neatly combed and showing the rapidly expanding traces of gray at the temples, dressed in an elegant silk blazer from his favorite Manhattan haberdasher, he accepted the gold medal and Open trophy from executive director Joe Dey, then turned to address the huge multitude that ringed the eighteenth green. Perhaps, considering all he'd been through, they expected him to speak frankly about what the historic turn of events meant to him. He now had won the U.S. Open three times, just one shy of the record held by Willie Anderson and his friend and hero Bobby Jones.

"Those of us who were there felt for sure he was going to really open up and talk about what this meant to him," Bill Campbell remembered. "But you could see him struggling to find the words. I've always thought this one meant the most to Ben, given the course and where he was in life. He said as much himself—in true Hogan fashion."

Faithful to his growing legend as the most self-armored athlete in American sports, Ben simply thanked the USGA and the fans and revealed precisely what was on his mind. "I'm glad I brought this course, this *monster*, to its knees."

He remained out of view for the next two months, resting up and planning a future life off the tour, then made a surprising appearance the first week of August at George May's annual spectacle in Chicago, the World Championship of Golf—where he'd run afowl of sponsors for refusing to wear a number on his back, and vowed never to return. His last-minute entry via the phone baffled the media but visibly delighted May, who warmly welcomed him back to Tam O'Shanter and told reporters that the magical name of Hogan guaranteed twenty thousand more spectators.

Perfectly in sync with Ben's calculating nature, and known principally only to a select few including George Coleman, Bing Crosby, Dallas tycoon Pollard Simons, and Marvin Leonard—Hogan's surprising entry was really about just two things: the opportunity to deprive Sam Snead of another Player of the Year honor and, more important at this point, to make money and further his dreams of creating a club-making firm with his perfect signature on them.

The first task was accomplished relatively simply. Ben went out and mugged Tam O'Shanter with four rounds in the 60s, shattering the tournament record and pocketing May's first-place check for $12,500, then slipping out of town without making a spare comment. Sam finished in a tie for eighth and, having done the math and decided that Ben was a lock for the honor he still coveted, decided to take the rest of the year off. He'd played just fourteen tournaments and won only twice, though this included his third PGA—going one-up on both Ben and Byron in that championship.

Ben, by contrast, won three of just four events—the Masters, the Open, and George May's Chicago extravaganza. His only disappointment was finishing fourth at the hometown Colonial National Invitational, where Sam had made himself persona non grata. Ben's strong winning percentage, and two major titles, proved the difference.

"Was the great Hogan even here?" asked one of Chicago's less impressed sportswriters. "He showed up, teed up, spoke to virtually no one, broke a scoring record or two, then vanished. What is Ben thinking?"

Whatever he was thinking, days before the members of both Ryder Cup teams of 1951 showed up in the Carolina sandhills at Donald Ross's masterful Pinehurst No. 2, his colleagues named him Player of the Year. During the opening dinner, a rapidly balding Sam Snead, the team captain, graciously joked about having to beat Ben "twice as much as he beats the rest of us to have a decent shot of winning the honors." Ben only smiled.

The next afternoon, in a cozy interview with broadcaster John Derr and the sports editor from his old paper, the *Greensboro Daily News*, an unusually relaxed Hogan described the home life he was currently enjoying with his "part-time" playing status, and hinted at "other interests" that were attracting a lion's share of his attention, refusing to divulge any more about what those might be. "We weren't sure what his plans were though we both came away from the conversation convinced this would be the last time we might see Ben in any kind of tournament," recalls Derr, who along with others had begun to take note of Hogan's struggles with a putter—chiefly by the amount of time he frequently stood over putts, especially short ones. "That only goes to show how we underestimated Ben once again," Derr added with a grin. "His best was yet to come."

With Sam as captain, the Americans routed Britain and Ireland 9½ to 2½, prompting Henry Longhurst to ruefully lament in his *Times* Sunday column that the only real surprise in Pinehurst was Jimmy Demaret's announcement that he was retiring from Ryder Cup competition with a perfect 6-0-0 record, prompting many on both sides of the water to wonder whether Great Britain and Ireland would ever win the cup again. Ben, who actually wore his pajamas beneath his golf clothes owing to the unusually cold weather, occasionally donning a topcoat between holes, teamed with pal Jimmy to decimate Fred Daly and Ken Bousfield in the opening Foursomes, and went on to beat Charlie Ward three-and-two in the Singles. In a subsequent article for *Golf Illustrated,* Longhurst gave his impressions of the Hawk: "Among the gallery in the fourth match, bearing no outward and visible sign connecting him with the proceedings, is a small dark man with grey raincoat, grey cap, grey trousers, and inscrutable expression, looking like a Pinkerton detective on watch for pickpockets. This is the world's greatest golfer, Ben Hogan, participating in a Ryder Cup match." Cup historian Dale Concannon concluded that this helped shape the British golfing public's enduring image of Ben.

In the event's aftermath, on the other hand, ebullient captain Sam Snead all but guaranteed his friends and fishing pals that 1952 would be his year. "There's no question that even Sam heard the clock ticking," says Bill Campbell. "Just like Byron and Ben, Sam was turning forty that year, which was particularly old for a player back then. Sam didn't drink or smoke, and he was the first player I ever knew who carried weights and did sit-ups and push-ups every morning. He was careful about what he ate long before that was fashionable. Gary Player and Frank Stranahan were said to be the tour's big health nuts. But it was really Sam Snead who showed them the virtues of staying in good shape. That's why all three—especially Sam—were able to extend their careers far beyond the norm."

Nobody sympathized with Ben's vexations on the greens more than Sam, who had determined that Ben's problem was an inability to initiate the takeaway, almost as if he simply couldn't decide on either the line or the strength of the stroke, often resulting in an abbreviated stab at the ball not terribly unlike Sam's own yips. Others who witnessed Hogan's lengthy pauses over the ball assumed he was merely taking more time to refine his thoughts.

Unknown to anyone but Valerie and his doctor back in Fort Worth, however, the cornea in his left eye had been damaged in the accident, and as he stood over putts that eye often lost focus along with depth perception. In these moments, he would wait until his right eye and brain could compute the line and distance, but by this point his tensing muscles were refusing to cooperate as they once had, causing an abbreviated stroke that sent his ball skidding toward the target. Since his comeback, he'd tried everything from tranquilizers and hypnosis to a host of new grips and putting techniques to subdue the effects of this steady deterioration, but to little or no avail. This proved costly when he showed up in 1952 to compete in his favorite tournament, the Masters.

For the stubbornly silent man who was at the center of all sorts of speculation in the press about his impending retirement plans, the lone highlight of this trip to Augusta was the Champions Dinner Ben proposed to Jones and Roberts and hosted on Tuesday evening, paying for the dinner for the next two years out of his own pocket until, as he put it, he "realized the tab came to more than the winner's share of the purse." Nine former champions showed up for the inaugural fete: Horton Smith, Henry Picard, Ralph Guldahl, Byron Nelson, Herm Keiser, Craig Wood, Jimmy Demaret, and Sam Snead—who reportedly broke the ice during cocktails by telling one of his blue jokes that got everybody laughing except Byron, who just shook his head.

In time, as younger Masters champions joined the dinner, Sam would illustrate his remarkable physical dexterity by standing flat-footed in the doorway of the upstairs dining room and then kicking the frame overhead, a feat that never ceased to amaze and amuse the newcomers. "Sam never grew weary of his role as clown prince of the dinner," says Arnold Palmer, who was invited after winning his first green jacket in 1958. "Some of us loved it, others not so much."

Buoyed by his role as host, Ben opened the tournament with a pair of two-under-par 70s, but Sam vaulted to the lead with rounds of 70-67.

Then the spring winds danced across the course on the weekend, wreaking havoc on everyone's score. Sam skied to a woeful 77, Bolt and Mangrum posted 75s, Julius Boros a 76, Jackie Burke a 78. Ben's 74 still gave him a decent chance, while Byron's 77-78 finish ended any hope he had of winning a third Masters title.

Ben's awful 79 on that windy Sunday was the talk of Augusta after Sam had held off Burke to win his second Masters. "Sam was walking on air," Derr recalled, "but the real buzz around the press tent was whether this was the end of Ben that everyone had been expecting. The fact that it appeared to be his worst finish in a major championship where he was contending spoke volumes to everyone on hand. There was a definite sense that the guard was changing in a big way. Ben was just the perfect symbol of that."

He also noted that Bob Jones, already suffering from syringomylia, the acute muscular disease that would eventually kill him, had begun relying on a motorized cart to ferry him around his club, and that Mangrum, Demaret and Harmon were all making noises about giving up the chase for good. Young guns like Burke, Bolt, Middlecoff, and Boros now featured routinely on the leaderboard, and others would follow.

"The idea that a Hogan or Snead might someday quit coming to the Masters was damn near unthinkable, something none of us wanted to believe," Tommy Bolt echoed some years later. "Given all they'd done, they didn't seem all that human to us. But time takes its toll on all of us, brother, and you didn't have to look too hard at either Sam or Ben to see their games were on the slide. Golf's an old man's pleasure, someone once said, but it's a young man's game."

Two months later, the inaugural National Golf Day held at the Northwood Club in Dallas—an ambitious fund-raiser sponsored by the PGA and *Life* magazine to capitalize on the significant growth of the game's popularity spurred by Ben's heroics and his ongoing rivalry with Sam—quickly became known as Beat Ben Hogan Day by the estimated 100,000 players who shelled out a buck at designated clubs and courses around the country to match their net scores against the reigning national champion's practice round at Northwood, a fairly new layout Ben considered unworthy of the U.S. Open scheduled there that summer. Those whose scores "beat" Hogan's would win a special medal from the sponsors.

Beginning at eleven sharp, Texas time, on May 31, 1952, as would-be giant killers from Bangor to Bakersfield teed off simultaneously, John Derr followed Ben around the five-year-old course built on rolling ranchland, once owned by the husband of actress Greer Garson, just north of the Dallas city limits. Displaying machinelike precision and no emotion whatsoever, Ben hit every fairway and green in regulation on the front nine. His only slip came when he pulled a one-iron into the cottonwood trees on the par-three sixteenth, prompting him to drolly remark to Derr, after the resulting bogey, "That should cost *Life* another 10,000 medals." He finished with an even-par 71.

Only 1,400 players across the country managed to beat him. But the organizers proudly pointed out that participants included General Omar Bradley, beloved TV cowboy Hopalong Cassidy, four sitting governors and one senator, not to mention the entire cast of the Broadway hit *South Pacific*. None beat Ben. A decent two-digit handicapper, Senator Robert Taft from Ohio, offered that playing in such a "wonderful democratic enterprise" probably didn't hurt his chances of gaining the Republican Party's presidential nomination in a few weeks. He was mistaken. A good friend of Cliff Roberts's and Bob Jones's paid his first visit to Augusta National about this time, and was chosen at the convention that summer and went on to win the election, taking his high-handicap game to the White House for the next eight years. Ike's passion for the game would dovetail beautifully with his country's growing ardor for the sport.

Despite his poor Masters finish, many oddsmakers calculated that the relatively flat and featureless terrain of Northwood would make this national open something of a cakewalk for Ben, and just days before the championship commenced, stars that included Ronald Reagan and Bing Crosby showed up to help him celebrate his induction into the Texas Sports Hall of Fame, prompting Charles Einstein of the International News Service to breathlessly predict that "this is the Open Hogan can't lose and Snead can't win." At his induction dinner, Ben singled out Valerie as the greatest inspiration of his life, crediting her faith and loyalty and good judgment with "seventy-five or eighty percent of my success."

Amid sweltering temperatures that caused hundreds to faint from heat exhaustion—many assumed the heat would ease the burden on Ben's fragile legs—he started well, and after two rounds shared the lead with old rivals George Fazio and Johnny Bulla and the easygoing newcomer Julius Boros. With three wins already under his belt that year, Sam opened with 70 and then skidded to 75. He was never close after that, complaining about the heat. Was it a good omen that *Follow the Sun* opened at two Fort Worth drive-ins that week? Many thought so, including former TCU player Dan Jenkins, who in Saturday's *Fort Worth Press* confidently predicted that the "pharaoh of the fairways" would break his own record of 276 and win his fourth national championship.

But Boros had a different idea, going out early and chipping and putting himself into the lead with a masterful 68 in the third round. By the end of Saturday's morning loop, with temperatures edging into the mid-90s, having uncharacteristically missed several fairways Ben found himself two strokes behind. "Even with that," Derr recalls, "there wasn't a thinking person on the grounds who didn't expect Ben to make a final-round charge and take the tournament. That had always been his way. Once in the lead, he never gave it up. That's a lesson he passed on to Jack Nicklaus and Tiger Woods."

But for the first time since his ordeal at Merion, Ben's legs betrayed him, his fabled iron will buckling under the high expectations and blast-furnace heat. One of the spectators who followed him briefly until things began to go badly was Byron Nelson, wearing his trademark straw hat. "It was apparent to me that Ben was out of gas almost from the start of that final round," he later said. "And goodness knows, who wouldn't have been?" Soldiers were ferrying collapsed fans to special cooling stations and hospital emergency rooms as Boros played his way home to claim the title. Ben's 74 left him in third place. Every move he made in public was now scrutinized for deeper meaning, and this collapse prompted a fresh wave of retirement talk.

For the record, an irritated Sam finished in a tie for tenth place and headed straight for his new Cadillac, though in a typical mercurial mood swing he bounced back the very next week by winning the Inverness Round Robin, where former head pro Byron still played as a special guest. They had a pleasant dinner and were overheard warmly reminiscing about their early days on the tour. Ben's name, according to Sam, never came up.

While hearing constant rumors about his own retirement, Sam finished 1952 with his second Masters victory and four more titles, clearly attempting to stake his claim before his greatest rival left the game for good.

After Northwood, Ben Hogan didn't appear in public for months. While he won his third Colonial National Invitational that year, he registered only two other finishes, a third at the U.S. Open and a tie for seventh at the Masters—his worst showing in more than a dozen years. Reaching its own conclusion, the Associated Press confidently reported he would soon announce his retirement, perhaps before Christmas and certainly before the start of the 1953 season.

True heroism is simply the courage to confront one's destiny.

Owing to his amazing physical prowess and his burning desire for a U.S. Open title and the respect of his peers—not to mention a poor boy's love of money that was as natural as his swing—Sam Snead was destined to go on playing, brilliantly at times, for the next two decades. With remarkably undiminished skills, and courage, he set records for playing longevity that likely will never be equaled, much less beaten. By the end of his incomparable run, he would be the only player to have won PGA events in six different decades.

Days after Sam won the Baton Rouge Open in March of 1953, A. S. Barnes, the same New York firm that produced Ben's best-selling *Power Golf* and Byron's *Winning Golf*, rolled out Sam's own long-awaited instructional book, aptly titled *Natural Golf*. An immediate hit, the book easily matched the sales of both Byron's and Ben's books.

In many ways, as 1953 got under way and Ben remained stubbornly silent on his immediate plans, this long-standing rivalry grew even more intense. Ben and Sam had won six majors apiece, and while Byron had won five, he had neither the ego nor the stomach to chase down another. From this point forward, his greatest legacy wouldn't be conducted in competition.

Golf Digest, which first appeared in 1951, had begun popularizing the notion long espoused by the cognoscenti that the truest measure of a player's greatness related directly to how many major titles he'd won. Bobby Jones, with four U.S. Opens and three British, had always been the gold standard of comparison, but he was distinctly from another time, as were Walter Hagen with eleven majors and Gene Sarazen with eight. Now, with professional golf arguably more popular than it had ever been, largely due to this American Triumvirate, millions were watching to see how the ongoing battle between Sam and Ben would wind up.

Which explains why—even as he was busy in Fort Worth setting up the infrastructure of his future life, with a new company devoted to making the finest clubs and balls available—Ben Hogan simply couldn't elude the burden of his own destiny. Entering his forty-first year, though the grind of championship golf was nearly too much to bear both physically and psychologically, his very nature guaranteed that he would do whatever was required to win at least one more major and improve his lead on his two greatest rivals.

Following weeks of practice down at Seminole, and a lucrative second-place finish in the club's popular Amateur-Professional Tournament, Ben finished in a tie for eighth at the Palmetto Pro-Am, forty miles from Augusta in Aiken, South Carolina. The man he'd tied, predictably, was Sam Snead, who was buoyant over the huge sales of *Natural Golf*. "Maybe we ought to go have a playoff somewhere down in Georgia," Sam later claimed to have told Ben. "I could give you a great book to help you with that swing of yours."

As Burke and Bolt were first to point out, young and veteran players alike often stood for hours watching Ben and Sam practice. This particular year, on the range at Augusta National, Mike Souchak, who'd turned professional in late 1952 but was here as a spectator, happened to observe a fascinating exchange between Ben and Toney Penna, the former tour star who was now a leading field rep for MacGregor Golf, the company Ben had signed on with in 1937 for $250. Violating protocol and Ben's own sacred practice space, Penna reminded him of the company's recent mandate that all its players use the new Tourney ball. Eight days after his fortieth birthday, however, Ben had paid a secret visit to rival Acushnet's factory to see how the Titleist balls he preferred were made.

Not surprisingly, on the practice tee at Augusta, he was hitting Titleist balls to a caddie stationed out on the range with a towel and a catcher's mitt. Penna was outraged by this bold defiance of company policy, not to mention that Ben was using MacGregor golf clubs that bore little or no resemblance to the ones the company sold under his name, two tiers down from their Tommy Armour Silver Scots and Byron Nelson Classics. These clubs, as it happened, were early prototypes of the new ones Ben hoped to bring to market within a year. Back in Fort Worth, he was already working with one of the game's most respected club makers to produce a finished model designed for better players.

"It got heated real fast," Souchak remembered. The recent Duke graduate was one of a handful of newcomers along with Ken Venturi, Gardner Dickinson, and Texan Dave Marr whom Ben would take a shine to about this time. "Penna demanded to know why Ben was being so difficult and Ben told him to tell Mr. Cowan of MacGregor that his balls and golf equipment were junk. That pretty much settled that."

Ben opened this seventeenth Masters with a steady two-under 70, missing a pair of short putts for par over the final two holes that left him two strokes behind Chick Harbert, and one ahead of Sam, the reigning champ, who drained a monstrous birdie putt on the final hole but erroneously signed his card for par and had to keep that higher score, a 71. Displaying his graceful unchanging swing, Byron went 73-73 but felt sharp pains in his lower back that caused him to withdraw after a third-round 78.

In the second round, where Ben typically made his move against the field, he hit every green in regulation and shot a 69 that gave him the halfway lead at 139.

Overnight, heavy rains pounded the course and softened up the greens, but ten thousand patrons trailed him and colorful journeyman Porky Oliver through the third round, observing one of the finest shot-making exhibitions ever put on by two players. "Word spread quick that Hogan and Porky were doing something really special out there," Mike Souchak recalled. "And by the back nine you had lots of players who'd already finished coming out to watch. They were both on fire and it seemed like some kind of record had to fall." Between the pair, Ben and Porky accumulated thirteen birdies and one eagle (Oliver's). Ben's final 66 was his lowest round ever at the Masters, and he beat Oliver by only a stroke.

A record did indeed fall that day, with Ben's 205 beating Byron's 54-hole mark by two strokes. In the clubhouse, Byron was among the first to congratulate him. Given his four-stroke lead over Oliver, not known to be a strong closer, the only real question in most minds was how badly Ben would beat the seventy-two-hole record of 279, shared by his friend Claude Harmon and Ralph Guldahl. Masters tradition dictated that the tournament leader be paired with Byron Nelson in the last round. But since he couldn't play, Ben got Porky instead, with Byron following as a spectator.

This was also a thing of beauty, a solid 69 that brought the vast Augusta gallery roaring to its feet with the final putt. Ben removed his cap and smiled, author of a new fourteen-under-par total of 274 that bettered the old record by five strokes and would stand for a dozen years. Byron was among the first to shake his hand and congratulate him. Sam, who shot 75 and finished tied for sixteenth, also congratulated the winner in the locker room. Ben reportedly thanked him and offered to send him a copy of his next instructional book. And so it went.

Before he left Augusta, reporters asked Ben if there was any truth to the rumor that he planned to play in the British Open at Carnoustie later that summer. That very week, both Bob Jones and Gene Sarazen had told him that he owed it to himself and the fans and the game to make a run at the Claret Jug, and he said that he would think it over. But the answer he gave reporters was typically Hoganesque—an emphatic "No."

Fearsome Oakmont was on Hogan's mind, that unclaimed fourth U.S. Open title that would tie him, at least by the USGA's math, with the great Jones himself. By his own calculus a victory in Pittsburgh in mid-June would be his fifth national championship, counting the disputed Hale America Open in 1942. Whatever else was true, he now had one more major title than Sam did, and two more than Byron.

Two weeks after the Masters, after riling fellow pros by demanding appearance money to play in the Pan American Open, he captured that event, too. Seven days later, at the new Sam Snead Festival in West Virginia, he three-putted the final hole from eighteen feet to finish third; fittingly Sam won with a record 268. Fourteen days later, the day after Native Dancer ran away with the Preakness, as questions about his British Open plans approached fever-pitch in the national sports columns, Ben won his fourth Colonial National Invitational. Accepting the runner-up check, Cary Middlecoff quipped, "I feel honored to play in the Ben Hogan Benefit here once again."

"Do I get to keep it?" Ben asked Marvin Leonard upon being handed the trophy.

"No," his mentor replied. "But you already own it."

In his mind, the year's only unfinished business before he got back to club making awaited him at Oakmont, that unforgiving masterpiece built by steel magnate Henry Fownes on the bluffs of the Allegheny River, with its 350 "sand pits," or roughly twenty bunkers per hole, and a well-earned reputation for having the toughest greens in championship golf. Shortly before the Hogans set off for Pittsburgh, Henry Picard phoned Ben to give him a bit of strategic advice. "The only way to handle those greens is to play for the collars in front," Henry said. "Otherwise you'll have no chance."

Heading east, the Hogans stopped briefly in Cincinnati so Ben could meet with MacGregor's head man, Henry Cowan, who made his pitch and showed him the results of detailed tests conducted on the new Tourney golf ball using a state-of-the-art mechanical robot—a prototype that the USGA would later refine and use for its own equipment testing, the aptly nicknamed "Iron Byron." Ben wasn't persuaded.

When Cowan angrily demanded to know how he could possibly deny all this scientific data, an equally irritated Ben reportedly looked at him and said, "If it's so good, I recommend you enter that machine in the U.S. Open," and walked out. Unknown to anyone outside his close circle, he already leased a fifteen-thousand-square-foot office building on West Pafford Street in Fort Worth. He'd also hired two talented club makers who were improving the prototype that had gotten him in trouble at the Masters.

Facing a new wave of stars including Burke, Bolt, Middlecoff, and Boros, Ben predictably didn't alter Open preparations one iota. He arrived at the club at nine o'clock sharp, signed a few autographs, then put on his spikes and walked with a caddie to a remote corner of the practice tee, where he smoked an entire pack of Chesterfields and went through his bag hitting every club for ten minutes. He also played practice rounds with Burke, Bolt, George Fazio, and young Mike Souchak, whose golf swings and personalities he liked. "One reason he liked us," Souchak said years later, "was we played fast and said little. Nobody wanted to be the guy who got in Hogan's way. We were all in awe of him."

As the players made their usual howls about Oakmont's difficult setup, Ben went out on a pleasant sunny opening day dressed in a gray sweater and his signature white cap, carving a masterful 67 out of the course, a round that included five birdies, and seizing a commanding three-stroke lead. Every other big name, it seemed, had a rough beginning. Host pro Lew Worsham could manage only a 78, while the seemingly ageless Sarazen and Runyan shot 82 and 79 respectively. The defending champion, Julius Boros, three-putted three of his last four holes for 75. Sam managed a 72. Meanwhile, a skinny, hard-swinging, and somewhat unorthodox young amateur from nearby Latrobe, who'd qualified on leave from the coast guard, also had a great deal of difficulty battling Oakmont's murderous rough. In his Open debut, Arnold Palmer slashed his way home in a discouraging 84 strokes.

In the second round, Sam recovered some of his old touch and needed only eleven putts on the back nine to shoot 69, edging two strokes closer by the end of the day to Ben, who shot 72 and took more time than usual over short putts as the tournament unfolded, oblivious to the slow-play penalties being handed out by officials.

Oakmont produced even slower play on Saturday, and the chorus of complaints grew louder. At one point, a disgruntled Middlecoff hooked his drive onto the Pennsylvania Turnpike, picked up his tee and stalked off the course. By then Ben Hogan was already in the clubhouse with the lead, having a light lunch of ginger ale and fruit salad in hopes of losing some of the fifteen pounds he'd put on since the accident.

Sam, meanwhile, after another 72 that allowed him to pick up another stroke on Ben, grabbed a sandwich and went to Worsham's pro shop to look at putters. "I was kind of agitated with my putting," he remembered, "but I was mostly worried about, well, the usual thing—the hex, the jinx, whatever you want to call it. Something always got me in the final round. I figured this might be one of my last good shots at the thing. And I was hoping Ben and I would be paired together that afternoon."

Most everyone else on the grounds was probably hoping for the same thing. "It was shaping up to be a classic U.S. Open in which the two reigning titans of the game, Hogan and Snead, would have the ultimate one-on-one for the biggest championship of them all," Al Barkow notes. "Sam's record against Ben in such situations was better than anyone else's in golf. In the three head-to-head major championship matches they had in their careers, Sam won all three. Joe Dey, an unapologetic Hogan fan, knew this. His personal dislike of fellow Virginian Snead was perhaps the worst-kept secret in golf."

When Sam arrived at the first tee for the afternoon round, he was dismayed to see that Ben had been sent out almost ninety minutes ahead of him and, in fact, was already on the ninth hole. His heart sank and his temperature rose.

What followed that afternoon was unforgettable for fans of both men.

Ben fired a brilliant 71 for a 283 that bettered the Oakmont tournament record by eleven strokes and officially tied him with Jones, whereas Sam was once more undone by the demons of self-doubt and staggered home with a 76 to his fourth runner-up finish in the Open. During the presentation, Ben playfully pushed the trophy toward Sam, who grabbed it and pretended to swoon, rolling his eyes. "I never felt worse than that moment," he said years later.

Outside Oakmont's elegant timbered clubhouse, reporters peppered a departing Hogan with questions about playing at Carnoustie, widely regarded as the toughest and most unforgiving course on the British Open rota. On the eve of play at Oakmont, Hogan had finally ended the suspense by announcing his intention to play the British Open, and one reporter pointedly demanded to know why he would want to subject himself to that. What he chose not to say was that wily Walter Hagen had tracked Ben down by phone and told him his greatness would never be assured until he won the oldest championship in golf—a feat Sir Walter had done four times.

"Oh, I don't know, fellas," he replied almost jauntily, eager to deflect any glimpse into his thinking. "Maybe because Sam probably won't be there."

Ben bought cashmere long johns from Abercrombie & Fitch for what he knew would be his final competitive trip abroad. Sam briefly considered going, too, but instead went home to focus on the PGA Championship.

Late on the afternoon of June 23, the Hogans arrived at their fully staffed private manor house in Dundee called Tay Park, an estate house arranged by Ben's Wall Street friend Paul Shields and owned by the National Cash Register Corporation. A Humber automobile and driver would chauffeur him wherever he chose to go, and during the ten days prior to the Open he made daily trips to reconnoiter vaunted Carnoustie and reacquaint himself with links-style play at nearby Panmure Golf Club, safely insulated from the rapacious British press. Meanwhile, Valerie was looked after by the staff at Tay House as if she were visiting royalty. On the recommendation of amateur Pinehurst stars Dick Chapman and Harvie Ward, Ben also secured a local caddie named Cecil Timms, a talkative young man everyone called Timmy.

Perhaps sensing the historic nature of his undertaking—and

its valedictory implications—Ben invited John Derr to follow him through every step of his preparation and the tournament itself. The broadcaster's bosses at CBS had initially balked at the idea of footing the bill for a fortnight in golf's holy land, but eventually sprang for the airline ticket and the hotel when some executive realized the potential bonanza of having their man on the scene if Hogan somehow accomplished the impossible. A deal was quickly hatched to use BBC equipment and engineers to transmit Derr's daily evening updates back to the States.

At the height of British summer, with daylight lingering until ten o'clock, Ben spent several evenings practicing on the Panmure course with Timmy and Derr as his sole companions. He never hit a ball, the latter remembered, from the gorse or heather. "Anyone who hits into that," he explained, "won't be contending anyway." Among other adjustments, he nipped shots off the firm wind-seasoned turf and hit low runners onto the greens using the smaller British balls he'd recently begun practicing with back home in Texas, also adjusting upward or downward in club selection depending on the strength and direction of the wind. One tranquil evening, he invited Derr—no slouch himself, a single-digit player—to borrow some clubs from the pro shop and play along with him, and even offered to give him a few pointers. But Derr politely declined, insisting he didn't want to risk distracting Ben from his meticulous preparation routine.

"I saw a new Ben that first week," he recalls, "or maybe it was the kinder and gentler Ben Hogan I'd heard really existed beneath his tough public reputation. I'd known him a fairly long time and perhaps because Sam and I were close—and Ben liked Sam and felt much closer to him than to Byron by that point—he felt he could open up and tell me a few things going on in his head. For instance, I learned this was likely to be his final championship before he announced his retirement, and that he intended to go into the equipment business very soon, although he didn't yield many details."

What Ben did relate, however, during one brief interlude, were several fundamental things he believed were essential for every golfer to master in order to play his best golf. He planned to feature these essentials, he said, in a new instructional book he'd agreed to do with Herbert Warren Wind of *Sports Illustrated*. "He made it clear that because every golfer was different—owing to variables in weight, height, build, strength and so forth—he had to develop his own game based on these fundamentals," Derr remembered. "The days after he told me this—we were having a sandwich at lunch at the time—he asked me not to share this secret with anyone until he was finished with tournament golf. Naturally I assured him I wouldn't. It would be *our* secret until he was ready to tell the rest of the world."

Ben Hogan made no secret of his grave respect for Carnoustie, a proud, tough, straightforward public seaside links course whose local sons prided themselves on being heirs to a distinguished line of players and teachers that included Tommy Armour and a host of fabled teaching pros who'd emigrated to club jobs in America from the Firth of Tay, among them Bobby Jones's mentor, Stewart Maiden. Claiming to date from 1500—supporting local assertions that it was even more ancient than the Old Course at St. Andrews—it had at any rate been shaped by three of golf's greatest figures: laid out initially by Allan Robertson in 1850, improved upon by Old Tom Morris two decades later, then brilliantly reconfigured in the early twentieth century by James Braid, the Scottish member of Britain's fabled Great Triumvirate.

It was, in sum, a fitting stage for an incomparable player's final performance, a noble 7,200-yard brute draped in glorious history and impossible gorse, so intimidating that a host of American contenders—including George Fazio, Johnny Bulla, Porky Oliver, and Gene Sarazen—all cabled their regrets to Carnoustie officials at the last moment, choosing to stay home. A few claimed later they wanted Ben to have the stage entirely to himself, though that didn't quite wash with anyone, nor did it prevent volatile Frank Stranahan and Tam O'Shanter gunslinger Lloyd Mangrum from showing up and registering a pair of nimble 66s in a final practice round that created the first media buzz of the championship. The other missing Americans, including Sam, were off in Michigan the week prior, playing in the PGA Championship at the Birmingham Country Club. With three Wanamaker trophies already on his shelf, Sam figured his odds of gaining ground on Hogan's total in majors would be greatly improved on home soil.

Three thousand spectators trailed Ben through the championship's two required qualifying rounds, an impressive one-under 70 followed by a 75 that made him question if he had the stamina for the duration. Complicating matters, the wind off the firth had shifted and cold rainy weather was forecast.

The next morning, July 6, wrapped in two cashmere sweaters, Ben started his Open quest. With no ropes holding spectators back, a dozen Scottish policemen needed to keep his path clear through the masses of fans. Unknown to Ben, the staff at Tay House had placed personal good-luck trinkets and amulets in the bottom of his golf bag—personal notes, an ancient British coin, a treasured family locket—that indicated their growing affection for this American the local papers were calling the Wee Ice Man. Owing to Ben's scratchy throat, the cook even gave him a packet of hard lemon drops to keep his throat moist.

Ben missed several short putts on the outward nine, causing the lanky and expressive Timmy to bend over and hold a hand over his eyes. At one point, Ben ordered Timmy to knock off the histrionics and stand perfectly still, and to quit eating all his candy. His opening 73 left him three strokes behind Frank Stranahan and one back of Roberto De Vincenzo, Bobby Locke, Dai Rees, and the Australian Peter Thomson, who would win the first of his five Open titles just a year later.

Following a Thursday morning downpour that rained out the early rounds, under clearing skies Ben shot a 71 that could easily have been three strokes lower. Still, he was just two behind Scotland's Eric Brown and Ryder Cup veteran Dai Rees at 142.

At Tay House on the eve of the thirty-six-hole finale, the head cold that had been sneaking up on him for days erupted with a fury, shooting his temperature to 103 and allowing only fitful sleep. In the morning, his feet were numb, his head dizzy, prompting Valerie to insist that he withdraw. When Derr heard about his condition, he chose not to alert his live radio audience back home. "We weren't even sure Ben would come out to play," he remembers. "But there he was at the start of round three, dressed in his sweaters and ready to attempt two rounds on the hardest course in Scotland in weather that had turned frightful. Valerie was worried out of her mind—and, truthfully, so was I."

A shot of the new wonder drug penicillin, administered by a Dundee physician, seemed to help a bit. Ben plodded under alternately rainy and sunny skies to a third-round score of one-under 70 that tied him for the lead with Argentina's Roberto De Vincenzo. Afterward, he retreated on aching legs to the men's locker room across the Links Parade Road, where he sat alone on a bench, took an aspirin with a glass of lukewarm ginger ale, and ate half a ham sandwich with a few orange wedges prepared by the Tay House cook. Feeling better after a brief rest, he calculated that another one-under 70 might secure the championship.

The gallery awaiting him at the first tee for the afternoon round had grown even larger, by some estimates half again as large as the morning as spectators following their favorites sensed the importance of the moment. After his opening drive split the fairway, they surged ahead and around him and Ben asked Derr to walk closer to him. "They knew they were witnessing history," Derr says. "They knew this was the greatest player of the age making his final walk into the record books."

On the fifth hole, at level par, Ben chipped in for a birdie and took sole possession of the lead. He narrowly missed birdies on eleven and twelve, then claimed one on the par-three thirteenth. When the gallery there released a thunderous ovation, he felt better than he had all week, lifting his head up in a manner Valerie said he always did when he was confident he'd win. Indeed, as he later confided, this was the precise moment he knew he had the Open in his grasp. No champion ever played better with a lead than Hogan. That's what Henry Picard said about him when he won his first tournament at Pinehurst in 1940, and it was just as true this day.

On the tee at sixteen, he asked where the other contenders stood, and Derr told him that Stranahan, who'd made a bold charge with six one-putt greens, had finished at 286. Three pars would put Ben in the clubhouse with 283. He then struck a brilliant four-wood shot to within twenty feet of the cup, safely two-putted and told him, "John, you can get ready for that interview. This tournament is over."

"It gave me goose bumps when he said that," the broadcaster remembers. "The certainty in his voice was absolute, almost chilling." Some twenty thousand spectators had gathered around the eighteenth hole, while an audience estimated at three million was listening to updates on BBC radio. Following a drive of 280 yards down the heart of the home fairway, the exuberant crowd closed around him, and Ben asked Derr to walk in front of him. "He grabbed the back of my pants, slipping his hand under my belt to hang on for dear life. People were trying to touch him and slapping him on the back. It was controlled mayhem. These people, the smartest galleries in the world, knew what they were doing following in his steps, walking with a legend who would never come again . . . immortality."

Up on the green, in a light drizzle, displaying little or no hesitation, Ben Hogan rolled home yet another putt for a birdie that gave him a 68 and a total of 282, which obliterated Carnoustie's existing tournament record by eight strokes. Hogan acknowledged the crowd's roar by removing his checked wool cap and giving a small wave and weary smile, slightly bowing to all four sides of the gallery. Future CBS commentator Ben Wright, who briefly went AWOL from his duties at a nearby military base that day just to catch a glimpse of him, recalled, "I'd never see a grayer and more exhausted-looking figure. He looked utterly and completely drained, a man on the verge of collapse. Still, the way the crowd quietly and respectfully parted as he approached—well, it reminded me of passing royalty."

Following their radio interview, Ben gave the broadcaster two Titleist balls. The one he'd finished his historic round with was headed for the USGA museum back home. The other, which he'd made birdie with on the thirteenth hole, was given to Derr, who told Ben he would give it to his infant daughter, Cricket.

Back at Tay House, the butlers, chambermaids, cooks, and groundskeepers lined up to bid the Hogans farewell. Only then did Ben discover the good luck totems in his golf bag, a moment that visibly moved the Wee Ice Man. The women kissed him on the cheek. The men shook his hand. In the Humber car on the way to a nearby airfield arranged by U.S. Air Force brass for a military flight to London to meet the newly crowned Queen Elizabeth, then on to France for a long-promised vacation, Valerie Hogan took her husband's hand, and broke down.

That same afternoon, at the train station in Edinburgh, a homeward-bound John Derr bumped into Bernard Darwin, the famous naturalist's grandson and himself the dean of British golf writers, a man who'd known the Great Triumvirate in their prime. Adding to the air of valediction, Darwin had just filed his final official story for the London *Times*. "You know, John," he was moved to say, "I don't think we'll ever see the likes of Hogan again. I distinctly got the feeling he could have done whatever was required of him in order to win. He could have shot 65 if he had needed it."

"That's what makes him Ben Hogan," Derr told him.

America agreed.

On July 21, when the Hogans arrived in New York harbor aboard the luxury liner *United States*, there was an impromptu press conference after they disembarked. As usual, Ben was peppered with questions about his immediate plans, and confirmed only that in 1954 he planned to play in the Masters and possibly the U.S. Open and certainly the Colonial Invitational. Asked if he would reconsider his decision to skip the Ryder Cup, scheduled that fall outside London at Wentworth, he tersely replied, "No." When a reporter whimsically asked if perhaps he'd follow his friend Byron Nelson's lead into cattle ranching, Ben stared blankly at him and dropped a bombshell of sorts—explaining that he was starting his own equipment company down in Fort Worth. This was as close as he would come, for the moment at least, to announcing his retirement.

"I think I have a revolutionary way of making clubs," he said. "We have several experimental models and hope to be in production soon."

"Won't this interfere with you playing golf?" an excited newspaperman asked.

"I don't plan to be a desk man," Ben told him, slightly mellowed from his quiet days at sea.

By the time the Hogans were riding down Broadway in an open Chrysler limo that afternoon, receiving the first ticker tape parade Manhattan had thrown for a golfer since Bobby Jones's triumphant return from Britain in 1930, word that he was retiring to make golf clubs had spread to newsrooms across the country via chattering press service machines.

Mayor Vincent Impellitteri read a congratulatory telegram from President Eisenhower and presented Ben with a citation that renamed Broadway Hogan's Alley for the day. "Here you are, the world's greatest golfer, and I am probably the worst," the mayor declared, fumbling a famous line Mayor Fiorello La Guardia had greeted Jones with in 1930. Almost simultaneously, Texas senator Lyndon Johnson got to his feet in the steamy un-air-conditioned Senate chambers in Washington to read a lengthy editorial from the *Lufkin* (Texas) *Daily News* declaring William Ben Hogan the greatest golfer ever. Johnson requested that the editorial and his own remarks be entered into the *Congressional Record*. Richard Nixon, who as vice president presided over the Senate, approved his request.

On the steps of City Hall, Ben addressed five thousand sweating spectators, many of whom had skipped work and got more than any stranger ever had before—a genuine glimpse of Hennie Bogan.

"Only in America and in New York City could such a thing happen to a little guy like me." He paused, glanced at his smiling wife and added, with a cracking voice, "I have a tough skin but I have a soft spot in my heart and . . . and . . . this tops anything that *ever* happened to me. Right now I feel like crying. This is the greatest moment of my life."

Following a dinner thrown by the USGA at the Park Lane Hotel, where Ben was showered with praise by Bob Jones and other dignitaries, the Hogans finally reached the refuge of their luxury suite and Ben pulled off his necktie and sighed.

"This has been the hardest day of my life," he told his wife.

15

LAST HURRAHS

A s HERBERT WARREN WIND put it in *The Story of American Golf,* 1953 was a year unlike any other, in some ways the equal of Bobby Jones's remarkable Grand Slam year in 1930 and Harry Vardon's 1920 farewell tour of America for the kind of rich human drama from which the game's sustaining narrative would arise. "The story of the next three years—the last three years—is the story of [Ben's] fortunes in six tournaments, three Masters and three Opens." Though he remained maddeningly silent on his retirement plans, Ben's near-triumphs in the only tournaments that now meant anything to him would punctuate his extraordinary career.

Beginning in April 1954, with the worldwide press unleashing every superlative imaginable on the heels of his triumph at Carnoustie, the last American athlete who somehow looked better photographed in black-and-white appeared as promised at Augusta National and played three brilliant rounds through the tsunami of excitement generated by unknown Billy Joe Patton only to wind up losing to Sam in a playoff.

As he later confirmed to Marvin Leonard and other intimates, this was one of his most frustrating losses. His concluding 75 was decidedly uncharacteristic, the result of his growing inability to pull the trigger on putts. But on the positive side of the ledger, in honor of his unique contributions, the Golf Writers Association of America unveiled the Ben Hogan Award at its annual gathering during Masters week, presented to the player who persisted despite serious illness or physical impairment. The first recipient, fittingly enough, was fellow Texan Babe Didrikson Zaharias, who was gamely battling cancer.

Following the Masters, perhaps sensing the sharp winds of change, Valerie Hogan's faithful newspaper-clipping routine abruptly ceased, almost as if she knew her husband would never attain a greater glory. In fact, he would win just twice more in his career, teaming with Sam to take both the individual and team honors at the 1956 Canada Cup, followed by a fifth Colonial title in the spring of 1959. The U.S. Open and the Masters remained his primary objectives.

"After 1954," said Mike Souchak, "every sighting of Ben was a special occasion, almost otherworldly to the younger players, who would always come around to watch whenever he was warming up or practicing. Many of the veterans did the same thing. Ben was living history, after all. We all sensed every time out could be his last. One thing I noticed, perhaps because of this, was that he grew a lot friendlier to people, even strangers who asked him for his autograph, especially kids. Ben loved kids. Most people don't know this. A lot of kids began showing up at the Masters and the Opens about that time. Golf was becoming a popular recreational sport thanks to the excitement Ben and Sam and Byron generated. It didn't hurt that you had a guy in the White House [Dwight Eisenhower] who loved the game and urged Americans to play. That combination really lit the fire in this country."

As his game dwindled and his appearances grew rarer, Ben's mind shifted to shaping his legacy in other ways.

Weeks after Ben lost the Masters playoff to Sam, a popular new Time-Life publication called *Sports Illustrated* borrowed unauthorized images of Hogan from *Life* and quotes from his peers to try to decipher the "secret" to his incomparable swing. Following the magazine's launch on August 16, an outraged Ben phoned *Time* founder Henry Luce and threatened to sue unless he was offered a written apology and a fee of $10,000. The savvy Luce, sensing an opportunity to turn a defeat into a victory, made a counterproposal to purchase Ben's book publisher, A. S. Barnes, and pay him $30,000 to either revise his best-selling *Power Golf* or perhaps do a new book altogether. By summer's end, the terms for an entirely new instruction book were hashed out; *Sports Illustrated* staffer Herb Wind agreed to serve as Ben's writing partner, and famed medical illustrator Anthony Ravielli was brought in to do illustrations.

More important to Ben, just days before he appeared at his hometown Colonial NIT in May of 1954, several hundred sets of clubs bearing his distinctive signature and crested emblem came off the assembly line at his newly refurbished West Pafford Street factory. Halfway through the tournament, however, he suddenly withdrew, offering no explanation. The reason, in fact, was his unhappiness over the quality of his clubs. Having taken hundreds of orders from leading pro shops, he made a bold decision to scuttle more than $150,000 worth of his new equipment on the eve of their release rather than allow what he believed to be inferior equipment bearing his name to reach the market. "He threw out castings and shafts and pretty well started from scratch," one early employee remembered. "Mr. Hogan wanted nothing less than perfection."

When his leading investor Pollard Simons angrily balked at this decision, Ben went to a Fort Worth bank and arranged to borrow half a million dollars on the strength of his own name. A group of investors that included Marvin Leonard, George Coleman, Paul Shields, San Francisco car dealer Eddie Lowery, Bing Crosby, and Dan Topping, owner of the New York Yankees, rallied to provide the necessary capital for the company to keep going. Leonard reportedly took the largest share.

If his business affairs were a bit more settled by the time he reached A. W. Tillinghast's splendid Lower Course at Baltusrol in New Jersey for the fifty-fourth U.S. Open in June, Ben's customary preparation routine and playing rhythm were clearly suffering. In yet another sign of how rapidly the times were changing, with ten former National Open champions in the field, this was the first to be televised nationally by NBC as well as the first where fairways were roped off to keep fans in control and out of the cameras' view. Most lenses and eyes were trained on the reigning champion, but after a promising 70-71 start the Hawk struggled to a sixth-place finish and confided to Valerie that he didn't know how many more U.S. Open efforts he could stomach. Though it was of no consolation whatsoever, Sam finished tied for eleventh place.

After his deeply satisfying victory over Ben at Augusta that spring, in fact, Sam's own competitive edge also appeared to dull rapidly. He entered just six more events that year and won only once—the unofficial Palm Beach Round Robin—and was a distant twenty-sixth on the money list, his worst showing in nearly two decades. "To be perfectly honest," he explained years later, "I was really questioning at that moment whether to keep playing tournaments or cut back the way Ben did. We weren't spring chickens, both of us forty-two and counting. I had good deals with the Boca Raton Club and the Greenbrier that provided a nice income. It wasn't the money that kept me coming back, no sir. It was that missing Open. The fact that Ben came out for just three events in 1955 kind of gave me some added motivation."

Following a winter of steady practice in Boca Raton before the 1955 season, Sam increased his daily exercise regime and entered twenty-one events, winning three and climbing back to seventh on the money list, a year highlighted by his fifth Greensboro Open title and a respectable third just a week later at the Masters, only a stroke behind Ben, the runner-up. Even as Cary Middlecoff lapped the field by seven strokes, Sam and Ben commanded the lion's share of attention, drawing record-breaking galleries.

Two months later, Sam launched a quiet assault on the fifty-fifth U.S. Open at San Francisco's beautiful Olympic Club, and one of the most formidable fields ever. Known for his quick Open starts, he commenced with an uncharacteristic 79 but fought his way back in round two with a brilliant 69 that left him just four off the lead held by Tommy Bolt and Harvie Ward, the sensational amateur out of North Carolina. "This place isn't a golf course," Sam quipped to a reporter following his impressive comeback. "It's a beautiful graveyard by the sea." His third-round 70 nudged him into second place behind former champion Julius Boros.

Yet once again, though, he was destined to be a forgotten man in the mist at Olympic, once more overshadowed by Ben and an unknown professional from Davenport, Iowa, who tied him with an eight-foot birdie putt on the final hole, forcing a playoff Ben dreaded more than anything.

At thirty-three, Jack Fleck was a journeyman pro who'd promised his wife that after this final shot he would give up a life on tour that had produced largely only frustration. A gangly, quiet fellow who listed a driving range back home among his primary club affiliations, he'd made his best finish on tour that year in Baton Rouge, an invisible tenth place, and unlike every other professional in the field he didn't have an equipment deal of any kind. On the other hand, the player he admired had given him a special gift—the second set of Hogan clubs ever used in competition.

Several weeks before at the Colonial, figuring the worst that could happen was simply a snub by his hero, Fleck brazenly showed up at the Hogan factory on West Pafford and introduced himself to the boss, explaining this was his do-or-die season. Impressed with his guts and honesty, Hogan gave him one of the first newly retooled sets of irons and woods and refused to take a penny. The only other set of Hogan clubs in play at Olympic that week was used by their maker.

The cruel and indifferent gods of the game decided that Fleck would deny his benefactor a record fifth U.S. Open. The Ben disciple, who prayed all week and claimed that an angel visited him while he was shaving at the modest El Camino Motel, went on to beat Ben in what is broadly considered golf's greatest upset. When Fleck, who looked shell-shocked, tapped in his final putt to win their playoff by three strokes, Ben Hogan came forward amid a sea of clicking cameras, removed his flat linen cap and shook hands with this sweet-natured man who would soon fade back into obscurity, playfully fanning his red-hot Bulls Eye putter. Later, at the awards presentation, with his face washed and his graying hair neatly combed, Ben's voice cracked when he said, "I'm through with competitive golf. I came here with the idea of trying to win. I worked harder, I think, than ever before in my life." He explained that he could no longer put Valerie through this grinding ordeal but left the door slightly ajar for another U.S. Open down the road.

"From now on," he added, "I'm a weekend golfer. I want to play for the pleasure of it because I want to be around the fellows and I want to be around golf."

It was his long-awaited retirement announcement. And with that he vanished.

"He'll be back," declared Tommy Bolt, disappointed at finishing third, just out of the playoff. "Ben needs this the way most of us need air to breathe."

For his part, Sam once again made a hash of the critical final round, spoiling an otherwise spectacular championship with a costly final 74. A 69 would have placed him in the playoff with Fleck and Hogan, and as his biographer Al Barkow laments, "What a playoff that would have been."

Three weeks later, two days before Ben's forty-third birthday, *Life* magazine's cover pictured him mid-swing under the bold headline "Ben Hogan Tells His Secret," and promised that inside the game's most mythic star "finally reveals the mysterious maneuver that made him a champion."

In fact, there was nothing remotely mysterious about it. As collaborator Herb Wind noted in the article and stressed decades later, the slight cupping of his left wrist at the top of the backswing was a technique that had been used since the days of Old Tom Morris and, accompanied by the weaker grip first shown to him by Henry Picard, was simply meant to open the clubface and thus "make it impossible" to close at impact and produce a "lethal hook." This revelation was illustrated by a nine-shot, freeze-frame sequence of the star's legendary swing. The public ate it up, with copies vanishing from the newsstands in record time.

Though the precise terms were never disclosed, Ben was reportedly paid $50,000 for this modest exegesis, the happy result of his tough negotiations with Henry Luce that led to his collaboration with Wind on *Five Lessons: The Modern Fundamentals of Golf*, the first serialized excerpts of which appeared in the pages of *Sports Illustrated* beginning in March 1957. The book appeared soon after and became an immediate best-seller.

That same year Marvin Leonard purchased two hundred rolling oak-shaded acres a mile or two from where Ben and Valerie Hogan were building a house in a prestigious neighborhood just off Roaring Springs Road in west Fort Worth. Robert Trent Jones was hired to design a golf course at this club Leonard planned to call Shady Oaks, his own private getaway from the more public Colonial.

To no one's surprise, Ben was the first member, and he also drove Jones crazy by constantly tinkering with his layout. Upon completion, Shady Oaks's beautiful clubhouse featured a large round table by the large window in the men's grill, where Ben and his closest friends and invited guests would have lunch together every day, five days a week, for the next thirty-seven years.

After the high drama at Olympic, Ben's next appearance would be at the centerpiece of events that would reshape the landscape of golf. Naturally, it involved his old friend and rival, Byron Nelson.

While touring the Northwest doing a charity exhibition in late 1952, purely at the suggestion of Eddie Lowery, Byron showed up at the National Amateur in Seattle to follow a promising young player named Kenny Venturi, whose father was the starter at San Francisco's public Harding Park course. After the polite, soft-spoken Venturi was eliminated in the first round of match play, the cattle rancher proposed that they play a round at the San Francisco Golf Club, where the youngster fired 66, and expected the legend to praise his game. Instead, Byron told him, "Kenny, Eddie said he wanted me to work with you, and if you're not busy tomorrow, you come out early because we've got six things to work on right away."

"But Byron had a way of putting things across like a Sunday school teacher," Venturi remembered. "Everything he said had a ring of absolute sincerity and truth. Naturally I agreed. It was one of the smartest decisions I ever made. Not only did I make friends with the finest gentleman golf ever produced, but I found a teacher who understood the golf swing better than anyone ever had. He also stressed how important it was to be the best you could be in anything you chose to do. The way you handled yourself in this world, and what you left behind, was really what mattered to Byron Nelson. That impressed me from the beginning."

In 1956, on the eve of Bing Crosby's Clambake at Pebble Beach, not long after the Seminole Golf Club made Ben Hogan an honorary member, Byron and Louise turned up at a cocktail party thrown by George Coleman at his home on the Peninsula, where another guest was his longtime friend Eddie Lowery, who rose to fame as Francis Ouimet's hustling caddie and later made a fortune with the most successful Lincoln-Mercury dealership west of the Mississippi, a three-showroom extravaganza that not only allowed him to invest in the upstart Hogan Golf Company but also to employ both young Venturi and Harvie Ward as floating salesmen, enabling them to compete on the national amateur stage.

In 1948, Edward Harvie Ward from tiny Tarboro, North Carolina, had knocked off an overconfident Frank Stranahan in the North and South Amateur Championship in Pinehurst, where he was hoisted onto the shoulders of his jubilant and rowdy Zeta Psi brothers from Chapel Hill, prompting an irked Stranahan to tell him, "If you couldn't putt, you'd be just another pretty fraternity boy." After his new boss Lowery arranged for him to begin working with Byron, he went on to win the British Amateur at Prestwick in 1952, beating Frank Stranahan six-and-five in the scheduled 36-hole final. Known for his brilliant touch with a hickory-shafted putter he'd found in the locker room of his father's golf club back home, and a playing style that was as silky as the cashmere sweaters he liked to wear, Ward demolished Bill Hyndman nine-and-eight in 1955 to capture the first of his consecutive U.S.

Amateur titles. Many considered him the most promising golfer in the country—possibly the next Hogan, as one national magazine put it.

Complicating matters for Lowery and both his protégés that winter evening, however, was a cancer growing inside amateur golf. This stemmed from a state and federal investigation that commenced following a widely publicized fixing scheme at New York's Deepdale Golf Club, where a pair of artful sandbaggers had waltzed off with thousands of dollars in the annual big-money Calcutta. Within weeks, while the USGA debated what to do behind closed doors, the scandal spread like wildfire. High-rollers everywhere suddenly found themselves being chased by state and federal tax authorities, especially those who spent lavish amounts on golf to entertain clients or woo customers and claimed those costs as deductions. (The tax code was maddeningly fuzzy on these matters.) Inevitably, Eddie Lowery, who didn't hide his liberal spending habits in golf and was underwriting the careers of Venturi and Ward, soon fell under suspicion in California.

Though certain ultra-private clubs like Seminole chose to simply ignore the growing controversy and still held their big-money games, among those who were seriously worried about appearances was Bing Crosby, who canceled his tournament's popular Calcutta in 1956, leaving Lowery—a guy who loved to make a bet—looking for a little action to fill the void.

Accounts vary on how one of the greatest competitive four-ball matches of all time came together. Byron remembered that not long after everyone sat down for dinner, Lowery and Coleman fell into a gentleman's friendly debate over Eddie's contention that his employees Ward and Venturi could beat anybody in golf.

"Anybody?" Coleman asked.

"Yes," said Lowery. "Anybody."

"Including pros?"

"Even pros."

Byron remembered that Coleman looked Eddie straight in the eye and said, "In that case, I'll take Nelson and Hogan."

This both surprised and pleased Byron—a match with his oldest rival against two of his own protégés.

"I'll do it if Ben will," he told them.

"What do you want to bet?" Coleman asked the car dealer.

"Five thousand," Lowery suggested. Coleman revised it downward to fifty dollars.

They phoned Ben at Bing's house and he agreed to skip a practice round at Pebble Beach and meet a few miles away at the Cypress Point Club. But he booked a tee time at Pebble anyway, purely as a diversionary tactic. According to Venturi, he didn't want the press or public to know that he and Byron were playing against amateurs, though Byron recalled that several hundred spectators caught wind of it and showed up to watch. Venturi's memory aligned with his mentor's, though Harvie recalled only a small cluster of folks at the start—Cypress members and friends of all four men. Whatever the truth of the matter, "The bet was down to just five or ten dollars," Byron said later, "far more about pride than money." Moreover, both Lowery and Coleman played along.

After Venturi rolled in a twelve-foot birdie putt on the final hole to potentially tie the match, Byron supposedly said, "Knock it in and we win, Ben." In the popular mythology surrounding the event his partner reportedly studied his final putt and mumbled, "I'm not about to be tied by a couple damn amateurs in front of all these people," though Ben's closest friends all dismissed this as totally out of character. Byron didn't hear this remark, though Ward and Venturi later recalled it. In his re-creation of this legendary match, writer Mark Frost relates that hundreds of fans hurried out to watch as it went along, culminating in a gallery worthy of a major championship at the final green, Ben's worst nightmare. Whatever the precise facts, the more important detail is that he took scant time to size up his slightly uphill ten-foot putt and, using a putter borrowed from the club pro shop, knock it into the heart of the cup for the winning birdie.

Cumulatively, the players were twenty-six under par, an extraordinary total that included twenty-seven birdies and an eagle. Just three holes were halved with pars. Ben tied his own course record at Cypress Point with a stunning 65; Byron had 68. Venturi and Ward finished with 69 and 70, respectively. And when they took out their wallets to pay off their wager, whatever it was, the Texans waved them away. One account has Coleman and Lowery canceling the bet on the spot.

Within twenty-four hours, the story was already spreading like an urban myth through the shops and watering holes on the Monterey Peninsula, and out into the wider world. The principals briefly considered a follow-up match, but it never evolved. Ben, according to Byron and Harvie, was uninterested.

"Ben and I talked about it, off and on, for several years," Venturi says. "Coming when it did, at the start of my playing career and the end of his, what happened at Cypress Point was deeply meaningful to us both. People have never stopped asking me about it. Whatever else can be said, I don't think the world will see anything quite like that again."

Wondrous as it was, the postscript to this otherworldly four-ball was merely the opening act of a much larger drama involving all four players, one that would force a sea change in America's perception of the game.

Weeks later, at the first Masters ever televised, in his second appearance there, Venturi took the first-round lead and established a new amateur record with a 66. The next day, playing with three-time champion Jimmy Demaret, he shot 69 to equal his mentor's record for the lowest score through thirty-six holes, and Byron was the first to congratulate him. Despite heavy winds that caused him to shoot 75 on Saturday, Venturi entered the final round with a four-stroke lead—instantly evoking fond memories of Billy Joe Patton.

As Augusta tradition dictated, Byron played in the final pairing of the tournament with the third-round leader. To avoid any embarrassment that might arise if his own pupil became the first amateur to win the Masters, Jones and Roberts asked him to step aside in favor of Sam, who was fresh off his sixth win at the Greater Greensboro Open the week before. Not unlike Ben, however, Sam intensely disliked playing with amateurs and made his feelings known immediately by giving his impressionable partner the cold shoulder. After all, he was still chasing glory himself—just off the lead when the final eighteen began, in quest of a fourth green jacket that would draw him closer to Ben in major titles. If he couldn't manage to win the U.S. Open, he told friends back home in Hot Springs, he at least planned to *own* the Masters.

When Harvie Ward finished his final round, he learned from Byron that Venturi was crumbling before the gallery's eyes on the back nine, further shades of Billy Joe. Harvie bolted back out, hoping just the sight of him might bolster his friend's fortunes. Instead, marshals threatened to eject him after several failed attempts to get inside the ropes, and Venturi staggered home with a horrifying 80 that included four three-putts and left him a stroke out of the lead held by the eventual winner, Jackie Burke. To his mentor's credit, despite a few inaccurate articles that portrayed him as a sulky sore loser, Venturi in fact handled the collapse with grace and humor, though it would forever haunt him much as the U.S. Opens did Sam. For the record, Sam finished tied for fourth and Ben tied for eighth.

Less than a month later, after visiting Ben's factory in Fort Worth to be fitted for new clubs and returning to San Francisco, Ward was confronted by reporters who informed him that Eddie Lowery had been indicted by a federal grand jury for tax evasion. Chief among many disputed charges was $11,000 designated as a "loan" to Ward that appeared, on the surface at least, to fully cover his travel expenses to the National Amateur, Masters, and the British Amateur and Open. The implications were profound, and potentially devastating to a player who supposedly symbolized the golden amateur ideal. Though Lowery and his attorneys passionately maintained it was all above-board and legitimate, the federal indictment claimed it amounted to a gift that should have been declared as such and taxed, not written off as a business expense. To some in the press, charming Harvie Ward suddenly appeared to be gaming the amateur code of ethics.

In fairness to Lowery and Ward, prior to the widening Deepdale and other well-publicized Calcutta scandals, the rules governing how amateurs' expenses got paid were politely overlooked in the general interest of promoting strong amateur play. Any number of emerging collegiate stars, for instance, could give examples of supportive patrons who assisted them financially. Otherwise, they argued, only wealthy players like Frank Stranahan could afford to play at its highest levels of competition. As Mike Souchak once noted with irritation, "This was the worst best kept secret in golf—we all had people who helped us along. Were they trying to violate the amateur rules of the game? Hell *no.*"

Five months after his collapse in Augusta, Venturi was eliminated in the third round of the U.S. Amateur at the Knollwood Country Club outside Chicago but loyally stuck around with Byron Nelson to watch their mutual friend Harvie Ward beat Chuck Kocsis five-and-four to claim his second consecutive U.S. Amateur title. For the moment at least, the firestorm around his boss's tax problems seemed to abate. Back home in San Francisco, there was a lavish party for the new national champion, and when asked if he might turn pro the way his old Atlantic Coast Conference rival Arnold Palmer had recently done, especially given Eddie Lowery's ongoing troubles, Ward gave his best Zeta fratboy smile and repeated his oft-stated intention to remain an amateur. He was, after all, approaching thirty, the age when Bobby Jones won his Grand Slam and retired from competition to make instructional films, a move that ironically resulted in his amateur status being lifted by the USGA. Whatever else is true, Harvie envisioned himself playing amateur golf into a comfortable dotage, purely for love of the game, the personification of the gracefully aging amateur champion, perhaps rewriting the record books along the way.

"Besides," he'd fatefully quipped to his good friend Richard Tufts shortly before his life took a wholly unexpected dark turn, "unless your name happens to be Hogan or Snead there really isn't any big money in golf. Why do you think Byron got out to raise cows?"

In the wake of recent events, Tufts—the incoming USGA president and grandson of Pinehurst founder and something of a father figure to Ward—had been charged with restoring amateur golf's tarnished image. In *The Amateur Creed*, a slim manifesto that laid out in elegant patrician prose the values of golf played for healthy competition and fellowship rather than money, Tufts expressed growing concerns about the rampant commercialization of the game, as reflected by his controversial decision in 1951 to end the professional segment of the popular North and South Open after the pros demanded a major pay boost. It goes without saying that Dick Tufts never envisioned this cleanup job would help destroy the career of the player he loved like a son.

Meanwhile, determined to prove his Masters success was no fluke, and perhaps nudged by Lowery's deepening crisis, Venturi turned pro in the autumn of 1956, following the lead of Arnold Palmer, who turned pro only weeks after his National Amateur win in 1954. Three months into the new year, Venturi finished thirteenth in the Masters but caught his stride by early September by winning back to back the St. Paul Invitational and the Miller Open in Milwaukee. In the latter, he withstood a furious late charge by none other than Sam, the bane of his Masters quest, who again apparently attempted more gamesmanship as they strode to the ninth tee of their final round by asking, "You ain't chokin' again are you, boy?" Reportedly, Venturi calmly replied, "I'll show you choking," and closed the deal by winning not only his second tournament in a row, but also claiming *Golf Digest*'s Player of the Year award. Following this encounter, so the story goes, Sam told other veterans not to mess with the young San Franciscan.

By this point, Venturi's pal Harvie Ward was in a state of disintegration. After a pitched battle against Sam at the Masters—where Sam slipped past Ward to wind up second to Doug Ford, though Ward again finished as low amateur, in fourth, his best finish yet in either a Masters or an Open—fallout from the negotiated settlement of Eddie

Lowery's troubles detailed in the newspapers proved too much to bear for Richard Tufts and the USGA. Within days, Ward was summoned by Joe Dey to answer questions about his expenses.

He consulted with a couple of high-powered lawyers but ignored their advice and appeared without benefit of counsel before the executive committee at a club in suburban Chicago, just days before the U.S. Open commenced, believing he would be vindicated if he truthfully answered questions and apologized for any mistakes in judgment he might've made in an otherwise sterling amateur career. In a nutshell, Ward maintained that the $11,000 loan was justified by the work he did selling cars for his boss at these golf functions, simply an advance against his salary so he could invest some money in the stock market.

The tribunal lasted for a full day, including testimony from Lowery and personal letters requesting leniency from a host of corporate leaders and politicians, all of whom regarded Ward as a shining example of amateur golf at its best. Some bluntly warned of a chilling effect if this charismatic young man were sanctioned for inadvertent mistakes. Dick Tufts sat silently throughout the proceedings, without meeting Ward's gaze.

In the end, it was Tufts's own misfortune to have to inform his protégé that the committee had unanimously decided that he'd violated his amateur status by being paid to travel to two U.S. Opens, three U.S. Amateurs, two British Opens, and three Masters. His standing was temporarily revoked, rendering him ineligible for the 1957 Amateur, though he was encouraged to apply for reinstatement in 1958.

"I walked out of that hearing room numb from head to toe, with a real burr up my ass," Ward recalled years later. "I simply couldn't believe what had happened to me. I never saw it coming and decided, unfortunately, that golf needed me more than I needed golf."

"I never felt Harvie got a fair shake at all," Byron agreed decades later. "The timing was very unfortunate. They were obviously eager to end certain bad practices and send an important message to other young players coming along in the game. But I don't think anyone could possibly have guessed what the consequences would be. I'd hoped Harvie would just accept the decision and move on. But he chose another path entirely, I'm afraid."

Within months, Ward began a long downward spiral that would end in a rambling life of booze and women and declining skills until his determined fourth wife, Joanne, cleaned him up in the early 1990s and he reclaimed a life in Pinehurst—"the only place," as he told friends years later, "I ever felt truly at home." Serving as director of golf at clubs both there and in Orlando, Ward blossomed into a splendid teacher and a wise elder of the game, working with a host of promising young players, including Payne Stewart.

In a much broader impact, the chilling effect Byron Nelson and others foresaw surfaced when a stream of top collegiate stars feared they might also face the same kind of inquiry and turned pro, sending a flood of talented young guns into the professional ranks, effectively thinning the ranks of amateur golf in America.

Fifteen years after this sea change ruling, Herb Wind visited his old friend Dick Tufts at his cottage beside Pinehurst No. 2 shortly before his death, and found him still grieving over the Harvie Ward affair, as it came to be called.

"He told me it broke his heart—his very spirit," Wind told me in 2001, three years before Ward passed away from liver cancer. "And it certainly changed the state of golf forever. I mean, at that very moment, you had Hogan and Snead and Byron coming to the end of their remarkable reign but amateurs like Billy Joe Patton, Ken Venturi, and Harvie making a great case for the validity of amateur golf. But taking into account what happened next, the year after Harvie Ward was sanctioned, Arnold won his first Masters and suddenly everyone wanted to be him."

Following his heroic efforts at Olympic in 1955, Ben Hogan made only two significant runs at the fifth U.S. Open title he craved.

The first came in 1956 at Oak Hill in Rochester, New York, when he put together four outstanding rounds over the rugged Donald Ross track and needed only two pars in the last two holes to tie Cary Middlecoff, already fidgeting in the clubhouse.

Once again, though, his putter froze over a thirty-inch putt on the penultimate hole. "I had my watch on him," John Derr remembers. "He stood over the ball for at least sixty-six seconds, an eternity, and finally made a terrible little stab at the ball. You could see he was in pure agony." He made bogey, followed by a par on the final hole, coming up a stroke shy of a playoff. He confided to reporters that he felt relieved and furthermore that this would be his last U.S. Open. Sam, also facing the verdict of time, finished tied for twenty-fourth.

On a far happier note, at the next Masters, Byron made his debut as a color commentator, paired with veteran announcer Chris Schenkel, behind the sixteenth green. Cliff Roberts had calculated that Byron's incomparable understanding as a competitor and former champion would be enhanced by his tasteful refusal to make any commercial references to crowd size or the money list or even a player's current rank on tour, all major taboos in the image-obsessed mind of Augusta's fabled majordomo. Though no particular moment stood out from that first nervous telecast—this was the year Doug Ford slipped past Snead and Ward to win—Byron's relationship with Schenkel would prove invaluable to his career, and Byron soon became the first player to work full-time on TV.

Ben's uncharacteristic 75-76 caused him to miss his first cut in thirteen years at the 1957 Masters, Byron's first in the booth, and—seemingly true to his word—he chose not to enter the U.S. Open at Byron's old stomping ground at Inverness, where reigning champ Cary Middlecoff lost in a playoff to Dick Mayer. His mind was absorbed by growing his equipment company and the challenges of moving into his new house on Canterbury Drive, not far from the Shady Oaks Golf Club's simple front gates. The next year, however, unable to completely let go of the dream of an elusive fifth, he ventured to Perry Maxwell's beautiful Southern Hills in Tulsa, where his protégé Tommy "Thunder" Bolt won his first major championship and Ben got paired in an early round with the newcomer and eventual runner-up, Gary Player. After their round together, the story goes, Ben congratulated Player and predicted that the hardworking South African would soon win on the American tour. Player thanked him and explained that he maintained a strong exercise and dietary routine.

"How much do you practice?" Ben abruptly asked, and when Player told him, he simply shook his head.

"It's not enough," he said, then walked away.

Among the first to view the Hogans' new four-thousand-square-foot dream house, a classic buff-colored brick ranch, were the Nelsons, who dropped in for supper with Marvin and Mary Leonard one evening in early 1958. The years of rivalry had caused the friendship that once existed between Ben and Byron to fray at the edges, but their wives remained in touch and relatively close. Though they enjoyed distinct different orbits in the Dallas–Fort Worth area—Louise maintained a broad range of friends and an active church life out in Roanoke while Valerie's narrowing world continued to revolve around her husband and a few social friends from Shady Oaks and Rivercrest Country Club—they occasionally talked by phone and more than once met for lunch and a bit of shopping in Dallas.

After they were given a tour of the beautiful home with its polished hand-laid pecan floors and stark white interiors—the basic color Valerie Hogan associated with "all things French"—Byron casually wondered why the spacious residence contained no guest room. "Because if we have a guest bedroom," Ben told him, "someone will want to use it."

"I always got the feeling," Byron mused later, "especially as the years came on to us both, that Ben was perfectly happy to withdraw from life. I'm not just talking about just public life, either. Except for his occasional trip out to a tournament and his annual spring visit to Seminole, everything in his life became centered around his office and Shady Oaks. It's my understanding from mutual friends that the increasing privacy may have actually mellowed him a great deal. I believe that is true. But his only real comfort seemed to come at home, especially over at Shady Oaks, where he could practice all day long and nobody would bother him."

Indeed, out of the glare of constant media scrutiny, Ben developed a highly structured routine that defined the rest of his life: at his desk on West Pafford by eight o'clock sharp every morning, lunch with his Shady Oaks cronies at the big round table overlooking the eighteenth green, an hour or two of practice at his favorite spot out on the course's back nine, then it was back to the office. By this point, he was getting several hundred letters a week, from invitations of every kind to letters from players seeking sponsorship and advice. Autograph seekers wanted his distinctive signature, and a budding generation of teachers inspired by his best-selling instruction book—golf's new swing Bible—wanted a personal connection with the game's most iconic star. Some of them received brief, courteous, and quaintly formal replies. Others he ignored.

During Masters week in 1958, Augusta National named the footbridges that spanned Rae's Creek in honor of Ben and Byron. Henceforth, in a gorgeous stretch of the course that Herb Wind poetically christened "Amen Corner" that same year, golfers moving to the twelfth green would cross the gently arching Hogan Bridge commemorating the Hawk's record-breaking total of 274 in 1953. Leaving by the thirteenth tee, they would walk over the Nelson Bridge, which memorialized his first Masters win in 1937, the first major title of his remarkable career.

Notably absent from these proceedings was Sam, who had one more green jacket than either of them. His partisans, considering the bridge dedications a snub, could point out that he'd won more tournaments in his career and his popularity and colorful style had done much to elevate the Masters's profile during its most challenging years. He was even on record as saying that, given the chance to win just one major championship, most players would choose this one.

These arguments, however, cut little mustard with Jones and Roberts, the determining deities behind the bridge dedications, both of whom felt that the less-dignified aspects of Sam's private life disqualified him for a similar recognition. "There's no question," says a long-time Augusta member, "that some of Sam's poorer social judgments hurt him tremendously with Jones and the rest. That's too bad. Sam was an American original and together with Ben and Byron he put a very human face on professional golf, including the Masters. Masters lore would be nothing without Sam Snead."

In the end, playing long and well was Sam's best and final revenge. That year alone, he entered fifteen tournaments, finished in the top ten in twelve and won two in playoffs, his own Greenbrier Invitational and the successful defense of the Dallas Open, an event that would come to play a defining role in the rest of Byron's life. And in a run for the ages that lasted another seven years, he entered at least a dozen tour events every season and won eight more times, concluding with a record eighth win at his beloved Greater Greensboro Open in 1965, at fifty-three the oldest winner in the history of the tour.

Ben Hogan's Last Hurrah came at the U.S. Open of 1960, a year of momentous change that began when four well-dressed black students sat down to be served at a segregated Woolworth's counter in Greensboro, North Carolina—sparking a nonviolent protest that would transform America's laws and racial attitudes and result in the election of a young, vigorous president, himself a golfer. In between the signposts of cultural change, the contraceptive pill was officially introduced, NASA launched its first communication satellite, and the first Playboy Club opened for business in Chicago.

If John F. Kennedy symbolized the nation's youthful anticipation of the future, so did young and brash Arnold Palmer, whose personal charisma and go-for-broke playing style unleashed the longest and most significant period of sustained growth in golf history. Not overlooked in all the fervor of "Arnie's Army," a phrase inspired by hand-lettered signs held up by soldiers from nearby Camp Gordon who manned the scoreboards at Augusta National that year, a gray and limping Ben attracted the largest galleries of the week and briefly rediscovered his putting touch, heading into the final round a stroke out of the lead at 213, tied with a group that included Billy Casper, Ken Venturi, Julius Boros, and Dow Finsterwald.

"The very idea that Ben Hogan was once again near the lead was enough to rattle probably everyone in the field, I guess, except Arnold," recalls Casper, who began his own run about this time, and went on to score more victories than anyone else in the 1960s. "Ben was a guy I'd watched and copied for years. People thought I was pretty boring because I never showed much emotion when I played. But that was the effect Ben had on me. He changed how most serious golfers approached the game. That same face is seen on most great players today. I look at them and I can't help but see Ben Hogan."

He faltered on Sunday, though, with a 76, which still gave him a respectable sixth-place finish. Sam won the new par-three tournament but finished eleventh, a stroke ahead of a beefy Ohio State junior named Jack Nicklaus, the reigning U.S. Amateur champion. And the charismatic, chain-smoking Palmer beat Venturi by a stroke to claim his second green jacket. In many ways, with his quick, easy, telegenic smile and playing style, Arnold was every bit as entertaining as Billy Joe Patton had been, and suddenly the public couldn't get enough of him.

Eight weeks later, at Denver's Cherry Hills Country Club, the game's golden past, thrilling present, and glorious future all converged on the sport's toughest stage. Mike Souchak, carrying a famous Jesuit prayer in his money clip for good luck and fresh off a putting lesson from Jackie Burke, shot 68 to seize the early lead while Palmer, who'd attempted to drive the green on the short downhill opening hole, finished four strokes back. Ben, suffering from headaches he attributed to the thinner air, and playing with the assistance of an oxygen canister, posted a woeful 75, while Sam made his customary decent start at 72. By the end of the second round, however, Souchak's 67 gave him a new thirty-six-hole record and he seemed to be running away with the championship.

For sheer blood-pumping drama, Saturday's double round proved to be the equal of Merion in 1953. The most intriguing pairing was Hogan and Nicklaus, who strangely enough had a mentor in common; as a young assistant at Glen Garden, Jack Grout may have straightened out Bennie Hogan's "hog killer" grip five and certainly encouraged him to take a shot at the early tour out west. Decades later, the same man helped young Jack Nicklaus shape his game. The aging legend and the future one went off at nine sharp and Nicklaus later remarked with unreserved awe that Ben put on a shotmaking exhibition that reminded fans of why he was the greatest of all time, hitting every green in regulation, three-putting none of them, and dropping two birdies for 69 that put him right in the heart of the fray.

Palmer finished his morning round seven strokes back of Souchak, with fourteen players between them, and was seemingly out of it. Stewing, he stalked off to get a cheeseburger and a Coke and bumped into Bob Drum, who'd covered his rise from the amateur ranks for the *Pittsburgh Press*. The veteran reporter was chatting with Venturi, Bob Rosburg, and Fort Worth reporter Dan Jenkins, speculating on what it would take to win. Arnold suggested that a 65 would put him at 280, then declared, "Two eighty always wins the Open."

Drum snorted and shook his head. "Two eighty won't do you a damn bit of good."

Palmer stormed out and hammered a few warm-up drives to the back of the range before he was summoned to the tee. Moments later, he lit another L&M and lashed his ball onto the green.

Ben had gone off with Nicklaus just ahead of him. Steadied by a bowl of chicken soup, ginger ale, and an aspirin, picking up where he'd left off in the morning—oblivious to everything but one shot at a time, one fairway after another, nearly picture-perfect golf, in full command of the game at forty-seven years of age, shades of the great Harry Vardon himself.

For Ben Hogan, the last reach for glory came on the seventy-first hole of the championship, the dangerous, moat-fronted par-five seventeenth hole. A little after five in the afternoon, now tied with the young Turk who'd miraculously made up those seven strokes and was waiting on the tee directly behind him, Ben struck what he believed was a perfect wedge to the scary front pin and saw his ball land six feet from the flag and spin back, pausing for an instant on the slope before trickling into the water. The vast gallery, estimated at 25,000, released a sustained groan.

Marty Leonard, Marvin's daughter, standing just outside the gallery ropes, covered her face in horror, then watched as Ben removed his handmade English golf shoes and socks, waded into the moat, and lashed his ball onto the green in an explosion of mud and water. Moments later, he two-putted for a bogey six that dropped him back into a tie with Nicklaus for second place. "He was still only one back," Marty Leonard recalled, "but I think all hope went out of him at that very moment."

He trudged up the eighteenth fairway with his head lowered ever so slightly, the telltale sign of her husband's mental state Valerie Hogan had perfectly described decades before. He was lost in the swirl of his own thoughts, after having made a calculated gamble far more typical of the man in the following pairing who'd taken his place atop professional golf. Attempting to cut the corner of the dogleg par-four eighteenth, he knocked his tee shot into the lake and finished with an uninspired triple-bogey, staring blindly at the ground the entire time. Grim-faced but still gracious, he shook hands with the brilliant young amateur he'd been paired with, wished him well, and left the green, barely acknowledging the long standing ovation.

Twenty minutes later, Arnold Palmer tapped in for the miraculous 65 that gave him his first—and only—U.S. Open Championship. By that point, Ben had already spoken with reporters and refused to second-guess his decision to go for the pin on seventeen—a moment, friends say, he would nevertheless spend the rest of his life replaying in his mind. By the time the new king of golf was talking on the phone with his appealing young wife, Winnie, back home in Latrobe with their infant daughter—"Hi ya, babe! Guess what? We won!"—Ben was being driven to the Denver train station. Years later, in the TV interview, he conceded to his friend Ken Venturi that the fateful shot at seventeen still haunted him. "There's not a day that passes that doesn't cut my guts," he said simply.

Safely ensconced back in his daily routines, Ben Hogan would not be seen again in public until the 1961 Masters, sadly finishing tied for thirty-second place with Byron. Sam, who nearly took Greensboro the week before the Masters and claimed the Tournament of Champions later that summer, finished fifteen places ahead of his greatest rivals.

By this point, Ben mostly had business on his mind. Earlier that year he had sold his equipment company to the American Machine and Foundry Corporation for an estimated $5 million, enabling him to bring forth a number of technical innovations including the first significant advance in shaft technology since the introduction of steel shafts. Now among Fort Worth's wealthiest citizens, he stayed on to run things.

The Apex shaft, as it was called, was expanded to five different flexes and soon became the standard of the industry. "The game," as Ben said in his advertisements, "is all about feel." When a curious reporter asked how his company tested clubs, he answered, "We have a testing machine here—me."

As living legends, however, Ben and Sam waged one last public battle for supremacy, which would have splendid repercussions for the game. It came at the Houston Country Club in the spring of 1965, when both men agreed to appear on Shell Oil's popular *Wonderful World of Golf*, hosted by Gene Sarazen and Jimmy Demaret, a series that began in 1961 and lasted nearly a decade.

The show was the creation of a visionary TV producer named Fred Raphael, challenge matches played between veteran stars going head-to-head on famous courses around the world, after which one or both would give a brief lesson. One of the earliest, appropriately enough, featured Byron Nelson and reigning U.S. Open winner Gene Littler at the Pine Valley Golf Club, with $3,000 going to the winner and half that to the loser. With cameras mounted on a station wagon, it took two full days to film the full eighteen-hole match and Byron eventually came out on top, shooting 74 to Littler's 76. The episode was broadcast on Byron's fiftieth birthday the next February. In effect, it was his last tournament.

The Hogan-Snead duel at the Houston Country Club was one of the most memorable installments. True to form, Ben showed up several days before the start of filming and studied the comparatively modest course from one end to the other, leaving nothing to chance. Likewise true to himself, Sam didn't show up until the night before filming, fresh from a lucrative exhibition in the Bahamas, relaxed and spinning his saucy tales.

Impressively, Ben hit every fairway and green en route to a 69 that beat Sam by four strokes, prompting Gene Sarazen to proclaim, a bit far-fetched under the circumstances, that the match was "the finest round I have ever seen." This brief, magical appearance was made even more special by the lesson Ben gave at the end, conveying a few of the fundamentals from his best-selling instruction book. For his part, Sam playfully shrugged off the drubbing by telling to a wire reporter afterward, "The real reason I can't seem to win an Open is that Ben won't really retire." On a more serious note, he expressed his belief that Ben Hogan was the finest player in the history of the game, bar none.

After the program went off the air in 1969, the producer dreamed up a new one in which stars of the past would compete in a three-day, fifty-four-hole best-ball affair. *The Legends of Golf,* as it was called, couldn't have enjoyed better timing. "The country was in a nostalgic mood," notes Al Barkow, who served as a writer along with Herbert Warren Wind. "Major league baseball was having its Old Timers Days, and Fred Raphael thought, why not a golf Old Timers Day?" The producer recruited Jimmy Demaret to help sell the show to his longtime tour mates.

As eager sponsors lined up, ultimately producing an initial purse of $400,000 that guaranteed every participant a $50,000 payday, the first phone call he made was to Sam, who agreed to play. When asked later why participation in a show that featured aging golfers well past their prime had any appeal to him, he gave one of his patented catfish smiles and explained simply, "I frankly didn't need the money. But there are other guys out there who did. I played for them." This comment earned Sam a lot of gratitude and respect from his former colleagues, many of whom were just scraping by.

In hopes of luring another old friend out of retirement, Demaret prevailed on Jack Burke—his co–founding partner at Houston's beautiful Champions Golf Club, which hosted the Ryder Cup of 1967 with Ben serving as nonplaying captain—to personally contact him at his office in Fort Worth. Apparently Ben listened to Burke's pitch before telling him he had no interest in a bunch of has-beens playing golf for a meaningless title.

But others jumped at the chance, including Paul Runyan. "Do you realize," he told Demaret, "I can finish last and win more money than

I ever won in any tournament I ever played in?" He'd been the first money winner of the tour in 1934, with a total of $6,767. *"The Legends of Golf* was a godsend to the players who made the game what it had become by the end of the 1970s," says Al Barkow. "Like manna from heaven. The public loved it."

In 1978, at the Onion Creek Golf Club in Austin, Texas, a dozen teams teed off in the first tournament. Two years later, featuring a new sponsor, the event expanded into the *Liberty Mutual Legends of Golf,* with sixty-six-year-old Sam and his partner Gardner Dickinson defeating Peter Thomson and Kel Nagle by a single stroke at thirteen under par. The TV viewing audience was impressively large, indicating the public's interest in these players.

As a direct result of this show's success, the PGA Tour established the senior tour in 1980, and acknowledged the vital role Sam Snead had played in its creation. During this same span of time, as if to emphasize the point, from 1963 through 1980, Sam won six PGA Senior Championships, five World Senior Championships, and a pair of *Legends of Golf* titles with Gardner Dickinson and another with Don January.

"Without Sam Snead," January told a gathering in Texas some years ago, "there would never have been a senior tour. He gave it instant credibility and made people come out and watch us play. For this reason alone, a lot of guys who never appreciated the antics of Sam Snead will be forever grateful to him."

Like Ben, Byron declined to participate in the rapidly evolving senior events, principally because he already had two full-time jobs.

Throughout the 1950s and 1960s, his active church life and cattle ranch continued to prosper and demand a great deal of his attention. For a while, he and Louise seriously considered becoming foreign missionaries. In 1963, however, after doing his TV work at Augusta and picking up some important broadcasting tips from John Derr at a tournament in Las Vegas, he signed a contract with ABC Sports and became the first player to do full-time commentary, starting out in the booth with Jim McKay at the PGA Championship at the Dallas Athletic Club where Jack Nicklaus captured the first of his Wanamaker trophies, then moving on to work with Chris Schenkel for nearly two decades.

His most cherished memories in this role, he later said, included

Ken Venturi's heroic march through the wilting heat at Washington's Congressional Country Club to win his lone U.S. Open in 1964, Lee Trevino's sudden emergence at Merion in 1971, and Nicklaus's brilliant one-iron at the seventy-first hole of the Open he won at Pebble Beach in 1973, all of which he commented on in his distinctive, flat—and highly audible—West Texas accent. During a tournament at the Firestone Country Club, after describing the severe break on a putt facing Billy Casper to his viewing audience, Casper drained the putt, turned, and wryly thanked Byron for helping him read the putt. Following this amusing incident, broadcast booths all featured Plexiglas screens to mute commentator voices.

"I think the fellows appreciated what I had to say," Byron said of his surprise career that provided him with the largest income of his life—allowing Louise to really decorate their modest home for the first time. "Among other things, I tried to speak honestly about the quality of a shot without being harsh or judgmental. Golf is the hardest game of all to master, in my opinion, and I always wanted the audience and the players to know how much I respected them."

He was finally appointed nonplaying captain of the Ryder Cup team in 1965, leading a strong squad that included Venturi, Palmer, Casper, Boros, January, Littler, Dave Marr, Tommy Jacobs, and Tony Lema to Southport's Royal Birkdale, where they defeated a formidable home team, 19½ to 12½. Inspired by the first-class preparations seen at the Atlanta Athletic Club during the previous match, Britain's hosts treated spectators and visiting press to the first tented village on a golf course, a five-star treatment that set a new standard for the biennial classic. Not to be outdone, when the Ryder Cup came to the Champions Club in Houston two years later, hosts Burke and Demaret rolled out an even bigger welcome mat, arranging lavish dinners, entertainment, and royal treatment for the wives—all under captain Ben Hogan's perfectionist gaze.

In the late summer of 1965, a spectacular private club called Preston Trail opened for play seventeen miles north of downtown Dallas, a true player's course that Byron had a major hand in shaping along with Ralph Plummer, a talented Texas architect (and former Glen Garden caddie). After Byron did radio commentary for the Dallas Open the next year, a group of dedicated business philanthropists called the Salesmanship Club of Dallas approached him with a novel idea—to rename the tournament the Byron Nelson Classic and move it to Preston Trail. Following some gentle arm twisting by a Who's Who of local business and religious interests, he agreed. He was impressed with the organization's camp for troubled boys and its other charitable works in the Dallas area. Following a gala opening, this was the first tour event to use a player's marquee name, and almost overnight the Nelson event became the working model upon which most PGA Tour tournaments operated. In the early days, the Byron Nelson Classic raised more than 80 percent of all money donated to charities by professional golf, prompting tour commissioner Deane Beman to study the excellent performance of the Salesmanship Club.

"It really became the best thing that has ever happened to me in golf," Byron told a visitor to Fairway Ranch in 1994, visibly emotional. "As surprising as this might sound, I rank that golf tournament even above my Masters win in 1937 or my eleven in a row in 1945. When I look back on my life," he added, "that will be the thing I'm proudest of accomplishing—because it helps so many people."

In his own humble way, Byron was saying, helping others was truly his Last Hurrah.

Epilogue

ENDINGS AND BEGINNINGS

I N LIFE AS IN GOLF, endings perhaps say even more than beginnings. So it was for the American Triumvirate. Following their deepest instincts, one achieved mythic stature and withdrew from view, another continued playing the game and chasing the public's affection until he quite literally dropped from exhaustion, the third used his faith and fame to become a leading ambassador of the game, a statesman who defined the notion of giving back.

During the last twenty-five years of his life, Ben made only a handful of public appearances and seemed to shun all adulation, which ironically stimulated the public's fascination even more. As time passed, his fans caught infrequent, fleeting glimpses of the little gray man whose mastery of the game and determination not to explain himself helped make golf seem like a monastic discipline and a scientific quest.

He effectively ended his career at the Masters in 1967, posting a 290 that was good enough for ninth place, and attended the Champions Dinner for a final time. Byron agreed to take over his duties as emcee.

That June, though, with little notice, Ben entered the U.S. Open at Baltusrol, where Nicklaus beat Palmer to the finish. In his final Open, Ben shot 292 and tied for thirty-fourth place. He wasn't seen in public again until the autumn, when he appeared as nonplaying captain of the Ryder Cup at the Champions Golf Club, his old pal Jimmy Demaret's club in Houston, an event he ran with his usual iron discipline, sparring with a jaunty Arnold Palmer, who flew in on his new airplane and was only a few thousand dollars from being the first player to win a million dollars in a single year. When Palmer playfully pointed out that he hadn't brought along any smaller British golf balls for the occasion, Ben snapped, "Who says you're playing?" and kept Palmer on the sidelines for the second-day morning tour balls. He insisted on long compulsory practice sessions and demanded his players be in bed by 10:30. During matches he was overheard grumbling, "I've never seen so many God-awful shots in my life." The Americans won in a rout 23½ to 8½.

Several months later, Ben underwent a series of operations to remove painful calcium deposits and joint spurs in his left shoulder. In June of 1969, he made another surprise appearance at the U.S. Open, also held at Champions—but as a spectator. "Fans saw Ben Hogan walking in the gallery and couldn't believe their eyes," said Tommy Bolt. "To tell the truth, neither could the rest of us." Over cocktails in the locker room with hosts Jimmy Demaret and Jackie Burke, Demaret casually mentioned to Ben that "some of the fellas are pulling their sticks out of mothballs and planning to do some exhibitions." He invited Ben to join them. "C'mon, Hawk," he prodded, "it'll be like old times. I'll talk and you'll say nothing."

His old friend shook his head. "There's no way on earth I'm going to let people see my game," he said. "Nobody but me should have to suffer through that."

And yet, there were traces of magic.

Two weeks prior to the start of the Champions tournament in Houston in April of 1970, following a return from Seminole, Ben suddenly showed up for several days of intensive practice with a caddie, taking a secluded cottage on the grounds. "Word of Hogan's entry," noted Walter Bingham in *Sports Illustrated*, "caused the normally blasé golfers to react like sightseers on Hollywood and Vine." Jackie Burke thanked Ben for coming, noting that there were players on tour who'd never seen him play, and Tom Weiskopf was lucky enough to be picked to play a practice round with him. "I was so terrified at the start, quite frankly, I was afraid I might miss the ball. But he told me to call him Ben straight off the bat, and we had a wonderful time playing together. Privately, I think this worshipful stuff the guys were doing embarrassed him, really got under his skin." Afterward, Weiskopf told his friends Frank Beard and Bert Yancey that he'd never seen anyone hit a ball the way Hogan did, still in absolute command. During the tournament itself, tour player Bob Goalby counted thirty-one players who came out to watch during his first round, a highly respectable 71. Using his own Hogan ball—at that moment the most popular ball on tour—Ben was paired with a talkative Lee Trevino in the last round. During the first seven holes, Ben nailed four birdies, prompting Palmer-like war whoops from the gallery, and placing himself in contention to win. Afterward, the Merry Mex told a reporter that with nine holes left to play he was certain the tournament belonged to Ben, but his putting nemesis returned with a vengeance and he wound up five strokes back of first place, tied for ninth.

During this effort, unknown to anyone but Valerie, he severely stressed his left knee and his pronounced limp intensified. Yet days later, he teed off in Marvin Leonard's Colonial event, prompting Red Smith to hail his surprising resurrection as the "top sports story of the year in America." But the gods were not kind at Colonial. After opening with a smart 69, briefly challenging for the lead, the blind stares and balky putter returned on a breezy Friday to produce a woeful 77, from which he never recovered. He finished in a tie for fifty-sixth place.

But still he couldn't let go.

In August, he showed up as a last-minute entry at the Westchester Classic, shot 78, and withdrew. Because the organizers sent him out so early on the first day, he was gone before most of the fans realized he'd even been there.

Days later, Marvin Leonard passed away in his sleep. One of his honorary pallbearers at the memorial service at Fort Worth's First Methodist Church, Ben later told his cronies around the circular grill room table at Shady Oaks that it was one of the toughest things he'd ever had to do.

A short time later, *Golf Digest* senior editor Nick Seitz was granted a rare opportunity to spend a day with him at his office and his home on Canterbury Drive. When asked about his remarkable return to the tournament circuit in Houston, Ben told him, "Time's runnin' pretty short if I don't play now." He paused and added, "Besides, I haven't really done what I wanted to do yet."

"What is that?" the editor wondered.

"I haven't won enough tournaments." Among other surprises, Ben told Seitz that he planned to start a ranch. The ranch never materialized.

The next summer, Ben showed up on his ailing knee at Champions for the Houston Open and hobbled painfully through twelve holes before his left knee buckled and he was forced to withdraw. A week later at Colonial, while playing a practice round with Mike Souchak and being trailed by a group of young pros and adoring fans, his knee buckled again and he nearly shanked his tee shot into the pond at the par-three eighth hole. "That's enough, Mike," Hogan declared, and picked up his ball. The two men walked into the clubhouse together making small talk. "It was a very sad end," Souchak remembered. "I had tears in my eyes, to tell you the truth."

Ben Hogan never hit another shot in public again.

That next winter, Bob Jones died in Atlanta, and Ben took it hard. He and Valerie considered attending his funeral but decided the crowds would be too large and they sent flowers instead. Around this same time, Ben's sister, Princess, a heavy smoker, died of lung disease and Ben told his daily lunch pal Gene Smyers that the world seemed to be disappearing before his eyes.

In 1973, he was invited by the renowned architect Joe Lee to lend his advice and expertise to the creation of a new course called the Trophy Club, out near Byron's Fairway Ranch in Roanoke. He threw himself into the project, but it failed to come out the way he envisioned. Though it was eventually completed, and today is called the Hogan Course, Ben rarely spoke of his lone foray into course design.

In 1974 Jack Fleck called Ben to invite him to appear at a charity event honoring the late Vince Lombardi. "I don't play in front of people anymore," Ben told him flatly, but sent him several autographed photos—black-and-whites, naturally.

That same year, the World Golf Hall of Fame in Pinehurst asked him to be one of thirteen honorees at its grand-opening event, and he agreed to go, in part because John Derr was serving as emcee, but also because of his abiding affection for Pinehurst—the place where he won his first professional tournament. The other invitees included Byron, Sam, and Arnold Palmer. "He seemed to have a good time and people were surprised and happy to see him there," Derr remembers. Arnold recalled, "The press always tried to trump up the tension between Ben and me, but the truth was, despite our differences, we really did like each other. He was one of a kind and it was great to see him again." When a reporter innocently asked Ben how it felt to be with so many "living legends," however, he bristled and ignored the question entirely. During the flight home, Ben confided to Valerie that he detested being thought of as an elder statesman of the game, a golden has-been. "In another five or six years," he later told Gene Smyers at Shady Oaks, "no one will even remember or even give a damn who I was." He never returned to Pinehurst.

In the spring of 1977, not long before Bing Crosby collapsed and died on a golf course in Spain, Ben and Valerie made a final trip to Seminole to see George and Dawn Coleman, and while there Ben agreed to let the family's longtime butler film him hitting golf balls from the Coleman yard into the Atlantic. A short while later, his beloved dog, Duffer, died, and for Christmas the Colemans sent Ben and Valerie a new female poodle puppy. They kept the dog a few days and then sent it back, noting that they were "too old to handle a puppy." The Colemans kept the dog and named her Bunker. "She lived many years and was much loved by our family," says Dawn Coleman.

Nearly a decade later, Ben sat for that rare TV interview with Ken Venturi, then a color commentator for CBS in the tradition of his hero, Byron. When asked about the modern tour, Ben replied with the faintest trace of contempt, "Everything is better nowadays, I don't care what it is. Whether you're talking about golf or baseball or hockey or automobiles, everything's better today. It will be better tomorrow than it is today!"

A short time later, he made a sentimental return to Riviera to film a series of TV commercials for his new Edge irons, the world's first forged cavity-back club. These spots began running before the start of the 1988 season, and over 100,000 sets were sold, generating an estimated $60 million in revenue for Ben Hogan Golf. The next year, the company was sold to Minoru Isutani, a Japanese billionaire, for $58 million. About the same time, Isutani also purchased the Pebble Beach Golf Links, for $835 million. When the two met for lunch at Shady Oaks, one likely apochryphal story goes, Ben looked at him and said, "You've just bought the family jewels, Mr. Isutani. Don't screw it up."

The next spring, Jack Nicklaus tried to persuade him to fly to Columbus for his annual Memorial Tournament. Former honorees included Old Tom Morris, Bob Jones, Walter Hagen, and Byron Nelson. Ben thanked Nicklaus but declined, asking him to put off the honor until he was dead.

Mike Wright arrived at Shady Oaks a short time later, a bright, recently married young assistant from San Antonio who enjoyed splendid rapport with the members and particularly Ben, who coached him on how to impress the club's board and helped him become the head professional. One of the first steps Wright took at Shady Oaks was stepping over a mixed-breed mutt named Buster, his second over a black-and-white border collie named Max. These were Ben's pampered friends, and both routinely accompanied Ben to his favorite practice spot between the thirteenth and fourteenth holes. Max—who made at least one appearance in a Hogan Company spot—always rode in the cart beside him, Buster following behind on foot. When Max was eventually killed by a UPS truck, "Mr. Hogan was completely devastated," according to Wright. "Buster meant even more to him after that."

Not long after his farewell trip to Riviera, Ben felt a sharp pain in his lower abdomen and had emergency surgery for a ruptured appendix, nearly dying. He spent almost seven weeks in the hospital, much of the time heavily sedated. When he returned home, Valerie began noticing serious memory lapses and grew concerned about his ability to drive to work and then to Shady Oaks for the afternoon.

These lapses, which she first attributed simply to aging, didn't prevent the Hogans from attending *Golf Magazine*'s big celebration of the one hundredth anniversary of golf in America at the Waldorf-Astoria the day after Curtis Strange defeated Nick Faldo in their playoff at Brookline in June of 1988. The black-tie affair drew forty-eight of the "Top 100 Players" designated by the magazine, including Sam, Byron, Jack Nicklaus, and Arnold Palmer. Earlier in the day, Ben spent over two hours chatting with people and signing autographs. At the dinner, Sam was prevailed on to tell a few funny and clean stories, and Ben got up and mesmerized the audience by talking for half an hour about the beauty of a good Vardon grip. "It was amazing," recalls George Peper, the editor who dreamed up the gala. "With all of the great stars in the room, Hogan was the one most people were watching. It was like seeing a legend come back to life." Though many assumed the "Golfer of the Century" award, a tightly held secret, would go to Ben Hogan, it instead was given to Jack Nicklaus.

Back in Texas, fans of all sorts began trying to catch a glimpse of their varnished hero, showing up at Colonial and down Roaring Springs Road at Shady Oaks. Some found Ben surprisingly receptive to their impromptu visits, though he never permitted them to intrude upon his daily practice rituals. Others got a chilly reception, often depending upon how they approached him. In 1992, a former Shady Oaks caddie named Jody Vasquez arranged for Nick Faldo, the British Open champion, to visit Ben at his company office and share lunch at Shady Oaks. At one point in their friendly conversation, Faldo asked his advice on how to win the U.S. Open, a prize that had recently eluded him. Ben stared at him and said, "Shoot the lowest score."

A year later, Hogan Golf got sold again, and its parent company decided to move the factory to Richmond, Virginia, putting more than three hundred employees on the street. "It was the saddest day in Mr. Hogan's life, like a death in the family," his personal secretary, Sharon Rae, remembered. "I'd never seen him more downcast." Ben spent the week prior to the sale, she and others said, just walking around the company floor talking with the staff.

A short time later, he failed to arrive home at his customary hour from Shady Oaks. Valerie anxiously phoned the club and discovered he had been gone for hours. Ben turned up around the cocktail hour appearing confused, but explaining he'd been scouting for a new place to build a factory and start a new equipment company and rehire his laid-off employees.

About this time, Buster the dog passed away. One winter evening when the Hogans came to the club for a rare dinner out, Mike Wright had something special to show them—a small stone marking Buster's grave just outside the pro shop. Ben stood looking at it for a moment, then did something quite extraordinary. "He removed his hat and gently knelt, kissed his hand and placed it on the stone," Wright said. "The tears came to my eye, let me tell you."

The next summer, he did something else even more amazing. Hogan hadn't been seen around Shady Oaks in many months, when Wright looked up and found him standing in the shop. Surprised and delighted, he offered to put his bag on a cart, but Ben waved away the idea. "That won't be necessary, Mike," he said, and then went into the club storage room and came out with his driver and walked to the tenth tee, after pausing to take three golf balls from a range bucket. He took a few warm-up swings before teeing up all three balls, striking them one, two, three down the heart of the fairway. "Each one was better than the one before it," Wright recalls of this extraordinary moment. "You could have thrown a blanket over all three shots." And with that, Ben put his driver back in his golf bag, and bid the pro goodbye.

He never hit another shot.

In advance of the 1995 Centennial celebration of the USGA, Museum Committee member and Foundation director Rayburn Tucker agreed to approach Hogan about the possibility of sitting for a taped interview. Initially Ben agreed to do the interview, but his declining health and other factors prevented him not only from making the film but also from attending. True to form, the most iconic player of his generation instead sent a simple letter of congratulations to the USGA on its birthday.

Ben Hogan died on a warm July afternoon in 1997, the eve of his wife's eighty-fifth birthday. He was eighty-four years old.

The cream of the PGA Tour turned out for his simple and tasteful memorial service at the University Christian Church near the TCU campus. Pallbearers included Mike Wright, Gene Smyers, and several of his Shady Oaks friends, along with Sam, Tim Finchem, Shelley Mayfield, Tommy Bolt, Judy Bell, Ken Venturi, and Rayburn Tucker, a Dallas real estate man and Ben's longtime friend on the USGA Foundation board and museum committee that helped organize a special Hogan Room tribute at the USGA's Far Hills headquarters.

The day Ben died, Byron had commented to a reporter, "After he left the tour, Ben basically just stayed to himself. I think that almost makes it a bigger news story. They're still trying to find out something about him, what made him tick."

Byron and his second wife, Peggy, were also present, seated about halfway back in the packed church with Ben Crenshaw, Bel-Air pro Eddie Merrins, and John Mahaffey. There was no formal eulogy, just hymns and an appropriate reading from Romans 5: "We glory in tribulation, knowing that tribulation worketh patience, and patience, experience; and experience, hope." The minister, Charles Sanders, talked briefly about Ben Hogan's remarkable life, concentrating more on his private generosity than the public glory, more about the man than the champion. Beneath the distinctive blue tiles and exposed beams of the mission-style sanctuary, the pecan-wood coffin was blanketed by hundreds of white roses. "It was dignified and simple," according to Rayburn Tucker, "just what you would expect from Ben."

During the ride to the cemetery, Sam rode with Valerie in her limousine, talking about Ben most of the way.

"I sure loved Ben," he told her at one point. She leaned forward and patted his hand.

"He loved you best, too," she told him.

Several years later, following a fire, over the strenuous protests by several older members, Shady Oaks built an entirely new clubhouse. In late 2004, a handsome new structure opened on the footprint of the old one providing, among other things, more displays of Ben Hogan's personal artifacts. Once again, Ben's circular table is back in place by the window overlooking the tenth and eighteenth greens, providing an even better view of the golf course he loved.

Ben's will left a million dollars to University Christian Church and another million to Fort Worth's Children's Hospital. He also gave a large undisclosed amount to the American Society for the Prevention of Cruelty to Animals.

Shortly afterward, believing it was important to perpetuate his legacy to golf, Ben's great-niece Lisa Scott had the idea of creating a nonprofit organization in his honor and invited Robert Stennett, a longtime Shady Oaks member and aerospace engineer, to serve as the foundation's director. And in 2007, a hundred influential citizens and friends gathered to launch the Ben Hogan Foundation. "Our principal mission is to promote the values of golf that Mr. Hogan exemplified and to improve children's lives," Stennett explained, citing the foundation's college scholarships to deserving high school students, education assistance to area military families, and financial support of Camp Bronco, a camp designed to improve the lives of asthmatic children. But its most enduring creation, many feel, will be the 5,500-square-foot Ben Hogan Learning Center that opened in December of 2011, a splendid facility of classrooms and practice grounds for the First Tee of Fort Worth, which boasts one of the fastest-growing First Tee organizations in the country, serving an estimated fifteen thousand kids.

"We think this is a beautifully fitting and lasting tribute to Ben Hogan and what he gave to the game of golf," says Stennett. "Ben loved kids and he loved golf. We think this is the beginning of something very special."

On Hogan's birthday, August 13, 2011, moreover, down in tiny Dublin, Texas, the Ben Hogan Museum officially opened, the joint creation of the Dublin Historical Society and the Hogan Foundation. According to one museum official, more than three thousand local residents have signed up to serve as volunteer hosts honoring "the greatest golfer who ever lived."

Somewhere, Hennie Bogan must be smiling.

Sam Snead remained a public figure almost until the day he died, setting performance and longevity records that will likely never be broken.

In the spring of 1965, he won the Greater Greensboro Open for a record eighth time; two months shy of fifty-three, he became the oldest player to win a PGA Tour event. By then, his 1962 memoir, *The Education of a Golfer*, written with Al Stump, had been a best-seller for more than a year, and he would author at least four more books on everything from how to gamble to the pleasures of golf after forty.

At the PGA Championship at Firestone in 1966, leading the tournament at the time, Sam suddenly abandoned conventional form and putted croquet-style for the first time. This seemingly larkish move paid quick dividends, as he finished tied for sixth. During the Masters in 1967, however, Bob Jones told him this new style "didn't look like golf" and most likely violated the rules. It did not. Yet after Jones took it up with Joe Dey, both the USGA and the PGA banned the maneuver. Sam's partisans howled but weren't the least bit surprised. In 1968, at the PGA Senior Championship, he used a modified "sidesaddle" style and won by nine strokes. The authorities considered banning this as well, but fearing a backlash from the public wisely chose to take no action. In fact, neither sidesaddle nor croquet-style violated golf rules, and several lesser-known tour players had been doing it for years.

Over the next fifteen years, Sam played a lot of golf in a great many places, a man in constant motion, traveling as much as anyone except perhaps Gary Player. He played with presidents and heads of states, celebrities and ordinary paying guests at the Greenbrier, where he served as head professional on three different occasions. "The thing about Sam," says his old friend Lew Keller, "is he would play with anyone, really regardless of their handicap. But there always had to be something riding on the match." Stories abound about Sam playing with hotel guests and later charging them for the privilege, though Keller and Sam's other friends say this is largely inflated by his reputation for penny-pinching. His most interesting casual matches occurred against skilled amateurs who sought out Sam knowing he could be lured into a money match, hoping to win a check from him that they could later frame. He rarely lost these encounters, however, and referred to these players as "pigeons," birds just waiting to be plucked.

Before winding up his twenty-year relationship with the Boca Raton Club, he paid for a membership at the Pine Tree Golf Club in Fort Pierce, Florida, where he owned property. A common story around the club holds that Sam routinely took five figures off a local millionaire every time they played, and had a regular game with a wealthy coal mine owner from Michigan and three other heavy hitters who loved to play a standard $25 Nassau with automatic presses. "Sam would clip them every time," remembers former Pine Tree head pro Bob Ross, who went on to teach using techniques he picked up from both Sam and Ben. He also remembers that Sam lent his name to numerous charity events and exhibitions to benefit other pros who were either sick or financially struggling, often waiving his appearance fee. "Sam was frugal to a fault," says Ross, "but also extremely generous, especially to others in the profession. He considered it a brotherhood."

The citizens of Bath County were also recipients of Sam Snead's anonymous charity. As his good friend Bill Campbell pointed out, there wasn't a church in rugged Bath County that didn't wind up with a new activity bus, roof, or fellowship hall thanks to an anonymous donation from Sam Snead. "Someone asked him once why he never wanted a soul to know about the things he did for people back home, and he explained that it wasn't charity if people knew who gave the money," says Campbell. "He had a point. That was Sam's philosophy to a T."

When a local school's band uniforms were looking a bit tattered, new ones mysteriously showed up. When a local high school won the state football championship, Sam paid for the rings. A teenager working two jobs at the Homestead to save for college had to scale back and take care of his sick mother; money soon appeared to cover his tuition. Another kid, working as a weekend doorman, once playfully asked Sam what he planned on giving him for high school graduation. "What would you like?" Sam asked. "That watch," the kid said, pointing to his Rolex. A few days before the ceremonies, he received one just like it. Several other deserving local kids had their educations covered by Sam as well. He also quietly took care of medical bills for ailing family members, old friends, and anyone who'd done him small favors in the past. Such stories are still commonplace around Hot Springs today.

Sam was a wealthy man, to be sure, worth probably far more than the society popinjays he'd resented as a caddie and shop apprentice, though because most of his transactions were made in cash and he never had a financial advisor, exact estimates remain hard to come by. "Everybody knew Sam was well off, but he was so private about money you never heard him say anything on the subject," says one of his oldest friends. "That's why he could afford, I think, to be so generous in a very quiet sort of way—maybe a little too quiet."

When a proposal was initially made to rename the primary road through Bath County Sam Snead Highway, the motion narrowly lost. Memories are long in the hills, and some people, clearly, never cared much for any of the Sneads, particularly Sam. "Every day I play with men who could buy or sell me," he wrote in his engaging book *The Education of a Golfer*. "But I own about 100 sports jackets, 75 pairs of shoes, 25 sets of clubs, 400 shirts, several houses, a Virginia ranch and five automobiles." It wasn't a boast, per se, because in the very next paragraph he talks about buying a fancy toupee from a Greensboro wig maker to cover his expanding bald spot when he played trumpet with a band at popular nightspots in Hot Springs and over the mountain near the Greenbrier. This was vintage Sam Snead—simply mentioning to anyone who was interested how far he'd come up in the world, with a note of sweet self-deprecation that said you could take the boy out of the hills—but not the other way around.

Over this same period, he won the West Virginia Open seven times, the PGA Senior Championship six times, and the World Seniors five times, and in 1971—the same year Ben Hogan's game broke down at Houston and he ceased playing in public—he claimed the PGA Club Professionals Championship. When the senior tour began in 1980, he agreed to serve as chairman, attending every sponsor dinner and cocktail party for half a dozen years. "Without Sam Snead," Arnold Palmer says flatly, "the PGA Senior Tour would never have gotten off the ground."

The last cut he made at the Masters, finishing in a tie for twentieth, came in 1974. Yet he continued to play until 1983, when he withdrew after the first round. Around then, he went in for an annual check-up and had a full body scan. At sixty-two, he still stood five-foot-eleven and weighed 185 pounds, more or less what he did in his prime. The doctors told him that he was in better shape than most men half his age.

He soon joined Byron Nelson and Gene Sarazen as an official starter of the Masters, striking the tournament's opening drives for the next eighteen years.

Meanwhile, the restaurant he and his son Jackie opened in the old-town bank building back in Hot Springs was going great guns. Sam Snead's Tavern opened for business in 1980, its walls covered with memorabilia Jackie replicated from his father's well-endowed archives, and there was an art gallery upstairs. A leading restaurant group soon convinced them to expand into markets where golf flourished, and a second Sam Snead's Tavern opened in Orlando a short time later. Fifteen more followed over the next fifteen years.

In the mid-1980s, Sam and Jackie purchased four hundred acres off I-95 in South Florida and considered building a daily-fee course in partnership with Robert Trent Jones, but nothing came of the idea. "Dad liked to say he was a golfer, not a designer. He loved classic courses and had very firm ideas about them. But at the end of the day, building a course never really interested him all that much. It meant he wouldn't get to play as often."

For a time, an ambitious plan to create a "Sam Snead Golf Trail" circulated in the golf world, and the Virginia legislature considered funding it, thinking his name might give tourism in southern Virginia a major boost. After years of delays and failed deals and a changing economy, this plan also fell apart.

By all accounts, Sam was never the most attentive of fathers to son Jack early on, but he made up for a lot during his declining years. "We grew to be good friends and very close," says Jackie. "And Dad never wavered in how he took care of my brother, Terry, who has had the best of care his whole life, first at various top schools and now living with a really wonderful couple here in the county."

In January of 1990, Audrey passed away. "It was the first time I ever saw my father cry," Jackie says. She was buried on a beautiful grassy meadow overlooking the sweeping hills that border the Old Snead Links.

A short time later, the Greenbrier offered him $20,000 a year to return as head professional emeritus, a largely ceremonial post that only required him to interact with resort guests and serve as host and play in a few events. He gave the occasional private lesson for $500. The resort also mounted an impressive display of his personal memorabilia, including replicas of his major championship trophies, medals, and scorecards. Guests were often treated to the sight of Sam and his beloved golden retriever, Meister, riding around the Old White Course together, greeting old friends and regaling guests with stories. At quieter moments, he could be seen fishing in the stream that bisects the famous course, and was said to have a pet bass in his own farm pond at home, a huge granddaddy that would come when Sam beckoned and allow him to stroke its belly.

Forever in love with the road, while driving his Cadillac from Florida to the 1992 Masters, Sam ran a stop sign and collided with the car of a young father of four, who wound up a paraplegic. "For a while," says Lew Keller, "I think Sam thought he might lose everything. He never denied culpability and faced up to the tragedy in a completely honorable fashion." Eventually, Jack Vardaman, Sam's longtime friend and a top Washington lawyer and Seminole member, negotiated a settlement with the victim and his family, the terms of which remain undisclosed. "Sam felt as badly about that as anything that ever happened to him," says Bill Campbell. "I'm convinced that shortened his own life."

Sam suffered a fractured shoulder and damaged knee in the accident but his refusal to go for treatment suggests an almost Old Testament sensibility. As his biographer Al Barkow suggests, this marked the beginning of the end for his vaunted golf skills, occasioning a rapid decline. Still, in 1995, Sam agreed to play a seventy-two-hole *Legends of Golf* event partnered with his friend Bob Goalby, the former Masters winner, and they placed second. "Pretty darn remarkable for a guy who was an eighty-three-year-old man," says Goalby. "Sam showed everybody that he still had that amazing golf swing and could play with the best of guys who were half his age."

It was Sam's final appearance in a professional competition.

Two years later, on a warm afternoon in August, he was playing golf with friends at the Lower Cascades Course when Jackie brought him word that Ben Hogan had passed away. Reporters were already calling, seeking his comments. "He looked at me with a glassy look in his eyes, a really faraway look, thumped his driver a couple times on the ground and mumbled, 'That's too bad, too bad.' You could see how deeply it affected him. He only seemed to brighten when I told him Valerie Hogan had called to ask him to be a pallbearer."

In spring of 1999, *Golf Digest*'s Guy Yocom accompanied Sam and Jackie Snead from Fort Pierce to the Masters, an extraordinary nine-hour journey in which Sam unreeled one great yarn after another, covering everything from the pleasures of driving in the moonlight on the back roads of the early tour to how to properly skin a deer. But near Jacksonville, he grew violently ill and threw up. When they reached Augusta in the early afternoon, he was sent straight to a local hospital, forcing him to miss his first Champions Dinner ever. The attending players all signed a menu and sent it to him. "It just wasn't the same without old Sam doing his routines," remembers Arnold Palmer. A battery of tests indicated that he'd had suffered a TIA, a temporary stroke that deprives the brain of oxygen, not uncommon among active seniors. According to Jackie, the tests also showed that his arteries were clean as a whistle. When Yocom managed to talk his way into his hospital room the next morning, he found Sam in his usual good form, eating heartily and raring to get back to the Masters to perform his honorary starter duties with Sarazen and Nelson. As Yocom poignantly recounted in *Golf Digest*, his warm-up swings were all rather sad, lacking the familiar grace and power of golf's finest natural swing.

After the elder statesmen were introduced by Masters chairman Jack Stephens and Byron and Gene produced serviceable drives, the first champion to don a Masters green jacket stepped to the tee. And what happened next speaks volumes about the legacy of Samuel Jackson Snead. As Guy Yocom wrote:

> *The applause for Sam is prolonged, and trebled in volume. Sam tips his hat, walks forward and tees his ball. He sidles alongside the ball, waggles beautifully—he always had the most beautiful waggle in the game—and cocks an eye down the fairway. Then it is as if an angel enters Sam's body, for he wheels away from the ball like the Slammer of old, his right shoulder stretching behind him, his left arm jutting into the sky. He pauses distinctly at the top and brings the club down like the arm of a locomotive.*
>
> *Pow! The ball explodes off the clubface like a bullet, arcing high and far toward the distant fairway bunker on the right. At the last moment it turns over and returns to earth, coming to rest in the exact middle of the center mowing stripe, 230 yards away.*
>
> *There is a moment of paralyzed silence, and then thunderous, sustained cheers shatter the morning. People jump, scream, back-pound and high-five each other. The fellow standing next to me shakes his head and his voice breaks as he mutters, "Unbelievable . . . unbelievable." He looks at me with tears in his eye, and he isn't ashamed.*
>
> *As for Sam, there always was a lot of ham in him, and with a broad grin he plucks the tee from the ground, doffs his hat, skips a few steps and kicks his right foot in the air. The crowd roars. Sam leaves the tee as if levitating, fans straining across the ropes to touch him.*

A kindlier angel would have let things end right there. But Sam went on for two more years, powerless to resist the stage of his favorite tournament. During this time, Jackie regularly drove him to speaking gigs at the Greenbrier and down to Greensboro to have supper with old friends. He attended a wedding in nearby Lewisburg, West Virginia, where he knew the words to every hymn sung. "Dad's short-term memory was completely gone by that point," says Jackie. "But he could recall the glory years of the tour—and even old hymns—like nobody's business."

Fittingly, the last ball he ever hit came at the Masters, on April 11, 2002, but it was a feeble drive that struck a spectator in the huge gallery, shattering his eyeglasses. Apologies were made, and Sam, who was disoriented at the time, was escorted away by Jackie and his wife, Ann, a short while later, his last trip down Magnolia Lane.

Within days, back at the Old Snead Links, he lost the ability to speak, though he still had his appetite and came to supper several nights wearing a jacket and tie. Ann made him chocolate milkshakes and cream chipped beef. Weeks later, his appetite also failed him.

Over the final seven days of his life, a bed was made for him by the fireplace. Sam wore a U.S. Marines T-shirt and drifted in and out of consciousness, monitored by a full-time nurse, his pulse ebbing. On May 23, four days before his ninetieth birthday, the nurse called Jackie on his cell phone and said he and Ann should come quickly.

"We arrived expecting him to be gone," Jackie recalls. "He'd been in a coma for days. But he suddenly opened his eyes, looked at me, pointed up and smiled as if he saw something. Then he shut his eyes and was gone. It still gives me chills to talk about it."

Three days later, Sam's funeral at the tiny Episcopal church in Hot Springs, on a beautiful spring Sunday in the hills, was an all-star gathering, with his childhood friends and cronies crowding in along with Curtis Strange, Tom Watson, Bob Goalby, Doug Sanders, Tim Finchem, and many others. Bill Campbell gave an eloquent eulogy: "He had a deep pride of place. He loved his family. He enjoyed his friends, and he exuded vitality until nearly ninety. Altogether, a great life, for which we will rejoice. Now he belongs to the ages, and his like will never be seen again."

Sam was laid to rest in the meadow beside Audrey.

Today, a curious traveler searching for clues to the indelible legacy of Sam Snead sees traces of the man in lots of places. The portion of U.S. Route 220 within Bath County is now called the Sam Snead Memorial Highway, and Greensboro has a Sam Snead Boulevard. Seventeen Sam Snead's Taverns lavishly display his memorabilia, as does the Greenbrier, including his original Masters jackets and one of his signature straw hats.

On August 2, 2009, Sam Snead and Bill Campbell were the first two inducted into the new West Virginia Golf Hall of Fame, the greatest amateur and finest professional the region ever produced. "Golf would have been a very different landscape without Sam Snead," says Al Barkow. "Without Sam, it's hard to imagine the golf tour being what it is today."

Byron Nelson never meant to become an icon.

In 1981, he began the longest stint anyone has ever served as an honorary starter at the Masters, not to reinforce his reputation as the player who created the modern golf swing and had the grandest winning streak anyone will ever achieve in the game, but to celebrate the sport itself and the many friends it had given him.

Perhaps no one had a bigger influence than Byron on succeeding generations of pro golfers. After shaping the game and values of Ken Venturi in the 1950s and '60s, he offered to work with Tom Watson after the young Kansan lost a heartbreaking Open to Hale Irwin at Winged Foot in 1974, which was one of his last telecasts as a commentator. In the locker room afterward, he pointed out to Watson that his leg action was out of sync in the final round, and invited him to come down to Fairway Ranch if he ever wanted any help.

Watson won Byron's own tournament in 1975, deepening their friendship, and took his advice on how to play Carnoustie in difficult conditions to claim his first Claret Jug later that summer. A year later, however, during a dry spell of wins, he finally took Byron up on his offer, and showed up at Fairway Ranch. "The minute you walked through the door," recalls Watson, "you could feel the love and humility of that house. Byron and Louise welcomed me like I was one of their own. She cooked great meals and Byron and I talked about the golf swing for hours. His understanding of it was incredible, probably as far-reaching as anyone who's played the game. No one ever hit the ball straighter than Byron, and his honesty in analyzing my swing was very rewarding. As much as anything else, though, it was the way this man conducted his life that served to inspire me. He helped set me on a path that helped boost my game to the next level."

In 1977, Watson won his first green jacket and outdueled Nicklaus at Turnberry to win his second British Open, finishing as the tour's leading money winner and the PGA Player of the Year, and went on to establish himself as one of the greatest players of modern times. As his career blossomed, Watson frequently referred to Byron's influence on his life and golf.

Many other young players found their way to Byron's doorstep and sphere of influence over the years, including Ben Crenshaw, Tom Kite, Corey Pavin, Scott Verplank, Justin Leonard and Payne Stewart. After getting to know Byron and working with both him and Harvie Ward—another of Byron's protégés—Stewart claimed two U.S. Opens and revived a dormant spiritual life that carried him to the summit of the game at Pinehurst in 1999, just before he died in a freakish plane crash.

"Byron's greatest legacy," Ben Crenshaw says with great emotion, "was the sense of integrity and friendship he passed along to everyone he met, tour player and average golfer alike—a love of the game that transcends all else. People couldn't take their eyes off Ben Hogan at play, and Sam made golf such a warm and appealing game to watch. But Byron made it a game of enduring friendships, and that's something everyone who loves the game understands."

In late 1983, when Louise Nelson suffered a stroke and was unable to speak or care for herself, Byron devoted every waking moment to her. "During the time he attended to Louise," says Charlie Summerall, a good friend from Preston Trail, "we almost never saw Byron. And when we did, it was shocking how much weight he'd lost. The toll on him was obvious. A lot of us worried about his health."

That same year, the Byron Nelson Classic moved from Preston Trail to Las Colinas in Irving, which would soon become part of the Four Seasons Resort, and by now this was the first tournament to have raised over a million dollars for charities. Jon Bradley, Byron's long-time accountant and business manager, recalls that he finally dipped into the investment account Cliff Roberts had set up for him decades before. Untouched until then, this provided Louise with the best possible care until her death in October 1985. Other funds were derived from the sale of a prime lot at Las Colinas that the owners had deeded to him. Up till then he had never accepted a penny of compensation for his involvement with the tournament.

A short time later, he founded the Byron and Louise Nelson Scholarship Fund at Abilene Christian University, where his younger brother, Charles, served as a trustee.

The next spring, a divorced mother of two named Peggy Simmons, a freelance copywriter who was preparing to enter the Methodist ministry, received a letter from Byron at her home in Dayton, Ohio, inviting her to come out and watch him play an exhibition match. She had briefly met him at an event in Dayton in 1981, and later wrote an appreciative fan letter. He had the bluest eyes she had ever seen, she later told him.

Five years later, they met again and romance sparked. She was forty-one. He was seventy-four. Byron's friends feared she might be a golddigger looking to take a famous lonely man for a ride. In October of 1986 he baptized her at his church in Roanoke, however, and less than a month later they were married in the same sanctuary and honeymooned at Byron's home on a course he'd designed—one of eight he had a hand in shaping—down in the Hill Country of Kerrville, Texas.

"Many had their doubts," says Jon Bradley, "but Peggy turned out to be the best thing that could possibly have happened to Byron. She brought love and vitality back into his life and extended his life for another twenty years. Anyone who knew them will tell you the same thing. They were like newlyweds." One of the deals they made early in their marriage was that Peggy would cook for him every day, and Byron would do the dishes. "He said the only dishwasher in the house was him," Peggy allows with a laugh. "He did the dishes every day, breakfast, lunch and dinner, and he never failed to thank me. When I started thanking him for doing the dishes, he got tears in his eyes and told me I didn't need to do that. If you can believe it, he told me he was afraid he could never do enough for me."

In 1990, Cleveland Golf rolled out a premium new set of Byron Nelson irons called the 68.3 Tour Model, in honor of Byron's record scoring average in 1945.

On his eightieth birthday in February of 1992, 150 guests were invited to a gala party at the Four Seasons Las Colinas, where a nine-foot bronze statue of Lord Byron leaning on a golf club was unveiled, an apt symbol of his towering presence in the game. Chris Schenkel served as emcee that evening, and most of Byron's star pupils and members from his Sunday school class attended. The USGA presented him with a replica of his 1939 U.S. Open trophy. That same year, Peggy collaborated with him on his delightful memoir *How I Played the Game*.

The Byron Nelson Foundation began quietly a short time later, aiming to benefit charities close to Byron's heart, including youth programs and after-school care in the metro area's most disadvantaged neighborhoods.

During the PGA Merchandise Show of 1995, more than 4,500 people turned out to honor him at a large dinner thrown by Cleveland Golf. Broadcaster Jack Whitaker served as emcee, and Sam Snead entertained guests with stories about his early rivalry with Byron on tour. "While Byron was out there he simply was the best," Sam graciously said at one point. "He didn't drink or smoke or dance, so I don't think Byron had any fun at all," he added, drawing a huge laugh from the crowd.

When Byron was called on to speak, he looked over at Sam and reflected, "You know, Sam is a funny man. But he was wrong when he said I didn't have any fun on tour. Sam, you don't think winning eleven straight tournaments was fun?" The hall exploded with laughter and wild applause.

Tributes began pouring in from every direction that year, the fiftieth anniversary of his incredible streak and eighteen wins. Among other things, a new clothing line called Eleven Straight provided him with the largest royalties of his long career, and protégé Corey Pavin captured the U.S. Open at Shinnecock Hills that June using a commemorative set of Byron Nelson wedges.

In 1997, the Nelson tournament climbed over the $4 million mark in charitable donations, in part due to the sellout triggered by Tiger Woods's first professional appearance in the area. Within five years, this figure would eclipse $110 million in donations to local charities.

Byron made his final appearance as an honorary starter at the Masters in 2001, stiffly poking a short drive down the right side of the fairway and calling it quits, a year before Sam did the same.

The final three years of his life were spent going to church two or three times a week and working in his woodshop to make birdhouses and cutting boards and coffee tables for friends, including a dowry chest for Tom Watson's daughter, Meg. "Golf was easy for me," he liked to tell visitors to Fairway Ranch. "Woodworking is hard. But I love doing it." He soon graduated to porch swings and coffee tables and clocks.

On the morning he died, Byron felt perfectly fine. It was September 26, 2006. "Before I went out to my ladies Bible study class," Peggy recounts, "I made him his favorite breakfast—sausage biscuit, scrambled eggs and coffee with cream." Byron was doing the dishes, and she asked if he wanted her to turn on radio minister Alistair Begg's morning broadcast so he could listen before he went out to the woodshop. He did, and the couple kissed. "Sweetheart, I'm so proud of you," he told her, then she went out the door.

Around lunchtime, she returned and found Byron stretched out on his back on their porch, like a man enjoying a peaceful nap. "I knew the moment I saw him that he was gone," Peggy says quietly. "I took his pulse and placed my hand on his cheek and thanked him. I told him, 'I'm so happy you're in heaven.'" He was ninety-four years old.

Several golf clubs in the area offered to provide food for the 2,200 people who attended Byron Nelson's memorial service at the spacious North Richland Hills Church of Christ, and tributes and flowers poured in from all over the world. A VIP room was set up to accommodate a large contingent of PGA stars former and current that included Tom Watson, Phil Mickelson, Ben Crenshaw, Corey Pavin, Ken Venturi and Tom Lehman. Byron's favorite hymn, "Blessed Be Thy Name," was sung and eulogies were given by Alistair Begg and Jon Bradley. "The funeral was everything you would expect for Byron Nelson," says Tom Watson. "Few men have earned the respect and love that he did in an incredible life. In the end, that was Byron's greatest legacy to the game."

Eight days after Byron was laid to rest beside Louise in the family plot in Denton, Peggy finally broke down and cried like a baby. "I'd been strong for days but I suddenly missed him so much," she says. "I asked God to please let me dream about him." A short while later, she did just that. "There he stood in a darkened hallway with light behind him. He told me it was very peaceful where he was and not to be sad. When I woke up, I finally felt at peace."

On October 16, 2006, Byron Nelson was posthumously awarded a Congressional Gold Medal of Honor by the Senate and House of Representatives, an act that passed unanimously and detailed twenty-five of his astonishing achievements.

Today, that medal and other artifacts that had belonged to one of golf's greatest ambassadors and gentlemen reside in a display case in the stunning atrium of the new Byron Nelson High School in Trophy Club, Texas, home of the Byron Nelson Bobcats, a name inspired by his famous quote that "Winners are a different breed of cat." Paintings of Byron in his early days also grace the beautiful school's public spaces.

Back at Fairway Ranch, Peggy Nelson keeps the house pretty much the way Byron loved it, wearing his 1937 Masters medal on a chain around her neck, a gift he gave her many years ago.

For anyone searching for a final bit of poetry and mythic symmetry in arguably the three greatest golfers of the twentieth century—this unique and incomparable American Triumvirate—it's intriguing to realize that they left this world in the reverse order in which they'd arrived, the youngest to the oldest, all sons of the same wondrous year—first Ben, then Sam, and finally Byron.

Acknowledgments

Though the late Herbert Warren Wind provided the inspiration and title for this book, the seeds were probably sown one rainy autumn afternoon in 1987 over a lunch with Henry Picard at the Country Club of Charleston, South Carolina. Picard spoke so modestly and engagingly about the early days of the professional golf tour—and specifically his unshakable belief that Byron Nelson, Sam Snead, and Ben Hogan played the pivotal role in its survival and growth—I was inspired to spend the next decade seeking out and interviewing players who shaped that era and laid the foundation for the early PGA Tour, a terrific grounding for the eventual writing of an authorized biography of Ben Hogan, *An American Life*. Sam Snead and Byron Nelson were tremendously generous with their time and unique insights, each agreeing to comprehensive interviews on at least two occasions. Over a period of years I was fortunate to gain many of the insights and stories contained herein from a host of great players that included Gene Sarazen, Paul Runyan, Tommy Bolt, Johnny Bulla, Jack Fleck, Jack Burke Jr., Shelley Mayfield, Skee Riegel, Johnny Pott, Johnny Palmer, Eddie Merrins, Ernie Vossler, Don January, Dow Finsterwald, Dave Marr, Billy Casper, Mike Souchak, Bob Goalby, Bob Rosburg, Cary Middlecoff, Jim Ferree, Doug Sanders, Jerry Pittman, Tom Weiskopf, Johnny Miller, Ben Crenshaw, and Tom Watson.

A longtime friend and mentor like John Derr was also an invaluable resource, a front-row seat to golf history at a key moment in its American evolution. Having spent more than a decade casually discussing these three remarkable men, John was good enough to permit me to tape more than nine hours of conversations on the American Triumvirate, all three of whom he knew on a close and personal basis. Needless to say, Derr's insights were critical to the process of this book.

Amateur greats Billy Joe Patton, Harvie Ward, and Bill Campbell were also invaluable resources, and Mike Souchak, Ken Venturi, and Arnold Palmer were especially generous with their time and insights at various key intervals during the writing of this book and the Hogan biography. From other corners of the golf world, I would like to thank several individuals for their valuable perspectives on the lives of my subjects: Bob Sommers, Ike Grainger, Barney Adams, Sandy Tatum, Peggy Bell, Jimmy Ballard, Sal Johnson, Robert Deaton, John Gerring, Frank Chirkinian, Ben Wright, Howdy Giles, Rhonda Glenn, Irwin Smallwood, Curt Sampson, Lee Pace, Furman Bisher, Jim Finegan, Dave Anderson, Jack Whitaker, Sid Matthew, Jim Deaton, Jack Vardaman, Bill Gilmore, Julius Mason for the PGA of America, the PGA Tour, and Rand Jerris and Karen Bednarski from the USGA. Once again, a warm thank-you to my good friends John Capers from the Merion Golf Club and Tim Neher, president of the Seminole Golf Club.

Additionally, I am greatly indebted to Valerie Harriman, Valerie Hogan's niece, who provided essential perspective and a bounty of personal scrapbooks belonging to Ben, as did her generous children, Lisa Scott and Sean Anderson. I wish to thank Robert Stennett of the Hogan Foundation for his generosity and assistance, plus a host of friends and former employees of Ben Hogan Golf, who contributed greatly to both books. They include: Dee Kelly, Gene Smyers, Gary Laughlin, Pat Martin, Bobby Goodyear, Marty Leonard, Sharon Rae, Elizabeth Hudson, W. A. "Tex" Moncrief Jr., Willie Mae Green, Ben Fortson, Charissa Christopher, Doxie Williams, Tom Stites, and Ronnie McGraw.

I'm especially indebted to Peggy Nelson and Byron's longtime friend Jon Bradley and Charlie Summerall, who graciously provided access to Byron's full and well-lived life. Ditto several members of the Salesmanship Club and officials of the Byron Nelson Classic, which still ranks as one of the tour's best-run affairs.

I must express deep gratitude to Jack Snead for helping me gain an intimate understanding of his father's complex and fascinating life, and to several who knew the Slammer as legend and man: Ann Snead, J. C. Snead, Lewis Keller, Robert Harris, Bob Ross, Don Ryder, Robert Harris, Paul Moran, and several residents of Hot Springs, Virginia, all of whom cherish their colorful stories of Sam.

A special thank-you to my dear friends Rayburn Tucker and Whitt Powell, a pair of discerning golf historians who read the manuscript and offered critical guidance and insights. I would also like to thank Al Barkow for reading the book in early draft form and offering his greatly appreciated thoughts. Anyone seeking a full understanding of the development of the PGA Tour would do well to read *Gettin' to the Dance Floor* as well as his splendid history of the PGA Tour and his engaging photobiography, *Sam: The One and Only Sam Snead.*

A quartet of friends provided other crucial resources: Tom Stewart of Pinehurst's Old Sport Gallery and Books for his classic books on golf and unerring advice; Bill Williamson, who arranged an unforgettable afternoon with Billy Joe Patton; and my colleagues David Woronoff and Andie Rose of *The Pilot* newspaper and *PineStraw* and *O. Henry* magazines. I would also like to thank Kelly Miller of the incomparable Pine Needles Resort in Southern Pines, North Carolina; Audrey Moriarity of the Given Memorial Library in Pinehurst; the members of the Biltmore Forest Country Club in Asheville, the members of the Hope Valley Country Club in Durham, and the members of the Greensboro Country Club in Greensboro, North Carolina; and the terrific reference staff at the Central Branch of the Fort Worth Public Library for assisting with research in this project.

It's every writer's ambition to have an opportunity to work with an editor like Gary Fisketjon. If this book succeeds in presenting an important story to a new generation of golf fans, Gary's formidable skills deserve much of the credit. He knows and loves golf—and can shape sentences—like few others I've met on the nonfiction fairways. A similar appreciation goes to my friend and longtime agent, Jay Mandel of William Morris Agency.

Lastly, a heartfelt thanks to my wife, Wendy, who lived with and encouraged this idea for many years before it found its way to paper, to my good friend Jeep, who never missed a morning of work, and to the ageless Miss Daniels, who is pleased to soon have this book in her shop.

Bibliography

Allen, Frederick Lewis. *Only Yesterday*. New York: Harper & Row, 1931.

———. *Since Yesterday*. New York: Harper & Row, 1939.

Alter, Judy, and James Lee Ward, eds. *Literary Fort Worth*. Fort Worth: TCU Press, 2001.

Barkow, Al. *Gettin' to the Dance Floor: An Oral History of American Golf*. Springfield, N.J.: Burford Books, 1986.

———. *Golf's Golden Grind: The History of the Tour*. New York: Harcourt Brace Jovanovich, 1974.

———. *The History of the PGA Tour*. New York: Doubleday, 1989.

———. *Sam: The One and Only Sam Snead*. Ann Arbor, Mich.: Sports Media Group, 2005.

Barr, Art Jr. *Ben Hogan and Buster*. Privately published, 2002.

Barrett, David. *Miracle at Merion*. New York: Skyhorse, 2010.

Bohn, Michael K. *Heroes and Ballyhoo: How the Golden Age of the 1920s Transformed American Sports*. Dulles, Va.: Potomac, 2009.

Bolt, Tommy, with Jimmy Mann. *The Hole Truth: Inside Big Time, Big Money Golf*. Philadelphia: Lippincott, 1971.

Brenner, Morgan G. *The Majors of Golf*. 3 vols. Jefferson, N.C.: McFarland and Company, 2009.

Buenger, Victoria, and Walter L. Buenger. *Texas Merchant: Marvin Leonard and Fort Worth*. College Station: Texas A&M Press, 1998.

Companiotte, John. *Byron Nelson: The Most Remarkable Year in Golf*. Chicago: Triumph, 2006.

Concannon, Dale. *The Ryder Cup: The Complete History of Golf's Greatest Drama*. London: Arum, 2001.

Corcoran, Fred, and Bud Harvey. *Unplayable Lies.* New York: Duell, Sloan & Pearce, 1965.

Cornish, Geoffrey S., and Ronald E. Whitten. *The Golf Course.* Rev. ed. London: Smithmark, 1987.

Darwin, Bernard. *James Braid.* London: Old Golf Shop, 1900.

Davis, Martin. *Ben Hogan: The Man Behind the Mystique.* Greenwich, Conn.: American Golfer, 2002.

———. *Byron Nelson: The Story of Golf's Finest Gentleman and the Greatest Winning Streak in History.* Greenwich, Conn.: American Golfer, 1997.

Davis, Martin, ed. *The Hogan Mystique: Classic Photographs of the Great Ben Hogan.* Greenwich, Conn.: American Golfer, 1994.

Demaret, Jimmy. *My Partner, Ben Hogan.* London: Peter Davies, 1954.

Derr, John. *Don't Forget to Wind the Clock.* Pinehurst, N.C.: Cricket Productions, 1998.

———. *Uphill Is Easier.* Pinehurst, N.C.: Cricket Productions, 1998.

Dickinson, Gardner. *Let 'Er Rip: Gardner Dickinson on Golf.* Atlanta: Longstreet, 1994.

Dodson, James. *Ben Hogan: An American Life.* New York: Doubleday, 2004.

———. *A Son of the Game.* Chapel Hill: Algonquin, 2009.

———. *The Story of Seminole.* Juno Beach, Fla.: Seminole Golf Club, 2006.

Duncan, George, and Bernard Darwin. *Present Day Golf.* London: George Doran, 1921.

Evans, Harold. *The American Century.* New York: Alfred A. Knopf, 1998.

Fehrenbach, T. R. *Lone Star: A History of Texas and the Texans.* New York: Da Capo, 2000.

Fleck, Jack. *The Jack Fleck Story.* J. C. Publishing, 2002.

Frost, Mark. *The Greatest Game Ever Played.* Self-published.

———. *The Match.* New York: Hyperion, 2007.

Graffis, Herb. *The PGA.* New York: Thomas Crowell, 1975.

Graubert, Julian. *Golf's Greatest Championship.* New York: Donald I. Fine, 1997.

Gregston, Gene. *Hogan: The Man Who Played for Glory.* Englewood Cliffs, N.J.: Prentice Hall, 1978.

Hagen, Walter. *The Walter Hagen Story.* New York: Simon & Shuster, 1952.

Halberstam, David. *The Fifties.* New York: Ballantine, 1994.

Heinz, W. C. *What a Time It Was: The Best of W. C. Heinz on Sports.* New York: Da Capo, 2001.

Hogan, Ben. *Power Golf.* New York: A. S. Barnes, 1948.

Hogan, Ben, with Herbert Warren Wind. *Five Lessons: The Modern Fundamentals of Golf.* New York: A. S. Barnes, 1957.

Jones, Bobby. *Down the Fairway.* New York: Minton and Balch, 1927.

Keeler, O. B. *The Bobby Jones Story.* Chicago: Triumph, 2003.

Knight, Oliver. *Outpost on the Trinity.* Fort Worth: TCU Press, 1990.

Laney, Al. *Following the Leaders.* New York: Ailsa, 1991.

Lawrenson, Derek. *The Compete Encyclopedia of Golf.* London: Carlton, 1999.

Lingeman, Richard. *Small Town America.* New York: G. P. Putnam, 1980.

Lowe, Stephen R. *Sir Walter and Mr. Jones.* Chelsea, Mich.: Sleeping Bear, 2000.

MacDonald, Charles Blair. *Scotland's Gift—Golf.* New York: Charles Scribners's Sons, 1928.

Matthew, Sidney L. *The Life and Times of Bobby Jones.* Impregnable Quadrilateral Press, 1995.

McMillan, Robin. *Us Against Them: An Oral History of the Ryder Cup.* New York: HarperCollins, 2004.

Miller, William. *How to Relax.* New York: Smith & Durrell, 1945.

Morrison, Alex, ed. *The Impossible Art of Golf: An Anthology of Golf Writing.* New York: Arkan, 1992.

Nelson, Byron. *The Byron Nelson Story.* Cincinnati: Old Golf Shop, 1980.

———. *The Little Black Book.* Arlington, TX: Summit Publishing, 1995.

Nelson, Byron, and Peggy Nelson. *How I Played the Game.* Dallas: Taylor, 1993.

Nelson, Peggy. *Life with Lord Byron.* Fort Worth: Creative Enterprises Studio, 2010.

Olman, John M. *The Legendary Golfing Life of Gene Sarazen.* Cincinnati: Olman Enterprises, Ohio, 1987.

Ouimet, Francis. *A Game of Golf.* Boston: Houghton Mifflin, 1932.

Owen, David. *The Making of the Masters.* New York: Simon & Schuster, 1999.

Pace, Lee. *Pinehurst Stories.* Pinehurst, N.C.: Pinehurst, 1991.

———. *Pinehurst Stories.* Pinehurst, N.C.: Pinehurst, 1999.

Palmer, Arnold, with James Dodson. *A Golfer's Life.* New York: Ballantine, 1999.

Peper, George. *Golf in America: The First 100 Years.* New York: Harry N. Abrams, 1988.

Price, Charles. *Golfer at Large: New Slants on an Ancient Game.* New York: Atheneum, 1982.

———. *A Golf Story: Bobby Jones, Augusta National, and the Masters Tournament.* New York: Atheneum, 1996.

Rapoport, Ron. *The Immortal Bobby: Bobby Jones and the Golden Age of Golf.* New York: John Wiley & Sons, 2005.

Sampson, Curt. *The Eternal Summer: Palmer, Nicklaus, and Hogan in 1960, Golf's Golden Year.* Dallas: Taylor, 1992.

———. *The Masters: Golf, Money, and Power in Augusta, Georgia.* New York: Villard, 1998.

Scott, Tom, and Geoffrey Cousin. *The Golf Immortals.* New York: Hart, 1968.

Snead, Sam, with George Mendoza. *Slammin' Sam.* New York: Donald I. Fine, 1986.

Snead, Sam, with Fran Pirozzolo. *The Game I Love.* New York: Random House, 1997.

Snead, Sam, with Tom Shehan. *Natural Golf.* New York: A. S. Barnes, 1953.

Snead, Sam, with Al Stump. *The Education of a Golfer.* New York: Simon & Shuster, 1962.

Sommers, Robert. *Golf Anecdotes.* New York: Oxford University Press, 1995.

——. *The U.S. Open: Golf's Ultimate Challenge.* New York: Atheneum, 1987.

Stirk, David. *Golf History and Traditions, 1500–1945.* Ludlow, U.K.: Excellent Press, 1998.

Towle, Mike. *I Remember Ben Hogan.* Nashville: Cumberland House, 2000.

Trimble, Frances G. *Colonial Country Club: The Diamond Jubilee Celebration.* Fort Worth: Colonial Country Club, 2011.

United States Golf Association. *USGA Record Book, 1895–1971.* Far Hills, N.J.: Golf House, 1971.

Vardon, Harry. *The Complete Golfer.* McClure, Phillips, 1905.

——. *My Golfing Life.* London: Hutchinson, 1933.

Ward-Thomas, Pat. *The Lay of the Land.* New York: Ailsa, 1990.

Wind, Herbert Warren. *Following Through.* New York: Ticknor & Fields, 1985.

——. *The Story of American Golf.* New York: Simon & Schuster, 1956.

Wind, Herbert Warren, ed. *The Complete Golfer.* New York: Ailsa, 1991.

Wright, Ben, with Michael Patrick Shiels. *Good Bounces and Bad Lies.* Chelsea, Mich.: Sleeping Bear, 1999.

Additional Sources and References

The personal scrapbooks of Ben Hogan, meticulously kept for nearly two decades by his wife, Valerie, were of significant help to this project. I am greatly indebted to the estate of Ben Hogan, in particular to Valerie Harriman and Lisa Scott, for allowing me unprecedented access and use of this invaluable source material. I also possess an extensive newspaper file, accumulated over many years, regarding the life and career of Sam Snead. What follows is a list of the known newspapers and periodicals that provided assistance to the formulation of this story:

The Arizona Republic, Asheville Citizen-Times, Associated Press, *The Atlanta Journal-Constitution, The Augusta Chronicle, The Baltimore Evening Sun, Boston Evening Transcript, Boston Evening Traveler, The Buffalo News, Chicago Daily News, Chicago Tribune, The Christian Science Monitor,* Cleveland *Plain Dealer, The Colum-*

bus Dispatch, *The Dallas Morning News, The Denver Post, Denver Free Press, The Detroit News, Durham Morning Herald, Dublin Progress, El Paso Herald-Post, El Paso Times, Fort Worth Press, Fort Worth Star-Telegram, Glasgow Herald, Digest, Golf Life, Golf Journal, Golf Magazine,* Golfing Magazine, *Golf Monthly* (United Kingdom), *Golf World, Greensboro Daily News, Greensboro News & Record, The Guardian,* International News Service, *London Daily Express, London Daily Herald, London Daily Mail, London Daily Telegraph, Los Angeles Evening Herald, Los Angeles Times, Louisville Courier-Journal Magazine, The Miami Herald,* Newark *Star-Ledger,* New York *Daily News, The New York Herald Tribune, New York Journal American, The New York Times, New York World-Telegram and Sun, Oakland Tribune, PGA Magazine, The Philadelphia Inquirer, Pittsburgh Press,* Raleigh *News & Observer, Reader's Digest,* Reuters, *Richmond Times-Dispatch, Rocky Mountain News, San Antonio Light, San Antonio News, The San Diego Union-Tribune, San Francisco Call-Bulletin, San Francisco Chronicle, The Scotsman on Sunday, Sports Illustrated, St. Louis Star-Times, St. Paul Press, St. Petersburg Independent, Time, The Times* (London), *Times Record News* (Wichita Falls, Texas), United Press International, *The Washington Star,* and *Weekly Scotsman.*

Photographic Credits

frontispiece: Courtesy of Snead Archives
facing the prologue: Augusta National/Getty Images

First Insert

Sam Snead, age seven (Courtesy of Snead Archives)
Sam Snead, Johnny Farrell, Billy Burke, Cascades Open, 1935 (Courtesy of Snead Archives)
Sam and Audrey Snead (Courtesy of Snead Archives)
Sam Snead circa 1930s, Masters Tournament, Augusta National Golf Club (Augusta National/Getty Images)
Sam Snead and Byron Nelson, 1940 PGA Championship (Courtesy of Snead Archives)
Sam Snead, 1939 U.S. Open (Courtesy of Snead Archives)
Sam and Audrey Snead, 1946 Open Championship (Courtesy of Snead Archives)
Sam Snead and Ben Hogan circa late 1940s (Courtesy of Snead Archives)
Sam Snead with dog, Meister, White Sulfur Springs, 1992 (Sports Illustrated/ Getty Images)
Sam and Jack Snead, 1995 (Courtesy of Snead Archives)
Opening Ceremony of 1994 Masters Tournament, (from left to right) Byron Nelson, Sam Snead, Augusta chairman Jack Stephens, Gene Sarazen (Augusta National/Getty Images)
Sam Snead at Snead Links (Courtesy of Snead Archives)

Second Insert

Byron Nelson in his early twenties (Courtesy of the Byron Nelson Estate)
Byron Nelson, PGA Tour (Courtesy of the Byron Nelson Estate)

Byron and Louise Nelson, circa mid-1930s (Courtesy of the Byron Nelson Estate)
Byron Nelson, mid-swing (USGA)
Byron Nelson circa 1937 Masters (Courtesy of the Byron Nelson Estate)
Byron Nelson, 1940 PGA Championship (Courtesy of the Byron Nelson Estate)
Byron Nelson and Ben Hogan, 1942 Masters Tournament, Augusta National
    Golf Club (Augusta National/Getty Images)
Byron Nelson and Ben Hogan (Courtesy of the Byron Nelson Estate)
Byron Nelson on his farm (Courtesy of the Byron Nelson Estate)
Byron and Peggy Nelson, circa 1984 (Courtesy of the Byron Nelson Estate)
Byron Nelson and Ken Venturi (Courtesy of the Byron Nelson Estate)
Byron Nelson in woodshop (Courtesy of the Byron Nelson Estate)
Byron Nelson tipping hat (Salesmanship Club of Dallas)

Third Insert

Baby Ben Hogan with father, Chester Hogan, 1913 (Courtesy of the Hogan Estate)
Ben Hogan, age sixteen (Courtesy of the Hogan Estate)
Ben and Valerie Hogan, Hershey Hotel, 1938 (Courtesy of the Hogan Estate)
Jimmy Demaret (left) and Ben Hogan, 1940 Masters (Corbis)
Ben Hogan and Byron Nelson, Augusta National, 1946 (Corbis)
Ben Hogan, Los Angeles Open, 1950 (Corbis)
Ben and Valerie Hogan, two weeks following accident (Courtesy of the Hogan
    Estate)
Ben Hogan, 72nd hole, Merion Golf Club, 50th United States Open Champion-
    ship (Time/Life)
Ben Hogan and Sam Snead, 1954 Masters (Corbis)
Ben Hogan Day, New York City, July 1953 (AP/WideWorld)
Jack Fleck and Ben Hogan following play-off, Olympic Golf Club, United States
    Open Championship, 1955 (Corbis)
Ben and Valerie Hogan, Shady Oaks Country Club, 1990 (Courtesy of the Hogan
    Estate)

A Note About the Author

James Dodson is the editor of *O. Henry* and *PineStraw* magazines. In 2011 he received the Donald Ross Award from the American Society of Golf Course Architects for his contribution to golf literature.

A Note on the Type

The text of this book was set in Palatino, a typeface designed by the noted German typographer Hermann Zapf. Named after Giovanni Battista Palatino, a writing master of Renaissance Italy, Palatino was the first of Zapf's typefaces to be intoduced in America.

Composed by North Market Street Graphics,
Lancaster, Pennsylvania

Printed and Bound by Berryville Graphics
Berryville, Virginia

Designed by Michael Collica